MAKING THEIR OWN WAY

Narratives for Transforming Higher
Education to Promote Self-Development

Marcia Baxter Magolda

STERLING, VIRGINIA

Paperback edition published in 2004 by
Stylus Publishing, LLC
22883 Quicksilver Drive
Sterling, Virginia 20166

**Library of Congress
Cataloging-in-Publication-Data**

Baxter Magolda, Marcia B., 1951-
    Making their own way : narratives for
        transforming higher education to
        promote self-development / Marcia
        Baxter Magolda.— 1st ed.
    p.   cm.
    Includes bibliographical references and
        index.
    ISBN 1-57922-035-5 (alk. paper)
    1. College graduates—United States—
    Attitudes—Longitudinal studies. 2. College
    graduates—Employment—United States—
    Longitudinal studies. 3. Attitude change—
    Longitudinal studies. 4. Education,
    Higher—United States—Longitudinal
    studies. I. Title

LB2424 .B39 2001
378'.01—dc21
00-066132

First edition, 2001
ISBN: hardcover 1-57922-035-5;
paperback 1-57922-091-6

Printed in the United States of America

All first editions printed on acid free paper

To my spouse, Peter, for being exceptional company on my journey

TABLE OF CONTENTS

TABLE OF ILLUSTRATIONS

Figures

ACKNOWLEDGMENTS

This book is about being better company for young adults on their journeys toward self-authorship, their journeys toward making meaning of their own lives. Following their journeys vicariously through annual conversations with them has taken me on a journey as well—one of exploring how I and my colleagues, as educators, can provide better company for young adults as they attempt to meet the expectations contemporary society places before them. Through this book, I invite readers to come along on both these journeys.

This book is possible, of course, due to good company I have enjoyed throughout this journey. The narratives of young adults' journeys belong to the 39 participants in my longitudinal study of young adults' learning and development. The richness of these narratives is available because these young adults are invested in this project and open to sharing their intimate reflections on their own lives for the potential benefit they may hold for others. My interpretations of their experiences are enriched by our partnership in this project, which shapes my thinking about our work. I continue to appreciate my participants' generosity, genuineness, and generativity and look forward to the insights their lives will reveal in the future.

Making sense of the participants' journeys for the purpose of my journey also involved good company beyond the longitudinal participants. My meaning making has been shaped by numerous intense dialogues with my graduate students as we struggle in our student development theory courses to make sense of college students' evolution of mind, voice and self. These dialogues open new avenues of thought and enhance my sense of possibility. Similar dialogues with alumni who are trying to transform educational practice to promote self-authorship keep me grounded in reality. I am particularly appreciative of extended conversations with Kevin and Trena Yonkers-Talz and Kelli Zaytoun Byrne whose perspectives have extended my thinking.

Many colleagues have provided good company in interpreting the journey toward self-authorship. Two colleagues—Lisa Boes and Michele Welkener—made invaluable contributions by reading transcripts with me and participating in extensive dialogue to explore possible interpretations. Our collective thinking sketched the initial version of the journey toward self-authorship. Their responses to manuscript drafts have strengthened the narrative contained here. Both continue to share resources and their thinking about our mutual interests in ways that enrich my work. Colleagues who share similar research interests have generously shared their insights in reactions to papers and long conversations. I am indebted to Blythe McVicker Clinchy and Patricia King for their generosity in exploring possibilities, sharing their research, and sparking new lines of thinking for me. Patricia King's careful review of this manuscript deepened my understanding of the journey and helped me articulate it more clearly. The support and feedback I have enjoyed from various journal editors and book publishers has also enhanced the quality of this longitudinal work. Gregory Blimling, editor of the *Journal of College Student Development*, has given me exceptional guidance over the years as did Joan Stark when she edited the *Review of Higher Education*. Gale Erlandson (Jossey-Bass Publishers), John Braxton (Vanderbilt University Press), and John von Knorring (Stylus Publishing) have contributed to my work through both their support and intellectual contributions. Many colleagues too numerous to name have contributed to this work via responding to conference papers and presentations as well as writing about similar developmental trajectories. My perspective on human development, as well as my interest in it, was significantly influenced by the work of the late William G. Perry, Jr., Mary F. Belenky, Blythe McVicker Clinchy, Nancy R. Goldberger, Jill M. Tarule, Patricia M. King, and Karen S. Kitchener. My ability to sustain this longitudinal project is also due to the support of my departmental colleagues, particularly Peter Magolda, Judy Rogers, Nelda Cambron-McCabe, Jan Clegg, and Peggy Bower.

My deepest gratitude goes to two people without whom my own journey toward self-authorship would have been impossible. My mother, Marjorie A. Baxter, consistently modeled self-authorship for me, supported my self-authorship, and invited me into a genuinely mutual partnership. As a result we have enjoyed a mutually rewarding mother-daughter relationship throughout our adult lives. I am thankful for this precious and unique gift. I am fortunate to have a second mutual partnership with my spouse, Peter M. Magolda. Peter is both a professional and personal partner. His expertise in qualitative inquiry has enriched my approach to the longitudinal project; his willingness to engage in extensive intellectual explorations of the meaning of the narratives has transformed my ability to make sense them. As my spouse, his patience with long evening and weekend interviews has made sustaining this project easier. His participation in our mutual partnership has created a context for my own self-authorship to evolve.

PREFACE

Successful journeys, even short ones, require good company. This point was reinforced for me in a recent visit to the Hawaiian Islands. While there, my spouse and I participated in an excursion called Maui Downhill. Maui Downhill was a 38-mile bicycle trek from the 10,000 foot summit of the Haleakala volcano to the ocean's edge—the key word here being downhill! The tour company provided us with bicycles, helmets, a van to follow us to collect those of us who might not make the trek, and a guide named Robert who would ride in front of our ten-member group. Robert explained how to lean into the hairpin turns, how to follow his hand signals to slow for turns and to let traffic pass, how to use our brakes effectively (particularly important on a downhill trip), and reminded us not to get too distracted by the scenery. Most of all Robert emphasized that we were in control of our own bicycles and thus our own and others' safety. Our journey was complicated because we were sharing the winding mountain road with automobile drivers who were also enjoying the scenery. Robert emphasized our role in the safety of the trek, noting that our varying weights affected our speed and that our attentiveness and risk-taking behavior mediated our ability to control our own bicycles. Yet Robert offered us autonomy to make good judgments in this complex situation and trusted us to act responsibly. We realized the complexity of our trek as we all successfully rounded the first hairpin turn. A rider not associated with our tour had just missed the turn and gone over the edge of the mountain. We stopped briefly as Robert went to assist the park rangers in rescue efforts and upon his return we paid more attention to his hand signals. Robert's good company resulted in our safe arrival at the ocean's edge four hours later.

Unfortunately the journey into adulthood is not downhill and good company is hard to find. The early years of the journey into adult life are particularly difficult because they are the years of profound transformation. College is viewed by many students as an experience that will ensure them a positive path into adulthood or in the case of returning adult students an experience that will lead to a more positive path than the one they are currently on. And although students may not initially conceive of college as a journey, educators know that it is. Educators have multiple expectations for the journey that is called a college education. For example, we expect students to acquire knowledge, learn how to analyze it, and learn the process of judging what to believe themselves—what developmental theorists call complex ways of knowing. We expect students to develop an internal sense of identity—an understanding of how they view themselves and what they value. We expect them to learn how to construct healthy relationships with others, relationships based on mutuality rather than self-sacrifice, and relationships that affirm diversity. We expect them to integrate these ways of knowing, being and interacting with others into the capacity for self-authorship—the capacity to internally define their own beliefs, identity, and relationships. This self-authorship, this internal capacity, is the necessary foundation for mutual, collaborative participation with others in adult life.

Educators provide students company on this difficult journey. We offer maps (e.g., the curriculum and cocurriculum) and highlight possible pathways (e.g., majors, leadership opportunities). We point out important stops along the way and activities to pursue at those stops that will make the journey more productive. We advise students when to slow down, when to let traffic pass, and when to use their brakes. We encourage students to explore on their journey, but at the same time to be mindful of others along the way. Educators also monitor travel difficulties. We help students who get stuck along the way and seem to have trouble getting back on the road. We deal with instances of road rage—travelers who violate others' rights in their exploration, or who lose control of themselves to their own detriment. Being good company for literally thousands of students, all of whom are on different journeys, is a complex challenge. This book is about how to be good company for college students on their journey toward self-authorship.

A Longitudinal Study of Young Adults' Development

My perspective on the need for good company for college students' journey toward self-authorship emerged from my longitudinal study of young adults' development from age 18 to their early thirties. I initiated the study in 1986 with 101 first-year college students to better understand learning and intellectual development during college. Annual interviews yielded a portrait of ways of knowing during college, which I described in detail in *Knowing and Reasoning in College: Gender-Related Patterns in Students' Intellectual Development* (Baxter Magolda, 1992). A brief overview here sets the stage for these young adults' continued journey toward self-authorship during their twenties.

Upon entrance to college, most participants were absorbed with finding out what the authorities thought—a way of knowing I called absolute. However, it wasn't long until most realized that authorities did not have all the answers, that some of what was to be known was still up for grabs. From this transitional way of knowing, participants realized that the search for knowledge was necessary in some arenas, but not having a process of their own to use they followed the lead of their teachers. Although most remained transitional knowers throughout college, a few participants adopted an independent way of knowing their senior year, assuming that most knowledge was uncertain and people chose to believe whatever they felt best. Only two participants adopted contextual knowing, a set of assumptions that included viewing knowledge as relative to a context and knowledge claims better or worse based on evaluation of relevant evidence. Independent and contextual knowing, both of which rose dramatically in the year after college graduation, marked the beginning of participants' awareness of the necessity for self-authorship in adult life (Baxter Magolda, 1994, 1995, 1998).

Thus participants left college having made little progress toward self-authorship, a circumstance that is typical according to similar research on college student development (Belenky, Clinchy, Goldberger, and Tarule, 1986; King and Kitchener, 1994). My interest in how this would affect their lives after college and how their development would proceed led to the post-college phase of the study. Recognizing that I had focused too narrowly on intellectual development (an issue in the overall college environment as well, as will become evident in this book), I expanded the focus of the study to include participants' sense of their identity and their relationships with others. Although our annual interviews still included conversation about the dynamics of good learning opportunities, we also discussed how participants' viewed themselves and their interconnections with others. These 300 plus interviews over participants' twenties yielded a more holistic portrait of the journey toward self-authorship (Baxter Magolda, 1999a, 1999e, 2000). Most importantly, the interviews revealed the central role internal self-definition plays in self-authorship. Internal self-definition is crucial to balancing external and internal forces in knowing and relating to others.

This book focuses on the stories of 39 participants who remained in the study through their twenties. These stories show the transformation from external to internal self-definition, the crucial shift in moving toward self-authorship.

Their stories of their twenties are important for college educators because they reveal the complexities and processes of the journey toward self-authorship. Understanding this journey and its complexities and multiple forms is the first step toward being good company. The stories are equally valuable because they describe the conditions that promote self-authorship, in essence giving college educators a framework for being good company. These stories offer useful insights to assist many of today's college students, the majority of whom are in their twenties, in their quest for self-authorship.

The participants' stories offer college faculty specific examples in multiple disciplines of how to be good company to promote self-authorship in the classroom and in faculty-student interactions. College student affairs educators will benefit from seeing how the framework applies to service learning, leadership opportunities, career services and academic advising, and a broad range of educational programming. Both faculty and student affairs educators will learn how to provide good company to promote self-authorship through paraprofessional positions in academic affairs, student affairs, and campus services. Current students reading these stories could also gain insight into how they are approaching the journey and identify experiences that would help them along the way.

An Overview of the Journey toward Self-Authorship

Although participants' journeys toward self-authorship varied in texture, form and pace, four phases of the journey emerged consistently in the shift from external to internal self-definition. The first phase, *following external formulas,* was prevalent in the early years after college. Although most participants realized the necessity of developing their own minds and voices soon after college graduation, they did not have experience in developing their internal voices. Thus they continued to follow formulas for knowing the world and themselves that they borrowed from the external world around them. Gwen conveyed this approach saying, "We're taught to make [our] plan. Plan your work and work your plan and you are going to get where you want to go." Some did in fact get where they wanted to go and found it less meaningful than they had anticipated. Others found that the formulas did not work to achieve their goals. This dissatisfaction with following the formulas, which emerged for most participants by their mid-twenties, led to the second phase, *the crossroads* of the journey. At this juncture, participants realized that their dissatisfaction stemmed from ignoring their own internal needs and perspectives and that they needed to look inward for self-definition. For example, in his midtwenties Kurt shared, "I'm coming from a position where I get my worth and my value from other people, which is, I think, wrong for me to do." Work on looking inward led to movement out of the crossroads into the third phase of the journey: *becoming the author of one's own life.* This phase involved deciding what to believe, one's identity, and how to interact with others. Dawn described it like this: "The more you discover about yourself . . . you become comfortable with who you really are. . . . You realize that it doesn't really matter if other people agree with you or not. You can think and formulate ideas for yourself and ultimately that's what's important. You have a mind and you can use it." Dawn's discovery of the ability to formulate her own ideas, to use her own mind, represents the process of becoming the author of her life. Continued movement in authoring their lives led participants to the fourth phase: an *internal foundation* that grounded them. Mark's sense of power over his own life characterizes this foundation. He said, "I believe I am the author of my life. I can make decisions right now that can change it in any direction. [That's] a tremendous amount of power; external influence pales in comparison." Mark's comment reveals the essence of self-authorship—that he manages external influence rather than being controlled by it. Yet self-authorship is not selfish or self-centered; it involves careful consideration of external perspectives and others' needs, but this consideration occurs in the context of one's internal foundation. The latter part of participants' twenties was occupied with becoming the authors of their lives; the internal foundation rarely solidified before age 30.

This journey from formula to foundation revealed how *three dimensions of development*—how we know or decide what to believe, how we view ourselves, and how we construct relationships with others—intertwined to contribute to self-authorship. How we know or decide what to believe, or the *epistemological dimension,* is often the primary focus of college. How we view ourselves, or the *intrapersonal dimension,* is viewed as important but not the central focus of a college education. How we construct relationships with others, or the *interpersonal dimension,* is often viewed as beyond the purview of educators. Participants' journeys through their twenties show that self-authorship requires growth on all three dimensions. Adopting contextual assumptions about how to know (via evaluation of evidence and choosing the best knowledge claims) was insufficient for self-authorship because participants lacked an internal sense of self or identity from which to choose what to believe. This intrapersonal dynamic also meant a shortcoming in the interpersonal arena; participants' relationships with others were constructed to please others with insufficient regard for their own needs. Without an internal sense of self, participants' beliefs, identity, and relationships were defined by external others. As Kurt and Dawn clearly articulated above, concern about others' perspectives was a key barrier to achieving self-authorship. Good company during their twenties helped participants make the shift to internal self-definition from which negotiation with others to form mutual relationships was possible, opening the way for self-authorship in all three dimensions of their development.

Good Company: Creating the Conditions to Promote Self-Authorship

Participants occupied diverse contexts during their twenties. Many pursued graduate or professional education in varied disciplines and types of institutions. Their employment settings included business, human service agencies, educational institutions and government posts. Leadership roles, volunteer work, and family responsibilities also framed their lives in unique ways. From an analysis of these multiple contexts and their influence on participants' journeys toward self-authorship, a framework of the conditions to promote self-authorship emerged. Despite diversity across contexts, environments that promoted self-authorship consistently operated on *three key assumptions*. These assumptions modeled the expectation for self-authorship in each developmental dimension.

First, these environments conveyed *knowledge as complex and socially constructed*. Whether engaged in a course assignment, job responsibility, or volunteer role, participants were faced with multiple interpretations, ambiguity, and the need to negotiate what to believe with others. This complexity modeled the epistemological growth—the capacity to wisely choose from among multiple alternatives—needed for self-authorship. Framing knowledge as complex and socially constructed gave rise to the second assumption—*that self is central to knowledge construction*. Participants were encouraged to bring themselves into their learning, work, and relationships. Encouragement to define themselves and bring this to their way of being in the world modeled the intrapersonal growth, the internal sense of self, needed for self-authorship. The third assumption evident in these environments was that *authority and expertise were shared in the mutual construction of knowledge among peers*. The invitation, and necessity, to participate as equal partners in this mutual construction modeled the interpersonal growth, or the ability to function interdependently with others, needed for self-authorship. These three assumptions were tightly coupled in environments that were most effective in promoting self-authorship.

These three assumptions were usually not explicitly stated, however. They were, instead, enacted through the approach educators, employers, or other adults took to interacting with the longitudinal participants. This approach parallels and extends three principles for educational practice I initially identified from the college phase of the study (Baxter Magolda, 1992). These principles were derived from college experiences that aided students' intellectual development, and further supported by an observation study in which their use in college courses promoted students' intellectual development (Baxter Magolda, 1999b). Participants' stories in their twenties provide further evidence that these three principles help educators join learners at their current developmental place in the journey and promote movement toward self-authorship. Thus they translate the three assumptions into educational practice.

The first principle, *validating learners' capacity to know,* was evident in employers' soliciting employees' perspectives and trusting their judgments as well as in educators' interest in learners' experiences and respect for their beliefs. This validation invited participants' into the knowledge construction process, conveyed that their ideas were welcome, and offered respect that boosted their confidence in themselves. The second principle, *situating learning in learners' experience,* was evident in educational and employment settings that used participants' existing knowledge and experience as the basis for continued learning and decision-making. Participants perceived the use of their current knowledge and experience as a sign of respect; it simultaneously gave them a foundation for enhancing their learning or work. The third principle, *mutually constructing meaning,* involved educators or employers connecting their knowledge to that of the participants to arrive at more complex understandings and decisions. This welcomed participants as equal participants in knowledge construction, helped them clarify their own perspectives, and helped them learn how to negotiate with others.

These three principles helped promote self-authorship by modeling it and providing participants the kind of support they needed to shift from external to internal self-definition. Because participants were at varying places along the journey, the company they needed varied accordingly. Situating learning in learners' experience and mutual construction of meaning helped educators and employers connect to and stay in tune with participants' development. Mutual construction helped educators and employers understand participants' journeys, an important part of being good company.

The Need for Good Company during College

The world in which college graduates will live and lead is becoming more complex by the minute. Survival in the 21st century requires flexibility, adaptability, the capacity to negotiate between one's own and others' needs, and the ability to cope with rapid change, ambiguity, diversity and complexity. If we expect our graduates to be leaders—in their work, personal lives, and communities—they need to achieve self-authorship. The participants whose stories are told here attended a quality university with a focus on undergraduate education, a caring faculty, and an extensive co-curricular program. Yet their college experience reinforced listening to authorities rather than developing self-authorship. They had significant responsibility in society in their early twenties—they held responsible jobs in both the public and private sectors; they became community leaders; they had children. They are our children's teachers, our accountants, our lawyers and doctors. Many had these responsibilities before they traversed the crossroads to become the authors of their own lives. They would have been better prepared for these roles, and have struggled less, had the conditions for self-authorship been created during their college experience.

Having followed their journeys from the beginning of college to their early thirties, I concluded that the missing piece of their college experience was the lack of emphasis on developing an internal sense of self. They learned disciplinary content and processes for thinking about it and applying it. It was not until after college, however, that their employers and graduate educators stressed that their thinking, knowing, and applying their perspectives to their work all hinged on their internal values and how they defined themselves. The crucial role of educators in providing guidance and good company while they constructed internal definitions is evident in their post-college stories. Inviting the self into the educational process requires moving away from the traditional forms of teaching and control-oriented forms of organizing student life that prevail on many campuses. This book describes how using the framework for promoting self-authorship in teaching, campus work settings, and the co-curriculum can move higher education practice in this direction.

Organization of the Book

A large part of our being good company is understanding students' journeys—listening carefully to hear students' perspectives on their experience and progress. I use participants' own words in part 1 to offer readers the opportunity to hear students' perspectives.[1] Chapter 1 introduces the themes and driving questions that occupied their twenties, the societal expectations they

---

[1]The story I tell here, of course, is my interpretation of participant's journeys. The issue of representation, or whose story is told, is addressed more extensively in the methodological appendix.

encountered, and how these themes and expectations translated to the need for self-authorship on all three dimensions of development. A brief overview of their college journeys serves as an introduction to the journey through the twenties. Chapter 2 offers an overview of the journey toward self-authorship using two participants' stories to illustrate the trajectory of the shift from external to internal self-definition. Chapters 3 through 6 then detail the four phases—following external formulas, the crossroads, becoming authors of their own lives, and the internal foundation.

Part 2 articulates the conditions that promote self-authorship and translates them into educational practice. Chapter 7 uses participants' experiences in graduate and professional education to show how the three assumptions and three principles can be used to transform pedagogy and faculty-student relations. Chapter 8 illustrates how the same assumptions and principles were prevalent in participants' diverse work settings. These assumptions and principles are then translated to campus work environments including research and teaching assistants, internships, student affairs paraprofessional roles in admission, orientation and residential life, leadership positions in student organizations and government, and service roles in campus libraries, laboratories, and recreational and food service facilities. Examples in both undergraduate and graduate work settings are included. Chapter 9 draws on a variety of participants' experiences to construct a cocurriculum that promotes self-authorship. Participants' volunteer work and leadership roles help frame service learning and student leadership opportunities around the conditions to promote self-authorship. Participants' experiences with career issues and decisions are used to conceptualize career services and academic advising practices to promote self-authorship. Finally, participants' experiences with relationship issues with partners, parents, co-workers, and supervisors are translated to forms of educational programming in interpersonal communication, diversity, relationship building, collaboration, conflict management, and community building. Collectively, part two offers a comprehensive framework through which to invite the self into the educational process and promote self-authorship during college.

An Invitation

The opportunity to observe my longitudinal participants' journeys from the beginning of college to their early thirties has taught me more about being good company for college students than I ever imagined. Their stories have had a profound impact on my own college teaching and the philosophy I share with my graduate students who are preparing to be student affairs professionals.

Encouraging students to control their own bicycles is difficult but, as will become clear in the following pages, well worth the effort. I invite you to come along on these participants' journeys through their twenties to learn how to become better company for young adults working their way toward self-authorship.

PART ONE

THE JOURNEY TOWARD SELF-AUTHORSHIP

I

COMPLEX LIVES

The five or six years that follow college are critical years for learning. Get out of the structured atmosphere; try your own wings; fly on your own! What is supposed to be good, what is important to me, what are my real values? For the first time I have a chance to listen to my own voice. I finally got to a point [in my mid-twenties] where I was paying a lot of attention to that. During that time I was processing all that I had been gathering for the prior years. I was finally able to see a clear path, chart a course, and now am on the course.

Gwen

If I think about the future too much it scares the living bejesus out of me.

Phillip

Gwen and Phillip are two of 39 participants in a longitudinal study of young adults' learning and development from ages 18 to 30. I open this book with their two comments because the driving questions of young adult life for the total group of participants are highlighted in these brief excerpts. Gwen's emphasis on listening to her own voice captures perhaps the most pressing issue this group faced during their twenties. Exploring one's values, processing information gathered from the external world in prior years, envisioning a path, and proceeding down that path mark the major themes of these participants' lives during their twenties. Phillip's sentiment conveys the emotion he and his peers felt during this age range.

This chapter portrays the complexity of young adulthood as a backdrop for the participants' journeys toward self-authorship. The pressing questions that occupied their twenties—"How do I know?" "Who am I?" "What relationships do I want with others?"—reveal this complexity from the participants' vantage point. The societal expectations they encountered—rapid change, ambiguity, and multiple lifestyle choices—sketch this complexity from the vantage point of contemporary society. I then use a student development lens to show the developmental complexity these expectations entail, essentially that they require self-authorship in the epistemological, intrapersonal, and interpersonal dimensions of development. Interconnections among the most complex phases of each dimension depict the complex transformation required of young adults in today's society. The role of higher education in stewarding this transformation is introduced next, followed by an overview of the participants' college journeys to provide context for their journey through their twenties. Thus the chapter closes with the participants standing at the threshold of self-authorship.

Driving Questions of the Twenties

As one might expect, the central concerns for most participants after college were career success, finding meaningful relationships, finding their way in the adult world, establishing families, and in general "being happy." Hearing variations on these concerns over time revealed a few driving questions that stood at the core of these issues. As mentioned previously these included: 'How do I know?' 'Who am I?' and 'What relationships do I want with others?' A key issue in all three questions was hearing one's own voice regarding each of these questions. The particulars of participants' experiences illustrate the essence of these questions.

How Do I Know?

Mark described the twenties as a time to articulate the questions, "What is causing my unhappiness? What would make me happy? Trying to understand that." These questions arose in Mark's life despite his success at the law school of his choice; they occurred to others despite success in their post-college careers. Heather asked herself, "What is the most important thing in my life? Is there one? Am I doing the right thing?" Dissatisfaction or lack of fulfillment in their initial career choices led to the issue of how one knows what to do. Gwen articulated the issue best by saying:

> The 'how you know' question was huge for me. Then career exploring, where are the answers? Learn to figure out what is important to you; learn to find what fits for you in work settings rather than thinking I have to work in advertising. Learning

where your values are first, rather than putting things first that you don't know about.

Gwen, as you will hear in chapter 2, followed the plan others had suggested for career success in her early twenties. During her twenties, however, she realized that "how *you* know" really came down to "how *I* know." She conveyed the struggle to know in weighing a marriage decision, saying:

> There are some things that just don't come with guarantees or instructions and you just have to trust your gut, take the leap of faith and muddle through with your instincts. . . . It's just one of those things where you set everything in line as best you can and then you look at it and you say, "Well, is it going to be a go?" And you go and you hope. And you just trust that what you thought was right. But again, that's totally against everything—I want a crystal ball. I want to know when and where and how and if.

Gwen wanted to know but she did not know how. As her quote at the outset of the chapter indicated, she discovered that listening to her own voice was the key to knowing.

Lindsey conveyed the changing nature of the "how you know" question throughout the years after college. Talking about changes in learning, he offered:

> A lot of these experiences are less technical than ones I talked about when I was a sophomore—then I was learning how to differentiate an algebraic equation. Ten years later you find yourself trying to quiet a baby. Eight years ago I was studying pricing theory and ramifications thereof; now I'm thinking about managing styles. I'm trying to learn to be a good daddy. It's ironic that when you have more knowledge than you have ever had, the types of things you are learning are less technical, less hard to learn. The process doesn't stop, it is just different. Also the ramifications back then if you didn't learn it, fine, try something else. Now, if you don't learn how to be a good parent, there are big ramifications. Or your career path goes to manager and you flop. The ramifications are pretty serious. Learning has become less intense, yet the ramifications become more intense. Different pressures. Different reasons for wanting to learn something; and different methods you use.

Although Lindsey did not label the difference other than technical and less technical, it seemed that he was describing the difference between learning and knowing in circumstances where there were tangible answers (i.e., the algebraic equation) and circumstances in which knowing was more subjective (i.e., quieting a baby). Encountering complexity and ambiguity in knowledge construction and learning facilitated movement toward self-authorship in how one knows (the epistemological dimension). The need to choose "how *I* know" from among the alternatives drew participants toward self-authorship.

Who Am I?

A closely related and equally pressing question was "Who am I?" Answering the "how I know" question necessitated defining who the "I" was. Al described changes in this arena during his twenties:

> In my early twenties, I was kind of out there swinging. Living for the day. Working and making good money, doing a lot of what I wanted to do. I didn't have anybody to account to or worry about. I was playing basketball, working out, and dating a lot of people. It was a much more selfish time for me. In my mid-twenties I figured out, okay, that wasn't fulfilling. When I focused energy on selfless things, I had more fun. I developed a more mature attitude.

Part of Al's decision about who he was related to changing from computer consulting to medical school. Al reported that when you realize you are going to be working for the rest of your life, the meaning of that work takes on a new importance. Another dimension involved volunteering as a big brother and becoming involved in his church. In response to a lack of fulfillment, he listened more carefully to his own voice in guiding life choices.

Barry described a similar experience. He recounted what happens when the "honeymoon" is over:

> You start settling into a job. The first year of working, the honeymoon of wearing a suit, when you look forward to doing that in the beginning. And you're not really thinking about your future; you're thinking about the next day. You're not thinking long term, you're like, "Okay, I have a job. Now let's see how I like it." But then after the first year, you start thinking about what you want to do down the road. You start saying, "Do I want to be doing this for the next twenty years? What do I want to be doing? If it's not this, what is it and how do I get there?" And where do you want to live? Not only what do I want to do, but also where do I want to do it and whom do I want to do it with? Do I want to spend the rest of my life with this person or do I want to give up my freedom?

Like Al, when Barry realized that these are long-term decisions, he began to question who he really wanted to be. Phillip was struggling with the same questions:

> If I think about the future too much it scares the living bejesus out of me. It would be nice to think something good is coming around the corner tomorrow. I have my own place, I'm paying the rent, it is stable, that doesn't scare me. But I keep thinking, "Am I going to be staying here the rest of my life?" I don't think I will, but I haven't opened up my eyes enough to see there is a niche for what I do. Being good at music doesn't matter here— that might be different in Nashville. A person invited me to Nashville for a training session. I went, and they are doing a lot of stuff there. I enjoy country music, but it is not my main thing. I'd like to be able to do a variety of things if I got into music production. Then other things, questions in my mind about people around me. The people living in my building are twenty- and thirty-somethings; some are going to prestigious schools, driving expensive cars, hoping to become doctors of various kinds, or professionals in the city. I don't see how, with my background, I can relate to these people. I hang out with my girlfriend on her side of town—row houses, working class people. A lot of people there are not college educated, do not speak English very well—for a kid from the suburbs seeing that is a shake-up. Nothing in common there either. It doesn't seem like a natural fit. I'm not trying to be snobbish; I can adapt to my surroundings and different lifestyles. These are a lot of things I do think about—I have periods of angst and periods of calmness.

Phillip was looking for a niche—for what he wanted to do (music production) and for what kind of person he wanted to or could be. Unable to find a fit either with his building mates or his girlfriend's community, he was still exploring.

Alice's dilemma was somewhat different, although still focused on the "who am I" question. Alice was satisfied with her career, but also wanted a child. She shared the dilemma of juggling the two:

> I have always known that [having a child] is something I want; the intensity of wanting it is increasing drastically. My spouse is on the same wavelength. We both have strong family relationships and want this. [The challenge will be] juggling. Honestly, my initial thoughts were "That isn't fair that I have to balance because I am the woman; nothing will change for him. Why should I have to give up what I have worked so hard for?" Probably six months I felt that. I felt that wasn't getting anywhere;

then my thinking became, "Family is priority one, so given that, how can I keep things I enjoy about professional life?" Child is number one, profession is two. How can I make number two as satisfying as possible? Being mad about [professional sacrifice] doesn't change anything . . . biologically determined. I've worked as hard as he has. We talked about it. Reality is, it affects me more. Since then it has been a matter of accepting and embracing it. Deciding that I wanted it, not feeling like it had to be. That is the biggest challenge right now. How will it play out to manage professional responsibilities while going through a pregnancy? We've talked about how we will do this with a kid. Something will have to change and something will work out. . . . I have always been confident [of my ability] to direct my own life.

Alice wanted to be both a career professional and a mother. Although she in some ways knew the answer to the "who am I" question, she was initially bothered by external constraints she faced and later concerned about what this identity would really look like. Participants' struggle with the "who am I" question (the intrapersonal dimension) stemmed from their discovery that self was central to knowledge construction. Clarification of their values and priorities was necessary for them to make good career and personal decisions.

What Kind of Relationships Do I Want to Construct with Others?

Once the internal sense of self materialized, it was necessary to incorporate it into relationships. Thus the flip side of the "who am I" question was "What kind of relationships do I want?" Lynn conveyed the reciprocal nature of these two questions:

I think it is a hard time relationship wise. Because you and your prospective other—you both are changing. I know as far as that goes with a lot of friends, they are divorced—got married too early. A lot of people make that mistake; happily it wasn't me. You tend to grow, a huge change time, especially the first three years out of college. Trying to find your niche in your environment—move to a new city, or start a new job, or, as in my case, to find that real job. Becoming independent, growing up. You are an adult now; you have to be accepting of all your situations that you put yourself into and sometimes that's not good. But I think that my twenties were a time of maturing and finding myself and becoming happy, becoming a positive person. I didn't just get to 30 and say, "Okay, I'm here"—it just didn't happen. It's a huge process and I think people get there at different ages and stages. I had friends who were ready at age 24; they found it, they got it, whatever *it* is-they got *it*. It took me a couple years more and that's fine. It takes everybody a certain time. Can't say you need to be here at age 25. You can't do it—too many obstacles in the way. I think independence and maturity are something that I would say sum up my twenties. Feeling all right, okay with what's going on.

Lynn articulated that as people grow and change who they are, they sometimes find themselves having difficulty with relationships. Many participants did struggle with maintaining, and in some cases dissolving, relationships due to their own self-evolution. Others struggled with whether they were ready for various kinds of relationships. Justin explained his worry about the upcoming birth of his first child:

It scares me to death. It is a major life change; don't know if I'm ready. We planned it, now it is really going to happen. There is no going back now. I'm anxious about it, it makes me nervous. It is going to be a huge time commitment; I am afraid about the normal stuff like we won't have enough money, or I'll screw something up and not be able to take care of it, or it might screw up our marriage. I'm nervous as hell. I'm in over my head. But it is exciting too. Sometimes I feel like things just happen to you. Things just roll. You just make decisions; it's weird. Time determines a lot of things—decisions are made because of something you did or didn't do. This whole decision making process—deciding to have a baby. My spouse had a big say in that; I kept putting it off. She was 30, and she said, "We can't wait much longer." There was pressure to do that because she was afraid if we waited it would be risky. I felt pressured there; but she was right. I don't want to be that old when my kid is in high school. Felt pressured, a little resentment, but then what can you do, because she was right. That is part of my anxiety— do I really want this? Too late now. I'm sure it will be great when it happens; I hope so. It is an overwhelming experience; all these thoughts and doubts will go out window when the baby comes.

Part of Justin's fear came from not being totally sure he wanted "this"—his fear of the relationship of father and child. He was also not totally sure about a career change he was preparing for—a move from classroom teacher to principal—due to his relationship with his father. He shared his issues:

There aren't many men in elementary special education. My dad is a teamster electrician, big union man. My grandfather was a pipe fitter, uncle was an engineer, and another was a maintenance supervisor—manly jobs. It is stupid that I care about that. [He laughed.] Wanting to be accepted by males in the family. I don't want them to think I'm a wuss. That is the biggest thing I don't like about my job; when I go to work, I like it. But I'm not doing some big industrial job. I don't want to do something because my parents want it. My dad is proud of what I do. But I've always thought in back of my head, of whether he thinks I don't have a manly job. It's a weird thing to say, but that is how I feel. Moving toward a principal position is a little more accepted. It sucks that I want to work for something that is more accepted; but that is not the only reason. I do want to make changes.

Justin did make career changes during his twenties, including going back to school to become a special education teacher and again to move toward a position as principal. He made these decisions based on an increasing sense of who he was, yet his concern about his relationships with others still affected his thinking.

Genesse, like Justin, struggled with what she wanted versus what others wanted for or from her. She found herself in a number of frustrating work environments in her twenties and often sacrificed what she wanted to meet others' expectations. Of her twenties, she said, "I try to stand up for myself more—not all the time, but more. If there is one underlying theme of my twenties, that is it." Relationship struggles (the interpersonal dimension) occurred in the context of the shift from external to internal self-definition. As Lynn noted, relationships were hard when both parties were changing. Bringing one's internal sense of self to this layer of knowledge construction altered relationships that pre-dated the external to internal shift. Standing up for oneself, however, was not a selfish matter of having one's own way; it was, rather, a matter of including oneself as a mutual partner in the relationship. Participating in mutual construction of relationships prompted interpersonal growth toward self-authorship. As Genesse noted, the process was not easy.

Complications

Finding their own voices and standing up for themselves was complicated for many participants by personal dynamics and external events.[1] Although all participants were engaged in a search for meaning around the three driving questions, some struggled under additional burdens. One participant shared the additional layer of the "who am I" question posed by exploring sexual orientation. Coming to an acceptance and celebration of this aspect of self also affected how to construct relationships with others in a society that marginalizes gay/lesbian/bisexual people. A few participants identified parts of who they were as problematic and sought therapy to reconstruct them. Sometimes these issues came from difficult family relationships or hereditary health conditions. External events also challenged participants in their twenties. A number of participants lost a grandparent or parent during this time, putting other life issues in perspective. Two participants experienced the murder of a family member, bringing the violence of contemporary society directly into their lives. Many knew friends or family members who suffered from terminal illnesses. Being in relationships with these persons prompted questions about the meaning of life. Others shared their concern regarding parents' divorces and their role in helping both parents while reconstructing their idea of what their family was like. These experiences also made them fear the future of their own relationships. One participant also faced an abortion decision due to the high probability of serious birth defects.

Regardless of their particular circumstances, all participants faced the fact that young adult life was not without struggles. Lynn captured this when she said:

> I've faced the facts of life that it's a cruel world out there. You hear it, but it's true. It's not this nice little piece of cake, you walk out of college and there's a job on a silver platter. I've been through a year of frustration and hard work and brown-nosing and the works to know that hard work doesn't always pay off like we all hoped it would. Dealing with politics, knowing who to work with and who not to work with, who to talk to and who not to talk to, who to trust and who not to trust.

Just as Lynn learned that life is not always fair in job searching, others learned that life dealt unexpected blows or involved struggles in coming to terms with one's internal voice. The driving questions were common among participants as was the complexity of each of their experiences in resolving the questions.

Societal Expectations of Young Adults

The driving questions of the twenties articulated by this group of young adults are not surprising in the context of contemporary society's expectations for them. In fact, the ambiguity of expectations contributed to these driving questions. Levine and Cureton (1998) noted that this generation of young people live "in a time of profound change—demographic, economic, technological, global, social" (p. 9). The U. S. economy generally declined during this period, technology expanded substantially, and organizational change that alters the nature of work emerged—all dynamics that affect the nature of work expectations for young adults. Oblinger and Verville (1998) articulated the skills they say business needs of higher education graduates—"initiative, persistence, integrity, the ability to communicate effectively, to think creatively as well as critically, and to work with others to solve problems" (p. 73). In describing these skills, Oblinger and Verville stressed the evolving nature of learning, the need for self-discipline, self-confidence, and self-direction as well as the interdependence that stems from more flexible organizational structures. Exploring more flexible visions of organizations, Zohar (1997) emphasized the need to cope with uncertainty and rapid change, the need for employees to be "cocreative partners" (p. 87) with employers, and the ability to work with multiple perspectives and supervisory styles. These expectations materialized in the work experiences of my longitudinal participants. They were often expected to work independently, to initiate their own work and problem-solving strategies, to cope with change, and to participate in the creation of their company's practice. Ambiguity was a common dynamic in their work, as was the need to work with others different from themselves. Thus the questions of how to know, self-identity, and relations with others were central to those complex work settings. An extensive discussion of their work experiences and how these contributed to their growth in their twenties is found in chapter 8.

Ambiguity in social roles was also prevalent for these young adults because of changing attitudes and gender roles. Greater higher education opportunities for women were coupled with changing attitudes about women establishing career as a priority. The women in my study, like the men, had high career aspirations and intended to put their education to work both due to their interests and the economic necessity of working. Yet most wanted relationships and families as well, although the timing of acting on this desire varied considerably. Most participants' families expected them to spend the first few years out of college getting settled in their careers and establishing financial security. They perceived that their college peers expected them to develop prestigious careers and demand high salaries. By the mid-twenties many also received the societal message that it was time to marry and have children. As Leah explained it, "you graduate college, then you get married, then you have kids. It's the next step in our lives." Despite growing acceptance of multiple sexual orientations, the overall societal pressure was still for heterosexual relationships.

As you just heard in Gwen's struggle with the marriage decision and Lynn's commentary on friends making marriage mistakes, the decision to marry was difficult for most. Divorce had become a common occurrence in this country as these young adults grew up; in fact many reported that their parents had divorced during their childhood or adolescence or that their parents were divorcing now that they were out of college. Many shared hesitation with deciding to marry—either working on the decision over a number of years, breaking engagements, or hesitating even after living together for some substantial period of time. Similar to young adults portrayed in a Newsweek article on marriage (Hamilton and Wingert, 1998), they questioned whether commitments could last and did not want to find themselves in a divorce.

Decisions to have children and the resulting questions of balancing work and advanced education were also complex. As Alice recounted above, even though she wanted children she still resented giving up her professional career for which she had worked hard. Many participants shared household roles with their partners, and in two cases the fathers took care of infants and pursued advanced education while the mothers continued their careers. In most cases, however, the mother made some adjustments in her professional role to raise children. The need for dual incomes and the importance of graduate or professional education complicated these decisions. Some participants put off starting families for financial reasons; others maintained dual careers after having children out of financial necessity. Mothers who kept active professional lives often worried about the quality of their parenting whereas mothers who made raising children their primary career often wondered what others thought about them. Some tried to excel in both roles. While this led to what Granrose and Kaplan (1996) call "role overload" (p. 7) for some, others found it workable. Much of the confusion in making these decisions for both mothers and fathers stemmed from societal expectations for career success, more flexible perspectives on male and females roles, yet strong messages that remained regarding traditional roles and issues around the quality of life for children.

Social roles in the community were also a factor in these young adults' lives. Perhaps due to the increasing diversity of their generation, or the growth of crime, poverty, and homelessness, or their own experience with economic struggle, they felt responsible for contributing to their community. Some committed extensive time and resources (both financial and emotional) to long-term relationships with young adolescents through Big Brother or Big Sister programs. Others participated in programs to help individuals with financial planning, community maintenance, and assistance to individuals in need. Some took official roles in their churches or community organizations to contribute to their communities. They engaged in these activities despite heavy work schedules and family responsibilities. Their experience seems similar to reports that this generation volunteers more than any other does (Bagby,

1998). Certainly contributing to community and helping to ease America's ills is a societal message they hear regularly. Both Bagby (1998) and Loeb (1994) report extensive service initiatives led by young adults committed to improving the conditions of others in the community.

The Nature of These Expectations: The Transformation to Self-Authorship

Meeting societal expectations and making one's way into young adulthood are complex tasks. Taking on adult responsibilities, managing one's life effectively, and making informed decisions as a member of a community require something beyond learning particular skills and acquiring particular behaviors. They require, instead, the "capacity for self-authorship—the ability to collect, interpret, and analyze information and reflect on one's own beliefs in order to form judgments" (Baxter Magolda, 1998, p. 143). Self-authorship is more than an acquired skill. As Robert Kegan (1994) explained, it requires complex ways of making meaning of our experience. For example, Kegan noted that as workers, adults are expected to:

> invent or own our work . . . to be self-initiating, self-correcting, self-evaluating . . . to be guided by our own visions . . . to take responsibility for what happens to us . . . to be accomplished masters of our particular work roles, jobs, or careers. (p. 153)

These expectations require self-authorship because they require the ability to construct our own visions, to make informed decisions in conjunction with coworkers, to act appropriately, and to take responsibility for those actions. As noted earlier, many longitudinal participants were asked to figure out the direction and details of their work independently and act on those responsibly. Similarly, in the private domains of parenting and partnering, Kegan sketched demands such as:

> establish rules and roles; institute a vision of family purpose . . . manage boundaries (inside and outside the family) . . . be psychologically independent from, but closely connected to, our spouses . . . set limits on children, in-laws, oneself, and extrafamily involvements. (p. 86)

Many participants shared their struggles with balancing independence and connection with partners, spouses, parents, and children. They struggled to create their nuclear families in the context of differences with parents and in-laws. These expectations, like those in public work life, call for understanding relationships in a complex way that allows adults to assess and contrast individual and family needs, determine a course of action in connection with, but not subsumed by, other family members, and take responsibility for those actions. These are not simply skills or behaviors; they emerge from how adults organize, or make meaning of, their experiences and their world.

The driving questions these young adults identified during their twenties—"How do I know?," "Who am I?," "How do I want to construct relationships with others?"—illustrate the intertwining of the multiple dimensions of self-authorship. "How I know?" represents the *epistemological* dimension of self-authorship—the evolution of assumptions about the nature, limits, and certainty of knowledge. The extent to which participants viewed knowledge as certain and the purview of authorities versus uncertain and within their ability to construct mediated the balance of external and internal forces in coming to know. The shift Gwen described from "how do *you* know?" to "how do *I* know?" conveys the emergence of the self-authored voice as the source of knowing, an internal voice from which to interpret and judge knowledge claims from the external world. This self-authored voice required an internal sense of self, the result of work on the "who am I" question. "Who am I?" represents the *intrapersonal* dimension of self-authorship—the evolution of how one thinks about one's sense of self and identity. Most participants initially adopted external expectations as their own without genuine exploration, constructing their identities primarily through external forces. The struggle in the twenties with the "who am I" question was one of finding, listening to, and constructing the internal self-authored voice as the source of self-definition and the internal compass to guide decisions about "how I know." The reciprocal question, "what kind of relationships do I want to construct?" represents the *interpersonal* dimension of self-authorship—the evolution of how one perceives and constructs one's relationships with others. As Lynn succinctly pointed out in her commentary on marrying early, relationships constructed before the internal voice emerged sometimes required reshaping after its arrival. Relationships constructed from an externally-defined identity emphasized what the other wanted whereas relationships constructed from an internally-defined identity brought what the self wanted into the forefront to be negotiated. This same negotiation occurred in weighing others' perspectives in deciding what to believe and how to view the self. This negotiation between external and internal forces (the latter emerging in the shift to internal self-definition) highlights the idea that self-authorship is not self-centered. Self-authorship could be described as "self-in-context," indicating that the self acknowledges external forces and takes them into account as appropriate, rather than "self independent of context," or having one's way regardless of others' perspectives (P. M. King, personal communication, October 2, 2000). The shift to internal self-definition allows the self, previously overshadowed by external forces, to join the external world in a mutual, interdependent partnership.

Although the driving questions emerged from an inductive analysis of the longitudinal stories, the three dimensions they represent are not a construction of this project. Extensive literature exists about each one. The longitudinal participants' experiences in their twenties, however, offer new possibilities regarding what these dimensions involve and how they interconnect. In the next section, a summary of the relevant literature provides a context for the new possibilities inherent in the longitudinal participants' stories.

The Epistemological Dimension

The epistemological dimension is grounded in the constructive-developmental framework of the Piagetian tradition. Jean Piaget (1950) described intelligence in terms of qualitatively different structures through which persons made meaning of their experience. These structures were characterized by particular assumptions about the nature, limits, and certainty of knowledge; assumptions that Kitchener (1983) labeled epistemic. The constructive developmental framework suggests that people construct sets of assumptions to account for their experience and that these evolve over time according to regular principles of stability and change (Kegan, 1982).

Perry (1970) offered the first theory of the evolution of adult epistemological structures based on his study of college men. This evolution involved a shift from accepting knowledge from authorities to making one's own decisions about knowledge claims. Perry described a period he called dualism in which younger adults regarded knowledge in the dual categories of right and wrong. Thus they looked to authorities for the truth. Discrepancies in knowledge and encountering authorities who claimed that knowledge was not dualistic ushered in a period of multiplicity, or the belief that some knowledge was uncertain. Dissonance between this view and experience led older students in Perry's study to adopt a relativistic stance. This way of knowing assumed that knowledge was uncertain and knowledge claims had to be made by judging the relevant evidence.

King and Kitchener (1994) reported a similar evolution in their Reflective Judgment Model, in which development moves from accepting knowledge from authority to making judgments based on evidence and reasonable inquiry. In the pre-reflective thinking they witnessed in late adolescence, students did not acknowledge, or in some cases even perceive, that knowledge could be uncertain. Pre-reflective thinkers relied on authorities much the way Perry's dualists did. In quasi-reflective thinking, which King and Kitchener's research suggests occurs later in college, students recognized the uncertainty inherent in knowledge claims but were not yet able to see how to use evidence in making knowledge claims. In reflective thinking, a phase more typical after college, adults assume that knowledge is relative. Upon arriving at this assumption, individuals rely on evidence and rules of inquiry (e.g., faith or scientific evidence) in a particular context to form a perspective. They later become able to compare and contrast evidence across contexts, leading to the realization that "knowing as a process requires action on the part of the knower; the spectator view of the knower that characterizes earlier thinking will no longer suffice" (King & Kitchener, 1994, p. 66). This ability to compare and contrast evidence across contexts leads to the final stage of reflective thinking in which individuals "take on the role of inquirers; they are agents involved in constructing knowledge" (p. 70). They realize that inquiry is ongoing and that conclusions are open to reevaluation based on further inquiry.

Belenky, Clinchy, Goldberger, and Tarule (1986) constructed a similar portrait of adult epistemological structures based on a study of college and adult women. Their theory involved a shift from taking in knowledge from others to constructing it oneself. In the early phases, women were either silent on the assumption that they were not capable of knowing, or received knowledge from authorities. Experiences that called these sets of assumptions into question led to subjective knowing in which women turned to their own voices. Eventually they turned to procedures to make sense out of their experience, a way of knowing similar to King and Kitchener's quasi-reflective knowing. When these procedures seemed to create a distance between the knower and the known, these women moved to constructed knowing, a concept similar to King and Kitchener's reflective thinking. Belenky et al. (1986; Clinchy, 1996) also described two forms of knowing that emerged in their procedural phase: separate and connected. The separate knower stood at arm's length from the object to be known and approached perspectives from a doubting stance in order to come to know. The connected knower entered into the object to be known, trying to see what could be believed about it. Belenky and her colleagues noted that women in their study demonstrated both patterns and that the separate pattern was more closely aligned with Perry's descriptions.

The possibility of gender-related patterns within epistemological structures was the impetus for the longitudinal project upon which this book is based. I used an inductive approach to the college phase of the study to construct a gender-inclusive model of epistemological development (Baxter Magolda, 1992). The model resulting from the college phase described the movement from absolute knowing (in which knowledge is assumed to be certain), through transitional knowing (in which some knowledge is believed to be uncertain), to independent knowing (in which knowledge is assumed to be largely uncertain). Although some evidence of contextual knowing (in which knowledge claims are made based upon relevant evidence within a context) emerged, this occurred rarely. Thus this model repeated earlier models in movement from accepting knowledge from authorities to constructing knowledge oneself. Two gender-related patterns emerged in that process—one impersonal and one relational. The impersonal pattern reflected knowing through separation or detachment, whereas the relational pattern reflected knowing through connection and getting inside the object of knowing. These patterns show some parallel to Belenky et al.'s separate and connected knowing, however they were evident in absolute, transitional and independent knowing. I concluded that they represented gender-related patterns within epistemological structures.

The Intrapersonal and Interpersonal Dimensions

The intrapersonal dimension is most often referred to as identity or self-evolution. Ruthellen Josselson wrote, "Identity is what we make of ourselves within a society that is making something of us" (1996, p. 28). Her comment reveals the difficulty of separating these two dimensions; I deal with them together here due to their close relationship. The concept of identity is most often associated with Erik Erikson (1968), who conceptualized identity as a psychosocial process involving challenges from the interaction of physical and cognitive growth with the demands of the environment. Arthur Chickering's (1969; Chickering & Reisser, 1993) theory of college students' identity emerged from this perspective as did Ruthellen Josselson's (1987, 1996) theory of women's identity development. These theories painted identity development as an evolving process in which we continually rework our sense of ourselves and our relationships with other people as we encounter challenges in the environment that call our current conceptualizations into question. Forms of identity in the early years of college, according to Chickering, Reisser, and Josselson, were highly dependent on external forces. The college experience offered opportunities for questioning and exploration, raising the possibility of constructing an identity separate from external forces. This often resulted in new identities formed on the basis of adult's own internal voices. Thus the formation of identity is closely tied to the relationships one has with external others.

Similarly, the relationships one has with external others are mediated by one's identity development. For example, Kegan (1994) describes a phase of self-evolution (called the third order of consciousness) in late adolescence and early adulthood in which identity is consumed by our relationships with others—we *are* our relationships in this phase. In the next phase, called fourth order, we become able to stand apart from our relationships and reflect upon them. Kegan described this as having a relationship to our relationships. In the early phases of identity development when external definition is strongest, young adults are most likely consumed by their relationships. In later years after the internal voice has emerged in other dimensions, relationships are reconstructed to account for the needs of the individual and the needs of others.

Judith Jordan (1997) spoke to this latter notion using the concept of mutuality. She has defined *mutuality* as "involv[ing] commitment to engage in the development and support of both people; it involves respectfully building a relationship together that both sustains and transcends the individuals engaged in it" (p. 32). As such, mutuality requires that each person be able to "represent her or his own experience in a relationship, to act in a way which is congruent with an 'inner truth' and with the context, and to respond to and encourage authenticity in the other person" (p. 31). Mutuality neither sacrifices self nor other too much. Jordan has suggested that in this new vision autonomy takes the form of being clear in our thoughts and actions, acting with intention, but at the same time recognizing the impact of our actions on others. The concept of mutuality constitutes interdependence.

The concepts of separation and connection emerging from study of the epistemological dimension also arose in the intrapersonal and interpersonal dimensions. Initially, identity development was conceptualized (based primarily on studies of men) as a story of increasing independence and individuation from others (Chickering, 1969; Erikson, 1968). This conceptualization called for the development of agency, or the ability to separate from others and function as an autonomous individual. Bakan (1966) initially coined the term *agency*, noting that it focuses on "the existence of an organism as an individual" (p. 15). He offered self-protection, self-assertion, and self-expansion as dynamics of agency. Thus agency is characterized by increasing individuation and separation from others to achieve control, autonomy, and independence in relationship to others. A focus on agency often leads to sacrificing others' needs in relationships to maintain autonomy. The individual freedom and achievement valued in Western, democratic societies led to a preference for agency as the guiding characteristic of maturity.

Further investigation of the identity development of women yielded another version of the story, this one based on communion, or the ability to connect with others and to function in a collaborative way (Brown and Gilligan, 1992; Chickering & Reisser, 1993; Gilligan, 1982; Straub, 1987). Bakan (1966) also coined the term *communion,* using it to refer to "the participation of the individual in some larger organism of which the individual is a part" (p. 15). Bakan described communion as "being at one with other organisms, . . . manifest in contact, openness, and union" (p. 15). Thus communion is characterized by connection to and fusion with others to achieve acceptance in relationships. This focus on connection often leads to behavior seen as dependent and self-sacrificing.

The question of how agency and communion related to maturity was most intensely discussed in the debate over Kohlberg's (1984) portrayal of the justice voice and Gilligan's (1982) portrayal of the care voice in moral development. Although many perspectives exist regarding the relationship of agency and communion, I find Kegan's (1994) notion of them as style, rather than structure, most informative. Kegan included his own work in the scholarship that, he argued, initially confused structure and style. He explained that autonomy and differentiation were initially viewed as synonymous with agency or separation. Autonomy constitutes the structural element of one's meaning making, whereas separation (or connection) constitutes the stylistic element or preference one has about meaning making. For example, one transitional knower prefers to stand apart from knowledge to assess opinions, whereas another prefers to get inside others' thoughts to assess opinions. Both share the same underlying structure of knowing, approached via different styles. The college phase data on gender-related patterns (Baxter Magolda, 1992) supports the notion that agency and communion are stylistic preferences within epistemological structures. Kegan has pointed out that the styles of connection and separation exist within the structures inherent in intrapersonal and interpersonal development as well.

Interconnections among the Three Dimensions

Perry (1970) noted that the shift from assuming that knowledge is certain to assuming that it is uncertain constituted a revolutionary restructuring in one's view of knowledge and oneself. Because knowing and valuing becomes contingent upon context, and because contexts constantly change, what one knows and values can potentially change as well. Perry believed that these realizations prompted restructuring one's identity as the one who chooses to what to devote one's energy, care, and identity. Moving through the relativity of knowledge and choice to make commitments about what to believe and stand for related more to identity than to new epistemological assumptions (King, 1978).

Belenky, Clinchy, Goldberger, and Tarule (1986) also emphasized the link between identity and ways of knowing in women's development. Their description of "constructed knowing" in which one integrates one's own experience and external information to construct a perspective became the basis of commitments to oneself, others, and one's community. Belenky and her colleagues noted that there was a paucity of this way of knowing in their college data. King and Kitchener (1994) also emphasized the role of the self as active knowledge constructor in the latter phases of Reflective Judgment.

Jane Loevinger's (1976) theory of ego development focused primarily on thinking processes that guided personal development, and she argued for integration of the dimensions involved in making meaning of experience. Robert Kegan (1982, 1994) articulated this integration clearly in his theory of the evolving self, finally bringing together the cognitive and affective realms of development in a constructive-developmental framework.

Kegan (1994) argued that people make meaning from various "orders of the mind," each characterized by a particular organizing principle that affects thinking, feeling, and relating to self and others. These principles are *how* we make meaning of our thinking, feeling, and social-relating, not the content of our meaning making. He described the core—or structure—of these organizing principles as the subject-object relationship. He defined *object* as "those elements of our knowing or organizing that we can reflect on, handle, look at, be responsible for, relate to each other, take control of, internalize, assimilate, or otherwise operate on" (p. 32). *Subject,* in contrast, "refers to those elements of our knowing or organizing that we are identified with, tied to, fused with, or embedded in" (p. 32). The difference, then, is that we cannot operate on that which is subject because we cannot stand apart from it. As Kegan stated, "We *have* object; we *are* subject" (p. 32).

Kegan (1994) emphasized that evolution of the subject-object relationship gives rise to evolution of the organizing principles we use to make meaning. Because what is subject and object for us is not permanent but rather changes as we adjust to account for new experiences, dimensions of our cognitive, intrapersonal and interpersonal meaning-making that are subject in one organizing principle, or order of the mind, become object in the next. For example, in Kegan's third order of mind one's relationships with others are subject. Identity is consumed by these relationships—we *are* our relationships in the third order. In the fourth order, relationships become object as we become able to stand apart from them and reflect upon them. Thus each new principle subsumes the prior one, resulting in a more complex way of making meaning. As Kegan explained, "Liberating ourselves from that in which we were embedded, making what was subject into object so that we can 'have it' rather than be 'had by it'—this is the most powerful way I know to conceptualize the growth of the mind" (p. 34). Kegan clearly stated that his use of the word *mind* does not refer to cognition alone but rather to the capacity of individuals to construct and organize meaning in their thinking, feeling, and relating to self and others. Kegan described three orders of mind from which adults tend to make meaning: third order, in which we are subject to and consumed by the external influences of others around us; fourth order, in which our meaning-making system becomes internal and thus mediates the influences of others; and fifth order, in which our meaning-making system itself becomes an object for our reflection.

Kegan's third order coordinates knowing through external sources, identifying oneself through external expectations, and constructing relationships based on others' needs. His research described many college-age persons as being in what he calls the third order of consciousness. The third order equips students with some of the cognitive processes to engage in knowledge construction (e.g., ability to think abstractly, hypothetically, and deductively). Yet the intrapersonal dimensions of the third order embeds the student in making meaning through shared realities with others who are external to the self. As a result the interpersonal dimensions also rests on external definition. Because the system by which meaning is made rests outside the self, self-authorship is not possible in any dimension. Deciding "how I know," "who I am," and "what kind of relationships do I want to construct" takes place in the context of what external others expect.

As was the case with previous theories of development, the increasingly complex phases of Kegan's theory described the emerging role of the internally defined self in knowing, identity, and relationships. Kegan's fourth order of consciousness is characterized by self-authorship, the new coordinator of the three dimensions. In fourth order, values, beliefs, convictions, generalizations, ideals, abstractions, interpersonal loyalty, and intrapersonal states of mind emerge from being coconstructed with others external to the self. Instead, the fourth order:

> takes all of these as objects or elements of its system, rather than the system itself; it does not identify with them but views them as parts of a new whole. This new whole is an ideology, an internal identity, a *self-authorship* that can coordinate, integrate, act upon, or invent values, beliefs, convictions, generalizations, ideals, abstractions, interpersonal loyalties, and intrapersonal states. It is no longer *authored by* them, it *authors them* and thereby achieves a personal authority. (1994, 185, italics in original)

This system brings the creation of belief "inside" the self, separate from the shared realities and coconstructions of the third order. The existence of this system that generates beliefs makes self-authorship of knowledge possible. It also makes possible identity formation that is more enduring than the earlier coconstructed versions because the internal self—rather than the social context—is the source of belief. The ability to relate to one's own intrapersonal states, rather than being made up by them, makes it possible to see oneself as the maker (rather than experiencer) of one's inner psychological life.

Mutuality, as Jordan (1997) described it, seems to require Kegan's (1994) fourth order structure and a blend of the styles of agency and communion. Mutuality is neither agency nor communion at their extremes, but rather an effective combination of individual authenticity and connection to others. Acting congruently with one's inner truth stems from the internal meaning-making system of the fourth order. Presenting one's own experience in the relationship represents agency, whereas responding to and encouraging authenticity in the other represents communion. Mutuality is a blend of agency and communion; too much of either does not constitute mutuality. Juxtaposing Kegan's and Jordan's ideas enables one to see the distinction between the structure of interpersonal maturity and the styles it requires. Contextual knowing also requires both styles as well as an internal meaning-making system that frees one to make judgments.

My longitudinal study focused on the epistemological dimension during the college years. During the post-college years, participants introduced the intrapersonal and interpersonal dimensions more readily and they moved to the foreground of our conversations. It seemed that they could not address the epistemological dimension, or the "how you know" question, without working with the other two dimensions. Stories from their twenties convey that adopting contextual assumptions about the nature of knowledge was necessary but insufficient for contextual knowing. In order to know and make decisions contextually they also needed to construct an internal self-definition that enabled them to choose what to believe and mediate their relations with the external world. The preferred styles prevalent in earlier portions of their developmental journeys also became more flexible as they moved from external to internal self-definition. Their collective stories told throughout this book extend our understanding of the three dimensions, how they interweave during the journey through the twenties, and what contexts aid in the transformation to self-authorship.

Higher Education's Role in Stewarding the Transformation

Establishing an internal belief system and a sense of self from which to join others in mutual relationships was the central challenge my participants faced in their twenties. Their career, advanced educational and personal environments demanded that they make the transformation from external definition to self-authorship. Their college education was intended to help them prepare for success and leadership roles in society. Educators hope that college graduates will experience a transformation from reliance on authority to complex ways of making meaning in which they are able to integrate multiple perspectives and make informed judgments. For example, Parks Daloz, Keen, Keen, and Daloz Parks (1996) wrote:

> The deep purpose of higher education is to steward this transformation so that students and faculty together continually move from naiveté through skepticism to commitment rather than becoming trapped in mere relativism and cynicism. This movement toward a mature capacity to hold firm convictions in a world which is both legitimately tentative and irreducibly interdependent is vitally important to the formation of citizens in a complex and changing world. (p. 223)

My longitudinal participants experienced the beginning of this transformation in college; that story is told in detail in *Knowing and Reasoning in College: Gender-Related Patterns in Students' Intellectual Development* (Baxter Magolda, 1992) and summarized later in this chapter as the backdrop for their journey through this transformation. The work, community, and personal contexts they encountered after college, however, called for them to complete the transformation to the mature capacity to hold firm convictions—to self-authorship.

Returning to Josselson's statement that "[I]dentity is what we make of ourselves within a society that is making something of us" (1996, p. 28), my study participants' focus during college seemed to be on what society was making of them, or more precisely, what they *should* become and believe to be successful in adult life. Like Gwen at the outset of this chapter, they were not aware until much later that they were not listening to their own voices. Their own voices were so entwined with societal voices that the two were one. At various points in their twenties, however, these young adults began to hear their own voices as separate from those of others, become aware of external forces they used to define themselves, and to actively construct an internally defined sense of self and belief system. Thus their focus shifted to what to make of themselves within the context of the society around them. Nearing the end of their twenties, many felt they were on a path of their own making; others were less certain about who had constructed the path.

The transformation to self-authorship was a complex task for these young adults. Much of what they learned in college called into question the values and beliefs instilled in them by their upbringing. Greater flexibility in gender roles opened new options for them, yet their families varied in the degree to which these new options were modeled or accepted. Taking risks to adopt new roles was often fraught with concern about unspoken expectations of masculinity or femininity, or with little conceptualization about how to adopt new roles yet keep old ones (e.g., career and family). Changing family structures left some at awkward crossroads—a place where choosing marriage and/or family was complicated by parents' divorce. Many of these adults learned that marriage and children were no longer a given but rather choices that entailed consequences. Their college experience conveyed a society different in most cases from the one in which they had grown up. Increasing diversity of perspectives, questions about the equity and justice in current societal arrangements, globalization, and technology all suggested that their adulthood would be different from that of their parents. Participants from working-class backgrounds were torn between pursuing success and maintaining their connections to their heritage. These dynamics yielded a tension between hopes and dreams developed in one context and how to live them out in another. The expectation and pressure for success were high, yet questions about the meaning of power and privilege complicated it. And while predictions and prescriptions for more complex social roles are plentiful, models for what they look like are few.

Despite the difficulty of this transformation in contemporary society, the need for self-authorship has never been greater. The diversity of our society and the global community requires that we be able to appreciate and work effectively with multiple perspectives. The recognition of inequity demands that we reevaluate the balance of our individual goals and our responsibility to the community. The increasing interdependence of people within our society and the world community makes addressing these issues imperative. The speed with which information and technology changes requires us to think in complex ways to keep pace. Self-authorship is necessary not only for survival in the 21st century but for the ability to offer leadership to model new forms of adult life and citizenship.

Stewarding this transformation—from naivete to commitment, from primarily external to primarily internal definition—is a complex challenge. Higher education has a responsibility to help young adults make the transition from their socialization by society to their role as members and leaders in society's future. The curriculum and cocurriculum of undergraduate, graduate, and professional educational settings are opportunities to steward this transformation. Willimon and Naylor (1995) wrote that a college education should:

> . . . provide a conceptual framework and a process to facilitate
> the search for meaning that attempts to integrate the spiritual,
> intellectual, emotional, and physiological dimensions of life,

> . . . encourag[ing] students . . . to formulate a *personal strat-*
> *egy* to address the most important quest human beings face—
> the need for their lives to have enduring meaning. (p. 130)

The workplace, the context in which most of my longitudinal participants experienced identity development and the search for meaning during their twenties, is also a site for stewarding this transformation. In many cases, these young adults found assistance with this transformation through connections with others in volunteer work, church, friends, and family.

Tracing their epistemological, intrapersonal, and interpersonal journey through their twenties offers insight into how contemporary society—higher education, workplaces within college contexts, and community within the college context—can be shaped to steward this crucial transformation. The stories of these young adults are particularly useful in this endeavor for two reasons. First, their growth during college has been documented, establishing a foundation for understanding their experience from the start of college. Second, by their early thirties, these adults' experiences covered a wide range of contexts including graduate and professional education in diverse fields, diverse work roles, and diverse family settings (marriage, divorce, children, and sexual orientation). The core themes of their experience as well as the rich texture of diverse experiences raise possibilities for mentoring people through the transformations of young adulthood. As concern grows over the ability of the next generation to assume leadership, the experiences of my longitudinal participants shed light on how these struggles might be approached.

Part One of the Journey: The College Years

I offer a brief synopsis of the college portion of these participants' journeys here as the context for their journey through the twenties (for an extensive report on the college phase of the study, see Baxter Magolda, 1992). They began college in 1986. One hundred and one students joined me for interviews during their first year; 80 of those interviewed all four years during college. Our annual interviews focused on their assumptions about the nature of knowledge; the role of the learner, instructor, peers, and evaluation in learning; and the nature of decision-making. Although the intrapersonal and interpersonal dimensions of development surfaced occasionally, the epistemological dimension took the foreground. This is most likely due to my framing of the study around learning as well as the learning focus of the college context. I constructed a portrait of the evolution of epistemology based on the college phase of the study.

Epistemological Reflection: Four Ways of Knowing[2]

The epistemological assumptions inherent in the four ways of knowing—absolute, transitional, independent, and contextual—are advanced here as relevant to the longitudinal participants. Because this study is constructivist in nature, I make no claim that this journey is transferable to other young adults unless their circumstances are similar to those described here. Methods and information from which to judge transferability are located in the appendices.

Absolute Knowing. Discussing his view of learning as a first year student, Jim offered a perspective that captures the essence of absolute knowing:

> The factual information is cut and dry. It is either right or wrong. If you know the information, you can do well. It is easy because you just read or listen to a lecture about the ideas. Then you present it back to the teacher.

The core assumption held by absolute knowers is that knowledge exists in an absolute form, or in Jim's words, is either right or wrong. They often assume that right and wrong answers exist in all areas of knowledge and that authorities know these answers. Uncertainty does not exist in knowledge per se, although it might exist in the student's lack of knowing the answer. The roles students describe for instructors, peers, and themselves as learners all hinge on knowledge being the purview of the instructor. As learners, absolute knowers focus on obtaining the information—a task Jim describes as reading or listening to lectures. They expect instructors to communicate knowledge clearly to them to aid in their acquiring it. They do not expect peers to have legitimate knowledge, although peers can share what they have learned from authority figures. Notice that Jim does not mention peers in his comment on how to do well. Absolute knowers' views of effective evaluation of students' work reflect the instructor's mastery of knowledge as well as the instructor's ability to determine whether students have acquired knowledge. When Jim presents what he has learned back to the teacher, she will know whether he knows the right answers. Students interpret discrepancies they encounter in the learning process as variations in explanations rather than true differences in knowledge. Finally, they approach educational decisions by looking for the right answers about educational programs, majors, and career directions. Sixty-eight percent of the longitudinal participants expressed absolute knowing during their first year of college. It steadily declined to 46 percent the sophomore year, 11 percent the junior year, and only 2 percent the senior year.

Two reasoning patterns were evident in absolute knowing: receiving and mastery. The *receiving pattern* was used more often by women than men in the study. A central characteristic of the receiving pattern is its internal approach, as shown in Toni's comment:

> I like to listen—just sit and take notes from an overhead. The material is right there and if you have a problem you can ask him and he can explain it to you. You hear it, you see it, and then you write it down.

Toni, a sophomore, makes it clear that this approach involves minimal interaction with instructors. Her receiving pattern peers also emphasized the importance of comfort in the learning environment, relationships with peers, and ample opportunities to demonstrate their knowledge. They resolved knowledge discrepancies via personal interpretation.

The *mastery pattern* was used more often by men than by women in the study. Mastery pattern students preferred an active approach to learning, were critical of instructors, and expected interactions with peers and instructors that helped them master the material. The active approach to learning permeates most aspects of the learning process. For example, Tim (a first year student), offered:

> I like getting involved with the class. Just by answering questions, asking questions . . . even if you think you know everything, there's still questions you can ask. When he asks questions you can try to answer them to your best ability. Don't just let the teacher talk, but have him present questions to you.

Thus Tim believes asking and answering questions is necessary to learn; he is not content to listen and take notes as Toni is. Tim and his mastery pattern peers reported engaging each other in debates to further their learning, showing the instructor they were interested, and resolving knowledge discrepancies via research and asking authorities.

Absolute knowers shared the common belief that knowledge is certain and held by authorities. Beyond their shared set of assumptions, receiving and mastery pattern students differed in three areas: voice, identification with authority, and relationships with peers. There was really no student voice per se in absolute knowing. However, mastery pattern students attempted to express themselves while their receiving pattern counterparts remained essentially silent. Mastery pattern students seemed to imitate the voice of authority and worked hard at reproducing it in an effort to join authorities as knowers. Receiving pattern students listened carefully to the voice of authority and repeated it in an effort to show that they had acquired the knowledge.

Although all absolute knowers viewed authorities as holders of truth and knowledge, receiving pattern students exhibited minimal identification with authority figures whereas mastery pattern students exhibited considerable identification with authority. Students in the receiving pattern exhibited a detachment from authority. They described learning as a transaction largely void of interaction with authority unless clarification was needed. Despite their motivation for receiving knowledge, they did not view identification or interaction with authority as a central part of that process. Students in the mastery pattern showed the beginnings of taking their place "next to" authorities in the arena of knowledge. Their learning behaviors resembled those of the active apprentice trying to master the trade.

Relationships with peers were a third point of difference for receiving and mastery pattern students. Receiving pattern students valued peers as providers of comfort in the learning atmosphere. Knowing others in the class made it more intimate, more comfortable, and an easier setting in which to learn and ask questions. For these students peers were a source of assistance in receiving knowledge. Collaboration took the form of support and sharing notes and information. Mastery pattern students valued peers as partners in striving for and testing achievement. They assisted each other in mastering knowledge and took turns testing each other's progress. Collaboration in this form was characterized by individual autonomy.

The path from absolute to transitional knowing involves the realization that not all knowledge is certain, and that authorities are not all knowing as a result. As the students' stories in transitional knowing reveal, mastery and receiving pattern students encounter this experience differently. Mastery pattern students' identification with authority prompts them to stay with certainty and logic as much as possible in the face of emerging uncertainty. Receiving pattern students' detachment from authority makes it easier to let go of certainty, thus endorsing uncertainty. Endorsing uncertainty leads to an increase in activity level over and above listening. Peers are important to students of both patterns but students endorsing uncertainty more readily assign legitimacy to peers' knowledge.

Transitional Knowing.   Uncertainty, upon its discovery, was usually perceived to exist only in particular areas while certainty remained in other knowledge arenas. Fran's statement reflects this perspective:

> Genetics isn't an opinionated kind of subject. Genetics is "These are the experiments; that's what happens. This is what we know now." You wouldn't sit around and have a discussion in calculus . . . or chemistry. In the AIDS class, it's just open discussion, and

it makes you really say what you want and think through what you want to think about.

Genetics retained its certainty for Fran, as did calculus and chemistry. On the topic of AIDS, however, uncertainty emerged. This shift in the nature of knowledge sparked changes in the roles students perceived for themselves and others. Students shifted their focus from acquiring knowledge to understanding it. This focus on understanding required that instructors use methods aimed at understanding, many of which included applying knowledge in class and to life in general. Peers took on more active roles, perhaps because understanding was described as requiring more exploration than that required for the acquisition of knowledge. Evaluation was perceived as appropriate to the extent that it measured students' understanding of the material. Uncertainty permeated decision making as well, as students struggled to figure out options for the future. Processes believed to lead to future success replaced direct reliance on authorities for educational decision making. All transitional knowers held these core assumptions. Transitional knowing assumptions were held by 32 percent of the participants during the first year. It increased to 53 percent the sophomore year and to 83 percent the junior year. Eighty percent of the seniors still used transitional knowing; it declined rapidly the first year after college to 31 percent.

Within transitional knowing some students, usually women, used an interpersonal approach whereas other students, usually men, used an impersonal approach. *Interpersonal pattern* students were involved in learning through a collection of others' ideas, expected interaction with peers to hear their views and provide exposure to new ideas, wanted a rapport with the instructor to enhance self-expression, valued evaluation that takes individual differences into account, and resolved uncertainty by personal judgment. Kris's comments capture the new expectations of peers:

> I get into discussions. Classroom discussions are better for me to learn. You have an opening lecture where you have the professor discuss. Then students can contribute—listening to other students contribute their ideas and putting in my own inputs—that makes learning better for me because it makes me think more and try to come up with more generative ideas as to what I would do in a situation. We react to the material, look at ideas and relate it to ourselves, look at what kinds of action we can take. It's a hands-on type class.

Kris clearly wants to hear the professor but only briefly; then she wants to hear her peers and express her own opinion. Interpersonal pattern knowers tended to focus on those areas that were uncertain and viewed this as an opportunity to express their own views for the first time.

Impersonal pattern students wanted to be forced to think, preferred to exchange their views with instructors and peers via debate, expected to be challenged by instructors, valued evaluation that is fair and practical, and resolved uncertainty by logic and research. Scott described the result of being forced to think:

> The debate and discussion process for me is really interesting; I learn a lot more because I remember questions and I guess I learn the most when I sit and I'm actually forced to raise my hand and then I have to talk. I have to sit there and think on the spot. I learn it better than in a note-taking class that is regurgitation.

Scott has rejected the absolute knowers' approach of presenting information back to the teacher, but he does not endorse Kris's interest in peers' comments. Instead he focuses on his own thinking about the material. Impersonal pattern students also demonstrated a dual focus on certainty and uncertainty and wanted to resolve uncertainty when it existed.

Students in both patterns exhibit development of their voice in transitional knowing as compared to absolute knowing. The impersonal pattern voice remains consistent in its closeness to the voice of authority, reflecting now the process of learning rather than the answers. The interpersonal pattern voice diverges more from authority than does the impersonal pattern. The discovery of uncertainty seems to be viewed by interpersonal pattern students as an opportunity to become involved in knowing, resulting in greater activity and exercise of personal judgment. Moreover, a subtle division remains between the interpersonal pattern knower's knowledge and that of authority. Some students remarked that their learning from other students did not necessarily help them learn the material in the book. Yet the interpersonal pattern voice has gained greater distance from authority than has the impersonal pattern voice. Using relationship with authority as a point of departure toward independent knowing, interpersonal pattern students would seem to be more ready to adopt their own voice.

The interpersonal and impersonal difference in the two patterns is clear. Interpersonal pattern students care about their peers' perspectives, want to know their peers, and want instructors to care about them. Relationships are central to the learning process because knowing others promotes sharing perspectives and sharing perspectives promotes adding to one's knowledge. If instructors are uncaring, teaching (and thus learning) is ineffective. For impersonal pattern students these themes did not surface. Although no student wants to be mistreated by instructors, impersonal pattern students prefer challenge to caring. Perhaps this reflects the impersonal pattern students' focus on individual learning whereas the interpersonal pattern students focus on the relationships made possible during learning. Considering peer relationships as a point of departure toward independent knowing, we could expect that interpersonal pattern students would have little difficulty accepting peers' views as valid. For them this will be an extension of knowing in the uncertain arena. For impersonal pattern students a shift will be required to add peers (and themselves) to the ranks of authority.

Independent Knowing.   The core assumption of uncertainty in independent knowing changes both the process and source of knowing substantially. The shift is evident in Laura's description of her discovery of uncertainty:

> Everything's relative; there's no truth in the world, that sort of thing. So I've decided that the only person that you can really depend on is yourself. Each individual has their own truth. No one has the right to decide, "This has to be your truth, too." As long as you feel—it feels right, then it must be right because if everybody is stuck on, "What do the other people think?" then you just waste your whole life. You just do what you feel like you have to do. That's why sometimes I felt that I had to get into business because everybody was going into business. I don't think the world rotates around the business world and money and materialism. Now I'm relaxed and I'm thinking of what I want, what's best for me and not for anybody else.

Given this newfound uncertainty, discrepancies among authorities represent the variety of views possible in an uncertain world. Authorities are no longer the only source of knowledge but instead become equal with students, who for the first time view their opinions as valid. The emergence of self-authored knowledge rivets the student's attention on thinking for oneself. Learning how to think independently involves expressing one's own views as well as hearing others. Instructors are expected to promote this type of activity in class. They are no longer responsible for providing knowledge, but rather providing the context in which to explore knowledge. Evaluation, likewise, should reward independent thinking and should not penalize the student for holding views different from the instructor or authors of texts. Peers become a legitimate source of knowledge rather than part of the process of knowing. Independent knowers emphasize being open-minded and allowing everyone to believe what they will, as illustrated by Laura's comment on how she decides what to believe: "I don't know (how I decide on my opinion). Something works inside my head and it's just there." Independent knowing was rare in the early college years (1 percent of sophomores and 3 percent of juniors). Sixteen percent used independent knowing as seniors; it rose dramatically the first year after college to 57 percent.

Gender-related patterns appeared in independent knowing as well. The *interindividual pattern* was used more often by women than men in the study. Interindividual pattern knowers believed that different perspectives resulted from each person bringing her or his own interpretation, or in some cases bias, to a particular knowledge claim. They simultaneously advocated listening to other interpretations or biases and espousing their own perspectives, describing how the interaction of the two helped them form their perspective. Alexus offered an example of this view during her fifth year interview. Reflecting on her senior year classes, she commented that senior year was a time "when you should be most open because you should be able to listen to what other people say and then come up with your own opinion on how you feel about a particular thing." When asked how she did that, she replied:

> I listen to their arguments for it and then I listen to other people's arguments against it. And then basically it's just my own personal view really, whether I can establish the credibility—so I guess it really stems from credibility of the person who's saying it also, as well as just the opinion on it. I listen to both sides. Really I usually throw some of my own views into it as well. So I'm influenced by other people, but in the end I think that each— like each member of the group should be influenced by each other. But then when the final vote comes in, you should go with what you believe.

Alexus clearly valued hearing others' ideas and felt people should influence each other. She simultaneously held her own view and tried to integrate it with the views of others she perceived as credible.

The *individual pattern* knowers, like their interindividual pattern counterparts, espoused thinking independently and exchanging views with others. However, their primary focus was on their thinking and they sometimes struggled to listen carefully to other voices. Fully acknowledging that everyone had their own beliefs, individual pattern knowers described the role theirs played when differences of opinion took place. Lowell shared an experience in which he and other students had different ideas:

> I'd consider myself conservative. And there was one guy in our group who was quite liberal and acknowledged it. I guess it gave me another viewpoint, another aspect to look at this. Like

it or not we're all kind of ingrained one way or another, whether it's to the liberal end or the conservative end. He looked at it in this way and I looked at it in another way. And everybody in the group had their own ways on it. It was a spectrum of—and to try to get your point across without sounding too dominating—I'm searching for words and not finding them. To try to listen to theirs, to really listen, not to just hear it and let it go through. And then to try to take that into account and reach a compromise. There was quite a bit of discussion. But I don't think the attempt was to try to change each other's mind. It was just, "Your point is all right, but you've got to look at this part, too, because this is as relevant."

Lowell's genuine attempt to hear his liberal classmate and his insistence that his conservative perspective also be taken into account stopped short of changing either perspective.

The equality of numerous views in the face of prevailing uncertainty made independent thinking possible. Equality of perspectives also changed the relationship of the knower to her or his peers and to authority. In the case of interindividual pattern knowers this prompted connection to peers and to authority. Connection to peers was evident earlier for interpersonal transitional knowers, but interindividual pattern knowers became more open to peers' views. Their exchanges became interindividual by virtue of the knower including her or his own voice. When the potential hazards to connection posed by criticism were removed by equality of views, interindividual pattern knowers connected more intensely with their peers. This connection freed them to express their voices, which appear to have existed internally prior to this point. For them, the adjustment to independent knowing came in the form of including their own voice as equal to that of peers and of authority. Interindividual pattern knowers reconnected to authority once their own voice was legitimized. Thus the interindividual pattern represents a union of one's own voice and the voices of others.

In the case of individual pattern knowers the equality of perspectives had a different effect on relationships with peers and authority. Peers' roles in knowing created a relationship that bordered on becoming a connection. Individual pattern knowers listened to peers but struggled to hear them clearly and also to keep their own voice in the forefront. The adjustment to independent knowing for individual pattern knowers came in the form of including other voices as equal to one's own. Thus their voices, expressed routinely in previous ways of knowing, were slightly threatened by the genuine consideration of others' voices. Their interest in and attempt to hold both voices in balance appeared to mark the beginning of genuine connection to others. At the same time, equality of views seemed to free individual pattern knowers from authority to pursue their own independent thinking. The individual pattern includes both self-authored knowledge and the views of others, with the balance of the scale tipped toward self-authored knowledge.

The variation in interindividual and individual knowing can also be cast in the language of communion and agency (Bakan, 1966) discussed earlier in the chapter. Communion involves connection and relationship with others whereas agency involves separateness from others. Both patterns moved toward communion: interindividual pattern knowers in terms of intense openness to others' views and individual pattern knowers in terms of genuine consideration of others' views. Both patterns also moved toward agency in the emergence of self-authored knowledge and for individual pattern knowers in separation from authority in the learning process. The degree of movement toward communion or agency is best understood in light of the degree to which either was reflected in earlier ways of knowing. Receiving and interpersonal pattern knowers demonstrated communion in previous ways of knowing but agency represented a shift for them. Mastery and impersonal pattern knowers demonstrated agency in earlier ways of knowing, such that communion represented a shift for them. Thus while interindividual pattern knowers still lean toward communion and individual pattern knowers still lean toward agency, both are moving closer together than in previous ways of knowing.

Contextual Knowing.   The fourth set of epistemological assumptions noticeable for a few students (1 percent of juniors and 2 percent of seniors) toward the end of college emerged more completely during the postcollege interviews. Contextual knowers looked at all aspects of a situation or issue, sought out expert advice in that particular context, and integrated their own and others' views in deciding what to think. Gwen, reflecting on her senior year, illustrates this perspective in her comment on whether to believe others' viewpoints: "I don't care if people feel this way or that way about it. But if they can support their stance and have some background and backing for that, to my thinking that is valid." Thus the student voice develops to the point of cognitive self-authorship; peers and authority both have valid knowledge if they can support their stance. The nature of contextual knowing, and the integration of the two gender-related patterns, is further explored in the remainder of this volume via the stories of participants during their twenties.

At the Threshold of Self-Authorship

The longitudinal participants stood at the threshold of self-authorship at the end of college. They recognized uncertainty in some areas and would recognize it as more prevalent soon after college. They left college with an initial awareness that they would have to make their own decisions, but without internal mechanisms to do so. I invite you to come along on the journey they shared from college graduation to age 30. Their stories offer rich descriptions of how the three dimensions of development intertwine, how the transformation to self-authorship is facilitated or hindered, and the intensity of the struggle to achieve an internal belief system and sense of self from which to join others in mutual relationships. As was the case with the college phase of the study, the post-college phase was approached from the constructivist perspective (see appendix for more details). Thus the transformation to self-authorship described by these participants is offered as a possibility rather than as a generalizable portrait of all young adults' experience in their twenties.

Notes

1. Despite using fictitious names for participants throughout the book, I share these dynamics anonymously to protect the privacy of the participants.

2. Portions of this description are reproduced with permission from Baxter Magolda, M. B. (1992). *Knowing and reasoning in college: Gender-related patterns in students' intellectual development.* San Francisco: Jossey-Bass and from Baxter Magolda, M. B. (1999). *Creating contexts for learning and self-authorship: Constructive-developmental pedagogy.* Nashville, TN: Vanderbilt University Press.

2

PATHWAYS INTO YOUNG ADULTHOOD

I could read a text at [college], and say, "this is a feminist critique of this text," then whip on the other pair of glasses and
say, "this is a Marxist critique of this text." I found conservative
lenses in law school. I could figure out what various kinds of
people would think. With Chinese philosophy, I've gotten closer
to understanding what my own pair of eyes internally and externally is seeing. It is more fundamentally true to my human
nature than political critiques. Getting toward more important
questions than what is a critique of this movie—getting to what
it means to be a human being with a soul.

                                                        Mark, age 30

Mark's shift from pairs of glasses to his own eyes forecasts the shift from following external formulas to self-authorship. The majority of participants left
college using transitional knowing, thus relying on the process authorities had
taught them for how to know. Finding multiple pairs of glasses from which to
view the world, however, led some participants near the end of college and
more in the year after graduation to independent knowing. From this vantage
point, it seemed that any pair of glasses would do. Despite the awareness that
they could choose a vision, in their initial exposure to work or advanced education participants had little sense of how to choose a vision. As a result, they
relied on the formulas they could glean from others.

The need to choose their own vision emerged from two sources. One was
dissatisfaction with the results of following the external formulas. Many participants were frustrated that their plans for success did not result in success;

others who reached the goals of their plan found them unsatisfying. Second, employment, educational, and personal contexts in which knowledge was conveyed as complex and socially constructed, the self was viewed as central to one's work, educational, or life decisions, and mutual construction of meaning was commonplace, called relying on external formulas into question. This portrayal of how to know (the epistemological dimension) brought the "who am I" question (the intrapersonal dimension) to the forefront of participants' experience. Up to this point, participants defined themselves through external expectations because they had not developed an internal sense of self. The notion of developing an internal sense of self, in combination with unhappiness from approaching life without regard to one's interests and values, called external definition in all three dimensions of development into question.

As the internal voice began to develop, it came into conflict with external influences marking the phase of the journey called the crossroads. From the vantage point of the crossroads, participants reflected back upon external definition and found it troublesome. They questioned the plans for success and formulas for knowing and abandoned transitional knowing and its reliance on external authority. They realized the dilemmas inherent in defining oneself through others and the need to define oneself internally. They realized that their relationships had been founded on acquiring others' approval rather than mutual negotiation of others' and their own needs. At the crossroads, participants realized that the pathway to knowing the world and oneself actually led inward to who they were and how they would choose to play out their lives. This was an exciting yet sobering realization. Because external definition had been their experience for so long, resolving the tension between the internal yet-to-be-developed voice and the strong external voices took considerable time and effort.

Looking inward, participants began the arduous process of choosing their own beliefs, as Gwen said in chapter 1, "how *I* know." At the same time, this necessitated constructing an internal sense of self by determining one's own values and philosophies. This internal self, although still under construction, had to be brought to relationships with others. Participants now acted in relationships in ways true to themselves, mutually negotiating how needs were met, rather than acting solely to gain approval. This marked the beginning of their capacity to construct authentic relationships with others in which both parties' needs were considered and negotiated. They were actively working on becoming the authors of their own epistemological, intrapersonal, and interpersonal lives. This phase of the journey was the beginning of self-authorship.

As the construction on all three fronts progressed, chosen perspectives coalesced into a belief system. This belief system was in part made possible by the coherent sense of self that emerged from choices about values and interests. Others' perspectives in choosing how to know or how to view oneself were genuinely considered from the vantage point of the belief system and coherent sense of self, resulting in relationships characterized by mutuality. I called this phase of the journey the internal foundation because participants became grounded in their internal belief system, sense of self, and mutual relations with others. From this phase of the journey participants realized that they had the power to construct meaning of their experiences, yet simultaneously realized that the world was beyond their control. Their own voices and identity—their own eyes—became the foundation for accepting the inevitable and interpreting the world in a way that was workable for them. The foundation from which they authored their lives yielded an internal sense of peace labeled "spiritual" by many participants. Many talk about the journey through the twenties as "coming home" to a feeling of being comfortable with themselves, settled on the ability to make choices even though their choices had not all been made, and at peace with the idea that they have the internal capacity to govern their lives.

Using their own eyes to make sense of their experience yielded self-authorship. This evolution from formula to foundation and external definition to self-authorship, hinged on progress on all three dimensions of development. Even those participants who had acquired the concept and language of contextual knowing could not live it as a way of knowing until the intrapersonal task of developing an internal sense of self was undertaken. Prior to the self becoming central to knowing, contextual knowing was a process detached from the self—pairs of glasses that could be used without regard to the set of eyes behind them. Likewise, the self was central to the interpersonal task of moving from acquiring approval to engaging in mutual relationships, which was in turn a central component of knowing the world contextually. Thus the participants' journeys through their twenties reveal that self-authorship can only be acquired through growth on all three dimensions of development. Although visual presentation of the movement of the dimensions does not adequately represent their fluidity and diversity among participants, the rudimentary visualization below offers a road map of sorts for the journey to come.

This chapter uses two participants' stories in-depth to offer an overview of the journey toward self-authorship. I first introduced these two participants, Mark and Gwen, in *Knowing and Reasoning in College* (Baxter Magolda, 1992), where I used their stories to trace the evolution of epistemology during college. I return to their stories now to illustrate how the three dimensions interweave along the pathway toward self-authorship.

FIGURE 2.1 Four Phases of the Journey toward Self-Authorship

	Following Formulas	Crossroads	Becoming the Author of One's life	Internal Foundation
Epistemological dimension: how do I know	Believe authority's plans; how "you" know	Question plans; see need for own vision	Choose own beliefs; how "I" know in context of external knowledge claims	Grounded in internal belief system
Intrapersonal dimension: who am I?	Define self through external others	Realize dilemma of external definition; see need for internal identity	Choose own values, identity in context of external forces	Grounded in internal coherent sense of self
Interpersonal dimension: what relationships do I want with others?	Act in relationships to acquire approval	Realize delemma of focusing on external approval; see need to bring self to relationship	Act in relationships to be true to self, mutually negotiating how needs are met	Grounded in mutality

Following Formulas for Success

Both Mark and Gwen left college having followed the plans for success offered to them by their external environments. Mark's attention to following the path to acceptance to law school paid off in his acceptance at a prestigious school that topped his list. Gwen's "plan your work and work your plan" helped her succeed in college and acquire a good position in the insurance industry upon graduation. Although both approached knowing near the end of college as contextual—acknowledging uncertainty and their responsibility to choose wisely based on evidence relevant to the context—they entered realms in which their experience was limited. They articulated making their own choices as they set out on the post-college journey. Yet, as is evident in their stories and later in their own reflections, they had adopted external formulas for success in the absence of their own internal belief systems.

Mark approached law school with what he had surmised was the "legal culture's map for success:"

> I came here and I tried to figure out what the legal culture figures is success. I knew that a Supreme Court clerkship was [success], so one of my goals was to aim towards that. So I got here to law school and I figured out, "Okay, well, to be a success here you have to get to know some professors who are influential with judges to get a good clerkship, to get in the pipeline, get in the star system here. Also get on *Law Review.* Write a paper here that you can publish." I thought, "Okay, this is kind of the plan then, step by step." The ultimate plan for success in the legal culture, I mean, go to [this] law school and do these things, then you've got it made. I would be in the *ultimate* position to do whatever I want to do because I will have done *everything* possible, and then I'd be in a position to make a choice that reflected exactly who I was, or at least more clearly.

Mark persisted with this map of success even when he was attracted to other activities. Describing his reaction when he went to a "fair" for various avenues of involvement, he said:

> I went right to the law journal, that big prestige thing. You know, I was thinking to myself "You've got to do this in order to get to being a law teacher." But on my way over to the law journal table, there was this street law, which is teaching in the high schools around here. I'm like, "Damn, that's what I really want to do." Real strong internal cues said, "Do this." So I picked up the information and was just like, "Damn! I just can't do it because it's not going to get me there."

This plan appeared workable, as had his plan for getting this far, in part because he was detached from it. Mark had leaned heavily on rationality and detachment in his approach to knowing during college and continued that pattern in his early twenties. He found it insufficient with personal and career decisions that were emerging on the horizon. He explained:

> Learning in a classroom is a wholly different process than trying to learn something in my personal life. Because when we talk about personal life, all of a sudden it seems to me the most important determinant is how I feel about it, my real gut reaction. And that's not the way I learn in a classroom. I really do not listen to my feelings in a classroom because I don't trust them. You're exposed to a host of new ideas. And to keep an open mind you have to check your gut reaction. So in a classroom to broaden my mind in the way I approach things, I just chuck the feelings and go with the ideas. It's really good in there. But, like I said, that's not the way you deal with career and personal life. It doesn't work.

The detachment that helped Mark learn became problematic as he tried to sort out personal decisions. He explained why he tended to shy away from his feelings:

> Nothing in college or in the classroom ever prepared me to really deal with those feelings. I don't know if that's good or bad necessarily. One thing I learned in my childhood is not to trust relationships very much. For instance, my parents divorced, which is so incredibly common. But it had a huge impact on the way I view relationships and marriage. In my life it was kind of devastating. Maybe that's why I did so well in the classroom is because I was used to not going with feelings. I can listen to radicals on both fringes, right and left, shove my feelings aside, listen to it, and then develop rational critiques of both sides. I can get to a point where I don't *feel* anything. That hurt me in the relationship, too, because I didn't want to *feel* love all the time because it's such—you're so vulnerable then. That came out of a few childhood experiences where I felt basically love was betrayed or wasn't able to come to any fruition.

Lacking preparation for dealing with feelings, he did his best to use the tools (and formulas) he had in making a decision about marriage:

> As far as personal life, I sit down and I write down things I know, pro and con, "Go into a relationship," "Don't go into a relationship," cost-benefit kind of analysis. Like I said, I don't leave my

rationality behind because I think that's really an effective tool. And then I think about all my options, and there's something about it. It carries on its own momentum. So I listen to those feelings, and I come to my room and I sit down and I push all my books away. I grab a sheet of paper or whatever and start writing things down, how I feel. And then when I feel like I've got a handle on those feelings and options, then I talk to the people affected. When you bring other people into it, you push your feelings down just a touch because then you want to be open minded again at that point. And then you talk to people unaffected by it, too, because obviously when people are affected by it they're invested in it. I don't let my feelings rush me into anything because . . . you're dealing with personal life more—if you do something rash, it can cost you a lot.

Mark clearly viewed logic and feelings as important factors in deciding. He used logic to check emotions, because he preferred to avoid doing anything rash on the basis of feelings. However, he had also discovered that the logical approach did not always lead to happiness. Summarizing how he felt about rationality and feelings, he said: "Rational thinking as best I can really gets me there. And then I get there and I see, 'Okay, here's the set of facts. What do I feel?' And then that carries me the rest of the way." These comments imply that Mark relied most on rationality, tried to approach his feelings from an objective stance, and acknowledged that feelings had to be included in the process. As he embarked on his initial decisions about law school and engagement, he believed these formulas were the best avenue to success.

Gwen was also in search of formulas for success. She explained, "We're taught to make [our] plan. 'Plan your work and work your plan and you're going to get where you want to go.' " She described the outcome of this way of thinking in her early twenties, saying:

Things always came very easily to me. I could kind of set my sights on something and it would happen. And I would generally know some of the things I needed to do to get there. "If you want this, then do this, this, and this," and it happened.

She was looking for these formulas in her work and initially frustrated that they were not readily available:

[I was] frustrated with not only a new job but also a new city and totally unfamiliar expectations. I hadn't had a chance to really get those ironed out, and basically they said, "We have faith in you; we think you can do this. Go ahead and do it." And I suddenly was saying, "Do what? What is it you want me to do?" I think that the best way, for me at least, is to have a clearly defined set of objectives and expectations. Then be given the tools that you need to accomplish them, and then just let it run and go ahead and do it. And I think that had I had a clear set of objectives in the beginning I wouldn't have been as frustrated. Not only was I trying to learn all this new stuff, but I was trying to figure out what I was supposed to be doing, which is kind of not good. I have actually found that what I learn through trial and error, although the process is a little bit more frustrating and a little bit more cumbersome in the beginning, I think I found better ways. I wasn't piggybacking off of what other people told me works that I may not find worked for myself. And I think I remembered it a lot better than having someone show me their way. Trying to figure out my way to do it, I think, was definitely better.

Gwen became more accustomed to figuring things out for herself over time, yet still relied on her supervisor to structure this process, as is evident in her story about her manager:

She helps me think through some situations as issues arise and I'm trying to decide what to do. Her management style I just admire immensely. I present the problem, then I say, "So here's where I am." Her first question always is, "So what do you read on this? What do you think?" In the beginning it was frustrating because I wanted her to say, "Okay. Well, here's how you handle that," because I didn't know. I'd never run across any of that before. She's very good at, "Okay, well, have you thought about this? Have you thought about this? Okay." And then suddenly everything is like, "Oh, so that's what I'm supposed to do." Very good at helping you reach your own conclusions.

Gwen was also looking for ways to figure things out for herself in her personal life. She reported having done some "housecleaning" in the last year:

Things that don't work and things that were bad for me, whether it was habits or relationships, I've gotten rid of. And it was just actually taking the time to step back from things and look at them for what they are instead of what you hoped that they are or what they can be. I realized I can't change the world and there are some things that you have to accept about that. And that's okay. . . . I woke up one day and I said "Is this all? There's got to be more than this." or "This is not good for me. Why do I do this?" I don't think I really allowed myself to spend a lot of time thinking about how things were. I just always thought about how I could make things be. I have always had an independent nature. But I really think I've had an opportunity to exercise that. I hate to say I put myself first—but I stopped trying to please everyone around me. And I really do things that please me. I find that I'm a much happier person. I wasn't an unhappy person before, but doing things for myself makes me just so much better. I feel like I have peace for the first time in my life, like I'm in control of the things that are happening to me. And I have worked at that. I think that a lot of that is just I'm really comfortable with myself. I'm comfortable with my direction and kind of my setup.

I asked Gwen how this change came about and she replied:

I think it was just all of a sudden here I was in a new job and it was kind of sink or swim. I think that there were just a lot of things and a lot of questions—not really even questions—but I just needed to come to terms with things on my own. And a lot of that was just exercising some independence and doing some things that I wanted to do just because I wanted to do them. All of that, and then finally, "If you're not happy, why aren't you happy? Find the part that's broken and fix it. And make sure that you maintain everything."

Meanwhile Gwen was involved with a man with whom she was contemplating marriage. He encouraged her to be an individual, and led her to be more comfortable with the fact that marriage wouldn't diminish her independence:

I don't think that marriage has to take away from your independence. In fact, in some respects I think it should foster a sense of that. I am with someone who allows me to be such an individual and encourages that. I find that just incredible. I think that kind of encouragement makes me even more inclined to do the things that I want to do for me because that makes me better for us, if that makes any sense.

Gwen's perspective here is hard to interpret. It could be the emergence of hearing her own voice and thus an opening to self-authorship. It could also be adopting a formula from an external source, in this case her fiancé. Although it wasn't clear to her or me at the time, it became clear later that external influence in the form of her fiancé's perspectives overrode her figuring things out for herself. Her perspective on being an individual was possible because her fiancé encouraged it.

Following these formulas for success turned problematic for Mark, Gwen, and their peers within the first two years after college, leaving them unhappy and unsure how to proceed. The formulas borrowed from the external world lacked connection to their voices and often conflicted with the internal voice that was starting to materialize. In the epistemological dimension both Mark and Gwen internalized external "shoulds" as ways to decide what to believe. This worked for Mark until his feelings entered the picture in the marriage decision. He tried to deal with these intrapersonal and interpersonal dimensions the only way he knew how—through the formula for knowing. Likewise, Gwen's feeling began to conflict with her formula. Her initial "housecleaning" is the first sign of an emerging intrapersonal sense of self. Yet it was overshadowed by external voices, particularly that of her fiancé. Increasingly strong internal cues prompted dissonance with their plans and led to the search for another way.

The Crossroads

Mark's struggle surfaced in the career arena. He found law school and the activities for success far less stimulating than he had expected:

> I started reading the books and I was like, "Whoa, this is pretty boring stuff." And it was painful, painful. I don't know. And then I thought, "I don't want to go through"—and this took a long time, especially first semester and then part of second semester too and then into the summer a little bit—I said, "Is this map of success given to me by the legal culture really a map at all to success?" And it depends upon your definition of success. A great résumé or accolades, yeah, that's the chart to a sign of prestige, that's the way to go. But I realized that I couldn't be a person who sacrificed happiness to that goal of prestige. I never *dreamed* that I would be unhappy working on the law journal. I didn't think it would be as tedious and boring as I found it. That never figured in. There was no way law school and its classes could be as big a turnoff as they were.

Mark's reaction to his work and his questions about the map to success led to a long period of reflection and a change of heart:

> It was a tough decision. I came here thinking about a Supreme Court clerkship. Now I'm not even trying for it. And it doesn't bother me that I'm not. I'm going in other directions that are more fruitful, I think. That kind of careerist perspective can get you in a place in ten years where you really don't want to be because you didn't listen to your internal feelings. . . . But, more importantly, the internal cues, which I never used to listen to and

which in the classroom I never listened to. I had to go to the internal cues because I'm getting to a point in my life where I could get locked into a situation and say inside I'm miserable even though objectively from the outside I've been quite a success.

These insights led Mark to consider happiness instead of prestige as his criteria for success:

I put major priority on "happiness success" now. That is my definite primary goal. And it took a lot of pain and thinking to change that, but for me you can be at the top of the prestige heap and life isn't worth living if you're not happy. And also—I mean, you should figure in my relationship to [my fiancée]. I know I talked about marriage like I was pretty certain in our last interview we were heading towards that. I bought the ring for her the October after the interview, got engaged Christmas Eve that year. And that definitely all fits in that big scheme of where I'm going. I mean, that relationship has provided me with more happiness by far than anything else in my life, other than perhaps just kind of family generally. Definitely in my adult life, that relationship has provided me with far more happiness than any other thing. And that's the key for me.

As Mark struggled to find happiness, he initially put his relationship with his girlfriend on hold. He later allowed himself to become more connected to her and become engaged. He also recognized the joy his younger brother brought to his life. He said, "I'm glad I've had a brother who was ten—well, who was fourteen years younger than I am because now I know how much joy somebody like that can bring to you." Mark was allowing feelings to become a more central part of his life. He was also connected more to his own internal cues.

His search for career direction led him to a summer position in a district attorney's office. He tried to figure out whether that met his happiness criteria, still leaning on his rational approach he had used for so long:

I definitely didn't feel happy being in a firm. And in a way that is something I put on my list and looked at objectively. Some of the things I put down, for instance, about working in a big law firm, on the pro side I'd write down "Gives you more downward mobility," you can always get a job in a smaller firm. So you can get flexibility that way. More downward mobility than the prosecutor's office, for instance. Now on the con side I may write down "Yeah, but I'm not happy here." And, you know, happy is a feeling. Or, "I feel tense here," because of the evaluative process that's constantly going on. . . . You know, one of the most important experiences for me at the DA's office was when

I went to the veteran prosecutor on staff and I asked him for names of prosecutors who had left the office who he respected a lot. And then I just went to talk to all of them and just asked them all kinds of things about being a prosecutor. Sometimes I'd press them on issues about family and how you juggle that and time constraints and whether they liked being a lawyer or not, all kinds of stuff. It was really a profitable experience; it was a great experience to go to somebody who'd been through something you hadn't but were considering and having him or her look back as I look back now.

Despite pursuing others' perspectives vigorously, Mark was weighing them carefully against his feelings and counting the feelings more substantively than he had in his previous cost-benefit analysis.

Gwen's struggle to be happy played out in her decision about marriage. She shared the growth she experienced in this process:

[It has been] a tremendous learning experience. It's been kind of a series of wonderful and not so wonderful. We're very excited. We got engaged last winter, about a year ago actually. And it was met with a response from my parents, like my mother just went through this little thing like, "I'm not a hundred percent sure I'm ready to have a daughter who's married." So we worked through that and we worked through a lot of these other issues. A part of it, too, with me was, "I'm not sure I'm ready to share all this with somebody. I'm not sure I'm ready for my whole life to change. I'm not sure about this. I'm not sure about that." I'm just really comfortable with that. It's not going to change. I mean, it changes, but it's not limiting. And I think that's the biggest relief, and I needed to know that, to confirm that. That it's going to encourage me to accomplish the things I want to accomplish and not hold me back from those things. I'm very fortunate because he's wonderful.

Gwen proceeded to talk about what she had learned about herself in this process:

I think my tendency whenever I make any big decision is to analyze to death and play out the "what ifs?" of every possible scenario. I about drive myself crazy doing that. I've really learned, and I'm trying to remember that I've learned this, to concentrate more on the living than on the analyzing. In some respects I'm just so carefree and everything is wonderful and fine. And every now and then something is just, oh, so big. And I just feel so overwhelmed by it. So from that standpoint I'm really just trying to focus on living this life and not paying so much attention to all the little components, just enjoy the parts of it. [I have to] remember that I don't have to understand everything one hundred percent, that I don't have to have total and complete control over everything that touches me, that it's okay to go with the flow; it's okay to face the unknown.

Asked how she learned this, Gwen replied:

Well, I think it makes me miserable for a start. My fiancé is very good about reminding me, "Hello. You're allowed to have your life to figure those questions out. You don't have to know today, at age 24, the answers to all those life questions." So from that standpoint, I think it's been just the sharing of perspectives with people that I care about and trust.

The influence of her fiancé became increasingly clear as she talked further about her experience at this point:

I think I'm just not beating myself up about it. And I just have to pay attention that when I start to feel like it's consuming me or when it stops becoming productive and I know that I'm not getting anywhere, that I can say, "Okay, that's enough." It's more manageable; I can't possibly expect that I have to understand everything now. It's not that I'm letting go of the controlling and it's not that I'm saying that I don't feel compelled to do that, just that I'm better at managing it and better at understanding when to say when. And particularly as it applies to other people, understanding when it gets in the way of other positive things in relationships. I think sometimes I pay a little bit too much attention, or I have a tendency to be so very concerned about other people's feelings that I let mine just totally go to pot. And I've tried to say, "Okay, I can be understanding and sympathetic and concerned about another's feelings, but take my sail out of their wind, so to speak. So that I hear you; you're not blowing me all over the place." So it's been a very powerful year for me. It was not an easy year; it was a lot of ups and downs. But I feel just so good about it now. And there's still a way to go; I'm not there yet. And that's something I'm probably going to work on for a long time. Because I can only control the way I feel. I really can't control how other people make me feel. . . . I was a master at shoving the square peg into the round hole. "Look, it almost fits. See?" So I think it's a lot of trial and error; it's a lot of just, "Okay, I deserve to be happy; I deserve not to beat myself up about everything and understand things." I guess understanding that there are limitations and you can't be all

things to all people. Those are some pretty sobering realizations. Everybody—it's just human to want to be liked by a lot of
people. And that everybody understands where you're coming
from and appreciates your thoughts. And that's just not true.

These comments reveal that she is aware of letting others' perspectives over-
power hers. She was trying to change this, but also aware that she wasn't
there yet.

The marriage decision led Gwen to abandon the external formula, even
though she still desired it, as is evident in her assessment of whether marriage
was the right thing:

I think it's just one of those things where you make your very
best wager; you set everything in line as best you can and then
you look at it and you say, "Well, is it going to be a go?" And
you go and you hope. And you just trust that what you thought
was right. But again, that's totally against everything—I want a
crystal ball. I want to know when and where and how and if.

Lacking a strong internal voice, she has no option but to "go and hope."
In her work Gwen was letting go of the formula as well. Reflecting on this
change she said:

I think in the past it was definitely, "What is protocol?" I was
interested in protocol. How do things happen? How does someone get from point A to point B? Because I could pretty much
follow the rules to get there. If these are the things you need to
do to be that, then I can do that and I can be that. I was pretty
confident that that's how it worked. And now, thinking a little bit
more outside the box, assuming I don't want to play by those
rules because I can't, I have to look for a different way. It has definitely been an evolution for me.

Having concluded that the "plan your work and work your plan" was a lie,
she explained:

If there's one thing I've learned it's when I don't feel comfortable
and try to force something, I always regret it. I'm learning to
trust my instincts more and more. Sometimes I think, "Oh,
that's okay," even though inside I'm going, "Nah." And it
always comes back to haunt me. My boss has said this more
times. He goes, "Your read on people, your read on situations is
always right."

She described learning to trust her instincts:

Make your little plan. Then check it out. Okay. Go on to the next step. Not that you are supposed to have this sequence of steps and then expect that you're happy with the end result. . . . It was learning to take smaller steps, look at things in pieces that are manageable instead of mountains that are overwhelming. I found myself writing a lot. That's a good way for me to kind of look inside a little bit more.

These growing internal instincts, and not forcing something, were heightening Gwen's self-awareness. Her connection to others, a mainstay of how she had approached life up to now, would have to be transformed to accommodate this new internal voice.

At the crossroads, the internal voice, or intrapersonal sense of self, gained sufficient strength to topple the external formula. Awareness of this tension between the external and internal press for who to be and the conflict between what others versus the self wanted lead to abandoning the formula. The dilemma, however, was that the ability to self-author one's beliefs (epistemological) or to construct oneself (intrapersonal) had not yet fully materialized.

As their lives and their ways of making meaning of them increased in complexity, participants extended their approaches from those they preferred in college. Gwen, who had relied on the connected pattern in college, was reshaping this pattern to balance it with the separation that stemmed from her internal voice. Mark, whose preference for separation is clear in his use of rationality and logic, began to incorporate connection to others with his logical bent. Arriving at an internal sense of self to guide knowing and interpersonal relationships would require an integration of both patterns (Baxter Magolda, 1995).

Becoming the Author of One's Life

Gwen's internal voice continued to grow, leading her to the realization that she was not ready for marriage:

I take a lot of responsibility for the things that happen in my life, the good things and the bad things. The decision not to be married as soon as I had originally thought was a grueling process to make a decision. For whatever reason I just did not feel comfortable with the plans as they were progressing. I went through a process to get comfortable, knowing the response I'd get from people—"What do you mean, you aren't getting married?" I learned a lot about myself in that process—I'm enjoying my space, the discovery of who I want to be, and I'm not sure I am ready to explore that as part of a committed long term relationship. I may wake up in a year and say it's him, or that I'm ready. I also imagine that the ball won't be totally in my court.

The process of making this decision was a matter of self-discovery and reframing relationships with parents and friends:

Last spring I probably felt like I was carrying the weight of the world around on my shoulders. I felt just that these decisions were weighing me so heavily. And the decision with work and the decision about marriage were all kind of happening at the same time.

Part of the struggle was working through her family's feelings:

And it was an awkward time as well with my family because I'd come from a very close family and we've always had very open communications. For whatever reason, at the time my Mom was just really not very excited about me getting married at all, just wasn't real sure that this was the kind of guy that she pictured me with long term, to the point where I don't even think she could be very objective about it. She didn't know him like she felt she would have liked. And that's her deal; that's not mine anyway. But it was adding to my [burden]. My parents were like, "Well, we'll support you. We're with whatever decision you make." But I didn't have my Mom being like, "Oh, honey, he's wonderful. You just have the nervous bride jitters." I had her saying, "Well, maybe you should think about this." It was really interesting. When I told my parents about my decision, I think they felt initially a lot of guilt about it as if somehow maybe they had something to do with it, when really I don't think they had anything to do with it. I think it was me, and it was my readiness.

Gwen also included her friends as part of her decision-making process:

But as far as process, I think it seems to be a real effective thing for me to do to—I have a couple of close friends that I trust just immensely. And one in particular often will help me kind of think through some things. I can kind of even talk nonspecifically about pieces of things and kind of kick around a piece of it and then throw it in the drawer and pick up another piece and throw it in the drawer and then hopefully have some of these pieces that begin to fit together and start to resemble something.

Talking about how various aspects of the process merged, she explained:

I think that it's changed some of my relationships with my friends for the better too, just in the sense that I feel I'm a little bit better listener. I'm a better sounding board as opposed to an advice giver. And I look for that as well. "I need you to listen to me talk this thing through." instead of "What do I do?"

The change in Gwen's interpersonal development is evident here. Rather than asking her family and friends to construct herself and her choices, she joined them in exploration. Her internal sense of self then coordinates the insights to make a decision.

Finally, Gwen also turned inward to sort out her feelings:

I found myself writing a lot. That's a good way for me to kind of look inside a little bit more. I think learning to look at things as far as what I can control and what I just have to pass off as not mine, can't do anything with it, might as well not get too bothered about it. I guess I used to think that I could carry a lot more than people really should, that somehow I could change people's feelings if they didn't feel good about something or that if I did something a little bit different then maybe that would change the perception of this. I spent a whole lot of energy doing something that I don't think is really productive that way. It was learning to take smaller steps, look at things in pieces that are manageable instead of mountains that are overwhelming. And in the past I don't think I ever really had big, important issues to deal with.

In the end, Gwen's internal voice remained in the forefront and she trusted her gut feelings in making the marriage decision.

It was very logical. And I didn't have a gut reading on it. I think that was my stumbling block. I didn't have something inside of me saying, "Yes, this is the right thing. Yes, this is what you're supposed to be doing right now." I just had this kind of logical voice in my head saying, "This makes sense for you to do." And I'm like, "No, no, this is not a decision I want to make sense. This is a decision that I want some kind of a gut read on to know." I was looking for some kind of a knowing, intuitive, gut thing.

After deciding not to marry, Gwen gave herself space to focus on herself:

Work is not the central part of my life. It's something that I enjoy, think I'm good at, and it gives me the opportunity to do other things I love and great experience. I'm trying to figure out what I'd like to do next. There are other dimensions—on the personal side there is a social sphere and a solitary, spiritual sphere. I'm not a churchgoer, but am becoming more spiritual in old age! An awareness and appreciation of that is energizing. It is empowering to decide not to worry—hand off to higher power. That has freed me up on a lot of occasions. Previously I would have been bogged down by trying to fix them. Socially, as friends move, family obligations change, dimensions of friendship change in positive ways, and in ways that make it harder. Substantial friendships become obvious. I'm fortunate with ones I have and have maintained; that energy is willingly given. Staying connected with groups to meet new people; try to continue to grow. I'm pretty carefree at the moment. I have lightened my load. I've chosen not to buy a house; unnecessary stress. Takes away financially and putting roots that I don't know if I want. I made a conscious decision to live lightly at the moment. I don't have demands in terms of relationships. It is different between being in a committed relationship and not. I have responsibility for just me. It might get old. I crave something that will consume my energy. I'm confident that I will find it. Don't have to find it by age 27. Meaningful things occurring outside of work, so not an issue. Want time to myself; maybe I'll never give that up. My expectation is that I'll feel ready at some point because I'll have a sense of who and what, and a more willing partner. Instead of figuring it out in the context of marriage.

In her explorations of new possibilities, she saw a new vision of life possibilities through others she knew:

I always thought you go to college, marry, have children. I don't know if it was that I was programmed that way, or if those were my own, but that is how I envisioned life. After being in a long-term relationship that ended, it was not all I had hoped it would be. It wasn't ever what I hoped it would be. There were always doubts that I chose to ignore; had mutual friends, had fun, covered up shortcomings between us. I reached a point where I realized, part of it was becoming friends with people five years older than me; wonderful, great, professional successful women who are single. Looking at them at 32 or 33—none of them have been married, not in serious relationships. I'm becoming comfortable with that reality that I might be where they are and seeing it as not so bad. It challenged me to think about life on my own as a single woman on my own for the first time. I never gave up faith that there was somebody out there for me, but it made the priority to find that person far less urgent. My life was about me, not about searching.

Becoming the author of her own life resulted in the end of her long-term relationship but the beginning of a vision of a life of her own.

Unlike Gwen, Mark was able to stay in his significant relationship as he became the author of his own life. He was also able to continue to refine his interest in the law. He grew in both areas through finding resources to establish his own internal belief system. He was following advice he had acquired from his mother: "A phrase that my Mom used to tell me, but I think is the best advice I've ever gotten is above all else 'to thine own self be true.' I think that that is really a key to who I am, definitely." Although Mark identified this theme as relevant to earlier points in his life, he was starting to live it in the context of his career decisions. This led to increased happiness and confidence:

> I'm a happier person, definitely. I am more confident than I was. I feel more in control of the decisions I'm making. I feel a lot more decisive. I'm definitely in much better shape than at any time in my life, definitely. Because I've solved a lot of these problems. And I know I have the tools to solve what comes down the road. I really know that and feel that. And part of it was because the problems that faced me were pretty darn big in the beginning. And I made it through and they're in my own historical memory. And, yes, I'm a much better person, much happier person. I see myself making strides as a better person too. So I'm really pleased.

One of the resources Mark found in continuing to author his own life was a book by Tony Robbins:

> One thing Tony Robbins talks about is you can choose and you can install certain beliefs in your belief system and become more productive for it. For instance, one belief he would say that would be good is the past does not equal the future. So what you've done in the past, what's happened to you, that doesn't necessarily constrain you. And my own take on that is whether or not that is true, having that belief is what can catapult you into a future you really, really like. Now maybe in fact the past does dictate some of your future. But by installing that belief, you're rationally manipulating your mind and your systems in such a way that you're going to succeed. But manipulating your own beliefs, I think that's really interesting stuff. I mean, making yourself into something, not what other people say or not just kind of floating along in life, but, you know, you're in some sense a piece of clay. And, of course, you've been formed into different things, but that doesn't mean you can't go back on the potter's wheel and instead of somebody

else's hands building you and molding you, your own, and in a fundamental sense change your values and beliefs. I certainly believe that's possible and I think it's really important that people believe they can do that.

Mark's ability to mold himself did not mean he ignored others as resources. But, as his stories of studying for the bar exam and learning the work in his clerkship show, he always brought himself to the process. Talking about how he approached the bar exam, he said:

Well, the first thing I looked at is how to study for it. How did other people, successful people, do it? So there's a role-modeling aspect. I spoke with people who had clerked and therefore worked like I was doing and passed the bar. And I said, "How did you do this? How did you allocate your time? What did you find to be effective?" And then you kind of role model them. But at the same time, you always bring yourself into it and in a way role model yourself when you were successful. So I'd think back to how I was successful. The older you get the more it would just be impossible not to bring myself to it now. Now if I was thrown into a totally alien situation when I was younger, maybe the move to college, I'm not certain, but I would be far more likely when I was younger to follow someone's recipe for success in a certain field. Versus now, it's just almost unimaginable to not judge it against your yardstick of experience, not bring yourself to it. Because you just have much more experience and an intimate sense of what works for you and what doesn't.

Similarly, Mark brought himself into his clerk role:

I'm the junior clerk. You always bring your personal style to it. At first you're a little more uncertain, so you follow the senior law clerk for guidance a little more. But then you're always asking why and you're asking why about certain things because you believe there may be a better way out there. And you want her input on it. But you kind of learn the rules of an operation just like any new job you go into. But as you grow into the job, I mean, you make it your own. There's no doubt about it. There's a personal style you bring to it. And then as far as one essential tool for a law clerk, you know, like writing style, I mean, that's all been—when I write something for a judge, I mean, it's all mine and I give it to the judge and the judge reads it. I mean, the judge hasn't tutored me in writing at all. He's been really very, very pleased with my writing, and that's made me very happy because you probably get less training in legal writing at [x] law school than any other school in the country.

Not only did Mark believe he could mold his belief system and his approach to work, but he also believed he could mold his everyday emotions by manipulating them:

> I think everybody has enough bad things going on in their life that if they focus on those, heck, you can feel bad very easily. Now I also believe that people have enough good things that if they focus on that and dwell on that that they'll feel pretty good about life. So the other thing is change my mental focus. And all these things are rational calculations I make to manipulate my emotions to make me feel good. And I do those kinds of things on a daily basis. Even like getting up in the morning or when I'm driving to work and saying, "What am I grateful for today?" Or if I don't feel particularly grateful, "What could I feel grateful about today if I wanted to?" When you ask your mind that question, there's a whole laundry list of things that can pop out of why you should feel grateful: grateful to your parents for helping you through school; grateful to your wife or spouse for, you know, blah, blah, blah. And so you ask yourself questions like that in the morning. So those are two examples of things I do on a daily basis or almost daily basis to manipulate emotion. The author of the work I read has particular gestures that he uses or that are common to him. I'd still bring myself to it and I'd still make up my own techniques too. So anyway I think it really increases your quality of life to do things like that because the bottom line is are you happy? And if you can take control of yourself in such a way that you can be happy in many different environments, that's wonderful. You've got a tremendous advantage. And if you're able to get out of unproductive emotional states—everybody's felt really sad or down or depressed. When you're like that, you're not a resourceful person, you can't accomplish things. You don't do anything. And if you can get out of those states, you're just a lot more productive.

Like Gwen, Mark was preoccupied with building his belief system and authoring his life. He maintained a healthy relationship with his new spouse, but shared a year later that he wanted to put more energy into strengthening relationships in his life.

Acknowledging the validity of the internal sense of self, participants looked for ways to develop it. Gwen's use of writing and reliance on her instincts helped her author major life decisions. In the process she re-visioned her sense of self and reorganized her relationships with significant others, parents, and friends. Similarly, Mark was finding mechanisms through which to organize his belief system in ways that maintained being true to himself. This in turn altered his sense of himself and his relationships with others. Becoming the author of one's life meant not only authoring knowledge, but also sense of self and relationships with others.

Internal Foundation

Gwen's trust in instinct to know had become the foundation for her internal belief system, as she described in our tenth interview:

> The biggest thing that has happened in the last six months is really coming to understand intuition. A couple things came up recently, and I probably knew the outcome long ago because I got little clues, but I ignored them—pretended I didn't see them. They keep coming back until they are taken seriously. I listened to those instincts because they are strong—[I'm] learning to listen and trust them. That's been significant both professionally and personally. I'm journaling every morning. It is amazing what is dumping out of my head first thing in the morning—things seem insightful and logical—ah-ha's. I used to ignore these; the message was inconvenient or disruptive to my lifestyle. Someone said the twenties are for defining who you are; still in growing up, but not in college. It's true—my perspective at 26 is so different than at 23. I feel a lot more centered, know about myself, my needs, the way that I am trying to pay attention to the way people interact, the way I do that consciously. Time gives you more perspective. I'm paying more attention to what my subconscious is stirring up. I don't feel as afraid. It makes me hold on less tightly to what I know and what's familiar, to make changes, take opportunities.

Comparing how this felt with how she used to feel, Gwen shared:

> I used to feel like I was on an out-of-control train—it was driving me. Now I have a lot more control over where I'm going and the speed. It's wonderful. In college I was going to be married by 25. It's ironic. I used to be planned and that was debilitating. It's tied into understanding who I am. I remember in college, and in late teens, what others were doing was important, I never wanted to miss anything. You think you are independent, self-directed, but there's a lot of group think involved. Getting away from that setting allows you to focus on your interests. I would love to live by myself for that reason. I went through a period, nine months or so ago, where I was very frustrated; not in control. And I was not sure how to get my arms around it. You can't change your whole life in one step. So change little pieces. [Now] I have a very anxiety free—I have a good sense of some of things I want to accomplish, I removed timelines, and set in-between goals. I

look for opportunities to help me get closer. Going back to the instinctive thing—I know when it is the right time. I used to live decisions, live the what-ifs; it's the quickest way to the loony bin! It took an inordinate amount of energy. I'm not completely free of it, but it is miles away in my thought. I'm accepting a decision and responsibilities that go along with it.

Gwen described how listening to her own voice helped her get off the train and onto a clear path of her own:

The five or six years that follow college are critical years for learning. Get out of the structured atmosphere; try your own wings; fly on your own! What is supposed to be good, what is important to me, what are my real values? For the first time I have a chance to listen to my own voice. I finally got to a point [in my mid-twenties] where I was paying a lot of attention to that. I talked about journaling when we last spoke—the book I was using (*The Artist's Way* by Julia Cameron) at that time changed my life in terms of hearing your own voice and giving yourself a forum to do that on a daily basis before you have a chance to let the censors in your mind and in the world step in. During that time I was processing all that I had been gathering for the prior years. I was finally able to see a clear path, chart a course, and now am on the course.

This path, or course, is Gwen's own now; it is not the external plan she originally relied upon to find her way. Gwen's comfort with herself enabled her to initiate a job change to further explore her career goals:

Last summer I was going to change jobs; I got a month off to look at other things; to get some direction—test drive possibilities. I was doing very well, well compensated, comfortable, well recognized, all the things people are looking for in a job. But I was feeling very unchallenged by it. My numbers were top in my district and I was barely trying. I thought, "this is ridiculous; if I am doing this with this little effort, what am I really supposed to be putting my mind to?" I decided to look for something to round out my resume and my experience. I work now for a CPA firm as the marketing director. They found me through a friend. I had been networking. It is a new position and they were looking for somebody to bring in a sales culture to their firm. My background was sales and the client management side. I hadn't done much hard core marketing. I was given an opportunity to come into a pretty small organization, and have a pretty big role to do things I haven't done before. I told them in the interview but they said I could do it. I said, "All right, if you are prepared to build this bike as we are riding it, then okay." My compensation structure changed dramatically. The old one was all base, the new one on base plus incentives. Initially that seemed like a setback. I thought about it like graduate school: an investment in me. I was looking for something that would round out my experience and to help me get focused. I've been there a year and it's been tremendous. I have accomplished the things I came in to do. It continues to be challenging—I have realized that long term, it has really helped me figure out exactly what I want to do—client development; client relationships. There are great things in the works that I hope will work out late summer or early fall. I am 28, seven years out of school, know people in positions of influence in interesting organizations, so have a network. It was going through more trying times trying to figure out so what next. The most important thing was giving myself the opportunity and forum to hear my own voice. I could stay moderately happy, continues to be rewarding, but I definitely have a strong sense it isn't where I need to be long term. I'll put things in place so I'll have other options.

Acting on her vision of living her own life, she also bought a house:

I bought a new home in fall, my first house! A friend was relocating, and I bought it. We did it all by ourselves. It was win-win for everyone. When I decided to buy the house, I was just feeling like I had been away from my former relationship for long enough and dated enough people and was starting to feel very comfortable with myself. I was no longer looking for the missing piece, something that was going to make everything whole and allow me to do what I wanted to do. I made the decision that I am going to do this, am going to buy the house, I'm tired of putting energy into other things, the energy is going into me.

To her surprise, once she was settled into her own life, a significant relationship emerged:

A couple of months after buying the house, out of the sky dropped a great guy I have dated ever since. Ironic how those things happen. Timing couldn't be better for either of us. We had the same experiences with former relationships and personal development and priorities. I think this is the guy! In fact, I know it's the guy. We are doing so well. This is what people mean when they say all these things—I thought it would never happen. Intuition—not something you have to sell yourself on. It's very rewarding because there is so much mutual respect and so little self-compromise. We both have a lot of respect for each other as individuals and understand the different things that are important to us that make us each other. Also we have a wonderful time together, a fantastic friendship. I feel very lucky. We are close and entangled with each other's families—all the things that make it feel like it is supposed to be.

The mutual nature of the relationship is clear in Gwen's comments about her internal voice:

I am much better, much more honest with myself, less inclined to base my actions and thoughts on what other people are telling me I should be doing or thinking. Another thing that is so helpful—things I used to worry about, now I can talk about with Steven—that is tremendously helpful. I know I can bear these burdens, but I don't have to. [That's a] liberating realization. It was frightening at first—I wondered if I should be afraid, then said "That is ridiculous, why would I?" It is more the Censor voice inside, the pessimist that says "Wait a minute" then other voices say "Okay, we are comfortable." [These are] all internal voices. There are external censors too—people telling you what you should do. People tell you what you should and shouldn't do—like buying a house without being married.

Gwen's internal foundation led her to feel settled and at "home:"

I probably feel more—not settled—but content with my life now than any other time I have talked to you. I struggle less. So probably, things we are talking about are a continuation of things I have found to be true rather than continuing to search. There is so much peace in just being rather than searching— frees you to enjoy so many other things. There are things that come up, but I have tools, I know how to handle them, so they are not as offsetting as they were. I roll with the punches better than ever. Nice when you feel like home is portable. It is not external, it is inside relationships. In years past, I had a big red flag about a relocation—wouldn't move for a relationship. Now where we live isn't the crux of everything; building life with him is. This is a good place and I didn't get here overnight, so I appreciate it.

This foundation, home being inside, guided her to marry a year later and change jobs. Talking about her marriage, she explained:

Definitely, he is the one. We met in October of 1996, were engaged a year ago tomorrow, and married two weeks ago. It was quite a ride! I *knew* immediately. There was just never, it was kind of like an old pair of shoes—you put them on and you say, "These are my shoes, they feel really, really comfortable." It was so—he and I are both on the side of being ultra communicators—we talk a lot. That is very rich for us. That is part of what made a big difference. No topics were off limits, as easy to be with him as anyone, even easier to be with him than anybody. We laugh—we never went through that stage of what is going to happen with us, no break up; met; dated; together ever since. A solid, grounded relationship.

Gwen's foundation was also apparent in her story about interviewing for new positions:

I had tremendous success with interviewing. I had sales, management, and marketing experience, all different kinds of things—at one point I had four different offers on the table. And that is a mixed blessing—it truly is. Be careful what you wish for because then you have to go through that exercise of how do you make those decisions? I was looking at project communication manager positions at financial companies, accounting executive positions with advertising agencies, and pharmaceutical sales, which is what I am doing now. They were jobs that had nothing to do with each other. There were common threads, and my experience fit nicely into all of those things. That was a great, really interesting exercise in decision making. Me making the decision, but also in a relationship that was very important to me, so that had to weigh in and instead of making a decision that was good for me, it had to be good for me but also good for us. For instance, one of the opportunities was with the company where Steven works. They have different companies, so we wouldn't have worked together at all, but promotions would mean relocation for both of us, and no way it would ever work. I also thought, we don't need to work for the same company. Options, that would be better. One of the things that appealed to me about going back into pharmaceutical sales is that again I am working out of my home, again I have flexibility to go out and manage my schedule, and it is a huge company that is growing like crazy—promotions and transfers happen all the time. That was something that was a factor—likely that I could keep my job with the company if he got transferred. And I really liked the company—it was the job I wanted the most. So everything came together.

Despite all this change in her life, Gwen felt grounded:

Marriage, job change, the thread that goes through there is feeling centered, grounded, knowing how to tap into and trust your intuition. Does it feel right? Okay, then off to New York we go. Going to New York [was] not logical— intuition is more important. We'll make more money, but it's more expensive; going from lots of space to little space. But having life experiences in other places is important. Whole world that is completely untapped for us. Life is wonderful here, but nothing stays the same—have friends here, but they won't always be here. Time to change and our time is now.

Gwen's internal sense of self, having developed strength to withstand external challenges, forms the foundation for her meaning making in all three dimensions. She has clear processes of her own to author knowledge and decisions. She is comfortable doing so because the internal sense of self is solidified. Her ability to connect to others is significantly different than it was earlier in her twenties because the internal sense of self can now be interdependent with others. Whereas her perspective was determined by her fiancé in her earlier relationship, she now determined her own perspective yet took her husband's needs and their needs as a couple into account in her decision making. Because the foundation is internal, Gwen is free to go anywhere—home is always with her.

Mark's foundation also allowed him to be centered; in fact, it allowed for a significant shift in the way he saw the world. The beginning of this shift is evident in his description of how he decided to accept a job in a large law firm:

Part of what you need to get through the process is time. Ask questions of self and various parts of the environment. Ponder the answers; refine the questions. My clerkship gave me a chance to accomplish goals—I need time to reflect. For example, what makes me happy? Where do I want to be five or ten years from now; is it profitable to think about ten years from now? Coming to an answer takes years, ask question over and over to get to the bottom of it. The key to the question of what makes me happy is how I answer it. I reflect on it more; it seems that I get different answers or conflicting answers. Keep pushing, ultimately comes down to judgment and experience. I have faith in myself and my decision-making processes. I'm comfortable in making decisions and acting on them. I'm very thoughtful. I'm confident once I've made a choice, but not to the point of blindness, I can revisit it.

This process is ongoing; it is in constant revision, yet Mark is confident with decisions made at points along the way. Constant revision was also a mainstay of how Mark approached his work at the law firm, explaining that he approached the firm as a university:

> Over time I've come more to the realization that I'm a lifelong learner and student—how I come to know anything is through that approach. I'm 100 percent dedicated to improving self and learning more. Role modeling a prior positive experience [college], makes me more confident than I would be. "I've done this before" idea. Even though I'm in a new environment, I'm comfortable because I made it an environment similar to an earlier one. Ultimately that will make me a better attorney. In order to learn you have to put yourself on the line, say what you believe, say when you don't understand. You're more likely to do this in a classroom than in work. In classrooms you are supposed to ask and learn. In the work world, people get concerned with appearing to know so they don't learn. You should reach a point of maturity to ask questions for self-improvement.

He offered an example of how he implemented this approach as a new attorney.

> If I don't understand, person may not think I'm very bright, but I still ask because my priority here is on education, not climbing the corporate ladder. For instance, when I was asked to write a position statement for client to the EEOC, I asked to see one that the attorney who gave me this thought was good. I role modeled from it, changed it according to what I thought was best. Writing is a creative act, invest yourself in it. If you are not seeing yourself in your work, you are losing something. You were hired to put yourself into work. I role model, but don't imitate. Another example is prioritizing facts in a motion for summary judgment. Got 8 depositions, 1500 pages, I do not have time to read all that. I chose the most important deposition, and scanned, skimmed, and read sections that were important to pick the story out of the plaintiff's deposition. The assigning partner trusts me to do this.

Asked how he felt about having this kind of responsibility, Mark said:

> My reaction to this kind of responsibility? Tremendous; it is what I have worked my whole life to do. I always wanted more, even as a child. There were too many rules in conservative Catholic high school! I was thrilled at [college] to get out of the oversight of my mother. I want to be the author of my own life; I am eager to do it. Can't imagine living any other way. Whatever I am in my life right now is primarily the product of deci-

sions I made. I feel like I am able to do it; if I need help, I'm not afraid to ask for it. People pick up values from parents, the environment, and never go through them to decide which ones make sense. My point is you are in charge of adopting that value; it might destroy you if you have adopted the wrong one. This is solely utilitarian. This may have been something I believed before, but it wasn't a core belief, not internalized [until recent years]. It has made a tremendous difference—impacted every area of my life: spiritually, politically, socially in relationships, career; I believe I am the author of my life. I can make decisions right now that can change it in any direction. [That's a] tremendous amount of power; external influence pales in comparison. As a child and young man, I felt much more at the whim of fate and am still at the mercy of fate, but I interpret fate, decide what it is going to mean to me and take action in my environment. My parents divorced [during my childhood] and there was nothing I could do. As an adult, if I hear devastating information, I can say "Okay, I can control my response and it won't affect other areas of my life. If it does, that is my choice." It's a radical responsibility in a way—authoring your own life. In another way, it is a radical freedom. You can construe it as either—I use freedom.

Mark's investment in learning and self-improvement opened the door to a significant paradigm shift:

I'm engaged in the development of a personal philosophy that goes beyond surface level understanding. For me, I am gaining knowledge in a way I never have before; by not thinking. It's completely an alien way of me understanding a way of life. In college I believed you had to analyze it. I believe there is a truer way to understand than through analysis. Forms of meditation. Turning your mind off. Then gaining an understanding of who you are and what this is around you, the world, without mental effort. I could read a text at college or law school, and could say this is a feminist critique of this text, then whip on the other pair of glasses. I found conservative lenses in law school. I could figure out what various kinds of people would think. With Taoist philosophy, I've gotten closer to understanding what my own pair of eyes internally and externally are seeing. It is more fundamentally true to my human nature than political critiques. Getting toward more important questions than what is a critique of this movie—getting to what it means to be a human being with a soul.

This perspective led me to inquire about Mark's traditional focus on rationality:

I'm not sure it is essential in knowing self. Who you are is as close as the tip of your nose. I can come to an understanding of that through silence, quieting of mind and body; that has no need for rational thought. Rational thought can act as a barrier between one's understanding and internal nature. I am less stressed at work than I would have been because regardless of what happens in any environments, there is a part of me that remains untouched by it. It has ripple effects throughout my life. In relationship with my spouse I am less concerned about things that may undermine marriage, like finances—because ultimately that is a mere piece of straw in one's existence. I have thought my whole life; it is shocking to read not to think, but at the same time I had a feeling of scales falling from my eyes. No bright light flashed, but it carried a lot of intuitive power to it. Maybe if I shut off idle chatter in my head about relationships, careers, and future I would feel better about self and have a fuller understanding. It is a paradigm shift, no doubt about it. I haven't gotten to a point with it—it is evolving, a work in progress.

Mark elaborated on the meaning of this shift:

Now I have an understanding that there is always a spiritual part of me present. Whether I consciously acknowledge it or not. I have a belief that this spiritual side will continue after my biological ceases to exist. I do feel that. Probably the first time I consciously reached out for it was after I saw Bryant Gumble interview Dr. Wayne Dyer on the Today show as I was running out the door. This Dr. Dyer said we shouldn't think of ourselves as human beings having a spiritual experience, but spiritual beings having a human experience. I carried that awhile. My dad visited and brought a book called *The Sacred Self* by Dr. Dyer. That book was the first conscious move in that direction. It talks about the detachment one gets when you have a spiritual understanding of who you are. Stepping back from one's physical self into a perspective and in knowing that what you are seeing in physical world is not the complete reality of your existence. You become much less invested in it. Stepping back from emotions such as worry, fear, doubt—[they are] unproductive. Some description and understanding of what part of you you are stepping back to—then it gets much more spiritual in terms of you are stepping back to part of you that has no end to it. When one believes that, spiritual component that is eternal, material problems in the world fall into dust.

In response to my question about what spiritual meant to him, Mark replied:

It has nothing to do with religion, and everything to do with one's soul. A part of you is a spirit; an intimate word. Not apart from you, an intimate part of who you are, have been, will be, after leaving [your] physical body. It comes from getting closer to [my] own spirit—not an overarching deity—a part of me that knows me better than I consciously know myself; it knows right for me. This is not a denial of responsibility for one's decisions, it is assuming one's responsibilities. I arrive at answers differently. I am still the author of my own life. No abdication of control over one's life. I could make a host of decisions to be different. I've found a truer identity that leads to understanding and informs important life decisions.

Even goals, which had always been a mainstay for Mark, now seemed artificial:

Something about goals is no longer valuable for me. A rewarding life can spring from life without goals. They seem artificial. Too many people are driven to distraction from their own carrots and stick. I don't know if I set goals anymore; I care less about them. That's another paradigm shift—worlds away from where I was. I used to tape goals to the mirror; now it is offensive and reductionist.

This internal foundation meant that nothing shook Mark's world. At the time of our last interview, his wife was beginning to explore locations for her residency. He had no hesitations about leaving his work to move with her:

If I wanted to exert some kind of control, or draw a line in the sand, I could—I have that kind of authority. But why would I do that? In terms of the process, Michele has ideas about where she wants to go. It may be best to go to Detroit, Kansas City, etc. I'd have to take the bar exam again, which is not something I look forward to, but I kind of accept Michele now as a kind of engine in part for my life. This move isn't just about her; more horizons for me just by going along with her to a new environment. You get more energy and enthusiasm from moving from one place to another. It is longer than a rush, an infusion—become focused, learn new things, grow. Her moving is an engine for me to develop as well.

He further explained how he has achieved this peacefulness:

One of the ways I have grown is to come at peace with anything that happens to me. It will happen—people passing away, injuries, things that are inevitable. So with a broader understanding of context in mind, it would probably take a lot to shake me down to my boots. As an undergraduate, intellect was my god. There is a syllabus for every class; you know when exams and papers are due. In life, there is no syllabus! No finish line, no set time for exams. I really had to expand beyond the intellect when I got more into the real world. Intellect is no longer my god; used to think I could solve anything by thinking. I don't know if it defrauded me or not, but it didn't lead to an understanding of who I really am. I decided to study more deeply emotions and spirituality. Have to go beyond intellect to understand those things, have to turn the intellect off.

Mark further explained how he was viewing intellect and rationality at this point:

I can see it [rationality, intellect] as a tool, a really sharp knife I can use to slice some things that are of importance to me. If you are using it constantly, 100 percent, you are cutting yourself off from yourself; you don't really understand who you are, and then you can't relate to others except the intellectual. That is not the way to relate to other people. One of the ways in which I brought the spiritual and emotional into daily life, and removed intellectual, is with arguments I have with [my wife]. Being intellectually right means nothing! First of all, the relationship is the most important thing and how can you extricate yourself from this without damaging that relationship? Hopefully it is through sympathy, understanding, a kind of detachment—I use this in just about any situation—when I am having a difficult time. Often times it manifests itself in detaching from intellect—it is chirping in my ear about career, money—those things don't matter emotionally or spiritually. There is no way to be at peace with yourself and often with others unless you turn the intellect off. It's like a waterfall of thoughts cascading down; you need to step behind that waterfall, no longer in the water, can see it go by, but at a point of stillness. Not thinking. Letting thoughts just pass right through. It took me a long time. Spirituality is the core—most important. Thoughts give rise to emotion. Intellect is not my master. I can turn it off. I was not like this when younger, before I learned meditative skills, and before I understood who I am. I [can] let the knife of intellect slip from my hand.

On how intellect, emotion and spiritual dimensions related, he offered this example:

These three things are always there—just because [I'm] not using right hand doesn't mean its not there. There is this interplay that goes on. For example, I was praised for my perform-

ance at this trial. I knew that they wanted to test me—the partners in the firm—in this trial. I'd never been in any kind of trial
before. They wanted to see if I would wilt, what would I do
under pressure? I did fine, and was praised for it. Prior to trial
we filed motions to get the case kicked out. If not, we would
have a ton of work to do. People got emotionally and intellectually invested in getting it kicked out. If you're dealing with things
from spiritual core, which I was, in a very self-conscious way, it
didn't matter to me if it got kicked out or not. I was going to go
through the process, whatever that was, and accept it. It
seemed like their self worth was determined by whether the
case got kicked out, or whether the judge disagreed with them
on something. Ultimately, to me it was irrelevant. So when I
stood up before the judge to make my argument, I was able to
do that successfully because I didn't feel that much pressure.
You can step through the waterfall and not be attached to
thoughts as they go by. You can't completely turn the waterfall
off, unless you're in deep meditation. Just because I am not
emotionally or intellectually invested in outcome, may impact
favorably on technical efficiency. It allows intellectual execution
to increase, just like oral arguments in court.

Mark's paradigm shift was so complete that he viewed this core as something he discovered, not created:

My understanding of it may be evolving, but quite frankly I think
it is a consistent thing. My own belief is that it has always been
there, it is just sometimes I haven't recognized it, or I thought it
was not there, or that there was no such thing. That is definitely
the intellectual talking there, slicing everything away but itself!
It was god; it gave life to everything. The spiritual core is not
something I created. That must come down to an article of faith
I have, I can't—in a way, one slice at it, there may be evidence
of me discovering it; intellect can create some amazing things,
but nothing I have created intellectually has given me peace or
stillness or silence. It is almost antithetical to intellectual thinking to have peace, stillness and silence. At least in the intellectual approach in my life, it's more chattering, thinking, logical,
slicing the layers of the onion. It seems very anti-intellectual, so
maybe that is one reason I say I discovered it. We explored it to
the best I can articulate it. It is beyond adequate linguistic
description.

Mark's sense of power and control is evident in his words. Yet it is no longer
the power of intellect alone. It is the combined power if intellect, emotion,
and what he calls spirituality, or a sense of being beyond the physical self.

Connecting to this internal core changed how he interacted with his wife and how he approached law cases. It also affected his overall outlook on how external events would affect him and how he could continue to pursue life-long learning.

The foundation, as described here by Gwen and Mark, is the achievement of internal authority of one's beliefs, self, and relationships with others. The power of this combination is audible in their language—"centered," "grounded," "at peace." Having found "home," they struggle less—not because their lives are any less complex, but because they know internally how to manage life's complexities. The merger of agency and communion is also apparent in the foundation. They connect to their internal voices, and in doing so achieve agency. Their interdependence with others reflects Jordan's (1997) concept of mutuality or the balance of agency and communion. Their reliance on internal sources in conjunction with analyzing external evidence to know reflects a merger of agency and communion in self-authorship. Thus self-authorship does not mean separation from relationships; instead it means connecting with others in ways that achieve mutuality rather than self-sacrifice.

The evolution from formula to foundation was an arduous process for most participants and occupied most of their twenties. Shifting from glasses acquired from the external world to their own eyes required determining what was going on in the minds and hearts behind those eyes. Although Mark's and Gwen's stories illustrate the trajectory of this evolution, their journeys are two possibilities among many. The next four chapters include many other participants' journeys to explore this evolution in greater depth.

3

FOLLOWING EXTERNAL FORMULAS

Upon leaving college, most participants found themselves in work, educational, and personal settings in which they were expected to function independently. Although a few had come to independent (12 percent) or contextual (2 percent) assumptions about knowing during the senior year, most still subscribed to transitional knowing and its accompanying reliance on authority to work through uncertainty. Postcollege environments, particularly work settings, emphasized multiple ways to approach tasks and reinforced the notion that participants had to think and function on their own. Participants adjusted their epistemological assumptions accordingly, coming to believe that most knowledge was uncertain and that multiple opinions were valid. During their first year after graduation, over 50 percent of the participants demonstrated independent knowing.

Participants who carried transitional knowing assumptions into their early twenties followed "formulas" they obtained from external sources to make their way in the world. These formulas took the form of prescribed plans or predetermined scripts for success in adult life that participants gleaned from others around them. Being unsure of themselves, they adopted these formulas as a means of becoming successful in their work and personal lives. This approach was consistent with the transitional assumption that following authority's lead results in resolving uncertainty. However, the growing number of independent knowers seemed to follow externally acquired formulas as well. Their epistemic assumptions that multiple perspectives and knowledge claims are equally valid might suggest abandoning formulas; I surmised that their lack of experience in working their way through ambiguity might account for their reliance on externally derived formulas.

Across their twenties, at varying paces in varying contexts, participants shifted to contextual knowing, assuming that knowledge was relative to a context, could be judged based on criteria, and better or worse choices made after an evaluation of relevant evidence. In both independent and contextual knowing participants were aware that they were now in charge of deciding what to believe and choosing their own paths. However, their way of being in the world up to now had been to rely on external authority and guidance. Despite their progress on conceptualizing more complex ways of knowing, they did not have the corollary progress on the intrapersonal and interpersonal dimensions to genuinely enact contextual knowing. In their attempts to function independently and contextually, they began to internalize external "shoulds" to decide knowledge claims. This resulted in adopting formulas or doing what others determined would be successful. Participants also internalized external "shoulds" to answer the "who am I" question; defining their internal sense of self through what they perceived that others thought was appropriate. Thus in the interpersonal dimension, other voices overshadowed those of the participants. Because they were focused on thinking for themselves and functioning independently, they framed their stories about all three dimensions as though they were internal. Hearing them in detail revealed that these processes were formulas—prescribed plans or predetermined scripts—adopted from the external world. Evan's and Kelly's stories are told extensively in this chapter to offer a map of this portion of the journey.

Evan's story illustrates internalizing external formulas for knowing how to do his work. Evan described his first postcollege job managing real estate as falling into his lap, and a context for which he had no formal training. Yet Evan's formula for success at this point was push yourself as much as possible, work hard and opportunities will present themselves. This attitude yielded quick responsibility in his new line of work:

> I could not find a professional tutor teaching me to learn more than I've learned with the mentors I have in my job. They not only teach me how to do things but why they're done and what effect it has or teach me a way to realize what effect the things I do have. At the beginning I had to ask a question on every single little thing. I could make a decision, but who knows how big a disaster it would be? At first there was no way that I could complete it from start to finish. They'd go through it with me the first time and then I would need to ask fewer questions each time. Now all I do is present them the paperwork and they sign.

> Now I know what they want and what's good for the company. I ask questions automatically that wouldn't have even gone through my head two years ago.

As Evan learned the questions himself, he became increasingly confident that no matter what he was asked to do, he could figure out a way:

> I want to make as much as I can of myself. There are times when I'm literally frightened to death to do something. But, I have no choice because if they expect me to do something, I've got to figure out a way to do it. Sometimes I underestimate myself and think that I'm at my limits. The next day you come in and your mind is fresh and you can do it. And you realize it's not as hard as you thought. You add it to your repertoire and move on.

Evan was forcing himself to learn to think and work independently because it was expected of him. His formula of pushing himself worked to help him succeed and to move toward an internal sense of self.

Kelly's story demonstrates how internalizing external "shoulds" helped her adjust to the freedom offered in her work. As a new kindergarten teacher she was anxious to apply what she had learned in her teacher education program. She was excited to find the opportunity in her first job:

> It was really neat because in the school district where I teach there are no textbooks in kindergarten. You have a letter a week that's the emphasis for language activities, and basically my principal just said, "Get the objective taught. Do whatever you want," which really—I found that I really, really enjoy being creative in the things I do when I'm teaching.

Despite enjoying this ability to be creative, Kelly was beginning to get concerned about whether what she was doing was right because her colleagues were not doing it. Attending a conference helped reassure her:

> In undergraduate, we studied things like using whole language. They told us to make a whole unit, but it was hard to do without the students and without having—there wasn't quite enough guidance as far as incorporating it into the classroom. And when I talked to these actual classroom teachers [at the conference] who were doing a book every week and a half and just different activities around it, and then this one lady who did Hawaii for a whole three weeks, and she had all of these using whole language, literature books that she used and math activities—I just got really excited. There was a unit on rain forests, but I

took some of her ideas and some of the ideas for the rain forests I did myself. I didn't lean as heavily on the literature I had gotten for the rain forest unit as I did on the Hawaii. And the Hawaii unit I also did a lot of stuff on my own. But as far as the outline for the unit, I kind of followed what she had done. But it was really reassuring for me to talk to all these other teachers and find out what I was trying to do and what I was doing part of the time, you know, trying to do most of the time, *was* right. Because I was kind of feeling shaky at that point in the year because I'd been trying to do all these whole language things, bring in the books, bring in additional activities, tie everything together. And I wasn't seeing that in the two colleagues. Being a first-year teacher, I was kind of insecure. But the conference really gave me a boost because here are all these teachers who have been teaching for 15, 20 years in kindergarten and they're changing with the times and they're doing the things that Miami taught me. They were able to let me see the whole picture.

Kelly wanted the freedom to plan her own teaching, yet was insecure about it when she noticed that her two colleagues taught differently. Hearing other experienced teachers talk about how they used the whole language approach reassured her that what she was trying to do was right.

Just as the participants internalized external formulas for what to think and how to do their work, they did the same to determine their identities or intrapersonal sense of self. Because they were expected to "act like adults" they tried to envision themselves that way. Again, having not had opportunities to develop an internal definition of themselves, they borrowed from external sources in trying to craft their identities. Evan's formula for managing his life was organization. He explained:

I like to keep things running smoothly. If something's broken, I fix it. If something's out of order, I straighten it. My checking account is always accounted for to the penny. I'm continually throwing out stuff that I don't want or need anymore, streamlining everything so that it's like a finely tuned machine, literally. I hate it when things go wrong and I try to keep my life in order so they don't.

This organization, in conjunction with Evan's "push yourself" formula, helped him define who he was. Similarly, Kelly described herself as in control of herself two years after college graduation. She explained:

I think I've just grown up. I've calmed down and I've just become more responsible, I think, for my actions about my bills.

You know, getting the bills in on time. Budgeting has been an incredible—oh, my gosh, what a learning experience. And I'm still comfortable with who I am and that makes me feel good. And that's just come back in the last week after getting through this relationship thing, which makes me think another reason that that was the right decision. So, I don't know. I think I'm more able to make decisions rationally than I was a year ago. And think about the whole picture. Do you know what I mean? I don't know. I feel like I can see things better. Rather than just thinking of just today, I can think down the road. . . . I've learned a lot. I'm never going to be in a relationship again where I'm going to allow someone to just control my life every single day. That's just not healthy. My best friend told me, she said [the relationship] was getting dysfunctional. She said, "You were just—there were just too many things; he was way too demanding." I don't know. I know he's probably pretty upset right now, but I don't know what else to do.

Kelly expressed a sense of self and confidence in herself in this discussion. Yet as the discussion continued, the role of external influences became clear:

I thought this guy was it. I thought he was really special. But I started to lose who I was basically at the end of the relationship. I was apologizing all the time for things I shouldn't say I'm sorry for. I really kind of lost who I was, and I'm a really self-confident person. I'm a very strong person. I felt so guilty this past week just because he's—he called me tonight. It was really bad because he just wanted a second chance. And I just—I don't know. I had to think of myself for once, I guess. I kind of have always thought of other people. I mean, after being a RA for two years and being a teacher, you always have to think of these 24 little people. And in the relationship it just got to be too much. I was not thinking of myself at all. And I was losing myself; I was losing who I was. I wasn't comfortable with who I was. So he would make me feel guilty for other parts of my life, like for singing in the church choir. I'm also now a senior high adviser for the senior high youth group. And making me feel guilty for the time I had to spend away from him. Whenever I was home he wanted to be here, every single evening. And it was just too much.

These comments show that Kelly has not typically thought about herself but rather focused on others. Even as she was extracting herself from this, her parents' approval of her decision weighed heavily, as she noted:

Mom said that four weeks ago now—she and Dad had been talking and they said that Mike was a really nice guy but he's not the one for me. My Dad said that I'm too independent for him. He doesn't have really the personality to handle it. So that made me really step back and think, too, because my Dad knows me and he knows how I am and knows how I work. I respect his judgment of people. And I'm not saying that that made up my decision because my decision was already made. I don't know. It helped to have my parents' support and have them not saying that I made this horrible mistake, "You had this wonderful guy."

Kelly in many ways conveys the same "be in control" formula that Evan described. She knows that being controlled by her boyfriend is not healthy. Yet she is not totally aware that she is relying on (and potentially controlled by) the perceptions of her friend and parents in moving away from his control.

Consistent with the expectations to be their own persons yet relying on external sources for doing so, participants talked about independent decisions in ways that revealed that other voices overshadowed theirs in deciding on life plans. Evan's account of how he decided to marry offers an example. Although Evan never used the language of external expectations, but rather doing things to make his life the way he wanted, his description of his decision to marry a year after college sounded very much like following the standard plan for adult life. Talking about it in retrospect, he said:

It wasn't that shocking to my system because I lived with Kristy for over a year before we got married. I've never been afraid to commit to something. It's no big deal. It was exciting; don't get me wrong. But it's not like some kind of mystical answers were revealed to me. When we first started going out I thought marriage would be neat. And then I was like, "Well, we live together, what's the big deal?" It was something Kristy wanted to do. And I wasn't against it. So we decided, we might as well, because who's kidding who? Neither of us was running away from each other. The biggest thing I could ask for is a stable life and when you're not dating, that's pretty stable. My grandparents are getting up there and it was something that I know they wanted to see. So I had no objection. The wedding is just something you have to go through. You don't have to, but it makes it more official. You feel worse if you want to split up with your spouse if you spent that much money. Instead of just saying, "Alright, let's go." It's not like going bowling or something.

His comments do not convey that Evan actively made this decision from some internal sense of what he wanted; rather they convey that he had no objection to what his fiancée wanted nor to his grandparents' wishes. Because marriage looked better than the alternative, he proceeded. Evan also knew in entering this marriage that he and his wife operated very differently. However, he believed that his organization of his life, and of their life together, would smooth over this difference. He described their differences and how they were approaching them:

> We both have different things we take care of. I handle money management, but she'll do other things, like laundry, that I don't like to do. If you look in our bedroom you can see the difference. My shirts are arranged in color order; hers are on the floor. We do our own thing and then we have our together things. So it's kind of like having three lives. We like a lot of the same things, so there's never really any arguments.

Evan was relying on his formulas regarding organization and relationships to overshadow these differences.

Kelly was also making decisions in which others' voices overshadowed hers. She explained her decision to pursue her Masters degree:

> And my parents have encouraged both my sister and I to pursue as much education and educate ourselves to our full potential and our full capabilities. And it was kind of weird to be having those thoughts in the back of my mind, you know, "Do I want to get this Master's? Sure I'll be making more money right now, but down the road in ten years who knows what's going to happen?" But I think my parents' values won out. I've always thought—even when I was a freshman in college I think that the Master's degree was a goal in the back of my mind rather than just the Bachelor's. That's what I'm going to do, and I'm going to live with the consequences I guess.

Kelly, like Evan, did not describe a decision-making process in detail; rather she described her hesitations and the strengths of her parents' values. Resigning herself to living with the consequences hints that she was not sure she wanted to return to school.

Despite coming to understand knowledge as uncertain and involving personal choice, participants in their early twenties were not prepared to act fully on these realizations. They had had so much encouragement to rely on authorities prior to this point and so little opportunity to develop their internal minds and voices that they could only rely on other voices when it was necessary for them to make important decisions. Knowing, however, that it was more complicated than just going to some authority for an answer, they worked hard at developing internal belief systems. Meanwhile, they became adept at finding formulas to follow. Most participants spent their early to mid-twenties in this external mode of self-definition. This chapter explores stories of formulas for career success (the epistemological dimension), formulas for adult roles (the intrapersonal dimension), and formulas for dealing with what others think (the interpersonal dimension).

Formulas for Career Success

Career and job decisions in the early twenties revolved around doing what one was supposed to do to be successful. Transitional, independent, and contextual knowers all realized that there were multiple career paths. Yet having no organized set of internal values to guide their choices, they relied on societal messages. Heather described (in retrospect as she prepared to return to school to change careers three years after college) her postcollege career choice:

> Education is quite a change from what I set out to do from college. I'm glad I'm making it. And another thing I thought about as I went through this is how I made my decision to go into business. I feel that I never really gave anything else a chance because, again, as part of my education and the goals that I set for myself it seemed to naturally push me into business. And I was encouraged to do so. I never really stopped to think otherwise, just always thought that's what I should do and that would be good and there are good things in business. I never really thought—I mean, I enjoyed several of my undergraduate classes, but never really thought through, "Is this really what I want to do with my life?"

Heather realized in reflecting on her experience that her choice of business as an undergraduate major did not come from an internal sense of self but instead from external encouragement.

Similarly, Kurt took his first postcollege job due to external influences, although they were somewhat different than Heather's. He explained his choice to work as an assistant in a law firm:

> I was motivated by wanting to go to law school. The law firm was also motivated by prestige. Being a lawyer would be good because I would get acceptance. [But then] I got a taste of the environment, and it was not one I wanted to be in. I was torn about it. I talked to my dad. I'll remember that conversation the rest of my life! Dad said he didn't like wet weather and might move upon retirement. And I thought, "I'm staying here to be near family, then you are moving?" It was an awakening—start living my life for myself. I decided to move out West.

Kurt also reflected that prior to the time of this conversation, he had always chosen to please those around him. He said, "A lot of times when pleasing others, there was a conflict along the way. Trying to please two parties who had opposing wants—my girlfriend and my family—I tried to choose the person who would be least mad." These comments clearly indicate that Kurt made choices based on what he thought others wanted from him.

Anne, an accountant, made career choices due to what others wanted from her as well. She was promoted in her job. In responding to my question about how she was selected for the promotion, she explained:

> I'm really not sure. I guess a position came open and they needed someone. My boss thought I would do a good job at it. I guess they figured that I had the most experience or the best experience or whatever. So they asked me to go up.

Anne's explanation shows that she had no role in this decision or seemingly any opinion about whether she was qualified or interested in this promotion. Even though she did not like traveling to another site for this new work, she did not even consider whether to accept the opportunity. Instead she accepted the decision of her boss that this was an appropriate move. Part of the external formula is that a promotion indicates success. Anne's pursuit of her CPA stemmed from external sources as well, as she explained:

> They want you to do it because they'll pay for it. But most of the accountants in my company aren't CPAs. Mostly they look at your performance, but I think it kind of matters a little bit, like if there are two equal people up for a job and you're a CPA, you'd probably have a better chance. There are a couple of jobs in my department that are really technical and you have to have a CPA. So if I ever wanted one of those jobs, I mean, they're probably ten years from now jobs I would want to have, I would need it. But that's only a couple. I don't know. I just kind of did it more for myself. I figure if I'm going to be an accountant I might as well be the best one and have the—I think people respect you a little more when you have that title. They think you know what you're doing. You never know what's going to happen. In today's world with companies and mergers, I just figure it would make myself more marketable if I needed to move sometime. I felt useful and felt like I was doing something to better myself. Because for a year I wasn't doing anything after I came home from work but goofing off and having parties or watching TV. It felt good to feel like I was bettering myself and learning and brushing up on things.

Anne views the CPA as a source of respect and something that will help her career.

Another formula that was evident was the notion that new professionals must "pay their dues" to get the kind of work they want. Describing the course of job decisions in his first years out of college, Will said:

> The first five months after I graduated from Miami I really wasn't employed anywhere permanently. And then I took a temporary position. It was only six months with a brokerage firm. While I was at the brokerage firm, I was really doing things that I wanted to do, marketing types of things, which is what my major was at Miami and what all my classes centered around. When I left there in March I took a job at a finance company, not doing marketing kinds of things. But I think that I'm going to stay here for quite a while. I've been there about eight months now, and the training has been, I guess, pretty good. I don't think the job market is too terrific. And there are always openings, I think, in this field. The pay was relatively low at the beginning, but with lots of potential, from the time I started in the first two years there's a lot of potential for pay increases, some of which I've already had. I'd worked for a brokerage firm, which was kind of in the financial services industry. And this is too. It's just, I think, in some ways another aspect of financial services, which is something I'd like to stay in. But I'd like to eventually get into the marketing end of it. I see it as being a means to an end. I don't know many people who start off with good marketing jobs. Usually you have to pay your dues. And I might not go to marketing. I might stay in this area. I'll just have to wait and see what happens.

Will was able to do what he wanted temporarily, but then had to shift to something slightly less desirable. He seemed somewhat tentative about the quality of the training and hesitant about the job market overall. Yet the earning potential sounded positive in the financial arena. He surmised that this was typical—a means to an end. His waiting to see what happens implies a heavy reliance on external forces.

Lynn spoke to reliance on external forces more directly in her version of paying her dues. Lynn was an education major and worked hard at finding a teaching job. Not acquiring a full-time position in the grade level she wanted upon graduation, she signed up to substitute teach. She expressed her hopes for the role this would play in her quest for a full-time position:

> I was thinking through my substitute teaching, going in and meeting the principal and telling them they're welcome in my

room anytime, that that would work out. But it didn't. And even after my long-term sub, I thought, "Well, you know, I've got it made. I made my name here. She [the principal] observed me; she gave me a great write-up." But she didn't do anything for me after I left the school. And that really made me angry that I put in my time and effort and energies and was creative with these kids and dealt with all of their mental problems of being shifted between teachers, that she would recognize all my effort, and she didn't, which was very disappointing to me. There were openings there, and the story I got was that she had to take transfers from within the system. That's understandable, but she could have said to other principals, "Look I had this great long-term sub. This is her name. Look at her." And I know she didn't do that.

Lynn continued to substitute, sent out resumes, and visited schools and principals. Still, no positions came her way. Talking about the tentative nature of a substitute teacher's life and this struggle three years after graduation, she said:

I feel like—this is a weird analogy—but I feel like a bull at a gate like at a rodeo. You know, just that anticipation of when the gate's going to open, and I'm waiting. I'm sitting there and I'm getting more and more antsy and more and more angry at the system. And the gate's not opening for me. And I'm trapped. You know, I mean, that's really how it is. I'm trapped in my position. It's gotten to the point of—I always thought, "Well, education's different. It's not who you know, it's what you know." And that's not the case. It's very much who you know. And that's a horrible thing to say about the world, but it's true. It really is. So it's been long and it's been hard. But I'm getting through it.

Lynn became frustrated that the formula everyone gave her did not work. She was angry to discover that it was really who you know rather than your performance that was important. The external constraints were very real to her as the gate thwarted her entrance into her profession. At this point, she was resigned to waiting, without a sense that she could influence the situation.

As is evident in most of these examples, participants encountered the shortcomings of following external formulas for career success. These formulas for knowing, translated to career decisions, did not result in meaningful work. The missing component was participants' own interests. They were so busy doing what others said would bring success that they had yet to define what success meant to them personally. Doing so would require progress on the intrapersonal dimension of development. These frustrations eventually led to the search for alternatives as will be explored in the upcoming chapters.

Formulas for Adult Roles

The tensions that were beginning to surface in the early postcollege years in the career arena were more obvious in participants' struggle to adopt adult roles. They consistently looked for external formulas to guide them but encountered issues with those formulas more quickly than with the career formulas. Leah articulated the general pattern of life most participants expected, saying, "It's like you graduate college, then you get married, then you have kids. It's the next step in our lives." When the pattern was disrupted, they struggled with unexpected changes. For example, Rosa explained her shock at becoming pregnant on her honeymoon:

> I was like, "Oh, there's no way." We took every precaution. I guess it's just meant to be. There's no possible medical way this could happen. I'm very organized. I have times written down of everything that's going to happen. And this wasn't on my schedule. I'd always known I wanted to be a teacher since I was in kindergarten. I knew I wanted to go to Miami [University] since I was a freshman in high school. I dated the guy 7 years before I married him. That's just the way I am. We were going to have kids, probably in about 2 years. So we were going to have kids shortly after, just not 2 days after. And that was really hard for me to accept because I always plan things. I'm not spontaneous. So that was really hard to spontaneously be pregnant. And there was nothing I could do about it. I think the biggest learning experience was just roll with the punches.

Prior to this "spontaneous" pregnancy, Rosa's life had proceeded as planned. She had acted on all her formulas. Being pregnant for the second half of her first year as a teacher also called her lifelong dream into question. She could not ascertain whether she was unhappy with teaching or whether her pregnancy was responsible for her reaction. This dilemma took a few years to resolve because Rosa "knew" immediately that she would quit her work to mother her child (another external "should" of how life was supposed to be for Rosa). Although Rosa was crystal clear on her life goals early on, her story left me feeling that she had not really explored the meaning of these goals for herself.

Anita was also concerned about relationships and how they affected her career. The uncertainty in following the formula toward a significant relationship is clear in her reflection on a break-up three years after college:

> I guess, when I'm involved in a relationship, I kind of leave a lot of opportunities open for me and remain flexible in terms of,

"Well, if we do this, then I can do this," or, "If we do that, then I can do that." Whereas I think men, or at least the men that I've been involved with, more or less have an idea of what they're going to do. And I don't think—I'm definitely generalizing here, but they're flexible to a degree, but they're not going to give up what they want to do career-wise really for a relationship. For instance, if this guy that I was dating got a great opportunity somewhere else and I refused to go, I think he would still go. And basically it would be looked at as, "I'm giving up the relationship because I'm not going." Whereas with me, if I had a great opportunity to go some place else and he was absolutely not going to go, I could see myself giving that up because the relationship would have more importance, I think, in my overall life and the type of life that I want than going off by myself for a career. Well, it's difficult because one thing that I kind of do is—in my mind, whether I do it consciously or not—I kind of picture what my life would be with this person, what I'll be doing career-wise, what he'll be doing career-wise, and the whole thing. And then—like, for instance, I just ended a relationship about two weeks ago with this guy that I'd been dating for a year. So now I'm kind of in flux between going back and forth from feeling like, "This is the greatest thing that could have happened; now I can do all these things I didn't really know I wanted to do, but I can do them now." Not that I couldn't have done them before, I just probably wouldn't have. And then I go to this feeling of, "Oh, my God, I'm going to be alone my whole life." And that's, I think, something that's—relationship-wise it's a big thing with a lot of people, my friends right now. They're ending relationships that have been going on for a long time, and they're scared to end them. They know that that particular relationship isn't right, but on the other hand, are they ever going to find something better? And, you know, we're getting older and, "What if I end up ten years from now and I've never found anything better and I give this person up?" It's kind of like, "Do I want to make this work come hell or high water or do I want to give it up and look for something else?" And it's scary.

Being in a significant relationship is an expected part of life for Anita and her friends. Having a career is also important, but secondary to the relationship. Knowing a relationship isn't right does not make it easy to give up because of the frightening specter of being alone. The formula is to be with someone, not to be alone. The other dilemma evident here is that two formulas exist—one for relationships and one for careers—and they potentially conflict. This was one way in which the utility of formulas was called into question and one condition that prompted the need for a system to manage competing formulas.

For others, the societal message was succeed in your career. Jim expressed his drive to succeed career wise through acquiring responsibility and authority:

> And I really see that the position I'm in can really expand. I mentioned the mortgage sales, and mortgage insurance. I'm hoping to pull that under my umbrella of activity. The computer function, I want to pull that in. And then the insurance side is already there. So I can really see this as just expanding a lot, having a lot of authority, and really making an impact on the organization. And, of course, if we increase income and I'm in charge of it, then that gives me the opportunity to shine.

Some of his efforts to put himself in a good position were not appreciated by his coworkers. He reported:

> I've had some problems with some people at the office because they see me as a brown-nose to the president. The president and I have a very good relationship. We shoot pool together and we go play golf. I take him to the airport or pick him up at the airport or whatever the case may be. So some people get jealous of that. A new employee came in, we started talking. Somehow it came up about my relationship with the president. And she said, "Well, everybody knows you're the president's pet." And I said, "When the president came in day one, I walked into his office and said, 'Do you want to have dinner?' And you had that same opportunity, but you didn't. So how can you judge me when I took an opportunity to get to know a man and probably put myself in a good position? I don't deny that. But it's not like I'm brown-nosing here."

Jim's formula for success, to put himself in a good position and acquire increased authority and responsibility, took precedence over his coworker's reaction, although he remained concerned that others thought he was brown-nosing. Jim was also concerned about lack of success in another arena of his life—significant relationships. He shared his concern:

> I think right now as far as personally I've been struggling a little bit with the male-female relationship because I do spend a lot of time at the office. I spend a lot of time on the road. And I spend a lot of time with a lot of older people. So I don't have a lot of time to interact with some younger people. And that's been somewhat of a personal struggle, you know, "Where am I going with that? . . . "Should I be"—my Mom always yells at me. She says, "You need to start acting 23 instead of 33." I'm like, "Yeah, but I've got a house now. I have to act 33." But that's a personal

struggle with myself. I think I was much more concerned with dating and that type of thing a year ago. Now I'm—it's an issue for me. "Should I be concerned about that?" I don't know. "Is it a good time now just to worry about your career, get to the point you want to be, and then worry about dating or seeing other people?" But I've made a decision to be committed to my work.

So despite different issues, Jim shared the dilemma others encountered in trying to figure out who he was and how he should be functioning in his adult roles.

These stories show that participants primarily defined themselves externally. When they ran into problems with the external formulas, they shifted to alternate formulas. Rosa first identified herself as a teacher and spouse. When she became pregnant, she put the teacher definition on hold to define herself as a mother. Because she had always known she would be a stay-at-home mother, it sounded more like an external formula than a considered choice. Anita was trying to follow two formulas—finding a significant relationship and having a career. Jim was doing the same only in the reverse. The core issue in these and other participants' stories was the lack of an internal sense of self from which to approach life choices and relationships. The external definition of self was integrally tied to struggles in the interpersonal dimension of participants' lives.

Formulas for Relating to Others

Reliance on external others for direction and definition yielded tension in relating to other people, particularly with the push for functioning independently and thinking for oneself ever present. Lauren encountered this tension in an acute way. Lauren shared a close relationship with her parents and trusted their judgment. She took her first job at her father's urging despite being hesitant about it. She found herself in a quandary when she became involved in a long distance relationship. She explained:

Right now I'm seeing somebody who lives far away. He came to see me and stayed with me. And my parents thought that was not appropriate. And I have to admit, in college they would have said no to that type of thing, and that would have been fine. But now since I've been supporting myself, I can make my own adult decisions. If I want him to stay with me, I will. In college I would have lied about it, whereas now I know that they're not approving of it, but I feel comfortable enough that I can say, "Well, I know you're not happy with it, but I am an adult, and this is what I'm choosing to do." I can be honest and I don't feel as bad.

Lauren's willingness to tell her parents came from the fact that she was supporting herself and thus could make her own adult decisions. How she came to this emerged when she explained how she decided to go against her parents' wishes and be honest about it:

> I think maybe also the influence of my sister. I'm very close to my sister; she's 30. And a lot of times I'll consult with her. And since she's closer to my age, I may be more willing to bounce something off of her and say, "Well, what do you think Mom and Dad will say?" She's even given me the okay, like, "Even if they don't agree with where your friend stays, it doesn't matter. You're old enough to decide." And so I guess getting that approval from her makes me feel better. So that has been one of the factors that has helped me along through this.

Lauren's own wishes, to have her boyfriend stay with her, were in conflict with those of her parents, whose opinion she highly valued. Being honest with them about her choice was made possible by the approval of her older sister, which still only helped her not to feel "as bad" about going against what her parents thought. Her sister reaffirmed that she was old enough to make adult decisions, essentially providing Lauren with a new formula. Lauren's source of self-definition remained outside of herself, even though she identified it as her own. Although she was able to make her wishes prevail over those of her parents, it was only through another external source of approval.

Amy conveyed this struggle with expressing one's own voice in the face of potential disapproval as well. She encountered it in graduate classes, in her social life, and in her work. Being pushed to express her own ideas in classes was a struggle, as she explained:

> That's one of my problems I have with writing things, you know, writing papers is actually showing my own ideas. I'm kind of scared of being completely off, and so I think I play the line very straight and I don't really take a lot of chances. And that's one thing I think I worked on in papers, trying to give my own opinion and not feeling that that was going to be completely off. That's one thing that—just in other things, not just in writing papers, but, you know, giving my own opinion or something, I'm always worried that what I say is not right. So I think—I know I'm always scared kind of about my creativity I guess, about how when something's in front of me and I have complete rein to do whatever I want, whether it's in a paper or doing

a project or doing something, that kind of scares me because I feel like I can do better when I have specific guidelines. You know, "You do this. You answer certain questions," rather than—I don't know—"Here, you have a paper and you can write it on anything you want." And then I'm just like, "Ooh." I'd rather have a specific question to answer and work it out.

It is clear in Amy's comments that fear of what others think about her ideas is a strong constraint. Her story conveys the strong connection between the interpersonal and epistemological dimensions of development in its linkage of what she thinks with whether others will judge what she thinks as useful. She offered:

I'm working on that I think. I had problems a lot of times when we would have "Give your own opinion on Jasper Johnson, Robert Rashenberg, were they pop artists or were they pre-pop?" or something like that. And I would be just be like, "Ooh," what in the world could I have to say?" I mean, it's probably already been hashed out and different people have different opinions. And it's so hard for me to say, "Well, this is my opinion." But, I mean, it just seems like it would be easier for me to say, "Well, these are the pros and these are the cons of different people."

Amy was more comfortable summarizing others' opinions who have already "hashed out" these issues. She described her fear of expressing her own thinking in a social context:

In social situations I rarely give my opinion because I guess I kind of feel that . . . like if people are speaking about politics or something that's been going on, if I don't feel like I'm right up to date on everything that's happening, I just listen. I guess I probably wouldn't give my opinion because I'm so afraid. You know, a lot of people when they talk they're very confronting. And if someone confronts me and says, "No, that's not right," I just kind of shrink away. And I suppose in some ways I probably avoid those kinds of situations because I feel that I can't articulate how I feel about that or what I mean. And I have trouble remembering things, like things that I've read. And I can remember parts of them and I'll start to say something, and then I'm just like, "Uh, well, you know, I can't really remember the exact"—and I don't feel comfortable saying things unless I can remember the exact facts and the dates and things like that. I don't like the feeling of people saying, "Well, you don't know what you're talking about." It's just even normal conversation, not even ones where the people are actually

really violently saying, "No, this is right, this is right." I just
stay out of them because, I guess, because I don't want to be
confronted like a fool who doesn't know what they're speaking
about. And then you run the opposite thing of people thinking,
"Well, you don't know anything about anything because you
don't talk about anything." So, I don't know.

Amy was clearly afraid of appearing foolish or unable to articulate what she
thought. Her lack of confidence in her own thinking inhibited her from
exploring her ideas with others, leaving her no place to "think with" others to
allow her internal voice to emerge. She was torn between being asked to
express herself and her intense fear of doing so. This tension occurred in her
thinking about her job as well. She explained:

I think I definitely have some insecurity about what other people
think. On a level I really don't seem to care. And there are a lot
of people, I think a lot of my friends who are doing the kind of
job that I'm doing. I mean, at least I have a job. That's what I keep
saying, "At least I have a job and it's not"—I don't know. And I
enjoy my job. But it's just sometimes I—you know, you the read
the Miami alumni thing, and everybody is just being promoted
and doing these—I don't know—kind of "corporaty" jobs. They
just seem like they're so successful. And I'm just like, "Oh, I'm
just kind of floundering. I haven't really got my bearing yet. And
I'm 25 and what am I doing?" But then on other days I'm like,
"I'm not in any hurry. I don't have any mortgages to pay or anything like that. I'm not really tied down, which I really like."

Amy was referring to her managing a retail store, a rather significant responsibility as she described it. Yet she wondered if her father was really proud to
tell his colleagues that she was a retail store manager. Her measuring herself
against her fellow alumni also indicated that external definition and the
importance of external others, even those she did not know, reined.

Gavin portrayed his struggle with how he saw himself in relation to others in his insurance sales job. He changed jobs within the insurance field to
reduce his discomfort with selling insurance. He reported:

I'm still in the insurance field. What I did before was—just an
agent out there trying to solicit business and calling on people
and trying to sell things to people who hopefully need insurance. I decided that that was not what I wanted to do any longer.
And a guy that I used to work with at [my previous company],
his father owns his own insurance company. So he asked me to
come down and interview with them because they needed

somebody else. So basically I decided to give it one more shot. Ninety percent of the way that I earned my money was sitting at people's kitchen tables and going out and seeing people during the day and mostly during the night. What I do now is we represent 12 or 13 basically life insurance companies. We, during the day, go out to various people who sell insurance, people that sell home and auto and financial planners and stockbrokers, and get them to use our companies when they sell life insurance. I'm kind of doing the same type of a thing, just with a person that to me is a little bit easier to deal with because they're in the same business that I am. I don't feel like I'm selling myself to sell a product. I feel like I'm just saying, "Hey, if you need help with any type of life insurance product or if you have a person that needs something kind of special, we want to be your backup." To me it's a lot less pressurized sales, which is, I think, the main reason I really kind of lost interest in what I was doing with [my previous company]. It seems like with the previous company also we constantly had courses and classes on, "Okay, if the person says no, here's how you get around that. If they say no at this juncture, here's how you get around that." It was always like you were to a certain extent trying to force something down their throat. And that's just not with what I'm doing now. You don't have to do that kind of selling where, "Okay, if they object to you this way, here's how you overcome that objection." That's just not something that I have to do, which I hated doing that. So I tried to combat that with—I could never tell people to do something they didn't want to do. I just had to see more people. And that's why I just ran myself ragged.

Gavin hated trying to overcome people's objections and did not want to force his product on them. He tried another type of sales, despite the fact that he had been considering going into education in the back of his mind for some time. He would later reflect that negative perceptions of education kept him from this passion for most of his twenties.

Amy, Lauren, Gavin, and others who were following formulas for relating to others had yet to develop strong enough internal voices to be willing to place their own perspectives on equal par with those of others. Thus their voices were constantly overshadowed by those of external others. As conflicts between their growing voices and those of others emerged in the mid-twenties, they faced these conflicts differently.

The Nature of External Definition

Following formulas was consistent with transitional epistemic assumptions many participants took away from their college experience. The lack of fulfillment from following these formulas, however, created dissonance with transitional knowing, calling its utility into question. Initially the reliance on external formulas for functioning in the postcollege world struck me as inconsistent with the independent and contextual epistemological assumptions most participants expressed as they gained experience in the post-college years. As the strength of external influences in how to know, how to view the self, and how to view the self in relation to others emerged in the early twenties interviews, I began to wonder if I had misinterpreted participants' epistemological assumptions or if they had returned to earlier ones in their adjustment to new environments and expectations. I have come to believe that the apparent discrepancy between independent and contextual epistemological assumptions and following external formulas addresses the interweaving of epistemological development with intrapersonal and interpersonal development.

In the early years after college, most participants came to understand the basic constructs of independent and contextual knowing. They knew that multiple perspectives were commonplace and that they had to choose from among them. The contextual knowers knew that decisions had to be made in context, and that wise choices stemmed from evaluating relevant evidence carefully. They also knew that they were supposed to be able to make choices in these ways. Functioning as an independent or contextual knower, however, required progress in both intrapersonal and interpersonal development that had not yet occurred. Fortunately, the postcollege interviews broadened to include participants' thoughts in all three realms, making this interpretation possible.

The stories in this chapter suggest that the "who am I" question (the intrapersonal dimension) was approached in the early twenties via general and particular external influences. General influences in the form of what institutes a successful career, expectations for marrying, gender roles in relationships, and implementing what one learned in college framed participants' visions of themselves in work and personal realms. These external influences came from societal messages, roles adults around them adopted, and comparison to their peers. Influences particular to individual participants included their relationships with their parents, significant others, and mentors they encountered. Because most participants in their early twenties made meaning of their experience in what Kegan (1994) would call a "coconstruction" with important others, their primary source of definition was external. The preceding pages convey numerous instances in which external voices overshadowed participants' voices.

Participants' stories suggest that they made sense of the world in a way similar to Kegan's (1994) third order of consciousness in which individuals "subordinate one's own interests on behalf of one's greater loyalty to maintaining bonds of friendship, or team or group participation" (p. 75). From this vantage point the answer to all three of the driving questions arose from sources external to the participants. Thus self-authorship of how one knows, despite awareness of the epistemological assumptions of independent and contextual knowing, was not possible from an internal vantage point. Amy's story earlier in this chapter most clearly conveys this connection between intrapersonal, interpersonal, and epistemological dimensions. She cannot work out what she thinks, or express it, for fear of how others will react. The fear hinders her self-authoring what she thinks, who she is, or how she relates to others. As she stated, however, she was "working on what I think" because an external source, her graduate school instructor, was pressuring her to do so.

The pressure to function more independently than they had previously in all realms of their lives created the need and opportunity for the emergence of the internal voice. As it gained strength, a clash with external influences was inevitable. That story is told next.

4

THE CROSSROADS

I've gone through most of my life being reactionary. Like those toy cars made in Taiwan in the '70s—battery powered, had a lever. You'd put it on a table, it would back up when it reached the edge of the table. Redirect yourself when you are going to go off a cliff. I was behaving like one of those cars. Somebody would put up a barrier and I would stop and back up; no progress. I haven't been working like that anymore.

Phillip

Phillip's reflection on his early twenties helps visualize the force of external sources of meaning making in these young adults' lives. Their experiences in their twenties revealed a significant story that fills the gap between Phillip's report of mimicking the toy car and his statement that he doesn't work like that anymore. The story begins when participants see the dilemmas inherent in backing away from barriers, a realization that comes with entering the crossroads phase of the journey.

Multiple paths led to the crossroads and although participants came from all directions, all arrived at some version of the crossroads. These junctures took on varied dynamics depending on the journeys preceding them, yet core threads were evident. External formulas did not produce the expected results, mainly career satisfaction and personal happiness. Some formulas led to crisis whereas others simply left participants feeling unfulfilled. The realization that external sources of belief and definition were insufficient for happiness brought acute awareness that internal sources of belief and definition were necessary. For transitional knowers this meant shifting to independent epistemic assumptions regarding the uncertainty of knowledge as they joined their peers in the process of developing internal definition. The process of developing internal sources of making meaning—or voice—was most often a struggle in light of concern regarding others' expectations and how one's internal voice would affect one's relations with others. Conflicts between what participants were coming to determine they wanted and what they thought others expected of them were commonplace. The crossroads was a turning point that called for letting go of external control and beginning to replace it with one's internal voice. All three dimensions required work on the internal voice. Let's return to the stories of Evan and Kelly to understand the key characteristics of this portion of the journey to self-authorship.

Evan's formula to make the most of himself landed him in trouble, as he described in our seventh interview:

> I overworked myself last spring. You know how every spring I run this hockey league. I didn't realize I was getting into the state I was in, and by June I had totally burned myself out. I walked around like a zombie and I was really depressed. I had worked on two really hard deals right before that, in addition to running that league. It took its toll without me really realizing it. I always thought I was Superman and could handle it. I did handle it, but I paid the price. That put things in perspective for me. I was placing too much importance on things that I really shouldn't have. Now I take it easier than I did. The world doesn't rise or fall on how I come through at work. I'm not a superhero, so I still do my best, but if something doesn't go through, I'm not going to be crushed. . . . I'm really glad it happened now because I've been able to do a lot of heavy thinking and just see what's important to me and what direction I want to take. One thing I did decide was that I really don't appreciate the industry that I'm in. Sure I make a lot of money, but if I could get into something that I would enjoy and I made less money, it wouldn't matter.

Evan was rethinking some aspects of his personal life at this point as well. He introduced this issue in talking about having been financially daring:

> This year our combined income will hit six figures. And we live from week to week. I was a little bit reckless, but I never was irresponsible. I was daring—my philosophy on it was if you earn the money and you can't enjoy it and you get hit by a bus, then what's the point? So we really went to town. You know, my wife has terrible credit. She had a lot of problems before I straightened out everything. When she paid her last car payment, they sent their bill that she still owed $3,000. I knew this was coming because she didn't have insurance on her car for three years, so they bought insurance.

Because his wife had also, in his terms, "cooked the engine" on her car, he bought her a new one and in the midst of it all got involved in straightening out her credit. He found some surprises:

> I was shocked. I was a little bit pissed off too. I knew she had credit problems before I married her, but I didn't realize the extent of how irresponsible she was. That sent me reeling a little bit. But I've started cleaning that up so when the time comes I'm able to get a mortgage. I've seriously flipped back and forth like, "Do I want to get a mortgage with her? Maybe I should hang out and rent for a couple more years to see if things last." I hope so, but I don't really deal with it right now because I don't have to. . . . I just—some days I'm like, "I wonder if I should have gotten married" just because of the way I feel sometimes. Sometimes I get in a mood like that. Not too often anymore. I guess it's just taken me a little longer to settle in than I thought. I must say we never get in fights, but I'm not jumping for joy all the time either, do you know what I'm saying? It is pretty difficult sometimes. Some of my friends want to be married. And I'm like, "Why?" That kind of sums it up right there. . . . My wife almost got transferred. She didn't get the position, so it was a moot point. But it raised certain points. I was like, "If you get transferred to San Diego or Miami, let's go. But if you get transferred to Canada, take your skis and write me a note because I'm not going." That was another thing that we had to deal with this year.

These struggles led Evan to conclude that he was becoming more his own person each year. He reflected on changes over the years:

> When the school year began each fall I would always realize, "Gee, last year, what a dork," you know. And I thought once you're out of school it really doesn't make a difference, but it's still like that year to year now. And I'm wondering if it ever does cease, if it ever does plateau. I become more defined year after year, become more of my own person. I'm a little bit wiser. I'm not a smart-ass, but I can find my way around a little bit better every year. I've become a little bit more organized every year, not that I'm not now, but I reorganize my goals all the time.

Even though he was reorganizing goals, Evan had given up on the formula. As a result of his experiences in work and personal life during this difficult year, he said:

> Nothing ever fits exactly the way you want. You have to compromise and adapt. I'm pretty patient now. I just will keep looking,

and when I think the right opportunity comes along and things click, it will happen. I don't like to force things.

Evan clearly planned to figure out for himself his goals and how he wanted things to be, but his approach was nebulous at this point due to the lack of a clear internal voice. He saw himself as becoming more organized and wiser each year, yet he had many questions about what to do with his work and personal life.

Kelly's external formula was interrupted by a significant event at the school where she taught. Lack of agreement between the board and the teachers led to a strike that placed Kelly in an awkward position. Because she had grown up in the community, her family considered members of the board as friends. As a teacher she could understand the two competing views but also trusted the board to work out a fair solution. She described her disillusionment with the teachers as a result of the strike:

> It got in the way of those old memories—it took away the student-teacher relationship and it forced me to see them as adults and human beings with weaknesses and opinions that I might not necessarily agree with, personalities that I might not necessarily want to associate myself with. It just kind of stripped away the barrier that was between the teacher and the student. It was just really a shock to my system. . . . And then the teachers—there were rumors circulated about me that—when I expressed my views and some of them came back and said, "Kelly, you know, they think that all your ideas are just coming from your Mom's mouth." My old teachers didn't give me credit for being able to think on my own, which really pissed me off. I thought, "My gosh, here I am, I've been through college, I'm a successful teacher. I'm working hard. I'm living on my own. Give me a little credit here."

Kelly recounted with great clarity the strike vote meeting and the stress it caused for her:

> The president of our association said, "Well, it's going to be a stand up-sit down vote. And if you agree, you'll stand up. And if you don't, you'll stay down." And here I am; I was scared to death. I raised my hand and said, "Don't you think an issue this important should be a secret ballot?" And people just laid into me, like, "Well, if you're going to cross the lines in two weeks we want to know it now. We want to see your face now." . . . I was the last person up. I was one of the last people up. I can't tell you how hard—I mean, it's like you couldn't stay down. I mean, I'm almost crying again just thinking of this. Being in a

> room where there are 70 people there, which is almost the full
> staff of teachers as far as professional teachers, it was just, you
> know . . . the pressure was incredible.

The external pressure prompted Kelly to act against her internal voice. As she tried to get her colleagues to think about both sides during the strike, external pressure again choked her voice and she turned away instead. Describing how she felt, she said:

> I think another thing that frustrated me so much, was I felt very
> helpless because I was one of the youngest teachers on staff,
> non-tenured, you know, and had those two strikes against me.
> Then once I heard that everything that I said they thought was
> coming straight from my Mom, I just said, "Forget it. Why even
> try to voice my opinion? Why try to make a difference?" Which
> isn't in my—it's not in my nature to kind of take that opinion. But
> that's the only way I could—I think that's the only way I could
> survive. I said, "I'm not responsible for the decision." I said,
> "My vote's not going to make a difference. I'm just going to sur-
> vive this thing the best I can."

Kelly tried to do what she could to survive the situation, not having a strong enough internal mechanism to process what was taking place. In addition to negating her memories, the strike also reduced her willingness to accept others' thoughts at face value. She explained:

> It's hard to put into words. I think my outlook's changed. I don't
> see everything black and white at all anymore. Nothing's black
> and white. I don't think I'm as naive as I was as far as trusting
> people. I've always been extremely trusting of people. And I
> consider myself able to judge people's personalities fairly well.
> And as a result I trusted my judgment. I was trod on a bit this
> past year, and although I still value my judgment, I'm not going
> to be as open as quick, I think, and involved in situations. So I
> would say it really—you know, it's made me realize the value of
> really thinking an issue through before you stand up and state
> your opinion. And maybe not because of what I said, but I still
> believe what I said was right, but things that I saw, you know, in
> the strike situation. You really need to look. I mean, there's a
> front and a backside to everything, and you've got to make sure
> you know what's going on. I don't think I can be as led as easily
> as maybe I could have before.

These realizations led her to relinquish the external formula for her life and to accept ambiguity. She elaborated:

> When I was in high school I thought "Well, by the time I'm 24 or 25 I'll know it all; I'll have it all. It will all be straight. My life will be set." Well, of course, we know that's not true. So I've kind of accepted the fact that I don't know what's going on, just have to take it as it comes and do the best I can. I've accepted the fact that I'm never going to have it all straightened out. You just have to take each day, take each year and do the best you can and educate yourself and do the best you can in your work and in your life.

Kelly realized at this point that she needed to find meaning within herself. The vague "do the best you can" reveals that she has not yet constructed an internal source of meaning making to guide her life.

Kelly's story highlights the intrapersonal dimension of the crossroads in the tension between expressing her internal voice and her colleagues not giving her the credit she felt was due her. Her discovery of there being "a back side to everything" illustrates disillusionment with the external formula and the need to figure things out for oneself. Evan's story also reveals how unexpected outcomes can show the shortcomings of the external formula. His internal voice was in conflict with his profession and possibly his marriage. Thus the crossroads was a portion of the journey that sparked the search for meaning across all three dimensions. Various dimensions were in the forefront for various participants, depending on when and how the external formulas disintegrated. The remainder of this chapter traces multiple pathways through the crossroads.

The Search for Meaning: Turning Inward

Kurt described standing at the crossroads with great clarity:

> I'm the kind of person who is motivated by being wanted, I think. I've gone to a couple of workshops and, either fortunately or unfortunately, I'm the kind of person who gets my self-worth on whether or not other people accept me for what I do or other people appreciate what I'm doing . . . I'm coming from a position where I get my worth and my value from other people, which is, I think, wrong for me to do. But that's where I am right now. I feel like whether or not I choose to be happy is dependent upon me and only me. If I say, "You made me mad," or the converse, "You made me happy," then I'm giving all of the power that I have to you. The power of choice is mine, I have a choice of how I want to perceive each and every situation in my life. . . . Obviously I'm not to that point yet because I choose to

make myself happy and make myself sad on what other people are thinking. But I think I'd like to someday get to a point where I can say, "Okay, that's your perception. I am not dependent on you for my happiness or my sadness." And I think that would be a very strong, very spiritual place to be.

Kurt's arrival at these insights stemmed from an external source—the workshops he attended. They helped him acknowledge that he did interpret his worth from external sources; he also determined that this was not the best way to operate. He stood at the crossroads knowing that he needed to exercise the power of choice that was his, yet not knowing how to do so. He could see his destination but was unsure what route to take to move closer to it. Kurt's story brings the intrapersonal dimension (his sense of his self-worth) to the forefront, although it is tightly interwoven with the interpersonal dimension (what others think of him).

Lauren was arriving at the same crossroads, albeit via a different path—her struggle in relationships. She described with equal clarity the awareness of co-constructing meaning with external others as she described an experience with her boyfriend:

He came home with me to [my parents' house] and I was totally gung-ho. I'm like, "This is it; I know it." And then after they gave me their feedback, they liked him but they were just not sure. And after they said that, all of a sudden I didn't like him as much anymore. It was nothing that he did to me; it was not the way he acted. It was nothing. But it was because of what they said, all of a sudden I started changing my mind. Yes, that's exactly true. But then my sister, on the other hand, is the opposite and is like, "Just go with how you feel." And my friends, my close friends here are like, "Just go with how you feel." So now it's gotten better. I'm trying to really think of what I want and not what they want. So this relationship is continuing, which they're not upset about at all, but I will tell you they have told me, "Come on, this really isn't going to work. It's too far." And that does affect me. But I'm really trying to take the attitude where maybe I need to find out for myself. But I will admit always in the back of my mind what they think still lingers over my decisions.

Like Kurt, Lauren knew she should listen to herself; yet she continued to struggle to do so because she trusted her parents' perceptions more than she did her own at this point. Her sister's and friends' influence offered an external support to encourage her to listen to herself. She became keenly aware that how she felt stemmed from how others who are important to her felt. Like Kurt, she was "trying to really think of what I want" and finding it a struggle. Her struggle is simultaneously interpersonal (in defining her relationships with her boyfriend, parents, and sister), intrapersonal (finding out what she wants), and epistemological (how to make decisions).

Kurt and Lauren turned inward in their search because they saw the need to be less dependent on others' perspectives. Kris turned inward for similar reasons, but under different circumstances. Despite being married two years out of college she felt no one wanted to listen to her. She explained:

> I look to others for gratification. And I know that about myself. If I do something good, I am always the first one to tell. And this has brought me to the point now where I say less about things that I've done one way or the other.

By "this," Kris was referring to her experience with her husband, mother, and coworkers:

> I feel like nobody ever wants to listen. And I've talked to my husband about this. He'll teasingly change the subject. If I really want to talk to somebody and I have something that I really need to talk about, I start my conversation and then immediately they want to tell me their situation. . . . I've really learned to deal with those kinds of situations. Rather than go to somebody else and try to talk about them anymore, I deal with them internally and spend a lot of time thinking about it. Just like all these decisions with the baby, at this point my husband and I really haven't discussed a whole lot. And I guess it's just because I've gotten so gun shy of going to somebody and saying, "Look, this is what I think." I really feel like I'm relatively intelligent. But it's almost like people don't value what I have to say, so why waste my breath? We talk about the weather and trivial things, but very rarely do I get into an in-depth conversation with anybody.

Kris struggled with the fact that significant people in her life did not seem to listen, but decided not to address it with them. Her reaction to not being listened to was to turn inward:

> It's good in that sense that it's made me a stronger person and more self-reliant, but it's made me really gun shy to look to other people for help because I don't get any help from them. And I think that it's hurt my relationship with my husband because we don't talk about things that I probably need to talk about as far as work is concerned. I used to have another

coworker that I would talk with. But she's gone now, so I don't even have a sounding board for that, so I keep all that daily stress locked up inside of me.

Kris was developing her internal voice and thinking internally about decisions because she had no sounding boards. Rather than risk confrontations, she turned inward. Yet with no opportunity to express her growing voice, she was limited in her ability to develop it. Like Kurt and Lauren, she was struggling with who she was and how to know in the context of relationships with those around her.

Searching for Meaning in Career Contexts

For many young adults in this study the breakdown of the external formula stemmed from experiences in their work lives. Participants whose internal voices conflicted with the career plan they were following found themselves questioning aspects of their careers. Al's growing internal voice led him to dissatisfaction with his work in computer consulting. Describing the situation, he said:

After you've worked a year or so, you start to realize you're going to be working the rest of your life. I mean, you realize you're going to have to get a job, but you really don't feel what it's all about until you get out there and do it. After a year, I learned a lot with the company I worked for. And I didn't dislike it. I just figured I'm going to work until I'm 65 anyway, I ought to do what I've always thought I wanted to do. And if I'm ever going to do it, I need to get started. Even that freshman year in college, I thought maybe I would want to be a doctor. But what was holding me back was (a) I wasn't sure I wanted to spend that much time getting there, and (b) I have never been a real science fan. Now I'm looking at the end of the road rather than what it takes to get there. I think the bottom line is, "Are you going to be happy in what you're doing?" The biggest thing is what am I really doing? In my job, I never really felt like it was the kind of help I wanted to give to people. How I can do a job faster to me is not as important as helping a kid get through cancer. So that's what I looked at in making the decision. I'm somewhat involved in the church. And at times I almost felt like I was cheating people. My billing rate was $120 an hour. And here I am, a year out of school and the company can charge $120 an hour for me to sit in a meeting. I was just like, "Great day! I'm definitely not doing work worth that much." And I just feel like I want to spend my life helping people more than just making companies more efficient, which is a good thing, but it's just not the kind of good I want to do.

Although Al did not leave computer consulting due to intense unhappiness, he did project that it was not going to make him happy in the long run. He also was experiencing some conflict between some of these workplace dynamics and the values he was constructing.

Lynn's career conflict was less a matter of what she was doing and more a matter of how she was doing it. After her lengthy struggle to find a full-time teaching position, she was determined to do her best when she acquired one:

> I was trying to be superteacher at first; it doesn't work. [I] can't be everything to everyone all the time. I took things personally last year that I know now that I shouldn't have. I drove myself crazy doing things; now I know my limits. You can't let yourself get overburdened. Summer was a learning time; I was not with the kids, so I had time to think. I vowed I would worry about me and my kids and not everybody else. First me, then kids. [You] can't perform when you aren't mentally and physically able. I was third last year—bosses, kids, then me. I wanted to make an impression, do the job. I ran myself into the ground; I was sick for four months. Living by myself has helped that, too. I put more importance in myself than in a roommate. This just happened through growing and learning—I was not aware of it necessarily.

Lynn's zeal to prove herself, much like Evan's plan to push himself, resulted in exhaustion. It also revealed the shortcomings of too much focus on pleasing others. Lynn translated this lesson to her search for meaning in the personal aspects of her life, saying, "Independence; a lot of it is living alone, doing what I want to do, not having to please people. I'm working toward my life more, not trying to please others." The fact that she raised the same issues two years later shows how hard it is to move away from the crossroads. She shared the following:

> My priority right now is me; that sounds egotistical. I need to do something to make me happy; instead of doing everything for everyone else. There's a point in time when you get to doing for yourself. I have yet to do that; I am going to do it. I made a New Years resolution that this is the year of me. It is hard to go after it because I don't know what to do. I have to make a decision and do it. I've never been a good decision-maker. It's hard to make a new process to do for myself. I would like to say, "this is how it is going to be." It's hard to change that focus. Want to

snap your fingers and have it done. . . . I'm more positive, sure of myself most of time. [she laughed.] I'd like to be all the time; have to do a little at a time; self-assured, healthy—mentally and physically—I'm working out a lot. Standing up more for what I believe in, sticking to my guns, voicing my opinion. I've become a little callous, not in a bitter way, but I don't let things get to me—used to take things personally. Sticking to my guns in all arenas of life—love life, family, professionally—won't let others tell me how to live my life. Gotta start standing up for yourself and saying no. My resolution was do things, go places I want to go even if I have to go alone—gotta live! Who's to say, I might die tomorrow in a car wreck. I want to go visit people and I'm gonna do it. I've got to live! I'm gonna start living. Or I might wuss out and stay home.

Lynn traverses most of the territory of the crossroads in this story! She established herself as the priority even though she describes it as egotistical. She stated her plans and resolution adamantly yet articulated just as clearly that she does not know how to proceed. She was "sticking to her guns" by not letting others tell her what to do; she just had not figured out yet how to do what she wanted to do. The struggle is obvious in her passion and commitment to living and her quick disclaimer that she might "wuss out." Like Kurt, she wants to move from where she stands but cannot see a clear path yet.

Phillip shared a similar account of his career struggles, although they differed from those above. Phillip wanted to be involved with music, ideally in a band but more realistically in broadcasting. He struggled to find suitable work and was thinking about giving up on his dreams. He shared the effect of moving back to his hometown after college graduation:

It was just, "Oh, the future is bleak and this and that." It was just a matter of me telling myself, "Okay, this is what I want. And what do I need to do to get it?" I can listen to other people's advice and take it with a grain of salt. I can do that until I'm blue in the face. Is that going to get me where I want to go? No. It takes action, not words. And the attitude of people in my hometown was just absolutely bleak. The main industry in there just plummeted really badly. So everybody's got this cloud of doom over their head, including my parents. I was expecting my parents to be a little bit more supportive, but my Dad kept telling me, "Well, you really ought to think about finding some type of career outside of broadcasting." . . . I continued to look for another job, but nobody wanted to touch me with a ten-foot pole. And I'm thinking, "What's going on?" I applied for a station position and they gave me the run-around, didn't hire me. I'm thinking, "Well, geez, why aren't they hiring me? I know I can do the job. I've got good credentials. I'm a Miami grad, for crying out loud. People know what that means around the Midwest." So I was just really in the doldrums. But I decided to just pull myself out of that and it took a lot of strength within to say, "Look, you've just got to get out of this situation." In fact, you know, going back down to Miami during November to visit some friends kind of convinced me because I talked to some of the faculty. They were really supportive. I told them that I was planning on leaving the Midwest and going out East. And they said, "Well, do it. What's holding you back? If you can do it, do it by all means because you just don't know what could happen to you. Things could be bad, but again, just think, something could happen after you're there a couple of months that could change your outlook, could be real promising for you in the future." So I kind of weighed the evidence and decided to come out. And it's been for the good. I think the whole experience has changed my outlook. I'm not going to ever get myself into a rut where I'm saying, "Oh, well, whatever I've done in the past is just worthless. I've got to pay more attention to other people's advice." Because if you do that, everybody's got their own opinion on something. If you continue to listen to everything that everybody says, you're going to be a chameleon; you're going to be changing from year to year, doing this, doing that.

Phillip's unhappiness prompted him to think about moving. The reinforcement he received from his former faculty helped make the decision. He was starting to value his own voice and wary of listening too much to others. It was not easy, however, as he explained:

But when it comes from your parents, there is a big impact. I don't know. I guess it's just the background that I have, but I wasn't very much of a rebellious child. So whatever the folks said was pretty much like, "Well, you've got to pay attention to that." I love them both to death, but the thing is that their interests are different from mine. They changed probably once I became an adult because, like I say, they probably had their ideas. My Dad probably wanted me to go into sales a long time ago. And I knew that wasn't for me. But once you're 20, 21, and you're out of school, it's like you just want to—you want so bad to take charge of your life and you want to have it turn out right. It really helps you to achieve that goal when you've got support. And especially, like I say, from your parents, from your good friends. But when they're telling you, "Oh, no, you don't want to do this. Why did you do that?" you fall into this role like, "Oh, well, bad boy. Slap your hands." I did for a while, too. Moving back home was not a—I think I regressed actually. I fell back into the role of the dutiful son and that is just not, it's not a positive outlook on life. It doesn't give you anything. It's just like, "Well, you're doing something for somebody else and not for yourself." And, granted, I'm a generous person. But where I want to go with my life is entirely up to me, unless I get married and have a family. Then I've got something else to worry about. I am the proverbial rolling stone right now, the free wind, or whatever you want to call it. I'm able to make my own decisions; I can take people's advice, but it gives you a sense of accomplishment, right or wrong, if you've made the decision, you know, and you have to live with it.

Phillip conveyed the desire most participants had to take charge of their lives, even when they were unsure how to manage external circumstances to achieve that goal. Phillip had to work through reshaping his relationship with his parents to move toward taking charge of his life while still respecting their role as his parents. He described how his family's way of operating affected this transition:

The family is very conservative. We don't do anything until we think about it for five years. Nothing is ever decided on a whim. It's like, "Let's see, I want to buy a car, oh, geez, next year. So I better start thinking about it right now," stuff like that. It can be really difficult to take risks in that kind of situation. It really can. And it takes a lot of determination to say, "Well, this is what I believe in and I'm going to continue with it come hell or high water." There were times when I said, "Well, they're right." I gave in and I said, "They're right. I should just forget about this." But I'm thinking, "Well, why are you going to do that? You don't know what might happen to you tomorrow. Suppose something comes along?"

Phillip did take the risk to move to another city and after a few months something did come along. It still was not exactly what he wanted, but it provided a living and presented the opportunity to hone some of his skills for broadcasting. Getting established in this city and job helped him take charge of his life, but he still wondered about what he really wanted. He explained:

Let's face it. If I were connected with my feelings, I'd be in a band, making no money, sleeping on someone's floor, no savings. Maybe I would be happy. That crosses my mind. You want to do music, you will live in squalor. Or you could go the way of the working world and make sacrifices that take away some of your personality, or the things that make you important, for the cause of a higher power—the almighty paycheck. I don't know—

could I give this lifestyle up? I don't know. I don't think so, because if I want a family, what am I going to have to do? Don't feel like having a relationship when wife makes money and I play music—a slacker. That's still a desire—common male instinct—to be a provider. Future Mrs. Widener, I want to show her that I am able to do that. By how I live. At the same time, I don't know if that is how it works.

I asked Phillip how he had been able to move forward toward taking charge of his life. He responded:

For me if I am surrounded by a bunch of positive people, I feel I can do things. In 1995 I went on vacation to see Aunt Arlene— a positive person in our family. She has turmoil, but comes out on top. She has a positive mental attitude. She was in ill health, but still spry. I told her about my dilemmas. She asked me why I didn't do what I wanted. She said there is a way. She told me not to give up hope. Taking that, I think I have learned to apply that in other areas of my life. Instead of being reactionary, I'm finding ways to get what I want without making bunches of waves that will be to my detriment.

Although Phillip had yet to live out many of the things he dreamed of, he was beginning to assert his own voice and clarify what the internal source of meaning-making meant in his life.

Although most participants who were engaged in the search for meaning in career contexts started from being unhappy in their work, the opposite was true for Genesse and Amy. Genesse had a number of unsatisfying jobs after college graduation, unsatisfying primarily due to poor treatment she received from others in these work settings. She finally found a position in a positive environment that she liked. She shared a dilemma that she encountered:

I loved working on the particular account I was on, I really enjoyed that. I dealt with customers on a daily basis, they were fun to talk to, and with internal people in the company. It was a high profile account, so I was invited to meetings, activities etc.—it was more interesting. Then they wanted me to take my own set of accounts; I felt I couldn't say no. I cut off my nose to spite my face. I interviewed with the manager. They picked me to take over a key account on that desk; the company contracts out to them. The territory was all of Florida and Puerto Rico; I took it over in June. It proved to be more than what I felt I could handle. I was staying until seven at night, I wasn't happy. Trying to expedite orders, it was a big mess. I let my boss know I was unhappy. She knew, there were all sorts of problems—they offered me the option to go back to the original desk; I did that two days ago. I feel like—I sort of failed—not failed, but not fulfilled about the whole experience. I'm not ecstatic about being back where I was before. May get back into it when rested. I'm not excited about anything. I felt badly that they had to train another person; the trainee liked it, and she had to move. When they moved me back, she had to move too. But that is business and I shouldn't feel bad about it.

Genesse's feeling that she could not say no led her to accept a promotion that she did not want. Her struggle in that role pressured her to be honest with her boss and to change back to her original position. Yet she had mixed feelings about that as well. Genesse reported working on developing her internal voice for most of her twenties. She called it "standing up for yourself" as she noted in this story:

Hopefully, I am a little more mature than I have been. The way I make decisions, the way I treat people, how I handle adversity, things that come up. I'm not so quick to jump into one course of action or another; sit back and think how it would turn out. It is not a good thing, well, maybe it is—to be less trusting of everybody. I've been naïve that way in the past few years. Feeling you can trust everybody and the world doesn't work that way and I need to smarten up—this came through work situations. It is unfortunate, but I have to stop being stepped all over and stand up for myself. And watch out. I stand up for myself more now. The way things happened this summer, on the job, I felt free to tell them when I didn't like something. Before timid me let it go by. I try to stand up for myself more, not all the time, but more—they respect me. If there is one underlying theme of my twenties, that is it. In work situations, one terrible one, I tried to stand up to that woman but she wasn't to be reckoned with; I should have walked out rather than taking it. In retail, same thing with being mistreated—why did I do that? In my twenties I let people take advantage of me. Related to trusting people—jobs sounded good, and I believed what they said.

Her experience with sharing her feelings honestly and those being met with respect from her employers helped Genesse start standing up for herself. Her previous negative work experiences hindered her from making progress on the journey through the crossroads.

Amy was making progress, but still not settled on her career situation. She dreamed of working in art museums but in the meantime found opportunities in retail. Her work resulted in her managing a store. She shared how she was thinking about her situation:

It doesn't feel right to leave here. It is a big thing I always struggle with. I know several others who live here and do these kinds
of jobs. My parents support me in what I'm doing. Other parents
tell their kids, we sent you to college to do more than work in a
store. Last year I had a lot of guilt, I should get my act together
and go to graduate school—but I'm happy here and didn't want
to leave. Last year I came to terms with it. I'm happy, making a
living, doing what I want to do—no one is pressuring me, why
should I? Going back to school, doing what the average American thinks is succeeding. A lot of that is wrapped up in living in
a city and having a job. Different levels of thinking about what
success is. . . . Having a job and making an honest living, being
happy—it doesn't seem like that is enough. I feel like I have to do
better. That message that comes through society. I worry that
my father—he must be embarrassed to tell people I run a store.
Sometimes I feel I should be doing more with my life. If I had a
job that was more fulfilling maybe I wouldn't. I like it here - can't
imagine being away from the water. Not a whole lot of options
if you want to live here. Hopefully find out what I want to do and
do it here. I don't know what it is. I felt by 27, I would know what
I wanted to do with my life.

Although Amy reported having coming to terms with her situation, she still
wondered if it was what she should do or wanted to do. She was happy, her
parents were supportive, yet societal messages continued to sway her. Without
a strong internal voice to guide her, she was in a holding pattern.

The theme of the career stories was attempting to integrate the emerging
internal voice with one's work, how one engages in one's work, and parental
or societal expectations about successful work lives. For some, like Al, this
meant career changes to bring work into closer alignment with developing values. For others, like Lynn, it meant managing work differently to balance one's
own priorities with those of others. For some, like Genesse and Amy, it meant
coming to terms with what they found satisfying versus what others viewed as
more successful. At the crossroads the emerging internal voice clashed with
career opportunities and expectations.

Searching for Meaning in Relationship Contexts

The career stories, while set in the context of career decisions and satisfaction,
also reveal the influence of relationships. For some participants, the crossroads
was primarily about defining one's relationships with others and the tension
between what others wanted versus what they wanted. Anita spoke to this
issue as she talked about her preparations and efforts to get into graduate
school. She offered:

The last thing I need, I don't trust myself, is to get involved in a relationship here and have to make a decision. In the past I would have chosen the guy; I might do it again. I don't want to have to make that decision. I have had difficult relationships in the past; now I am getting to know myself. I'm happy with the way life is now. It might be better if I opened myself up and take chances. But it could be worse. At the moment I'd rather take the safe road. Men are just like women; guys think I am trying to be aloof. It becomes a big challenge to them. I used to be that way with them. Men are more like women than I ever thought they were. As I am meeting older men, I am getting older, I thought I was ready to settle down years ago—now I am thankful that I didn't. I always thought I would be married by 25; now I am 26 and mom is starting to worry. I know in my gut that I am not ready. I see in my guy friends that they are ready; it is scary. It feels like they are setting their sights on you; thought it would be other way around. What I pictured women to act like. They are trying to convince me of what great husbands they would be.

Anita made some decisions about career directions, but did not trust herself to stick to them in the face of a possible relationship. Recall from chapter 3 how she envisioned herself in various relationships to guide her decisions. Now she has determined that she is not ready and enjoys getting to know herself. She was moving toward developing her internal voice but knows it is not ready to stand up to competition in the form of a relationship. She was uncomfortable with men who were ready for relationships, fearing they were "setting their sights" on her.

Heather spoke to searching for meaning in the context of marriage. She, like many of her counterparts, was contemplating a significant career change, in her case from business to education. She reported how difficult this was in the context of marriage:

And then especially when you have someone else who counts on you and who is involved in your life and your decisions affect his life as much. So there's compromise involved. You know, it's another dimension there also. . . . It's caused me to get angry a lot. It's forced me for one to think things through more because there's someone there who's always got—I mean, he's got a different perspective and challenges me to think of things that I might not think of if he wasn't there. It also—I mean, I think the art of compromise and the communication that goes into that compromise is something that, I think, you're continually working on. Every time we have to make a decision like this, we have to talk about it, figure out what we want to do and not just what I want to do. Sometimes it's not so pretty, but in the end you learn more about how to compromise and how to communicate and how better to communicate, what you might have done wrong. So I think that it's a huge learning process. And also learning what the other person needs and learning that people change. And my poor husband, you know, he's known me for a long time and it's always been business, business, business. And then one day I come home and say, "Gee, I think I'm going to teach." He's like, "Okay, where did this come from?" It's like, "Well, do I just ignore her and she'll change her mind in a week or is this something we really need to discuss?" It's just—I don't know. I think it's pretty amazing how much you continue to grow because the other person changes and you have to bend and realize what they're going through and what they need and how you're going to work together to make it work. A lot of growth, I think, there. And learning to give up things.

Working together to make it work is hard when both parties voice their needs and desires and when both simultaneously change. Heather was coming to understand some of her desires and translating them into a career change. This complicated decisions with her husband because her transition would mean going back to school, an option that was on the horizon for him as well. Although Heather recounted expressing her needs in the relationship, she also noted that she had to think harder about things, was sometimes angry, and had to learn to give up things. At this point Heather had yet to articulate a fully developed internal source of meaning-making that guided her negotiations with her husband.

Lowell's search for meaning came from a relational crisis. Lowell spoke to the issue of external pressure in his marriage, something to which he initially succumbed:

I knew that my going to school was prohibiting us from living a somewhat better lifestyle and that my being in school took a lot of time. So, I guess I tried to make that up to her. I did things [that we could not afford] just to try and make her happy because I knew she wasn't.

Lowell's awareness of this came as he tried to sort out the reasons for his separation from his wife. Financial woes were a big part of the story, as were disagreements about his career. However, it became clear as he talked that sacrificing his own needs was the crux of the matter. After numerous disputes in which he gave in to his wife's wishes, he reported:

I felt, "I've had enough; I'm sick of sacrificing everything that I want or need or value just for someone else. It's just not worth it." I just couldn't take it anymore. My mother was really questioning me, you know, "Lowell, you made a commitment to this woman. You can't just get up and walk away because one morning you don't feel like it anymore." She's absolutely right. I did try to discuss these things. If you talk to a brick wall so long, only so many sane people will continue. I know I shouldn't have sacrificed my own feelings all along. She wasn't the only one who didn't know how to be married.

Lowell's decision to assert himself and act on his own needs was difficult because one of his internal values was to stand by his marital commitment. When it became apparent to him that he could not do both, he chose to separate. In the end, his growing internal voice required that he take himself out of the relationship. He was able to see in retrospect what he could not see during the relationship:

Another flag that I think I should have seen: She basically went home every weekend—a half-hour drive away. I look back and say, ". . . How could you be so stupid?" You know. Hindsight is 20-20. Those are the types of flags that I keep thinking in my mind. . . . They're just popping up all over the place; the landscape is just littered with them. But you know, it is really easy to see once you step aside and take a look back. . . . And all those flags I talk about—they were logical things that if I had thought about them logically would have . . . I mean, I am still a human being, and I have emotional feelings . . . I don't disregard that. . . . I was blind to a lot of things. I don't think that it was that I chose not to see; it's that I was just blinded by it.

Lowell was so busy trying to please his wife and work out her concerns about his career (which she had not expressed before they married) that he missed all of these clues. Not being able to take it anymore brought him to the crossroads; his decision to act on his inner voice was the pathway to self-authorship. The theme of the relationship stories is the futile attempt to please oneself through pleasing others. Most participants came to the realization that the only way to resolve tension between their own and others' voices was to act in ways that were true to their own voices while mutually negotiating how needs are met. At the crossroads, they stood at the turning point, wondering if they would be able to maintain relationships from this new approach to constructing them.

Searching for Meaning: Establishing One's Own Beliefs

For some participants, the epistemological dimension took the forefront as they entered the crossroads. Letting go of external formulas for how to know left them with the task of figuring out how to know for themselves. The struggle to establish their own beliefs when they had learned so well how to adopt those of others was substantial. For Reginald, who described the struggle as part of his experience in seminary, the task was to establish his perspective and simultaneously remain open to new ideas. He explained:

I think what I struggle with . . . is to claim the experience. . . . I have to have that identity of what I do believe. . . along with the open mind and the openness to other views and respecting that. Because if not I'm just sort of wishy-washy, flimsying around,. . . [claiming your experience] is part of what makes you who you are. That's perhaps the intellect and then when you live it that's the emotion or the passion perhaps that you bring to what you do. . . . The belief is sort of a clay that is not hardened, that is always being molded. It can shift; it can take new forms. But it's still the same, still a belief system within your self-identity, within your experience that won't deny your experience. It won't completely just blow away like sand, but it will form and it will be consistent—it has some weight to it.

Reginald struggled to claim what he believed, not wanting it to restrict his openness to others' ideas. Yet he was aware that he had to have some "form" for his perspective so it would not "blow away like sand." Reginald was working to accept that his experience could be the basis of what he believed. This helped him in forming an identity from which to balance accessing others' thoughts and acknowledging his experience—the central challenge of the crossroads.

He explained this notion further through the idea of boundaries:

In defining that self, identifying that self, is the creation of boundaries in what we do personally and publicly. . . . If I didn't have that boundary, I might not bring out what it is that I need, what it is that I do believe. . . . If I disregard the boundary, I can be overwhelmed . . . I always considered the word *boundary* as a barrier. And so if I created these [barriers] I would be . . . a closed-minded person;. . . there wasn't a meeting place because there was this wall in the way. The other person would come to one side of the wall, I'd come to the other side of the wall, and we'd look at brick. And there wouldn't be a place where I could meet them. . . . But also, if I don't have anything, if I don't have boundaries, I lose the sense of who I am and I can't learn.

Reginald was trying to construct boundaries for his identity to keep himself from being consumed as he met others in dialogue. His story shows the close link between how one knows and how one views oneself. He argued that he could not learn without a defined self-identity. Like others in the crossroads, Reginald could identify how he wanted to be but conveyed that he was still working on getting there.

Anita's search for her own beliefs was brought on by her volunteer work on a crisis hotline. Part of her dilemma was whether she had a right to have an opinion, as she explained:

> I'm getting used to not knowing at the switchboard; there is nothing you can say that is wrong, as long as you are trying to help. The same call could be handled differently by different people. Like with one situation, I feel like I shouldn't have confronted a person, but others said I had to do it. I'm learning to let them go. I'm better at realizing and admitting when I make mistakes. More humble. I agree with the philosophy that if you are helping, it is okay. Sometimes I hear other calls and I wouldn't have done something that way. Sometimes they do tell people what to do. I'm trying to figure that out for myself, I don't have the right to an opinion. Then sometimes I think I do. Like if someone hits [the caller], I have a hard time saying it is wrong. It can lead to an arrest, and make a bigger mess. I have a hard time being as directive as I should. I have to figure out for myself what my own beliefs are. I do have the right to have an opinion. But I don't know enough about the department of family services. I know molestation is wrong, but what will the caller's life be like if I report it?

Anita knew she had to settle on her own beliefs about these matters. She debated whether she had the right to an opinion, or whether she had the right to make decisions that would affect someone's life. She found herself in a quandary with some calls because she had not sorted out what her beliefs were on these issues. Because this work was in line with what she hoped to do after attending graduate school, she knew she would have to work out her beliefs.

Barb was working on what she believed and how to express it in the context of her career preparation in law school. She reported that it was changing who she was and how she interacted with others:

> I think I'm getting more aggressive, but not so much. But I think it's maybe more aggressive. I'm more likely, I guess, to argue or

state my point of view. Maybe it's because when I have conversations with people I understand what they're talking about
more, like business type things. When our friends talk about
their work, I understand it a little bit more now. So I feel like I
can put in my two cents without feeling shy about it. I guess its
just confidence again. Plus I hear attorneys make arguments all
the time, so I guess I'm always trying to think of an argument to
make. And not necessarily argue with someone, but just keep
the conversation going.

Barb was quick to clarify that she hoped not to become arrogant like many
attorneys she knew. She surmised that they became arrogant because they
knew things that others did not. Asked how she would avoid this fate, she
offered:

I guess just recognizing that. I see it in other people hopefully. I
don't know. I say I'm more aggressive, but I think I'm still pretty
much a wimp. I don't think I'll ever get to that extreme. I hope
not, anyway. No, I don't think I will. . . . My Dad always calls
me a big wimp. Like when it comes to arguing with salespeople,
he always calls me a wimp. I think I'm getting a little better. I feel
like I'm being arrogant just talking like this. Do you know what I
mean?

Not only was she unsure of her movement toward what she called aggressive
in light of her father's assessment, Barb even became concerned that I would
view her as arrogant for implying that she knew things others do not. When I
responded that I was unsure of what she meant, she added "Well, I mean, I'm
sort of bragging about 'Well, I know things that other people don't know' type
of thing. It sort of makes me a little uncomfortable." It came as no surprise to
me that she concluded with "I have this problem about worrying what other
people think." Barb's experience in law school and her job as a clerk were
forming her voice, yet she was very uncomfortable expressing it for fear of
how others would react. Her tentativeness in viewing herself as more aggressive was apparent throughout her story.

Near the end of the journey through the crossroads, participants felt an
increased confidence and sense of direction, even if they had not yet acted on
it. Justin talked about this experience at the point of making a tentative decision about his career:

I think my self-confidence has increased. I think my self-esteem
has increased. I think my ability to form clear perceptions of
what I interpret as reality has changed. I feel like I'm able to

think a little more clearly now for some reason. Just to formulate perceptions of things has increased. I guess I could say my insight has increased. I think I'm less influenced by what goes on around me. I'm able to form my own perception of what's happening instead of being so influenced by people. I think a year ago I was pretty influenced by different groups of people. And now at this point in time I feel like I'm more myself and I'm able to form clear perceptions that are unbiased in regard to these other groups of people. Maybe this is because I've gotten sort of a direction now, or can kind of see myself moving in a direction. I'm a little more goal oriented this year. Last year, I mean, I was lost. I didn't know what I wanted to do; I didn't know anything. Not that I know exactly now, but at least I have a little clearer perception of where I want to go. I have goals now, which really kind of feels good. And I'm feeling more self-confident like I'll be able to meet these goals. The future seems a little more bright.

Justin's description of his earlier experience at the crossroads is one of being lost and not knowing anything. Having a sense of direction is the path out of the crossroads and into internal self-authorship. Although he had yet to set off on that path, the future seemed a little brighter just knowing it was there.

Scott was in a position to start down the path. He had amassed knowledge needed by others in his work, and thus found himself able to express his ideas. He explained:

I'm willing to get in a lot more fights in the office over certain issues, but at the same time there are some times when you have to back down. I know my position in the office. It's a little bit more stable because of my projects. Therefore, the knowledge I have, people need. They know that I do a semi-decent job, so I can stay around and produce reports that are good. Therefore I can defend my points. Whereas probably a year ago I didn't feel that secure. My position wasn't always quite as strong and defending my point of view was a little bit harder.

His increased confidence in expressing and defending his views came from having acquired the relevant knowledge. Scott still monitored when to take a stand because his "position in the office" was still determined by others.

Establishing one's own beliefs, perceptions, and knowledge was a challenge at the crossroads. As Reginald described, it was hard to accept that one could know based on one's experience. Some, like Reginald, Anita, and Barb, were just beginning to get comfortable with this notion whereas others, like Justin and Scott, were a little more settled with it.

Movement toward the Horizon of Self-Authorship

The crossroads represented progress on all the driving questions of the 20s. Altering career choices to align with developing values came as a result of progress on the "who am I" question, or the intrapersonal realm of development. Standing up for oneself in relations with others and making the self equal to others marked progress in the interpersonal realm, or the "what kind of relationships do I want to construct" question. Establishing one's own beliefs, perceptions, and knowledge indicated progress on the "how do I know" question, the epistemological dimension. Yet the gains in the internal voice were not yet sufficient to take priority over external influences.

Transitional knowers abandoned their epistemic assumptions about some knowledge remaining certain in exchange for the independent assumption that most knowledge is uncertain. This progress on the "how do I know" question was essential in light of the growing recognition of the internal voice. It was possible to function at the crossroads with independent epistemic assumptions; participants who did so focused on translating the assumption that various knowledge claims are equally valid to making their internal voice equally valid to external influences. For those who had already adopted contextual assumptions in response to the "how do I know" question, their focus revolved around the "who am I" question—essentially wrenching the sense of self-definition from the external world into the internal realm. For all participants, the "who am I" and the "what kind of relationships do I want to construct with others" questions were integrally intertwined.

Stories about the crossroads part of the journey are filled with pronouncements about what is going to be. Participants appeared to be trying to convince themselves that they really were going to stand up for themselves, that they really were going to start following their own voices. Some were at the threshold of doing so; others had taken initial steps to act on their resolutions. External influence, so strong prior to arriving at the crossroads, was weakening, but had not yet lost its grip on these young adults' sense of themselves. Self-authorship was on the horizon and they were steadily working their way toward it.

The "Snapping" Point

I conclude this description of the crossroads with Cara's story because she clearly articulates standing at the threshold of self-authorship. Like Kris earlier in the chapter, Cara found few people to listen to her. Pursuing her graduate work in a predominantly male setting, she found few people who understood her concerns. One major concern arose when a professor expressed a romantic interest in her. She rebuffed him, but it damaged her chances to work in a particular area of interest. Of the experience, she said:

> This experience has made me more guarded, colder, harder. I am more confident now than I have ever been in my life. Being away from home, more independent, that has helped a lot. Day to day, making my own money, has made me feel pretty good. Feedback I've gotten—a nomination for a teaching award and papers accepted at better conferences—outside things. I'm in a healthier relationship with my boyfriend than I've ever had. I used to be in ones that didn't do much for my self-esteem; that carries over into everything else. This is so much healthier. I have tried to make sense of that; they were not abusive, just put me down. My boyfriends were alcoholics, jealous. They are charming at outset; I was attracted to something in that. I always did well in school, had girlfriends, why did I turn to these people? I would date nice guys, then go back to the bad guys. When got here, I was so stressed out with this crazy man at work, I reached a snapping point; I said to myself, "I won't do this again. I am in a Ph.D. program, what I wanted my whole life; I am making myself ill because of this. I am ruining my own dream." I decided not to do it anymore. I just reached a snapping point. I was running one day; I decided I didn't have to do it anymore. Went and told my advisor about this guy; got it out.

Cara hesitated to tell her advisor, for fear that he would think she was crazy, or that she had done something to provoke the professor's advance. Her boyfriend supported her, telling her it was not her fault. Despite her statements about self-confidence, being in a healthy relationship, and deciding not to be in unhealthy relationships anymore, Cara was still stuck at the crossroads, as is clear in these comments:

> A lot of my friends are married, have children, and houses; they have definite jobs they will keep. My future is ambiguous; I think my boyfriend and I will marry, but I'm not positive, and I don't know where I'll be and whether I'll have kids. Until I get married and have kids, I'm treated like I'm not a full member of society. People ask me when I'm getting married; mom says the clock is running out. It gets to me a lot. I've noticed that no one asks my boyfriend these questions; being a single man is normal. I don't want a child now, but I don't have forever. After I get my dissertation done, I'll want tenure, and will be poor. There is no ideal time. I worry about it a little—frustrating that my boyfriend doesn't have a biological clock to worry about. I don't want to be married and have kids now; can't imagine it. When I listen to people, I wonder if they know something I don't. If I went on my own intuition, I'd be okay.

In response to my question about the importance of intuition, Cara continued:

> I have had a good intuitive sense but have ignored it; like in bad relationships; my stomach would clench. Then I'll have a logical or rational voice saying you are overreacting. In the last six months I've tried to listen more; spend 20 minutes a day and do breathing exercises. I'm used to reading to help myself; read what someone else is saying rather than listening to myself. The more I'm listening to myself, I'm allaying fears. I'm paying more attention to me than to other people; I made some bad decisions as a result of listening to others. I changed my major to psychology to stay at home with a boyfriend. I'm sick of listening to others! Then I think, "I'm not honest with my parents." When am I going to stand up for myself and be who I am instead of trying to make people happy? Or share my reaction when people aggravate me? Expression of my opinion is seen as creating a scene. If a man said it, they'd say "good point." I am at the start of this—not there—an invisible force, I'm pushing against it, what is it? I don't know, but it is there though.

Cara's experience of the snapping point made it impossible for her to return to listening to others, yet she felt some force interfering with her standing up for herself. She did later find a guide whose understanding helped her move forward—a female colleague who understood some of Cara's experiences with men helped her think more clearly about others' influence. She also had sustained support from her boyfriend, whom she did marry. Cara reported:

> Patricia has a quote on her desk—"care too much about others' opinions and you'll be their prisoner." I obsess about what others' think. I think about that, and say to myself, "don't go there." My husband said the same thing to me, but I discounted it. Of course he is going to say that, he's married to me. It had more validity to me coming from her; he said it because he never felt that way. He is external—if someone does something, it's their fault. Nothing interferes with his focus.

Cara's description of her husband suggests that he is internally defined, the place in the journey for which she is striving. The snapping point marks progress for Cara in this journey because she can say to herself, "don't go there." Standing at the threshold of self-authorship, Cara continued to push against the invisible force and resolved not to go back into the crossroads. The next chapter describes her and her peers' journey forward into self-authorship.

5

BECOMING THE AUTHOR
OF ONE'S LIFE

Making yourself into something, not what other people say or
not just kind of floating along in life, but you're in some sense a
piece of clay. You've been formed into different things, but that
doesn't mean you can't go back on the potter's wheel and
instead of somebody else's hands building and molding you,
you use your own, and in a fundamental sense change your values and beliefs.

Mark

Mark clearly articulated the move into self-authorship he and his peers made
in their mid- to late-twenties. During this time, the tide turned in the clash
between internal voice and external influence. Participants' internal voices
grew strong enough to supercede external influence, and although external
influence remained a part of their lives, it was now relegated to the background as the internal voice took the foreground. The internal voice, or self,
became the coordinator and mediator of external influence. As Mark said,
participants began to use their own hands to build and mold themselves and
their beliefs.

Becoming the authors of their own lives involved reshaping what they
believed (epistemology), their sense of self (intrapersonal), and their relationships with others (interpersonal). Participants shifted from "how you know" to
"how I know" and in doing so began to choose their own beliefs. They
acknowledged the inherent uncertainty of knowledge and took up the challenge
of choosing what to believe in this context. They also attempted to live out their

beliefs in their work and personal lives. At the same time, "how I know" required determining who the "I" was. Intense self-reflection and interaction with others helped participants gain perspective on themselves and begin to choose their own values and identity. This emerging sense of self required renegotiation of existing relationships that had been built on external approval at the expense of personal needs and the creation of new mutual relationships consistent with the internal voice. Both the content and the language used in the stories in this chapter reflect participants' self-authorship. The dynamics of this juncture in the journey is evident in the continuing stories of Evan and Kelly.

Recall from chapter 4 that Evan had decided to be patient, waiting for something to click in the career arena. Something did, as he reported:

> Earlier this year, I and 4 people from my company were "sold" in the merger to another company in the city. Now I take the train everyday. It is a wild ride. I'm getting settled in—I like it a lot. I was thrown into a brand new environment; Madison Avenue—playing with the big boys. It is not a new job, but tripled the responsibility for me. I didn't go unwillingly, but not by choice; I am in the river and that is where it flowed. I'm grateful for it, there are no problems, but I had feared it. It is a big pond. It amazes me at how big it is. If you think about it too often, it is overwhelming. I'm used to the suburbs, five minutes from the office, not wearing a suit. Now it is high theatrics. If you are going to advance, you have to go to the city.

Evan conveyed that he had changed his attitude and was letting go of keeping things perfect:

> More with personal stuff than with the job, I get the attitude that you do what you can. In the past I always tried to keep things perfect. It is a waste of time. Expect things to go wrong and you'll be better prepared. Things were going good for me—the power went to my head—I felt like I was in more control than I was. Now I'm at the attitude of screw it, but I'm not irresponsible.

Having given up his notions of keeping things perfect, Evan seemed to swing the opposite direction in going with the river he was in. As it turned out over the next couple of years, Evan began to formulate his own ideas of what was good for him and how he would shape his life. Talking about his work, he noted that he had come to accept it as who he was:

> The most important thing has been work for the last year and a half. It has taken over; I've gotten way more serious about it. I

focused on improving myself in the work place; this is my career now. I've come to terms with it and accepted it. Fortunately for me, I have grown to like it because I've become good at it. I'm extremely lucky that I have had knowledgeable mentors who gave me responsibilities, afforded me the opportunity to learn and grow. I work hard, I'm dedicated to the venture I'm in whether I like it or not. My liking this was a gradual thing; probably happened when I left the company I started with, and went into a situation where I was not challenged. I grew to really enjoy this when I was asked back to my company, made an officer, and allowed to become heavily involved. I realized I had learned a lot, proven that I can function in this environment. That gave me confidence to do well—I look forward to going to work. It is less of a chore and more my life. It has become what I am.

Coming to an acceptance of his career was part of Evan's growing internal voice. Another part was doing his best and doing things his way. He described having done so under less than ideal circumstances:

When my company merged with this company, they planned to ditch me at the earliest opportunity. I dug my heels in and rolled up my sleeves down there. Now, the whole staff that worked on properties was reduced to me. I am organized to a point that is maniacal—which they like. I got a raise, they saw how I did this; they gave me more properties. The company has continued to grow; for right now I still have much to learn. I like to learn hard things. It is beyond my control but in a way I'm comfortable with it. I am given the time and space to learn on my own without being forced to do it one way or another. I've done it my own way. I've made lots of mistakes; learn not to do it again. I obsess about it until I solve it; or adjust that this is the situation now and I can't change it.

Evan's passion for learning, and his dedication to being able to describe it to me each year, led him to an understanding of how his mind worked:

I told you about this feeling that I had once I became "aware." That is the best word that I can use to describe the difference between how I view my intellectual level now, versus how I felt prior to "noticing" my surroundings and my relationship with the world around me. It was like I woke up one day and things just clicked in my brain and things became clear to me for the first time. The most dramatic difference between before and after was my ability to think, and the subsequent confidence in my abilities and trust in my decisions. I have developed my own

> approach to solving problems, one which has proven to me to be a good one, and one which has proven to be a good teacher. When it becomes apparent to me that I have relied on this ability, I often try to remember what I did before I began to understand how *my mind* worked.

I think what Evan was describing here was his shift to self-authorship. He was able to articulate to himself, and to me, the details of how his mind worked in solving problems. In doing so, it was apparent that his own voice was at the center of every step in the process:

> I clear everything away from my eyesight to focus on the issue; this allows me to jump in and roll around in it. I take pieces of information, move them around, change them; break them down, group them together by similarity. I like to figure out what the problem is, state it to myself. Problems are more overwhelming in your head than on paper. Sometimes I have to put it off for a day. Sleep on it. Regardless of outside influences, I have to do it my way. Once I can establish what it is, I determine what I have to do to correct that. Then figure out a way to get from A to B and who the players are in that, what role they have. I'll orchestrate solving the problem by using people and tools I have available, using the least amount of time and money.

In addition to being aware of how his mind worked, Evan was increasingly aware of himself.

> As my personality and sense of self have really begun to develop and become more refined, my ability to direct my life accordingly has become increasingly confident. As I realize who I am, and what is important to me, it becomes easier for me to establish my priorities. Identifying and arranging my priorities has helped me to develop a "road map" for reaching short and long-term goals. Don't get me wrong, I am not trying to predict the future and I by no means know exactly what I want, but I have developed a general idea and use my knowledge as a guide.

Along with this refining of who he was, Evan was refining relationships with others:

> I find that I am constantly rebalancing my identity in relationship to others. With my parents' divorce two years ago, and the purchase of my home, I am becoming a central figure in the extended family and have left behind my "youth" oriented iden-

tity. At work, my identity continues to grow almost as fast as my personal identity. Since I began with the current crew two and a half years ago, I have been titled Asset Manager, Senior Asset Manager, Assistant Vice President, and now Vice President. My identity within the group has changed very much. I owe this to my abilities in being aware of how my mind works and dealing with my personal set of realities.

Evan's increasing comfort with himself and his identity, as well as his ability to reflect on this own thinking, seemed to be helpful in his continued differences with his wife:

I find comfort in organizing things. My wife is the complete opposite. I'm at my wits end with her sometimes because of her habits around the house. Everything I own, I know where it is at all times. Her car is a disgrace—it is an extension of her closet; my stuff is in my trunk in an Eddie Bauer bag in compartments. Every once in awhile it comes to a head; never gets resolved. Then other stuff occurs and you stop focusing on it. I've learned that criticism doesn't help; I don't worry about it; we have our own rooms where we can go where the other isn't forbidden, but we keep our stuff there and respect that. That's one way of dealing with it. When it becomes a problem, it becomes a problem. It is not easy to be married. There's no way to describe how I handle it; I do what is most right or convenient at the moment. I'm more focused on myself than on partnership problems. I have enough to contend with during the day; personal stuff builds up in the week, I can't deal with it. Whatever happens, happens.

Evan's story demonstrates that achieving self-authorship is an evolving process and does not mean life is without struggle. He was actively setting his priorities and dealing with issues as they arose. Knowing how his mind worked and refining his sense of himself gave him confidence to direct his life.

Kelly was also paying attention to the ways her mind worked as a central part of her search for internal meaning. She found the opportunity to explore this in graduate school:

It means a lot to me that I'm hearing that other teachers are experiencing the same things I am. And also hearing the way other teachers do things. The biggest thing now is all the workings of my mind whenever I hear something, I've got something concrete to link it back to in my classroom. It makes it more meaningful; it makes it tangible. And it makes it important to me. Finding common ground and being able to apply it. Then we can take the theory or strategy and take it back to our own respective situations.

Connecting what she was learning to her own experience and deciding what to do with it led Kelly to feel more secure as a professional and as an adult. She explained:

I'm more secure professionally, as a teacher. I've very secure in my knowledge. I'm more secure when I talk to parents that I know what I know. I think I know more than a lot of other teachers who aren't working on their master's or don't have it. I can back up what I say to the parents with theories and "This is why your child is this way," and "This is what I read in the research." I feel like that gives me a little more credibility rather than just telling them, "This is the way it is." Every year I get more secure as a person, as an adult, more confident in just living as an adult.

Kelly also had an opportunity to prove herself at work, both to herself and to others:

I'm proving myself. This past year we participated in a scientific literacy grant. We were chosen as a target school. We have a lead teacher go with the principal to meetings every month and learn about new science procedures. I was chosen to be the lead teacher from our school. I brought information back to teachers in three grade levels. We chose a whole new science curriculum, 1 to 8, so I was a big part of that committee in choosing a new curriculum. That was a good thing because I had to lead the meetings with the other grade-level teachers, and I also helped the principal with some in-service meetings. They could see that I was knowledgeable about this. I think it's helped them see me in a professional sense.

Kelly was seeing herself as knowledgeable and this was reinforced by her opportunity to exhibit her professionalism to her colleagues. She had come a long way from the beginning teacher who needed affirmation that she was teaching in the right ways and who was unable to "stay down" during the strike vote. Kelly's sense of herself as a knowledgeable professional and as an adult also led to a transformation in her relationship with her family:

Family's become a lot more important to me over the last few years. My relationship with my family is on a totally different level now than it even was in college. Like with my aunt, I feel that she's more of a sister to me now, even though she's in her mid-forties, than an aunt because we've just got a really open relationship. The same thing with my Mom, although it's not on the sister level. She respects me as an adult, and she respects my life. She and my Dad are very careful; they don't come over unless they call first or they are invited. They respect my privacy in my apartment. They're very respectful of my adult life.

The emergence of Kelly's internal voice allowed her to join her parents and aunt as an equal in the relationship.

Another dynamic of Kelly's self-authorship was the increased role of faith in her life:

Church has become larger part of my life, both physical and mental. A big change in faith over the past two years. My eyes have been opened up a lot. I was raised in a Presbyterian home, with Christian values. For three or four years after college, I was just going through the motions. I had a conversation with a guy; we started talking about faith. I hadn't talked about my beliefs out loud. My family believes you don't talk about it, you live it. I needed to experience that. I started listening to Christian radio—I was curious about it. Listening to Christian singers every day really connected me. I think about it every single day. I started reading more things, talking to people that would help me through it. I read the Bible; everything started falling into place. Everything has happened sequentially; everything happened and I could handle it. I wouldn't have known how earlier. I talked to a friend about it; she said it seemed to be a series of answered prayers for me. I learned a lot about myself and where faith belongs in my life. I'm more comfortable, centered. It is neat. My aunt has been a catalyst; supportive, very open. . . . Right after I talked with the guy that got me thinking, I had a scary couple of months—I started doubting my faith. It was a scary feeling after growing up believing Jesus is the Son of God etc.—too huge, I couldn't fit it together. I picked up my Bible; I had never just read it. I read a little before bed at night to see what would happen. It took less than a week; I had my head screwed on straight—this is the way it is. It is powerful. The more I read, the less I know. I am amazed at how little I know about what is in there. I talk to people, find out how knowledgeable they are and that makes me thirsty, want to know more. It has been a significant experience.

Although the impetus for this move toward faith was external in the form of a friend and Kelly's aunt, she started acquiring more knowledge about her faith. Her story here was the beginning of a concerted effort to explore and decide what she believed. Kelly's finding meaning through her evolving faith, her increased confidence in her work, and her understanding of how her mind worked, all combined to help her make meaning of herself and her adult life. Whereas Evan's awareness of how his mind works guides his meaning making, Kelly's faith guides hers. They both illustrate what the majority of participants were experiencing in their late twenties—having found a process for authoring their own lives.

It is probably apparent by now that the three dimensions of self-authorship are intricately intertwined. Participants' stories, however, often placed a particular dimension in the forefront, depending on what was uppermost in their minds at the time of our conversation. Becoming the authors of their own lives meant doing so in all three dimensions, but most participants spoke to the dimensions most salient in their experience. Although the complete stories include all dimensions, I use stories that highlight each dimension in this chapter to illustrate the specifics of authoring one's sense of self, relationships, and beliefs.

The Intrapersonal Dimension of Self-Authorship

For those adults who had struggled to accept their voices and hold them as equal to those of others, leaving the crossroads prompted a focus on the intrapersonal dimension, or their sense of themselves. Recognizing that they needed to develop their internal thoughts and decide whom they wanted to be resulted in intense self-reflection. Through analyzing various aspects of their experience, they began to build frameworks to guide their lives.

Self-Reflection

Arriving at a sense of the capacity to actively construct themselves and their lives, participants in their mid- to late-twenties talked freely about self-reflection. Because they were thinking about who they were and wanted to become in all aspects of their lives, soul-searching had become important and surfaced quickly in our conversations.

Recall Kurt's statements at the crossroads regarding wanting to act on the power of choice to make himself happy rather than getting his worth from others' thoughts. He had continued to work toward that goal and articulated his departure from the crossroads:

> It has been like my own personal spiritual path—exploring, trying to understand why I am here, what I have to contribute to life on earth. I am motivated by personal satisfaction, I kind of abandoned [external reassurance]—[I have] more of a self-

acceptance rather than external. I'm letting go of external influence to a large extent. I've done personality assessments, and one of the tenets of self [for me] is gaining acceptance through pleasing other people, sometimes sacrificing my own needs. I'm letting go of that to become more in tune with who I am and what makes me happy. I would not have imagined working for a hardware store three years after college. I came to an acceptance of what *is* in life, rather than changing externals. It's a great job, and I have fun doing it. Self-acceptance, being able to say, "Yes, this is my choice, and I'm happy with it." By doing what I want I have abandoned [self-sacrifice], but fall back into it sometimes. Learning is a process, slow and steady. It is still hard to stand up for my needs and too easy to meet others'.

Two years later, Kurt was feeling this even more deeply and drew the distinction between talking about it and living it:

My philosophy, what I'm looking for out of life, is the same: The ability to influence the world around me in a positive way. What has changed is that it has further unfolded in my life—two years ago I was talking about it; now I'm living it. That's a totally huge difference. I probably thought I was living it then. What is inside impacts what is outside, but it comes from inside. The inside is not influenced by others. You have to learn that it does come from inside. For awhile you think others can make decisions; you learn in the end that it comes down to you. There is a poem, something like "Man in the Glass." It talks about going through life, but the only person you answer to is the man in the glass— the mirror, looking at yourself. I can't remember the exact lines, but one is that the most important person is the person in the glass. My parents have instilled that a lot. They never gave answers, just said, "You get out on your own and we'll support you." My experience with the law firm set me on the road to where I am now. I thought it would bring me happiness, I tried to live society's plan for me; no way! Then it was like, "Okay, I don't think there is any self-actualization in what society has planned." In order to self-actualize yourself, you have to look inside yourself.

Kurt was accepting where he was in life at the moment, not worrying about what other people thought regarding his working in a hardware store three years out of college, and working on developing the internal voice that would guide him to the future. Despite occasional struggles with others' expectations, his internal self-definition remained in the forefront of who he was, allowing him to achieve self-authorship.

Phillip was soul-searching as well and reported having had an awakening. Asked to talk more about it, he offered:

It is the culmination of several experiences in my life. In high school when you break away from family and get involved in friends—for me, I had tons of friendships, and I thought they were the Zenith. Then a couple bad experiences and you say, "that's not it." Then you graduate from college—maybe the career is it. Then you see you are dealing with all types of people who don't think like you. Every day is not a shining success. That is not it. For me, just being sensitive to what was happening in my life and not just backing up like proverbial car and hitting the edge again. I've tried this, it isn't 100 percent satisfying, so put the amount of effort in there that will give you that satisfaction. Put more in only as far as your priorities go, calculating the cost-benefit analysis. For me, I know that I can continue to do certain things, put effort into it, but it isn't all it is cracked up to be. There are some rewards, but worshipping in the temple of the career—I'm not there. The same thing with relationships.

Phillip's awakening hinged on realizing that his happiness did not reside outside of himself—in his career or his relationships—but rather inside. He continued the story of where self-reflection had taken him:

I got a sense of what is good for me; put more into what is good and less into what isn't. Getting out on your own and trying things—you have to kind of say, "The way I've been doing things has to change to be satisfied." Adjust as you go. I didn't come across that until a few years ago. It was a shift of what is possible. I thought I couldn't write a song, but I did. In grade school I used to put together models. I made a wooden model of a car but when I got it done, I didn't like it. I tried it again; Dad said, "Just buy the plastic model of that car." So I put it away. It sat at our house for 14 years; I noticed there are a lot of things I needed to complete. Here was one of them; a small thing. Going through life dabbling a little, then say "I can't finish it." No! Then I thought, "Stupid piece of wood, I'm an adult now, I should at least be able to finish that." I wanted to. I had dad send me the miserable piece of wood. I spent five months on the thing, swearing and cursing, fingers glued—my parents said "why?" It started to come together; motivated me to complete it. It is sitting on my dresser in a case—I'm waxing poetic—it is a symbol to me. I think, "At one point in your life you said you couldn't finish this; you aren't at that point anymore; it isn't perfect, but you have completed it and can move onto something else." In doing this little project, I not only completed something, I brought it to its end and learned something. After I got that finished, I was able to take that to other areas in my life, like writing songs.

Phillip's reflections led him to put career and relationships in perspective, allowing his internal self-definition to guide his approach to these dimensions of his life. He recognized he had some personal work to do and his story about the model car illustrates his working through his own doubts. His "little project" in the form of the model car represented a much larger project—convincing himself that he was capable of doing things he wanted to do.

Like Phillip, Heather discovered that she needed to do some personal work and had acted on her discovery. Heather had previously reported that she knew herself and was in control of her life. Encountering difficulties with her biological sister and a little sister from her volunteer work, however, called this all into question. Heather told this story in our twelfth interview:

> I'm a different person. I was externally driven by a weird force telling me to live up to what I thought was right. I thought I knew what I wanted. But I didn't. The biggest thing is now I'm internally driven—that freed a lot of things. I'm much freer emotionally, more expressive when I speak. I'm learning to listen to my emotions; when I was externally driven I didn't pay attention to them, to what made me happy. I focused on what was supposed to make me happy versus what I felt. I'm more comfortable in my own skin; living by what I think and feel rather than some standard.

Asked how this shift took place, Heather continued:

> It started by trying to figure out how to help my sister, and it snowballed from there. All of a sudden it hit me when I was driving to work one day. I was thinking about my sisters, what went wrong, analyzing it. I did a lot of reading, some self-help books were good. A couple slapped me in the face. The book *Dance of Anger*—I read it because my sister was reading it—I hadn't thought about my own anger. It hit me—I could see myself there. I started seeing how that related to my interaction with my family and my husband. Before, I wasn't aware of how I was expressing things. Before I felt like I had to be the strong one for my family, for my little sister; I never stopped to think about whether that was fair, or how it was affecting me. I'm realizing that I have very similar behaviors that drove my sister's behaviors. I used to intellectualize solutions to problems; I'm learning not to do that. Logical relationships and meaning, I still do that, but I'm learning to let myself sit back and feel for

awhile. Just learning to deal with my sister; how to set boundaries with her. Realize things I was doing; I had to become much
more honest in relationships—I hadn't been before. Honest
about what I was feeling, not being passive-aggressive. . . .
The other thing is, once I stopped and tried to figure out what I
wanted, I couldn't tell you. Someone asked what I wanted—I
had no idea. I had defined my life externally, and when the
structure was gone, I was just lost. I realized external wasn't
what I should define life by, but I hadn't had time to explore and
figure out internal thoughts. I was lost for awhile.

Heather's concern about her sister led her to a concern about herself. Seeing
herself in what she was reading and in her own sister prompted her to reevaluate who she was. Figuring out her internal thoughts helped her become internally driven.

Andrew was also becoming internally driven, a shift impacted in large part
by his mother's death. In our seventh interview he shared his loss and its role
in his self-reflection:

I just found myself in so many ways changed, just the way I
approached and reacted to things. I think I deeply changed
because my Mom was probably my best friend. For me it was
just a drastic change in my life, even just beyond losing a family member. It's kind of hard to pinpoint exactly what it made me
do. But I think it oddly enough made me realize that I, in a way,
had nobody else to lean on and I had to, I guess, pick myself up
by my bootstraps. My father's still alive. He was never the one
that I'd lean to for support. So I found myself going a lot more
to internal support, congratulating myself for a good job and
doing things to please myself rather than to please somebody
else. If I got a B on something, but I thought I had done a good
job, I was much more comfortable and able to deal with it
because I knew I had given it my best. I guess in a way I just felt,
"Well, that's just one other person's opinion." Pushing myself
internally made the As come easier because I might have set my
own personal standards higher. It's kind of hard to pinpoint
exactly how it affected me.

Losing his mother prompted Andrew to realize that support and personal standards had to come from him. As he gained strength in constructing his standards and supporting himself emotionally, he was able within the next couple
of years to accept the loss of his mother. He said this about it:

For me personally I have finally come to grips with losing my
mother. She was my best friend. Positive things happen to me

since she died, and the first person I wanted to tell was her. Getting a graduate degree, getting married, getting this business. It was not one to one—but I always told her. I've learned to deal with it more; appreciate dad and grandparents more. I've become closer to dad, talk to him several times a week. I share everything with him. I never had done that, but I'm slowly getting to the point that he is the sounding board my mother once was. I never stop missing her. But it made me realize that you have to go after what you want, not what others want you to do; do what you feel is right. I found myself, keep up with relationships with friends that meant something to me, and others I dropped. That isn't what is really important. Having everyone like you is not that important. I have never felt that way that much; I'm me, like me or not, I was never uncomfortable with people not liking me. Learning to accept that has been another aspect—relationships that really matter you need to hang onto.

Self-authorship, or finding himself, allowed Andrew to determine what was important in his life and pursue it. After finding his internal strength to support himself he was able to build a new relationship with his father. Although he reported never being too concerned about others liking him, he still experienced the shift from external influence to internally guiding his own life.

Ned was able to talk more specifically than some of his counterparts about how self-reflection played out in the shift from external to internal influence. He identified how he used introspection to build a framework for his life:

I have a friend, he and I always go off when we get together and have a beer and talk for six hours about life and really sorting things out. If you don't have that person to bounce your things off of, I don't think it forces you to assimilate them and take that next step. I've been fortunate to have this guy and my wife to ask them what they think about what I did. Not judgmental; learn about myself in process—Aha, know what makes me tick. Those people have helped me keep my focus on knowing myself. Otherwise, life is just a lot of experiences that you don't connect—it helps to get to a framework. But when you are going through it, you have to have a learning experience to connect it to who you are and what you are about. It is not as fast and easy as having somebody tell you; you have to bump into a few rocks. The latter might be more meaningful because it is an internalized thing.

Ned's introspection involved analyzing his experiences, collecting feedback from his friend and his wife, and deciding how that fit into the framework he was constructing for who he was and how to live his life. He used new experiences to build onto the framework. He even regarded our conversation as an opportunity for introspection. At the close of this conversation he said:

> A good example of this introspective stuff is what I'm getting out of this conversation right now. I don't often get the opportunity for someone to ask these tough questions to figure out my framework. It is very parallel to discussions with my close friend—at the beginning I had no idea what I'd say; then I recognize things I need to think more about. One of those is developing my framework for making people decisions. What do I need to do to develop my framework, my theory about this? It kind of calmed me a bit—feel like now it isn't as scary as I thought. For me, personally, it is helpful for us to talk.

The issue of making people decisions arose in the course of conversation about Ned's promotion from the technical side of his work to management. He already had the framework for the technical side (as you will hear later in the chapter) and realized in our conversation that he had not yet worked through his framework for managing. Yet he knew how to use resources and experiences to work that out. He realized his capability for self-authorship would help him develop this new framework.

The common thread of the self-reflection stories was getting to know oneself. Sometimes this was the culmination of multiple experiences and disappointments; other times it was the result of some specific event or crisis. Regardless of what started the self-reflection process, the outcome was the continual authoring of the internally defined self—the answer to the "who am I" question. The stories shared thus far focus on resolving this question by looking inside oneself. The next set couples this with gaining perspective from external environments.

Gaining Perspective on Self

Self-reflection and constructing a framework from which to guide one's life often resulted in what participants called "gaining perspective." For some, this translated to approaching experiences in their lives from different vantage points than they had previously. Lynn offered an example in talking about going through the search for a full-time teaching position—something she had struggled with five years earlier. She explained:

> This summer my mother was the negative factor in my life—have you done this, how about this? I had to just tell her—I was finally old enough and strong enough to say this—"Look, just back off. This is something I need to do myself" and I had to

stay positive. It is tough being rejected. It is humbling to have someone say "sorry;" or it was down to two people and they hire the other person. I had many interviews this summer, and nothing—it can be depressing. But I didn't let it get to me this time, and before I did. The difference? Maturity. It is not the end of the world that I don't have a fulltime job. Knowing that I am a capable teacher; I have positive reports from my past principals. Knowing that I am good at what I do. Being able to admit that. When you are 22, you aren't quite sure—still feeling your way out there. Even at 24, maybe even 25; first couple years out of school are a big change, you're not there yet. I think I'm there; I've got the picture. I've got the grasp as to this is who I am and this is okay. Yes, I have my faults and so does everybody else. And I can accept the situation—just knowing that something right will come to me. Just having that feeling.

The major contrast between Lynn's experience this time around and the earlier one (recall her being "at the gate" in chapter 3) is her knowing that she is a capable teacher and knowing that she can influence the direction of her life. She no longer needs the full-time teaching position to define who she is; that definition is now her own. Authoring who she is helped her confront her mother, stay positive, and trust that something would work out.

Barry was revisiting a past experience from a new vantage point as well, although it was more of a journey in his case. The experience was the loss of his father earlier in his life:

The last major thing that has happened to me is my father passing away when I was 10. I am really looking at it for first time from my parents' point of view. This is last journey with that, the last step will be when I am a father myself. First, I looked at it as "How could this happen to me?" Then in my teens, I looked at it from my mother's point of view—mom being alone, but not knowing what a significant other even meant. Then the last couple of years, I've looked at it from my father's point of view. I didn't get to talk to him about it—he had cancer. Thinking about what he had to go through. Knowing that he wouldn't see me graduate from high school. Thinking what that meant—feeling closer to what those feelings were. It is a long journey. I don't know how to capture it somehow—it is different than losing a parent later in life. It is different when at 11 you don't have a dad on Father's Day. Can't ask him what it was like when he was a teenager. At the rehearsal dinner before our wedding, had close people there, I stated in my speech that there was a consultancy of people filling that void—mainly my mother. Recognizing that, but there is one final step—maybe it never will be, but when I am a father, when I turn 45—that is when he passed away. I am finally looking at it from different points of view and coming to terms with it.

As Barry revisited his father's death from various events in his own adult life, his evolving understanding of himself allowed him to see the experience from other perspectives. His ability to do so and to reflect on those perspectives helped him through the long journey of coming to terms with the loss.

Gaining perspective stemmed from looking at on-going life events through a new lens (the internal voice). Lynn and Barry revisited events in their lives from their new lenses and thus reacted differently than they had previously. Seeing things from new vantage points helped participants reinterpret the affect of such events on their lives—a notion similar to the one Mark advanced in chapter 2 of authoring what meaning events will hold for a person. Becoming the author of one's identity was a process of analyzing (and often reinterpreting) past experiences, reflecting on feelings about the self, and interpreting new experiences to build onto one's evolving identity. This process, of course, involved reshaping relating to others, the topic taken up next.

The Interpersonal Dimension of Self-Authorship

The ability to self-reflect and author one's own sense of self played out in the interpersonal dimension of participants' lives. Prior to this point, relating to others had been defined on others' terms, with the internal voice in the background. Their decisions about the kind of relationships they wanted to construct with others—coworkers, life partners, parents—were all mediated by the internal voice moving to the forefront. Renegotiation of relationships was necessary to allow participants' self-authored identities to join the other as an equal partner. This dimension was front and center for those who were in the process of renegotiation with parents, coworkers, or significant others. It was also a salient dimension for those who were trying to make marriage decisions.

Renegotiation of Existing Relationships

Lauren, whose story about liking her boyfriend less after her parents expressed hesitations about him appeared in chapter 4, found a path out of the crossroads. Her story illustrates many participants' reshaping of their relationships with their parents. Lauren followed her inner voice to further develop her relationship with her boyfriend and in the process had to renegotiate her relationship with her parents. Lauren explained how she came to act on the inner voice:

We continued seeing each other for a year and a half. And I got to a point where the distance was really a barrier [personally] as well as financially. So I decided if I'm going to make this work, I need to just try it for myself. He didn't ask me to come, but I knew this was what I needed to do to make a decision. I have gone through a lot in the past year, the personal side of finding out what Lauren wants. In the past, it was, "Is this okay with Mom and Dad? What will they think and say?" Last June I went home and said, "This is what I'm going to do." As I get older, I realize I need to make my own decisions. They said "Do it for yourself, make yourself happy." It is the hardest thing to leave them. It is the biggest decision I made in my entire life. I looked at options, pros and cons, and went with my heart—I never felt this way toward a man. I've grown in that area as well. Hopefully it will improve my judgment skills. I always ask for advice.

Lauren's decision was about a relationship she wanted to pursue, but the dilemma was really about relying less on her parents' thinking in important life decisions. Despite her parents' support, she had difficulty moving away from them, even though she already lived four hours away from them. The difficulty of "moving away" had more to do with moving away psychologically from her parents than moving away from their geographical home. Lauren's decision also demonstrated her acting on her self-authored sense of self because her boyfriend did not ask her to come; she made the decision to find out for herself. Her decision represented both acting on her voice, and choosing to put herself in a context to further develop her ability to act on it. Her parents' support in recognizing her as an independent decision-maker helped her further this vision of herself.

Given the importance of career in most participants' lives, and the fact that most had entered into their career settings from the external formula perspective, it was not surprising that many found themselves renegotiating how they related with coworkers. For example, Megan was expected to take over when her boss was absent. She reported how this contributed to her self-authorship and to changing relations at work:

I've become more assertive just because I've been in situations now where I have to stand up for myself and for what I need. I can't just take a back seat to things because I'm expected to take over when my boss is gone. And as things come up I have to be able to handle them. I'm basically a shy person, but this job has been good for me because it's forced me to come out and say, "I can handle this situation. I'm in control here. These people must listen to me or we're not going to do this right." And I would like to be more assertive than I am now. There are days where I'm very confident and I feel very good about things. And then I have bad days, too, where I feel like I don't want any confrontation at all and I just want people to just give me all the information I need and not ask too many questions.

Megan's story suggests that she was pushed into assertiveness in her role, yet she was happy about being able to handle events in her work.

Renegotiating work relations was mediated by dynamics of the work context. Just as Megan was pushed to be assertive, Pamela was pushed in the opposite direction. She felt the external forces at her workplace restricted her ability to act consistently on her internal voice. Discussing disagreements at her school, she offered:

I kind of just step back and watch what other people do because at this point I'm still a new teacher and I can't afford to say much. I don't have tenure yet. I just kind of go with what's happening and do what's expected of me. I'm not trying to make any waves at this point. . . . I have a curriculum that outlines what content I need to cover. But I can choose how I want to teach that.

Perhaps some of Pamela's hesitation stemmed from her ties to the local area via her husband's business; some undoubtedly came from the tenure process. Pamela expressed her self-authorship in her teaching but hesitated to do so in school disagreements. Her story demonstrates that renegotiation is context bound.

Whereas Pamela's survival in her teaching position hinged on monitoring when to express her internal voice, Sheila reported that her survival necessitated expressing hers. Sheila enrolled in cooking school and found the kitchen experience challenging:

I was able to adjust to get what I wanted. It was not my way of learning, or one that I would choose. I was threatening [to the other students]. I couldn't cook but if anyone would make it, it would be me due to intelligence or financial backing. I could do the schmoozing—that is important. I was threatened by their ability to cook. We formed a symbiotic relationship. I gave technical information about cooking; they helped me with knife skills and speed. Some never accepted me as a woman. I had never faced sexism like this. Some couldn't respect me; it was good for me because I stood up to these people. I had ability with words that they didn't have. When they made sexist comments, I would come back at them and knives dropped all over the kitchen. This was a turning point for me; they respected me for fighting my own battles. It was good for them to understand that women aren't the image that they have of them. It was a men's club in the kitchen. Part of my evolving—I could stand up for myself and take care of myself. I realized I had accomplished something. Finding my way of empowering myself. . . . pushing myself in areas I never thought I could cope with. You get to an age where you realize you aren't doing anything to develop yourself. That pushed me into cooking school.

To survive this sexist atmosphere, Sheila stood up for herself. In doing so, she was able to form productive relationships with other students to get what she needed. Because she entered cooking school having already begun to author her sense of self, she asserted herself to further her goals. Doing so helped her build on her self-authorship.

The confidence Sheila gained through empowering herself in the kitchen helped her in other interpersonal dimensions of her life, particularly in marriage. She explained that finding her way to empowering herself helped her through divorcing her first husband. Reflecting on that situation, she said:

I spent five years trying to create [my first] husband; now I'm trying to create myself. I have allowed things to happen. I have ambition and drive, but I haven't focused them the way I should have. I focused most of my drive on both my husbands; it is despicable. I don't know why I do this. My ex-husband has a good job because I wrote his cover letters. I blew three or four years of my life on that project. I backed off that with my current husband—I'm not his mother, he can do what he wants. I'm not going to do that again. I have only one life and I have to make myself happy. I don't know why I decide to be June Cleaver when I have a ring on my finger. I need to focus on what I want and what makes me happy. . . . Trying to swim against the stream. My eyes are wide open now about what is going on, I'm more able to fend for myself, and to go get what I need, whether it is information or support. I feel more responsibility for myself; I hope to get to a place where I can feel more responsible for other people—to help others.

Sheila's focus on what made her happy resulted in divorcing her first husband. It is clear from her story that she was focused on him rather than on herself in their marriage. Sheila articulated the dilemma many participants faced as a result of their socialization regarding appropriate gender roles and the strength of the image of June and Ward Cleaver. But Sheila had overcome those notions, and despite self-authorship requiring swimming upstream, she was making progress. She could even envision turning her attention back to helping others once her internal work was accomplished.

Candace also realized that a good marriage required self-authorship on the part of both parties. Fortunately for Candace, she came to this conclusion prior to marriage. Describing a difficult decision, she said:

> I did choose to break off my engagement. At first I moved it back, then I broke it off. I was the dominant person in the relationship; my fiancée was doing everything possible to please me and it was driving me nuts. He was not going anywhere with his own life. He had several jobs; he just continually tired of one, was always changing to something else. Searching for something that was never there. That was the way it was going to be; if he was trying to please me he wasn't going to be happy. The best thing was to break it off for awhile.

Because Candace had come to self-author who she was, she was not satisfied with a relationship in which her fiancée was unable to do so. Her initial thinking was to break it off "for awhile" but she quickly learned that renegotiation to a new relationship was not possible after some rather desperate attempts on her fiancée's part to save their relationship. Seeing that his self-authorship was some way off, she moved ahead with her own life.

Heather's story of renegotiation with her spouse represents the stories of those who were able to reinvent and maintain their partnerships. Earlier in this chapter I shared part of Heather's story of self-reflection in the context of difficulties with her sister. You will recall that through her reading she was learning about anger she was harboring. Her self-reflection spilled over into reflection on her relationship with her husband, and to working through issues she had not previously seen clearly. She described what had taken place with her buried anger:

> I took it out on my husband. When he would say it wasn't fair that I was doing this, I would get mad at him. Probably because I felt that [it wasn't fair], but I felt I had to do it. If you would have asked me before this happened, I thought I was in tune with myself emotionally. Before this happened, I would have never thought I had problems in this area. In hindsight, I know I didn't express myself well; I bottled [anger] up and took it out on my husband and couldn't clarify why I was angry. When I started clarifying why I was angry, I could adjust. Before I just got angry, and it never moved beyond that. I thought I had a right to be mad; now I know I have a choice in the matter too and a responsibility to myself.

Learning about her anger led Heather to work with it in her relationship with her husband. This work to renegotiate the nature of their relationship was complicated though by issues he had as well:

> My husband was willing to own up to some of his stuff. Given the issues I had, he was the worst person for me to marry. We are exactly alike—I was compulsive about social things; he was compulsive about financial things. We joked about making the perfect world. It could have been bad. He has also been able to recognize that and decided that it is not healthy. We grow through this together. We are still in practice mode, going back to the structure. We are both fighting it, so it is not easy to help each other out of it. So far it has been worth it. We [are] two people who have defined ourselves externally; had intimacy issues because we don't know what to do with emotions. When we get to the emotional thing, it is kind of difficult. We are enjoying it; it is fortunate we decided to take the same path. Because I am defining myself internally, I have better relationships.

Heather clarified in this part of the story that there is more than just learning to deal with anger going on here. Because she was starting to make decisions about what was best for her in her relationships with her family, sister, and spouse, she was becoming internally defined. She talked about the on-going difficulty of achieving "better relationships:"

> I still have to remind myself about it. I've gotten a lot better. Part of it is my husband is still there [externally defined] and we conflict a little bit. If he is a little fearful and goes back—his comfort zone is back in that structure—if he goes there, I'm not strong enough to stay where I am. I get pulled back there. I'm not there yet; I know what it feels like, know where it is heading. I feel like I will get there. I recognize when I'm being pulled; at first I didn't realize it. I would get mad at him for being where he was; then I realized I was mad because I couldn't keep myself from going there. Now I can recognize that. Since I have gotten to that point, we can work on it easier. Recently figured that out; now we are working on that.

Heather's insights demonstrate that self-authorship is a long and sometimes painful process. She has seen it and does not plan to let it go. On occasion, though, she is pulled back from self-authorship in her relationship with her husband. Her ability to recognize when that happens is due to her having already begun the self-authorship process. Thus she is able to look at experiences from a new vantage point and trust that she will become more solid in her ability to self-author. The insights she is able to gain from her self-reflection ability, in conjunction with her husband's willingness to work toward self-authorship, make their success in renegotiating their relationship look promising.

Considering Relationships that Maintain the Intrapersonal Self

Participants who had already begun authoring themselves were careful in choosing relationship commitments because they knew these commitments had to honor the self they were constructing. They were uncertain, however, how to go about making these choices. Barry recounted the process he experienced to determine whether a woman he was dating was the one he wanted to marry:

> The variables are difficult to put in categories. I'm coming to grips with emotions and how to display them. For as much as I like creativity, I'm a pretty rational person. I can come up with great toys [at work], but when I look at my decision making, it is very rational. There are no facts in relationships! The only way you do that is through trial and error. Looking for it until it felt right. I try to think of life without her, and I don't like it. But I wanted to find out that this is the correct person. "Kay is perfect for you." I wanted to find it in a book. Then there were temptations; feelings for other people in the past year and a half; that is difficult. What does that mean? Does it mean I don't love her? Nobody to say yes or no. Others say you know! That's great; it didn't happen for me. People say, "Then you aren't in love." It is a big decision. I thought I knew two times before; then I didn't. Everybody wants to give their opinion—friends and family. I ask myself if I am happy. Okay, exclude all that, how do I feel? I put it in its place; it took awhile. I am influenced by a lot of people. I really have to say that I am very, becoming less [influenced], trying to do that. Sometimes I am too influenced, but I take bits and come up with my own ways. It is important not to be overly influenced because you'll never be happy making somebody else happy. You'll be confirming what they believe, and you have to get to what you feel. Make sure it is your decision.

Barry was more comfortable in his work decisions where he could organize variables into categories. Like Gwen (who told a similar marriage decision story in chapter 2), he wanted the crystal ball, or in his case a book, to know she was the one for him; yet he knew this was impossible. The vague nature of his trial and error process showed that he was uncertain how to make use of emotions in decisions, but he was convinced that it had to be his decision and one that made him happy.

Al also discussed making the marriage decision, but unlike Barry he leaned more heavily on logic than on emotion. He told this story about an unexpected relationship that emerged during medical school:

> I wasn't looking for a wife by any means. I met this girl; and then I started thinking about it. She was different than a zillion I had dated. I started to think about "Do I want to risk losing her?" After evaluating that, I said, "No. I don't want to be without her." Once we were engaged, it didn't make a difference to me when we married. Looking back, we would have had more time to grow if we had dated during these difficult times [when school was in session]. We dated during my summer; we could have seen what it was like in the crazy schedule. We could have gotten some growing pains dealt with. I used the same [decision-making] process I usually use. It was a logical decision; it wasn't spontaneous. I know it sounds that way, but it wasn't in my head. I am not Mr. Emotion; it wasn't like I was swept over, wasn't gaga—I don't get like that. I don't have emotional swings in either direction.

Al approached the marriage decision from a self-authored vantage point. His strong sense of self was even more evident as he talked about learning to make decisions together with his wife:

> I'm not used to making mutual decisions. Being able to make decisions and feel comfortable—there are two things there. One is coming to competence, a sense of self that you have confidence in yourself to do these things. Do your best and feel good about it. [Second] in some situations you can't get that level of comfort without being well informed—in my situation, I can't get that yet. It is more than an attitude; it is getting a knowledge base. I know I will be comfortable, but still need that knowledge base. The thing I'm going to be dealing with—adding kids into my life—I've been a cowboy kind of guy, never accountable to another person in time and priorities; it is a struggle. I'm still working on it.

Al conveyed that he had competence, but in mutual decisions he had yet to develop the comfort level due to lack of knowledge. Joint decisions and managing his priorities with those of his wife was something he was working on. It was clear that he was not giving up his priorities in learning how to function with another person.

Al's decision-making process differed from Barry's in form; yet both men approached the decision from the vantage point of self-authorship. Both men viewed these relationships as enriching their lives but neither made mention of changing who they were in joining these unions. Their ability to self-author who they were helped them learn self-authorship and its accompanying mutuality in the interpersonal arena.

The question of what kind of relationships to construct with others was altered by progress toward self-authorship on the "who am I" question. Existing relationships were viewed from a new vantage point—the internal sense of self that was gaining strength. This internal self-authorship mediated the renegotiation of those relationships as well as the choice of new ones. The core nature of the internal sense of self made it necessary to organize all of one's relationships—with significant others, parents, siblings, friends, co-workers, supervisors—in ways that supported the internal self. In some cases, as Al described, the celebration of this new sense of authorship (and perhaps the fear of retreating to external control) made it hard to engage in mutual relationships.

The Epistemological Dimension of Self-Authorship

With the internal voice in the forefront in both the intrapersonal and interpersonal dimensions, participants gained the capacity for implementing their contextual assumptions about how one knows. The key shift, as described in chapter 1 by Gwen, was from how anyone knows to "how *I* know." The "I" had become increasingly distinct as participants worked their way out of the crossroads. Their progress in self-authoring who they were and how they would relate to others dissolved the external barriers to self-authoring their beliefs. The struggle in self-authoring who they were also revealed that all perspectives were not equal, ushering out the ability to achieve genuine self-authorship from the vantage point of independent epistemic assumptions. As was the case in other dimensions, the journey to self-authorship was a gradual one.

Deciding What to Believe

Reginald was still wrestling with his beliefs near the end of seminary. He shared his experience with an assignment and how it affected him:

> I was just really struggling to write down the actual "what did I believe?" So what I thought had been a breakthrough in that one year—I guess I realized that it's a continual struggle to be

consistent in terms of getting out your own ideas. I think the nature of the breakthrough was a combination of things. One was that I finally was able to accept that I could have creative, new ideas and present them. I could accept that in a process of previous knowledge, of being able to do research. Now I finally understand that supporting my ideas is not this awful thing that I have to do just because someone else told me to do that. Before it was sort of like a nuisance. I finally realized the importance of that. So I felt good that the creative process does not necessarily have to be new and totally unique. I think that was the breakthrough. And then that gave me a little bit more confidence in what I had to say.

Reginald discovered that self-authorship extended beyond coming up with a new idea to supporting its importance. He also realized that self-authorship did not require totally original knowledge but rather what he thought in the context of existing knowledge. These realizations allowed him to proceed to author his beliefs, as he described:

I guess it was, "Do you really believe this?" a self-questioning. No real books to fall back on. I mean, I could fall back on someone else, but that was what *they* really believed. But when I fell back on my paper, the only person I had to ask was *me*. And I had to say, "Yes, that's what I really believe." Basically I found who I liked, who had similar thoughts to myself in terms of some of the things, again that research idea, doing some background work, seeing what other people thought. And realizing that I did have something there to begin with long before I ever took the class. And then drawing that out, "What is that, really?" In fact, I found out that that paper I did before was really my theology, a beginning of it, the theology of relationship. So I had something going already; I didn't have a name to it. I guess it's a naming process, gathering thoughts that you have about a certain subject, a certain group of knowledge events is what we can call it, then naming it. And naming it as my own and validating it.

Through continually asking himself what he really believed Reginald was able to pull out ideas he had been constructing, merge them with existing knowledge, name the outcome and claim it for his own. This construction of his beliefs, and of the boundaries that identified him that he described earlier (see chapter 4), readied him for taking his place as a community leader after seminary.

While Reginald was figuring out his beliefs in order to function as a pastor, other participants were thinking about spiritual issues as part of their belief systems to guide life decisions. Barry raised the notion of spirituality as he struggled with the marriage decision discussed earlier, saying:

The one thing you don't choose [as a child] is religion. At college there was an absence of religion. It had been forced upon me, and I needed a break. Then you come back to "what are my beliefs?" That's why that takes the longest. It is the most difficult question; nobody has answers for it, but there are a thousand out there! Mohammed or Brigham Young—who's right? It is not a rational thought; a belief—a feeling, or an emotion. You can't touch a spiritual being; that is difficult. That will continue evolving.

And it did continue evolving. Barry raised spirituality again in more detail after he married and was anticipating children in the future:

One thing that is an issue—not major—is we come from different beliefs in some areas—I'm Roman Catholic, she is Presbyterian. It is interesting how we deal with, talk about that. We've been going to Catholic masses, and she said, "Let's try others." I'm open to that. I'm not a real practicing Catholic, because there are certain things I feel are difficult. If I have a daughter, I don't know if I can raise her in the Catholic church [due to their views on women]. It is very important to me overall—when my dad passed away when I was ten, the church was there for me. If it is a more liberal Catholic church, then I may be more willing. We have talked, she doesn't want them in Catholic school. I went to public schools and was fine. Our number one priority will be our children.

Barry still was not certain how to merge his thoughts about women and tenets of the Catholic church, or how to handle differing beliefs between him and his wife. Because the Catholic church had served him well, he was still drawn to it, but his emerging beliefs were clearly going to take precedence over those feelings.

Al had been thinking about spirituality and talking about it in our conversations since soon after college. By his late twenties he had settled the question of faith in his life. He described it in talking about the way he thought about decisions:

I don't second-guess decisions; that has changed. I used to have stomach trouble! I've gotten better at this over the last three to five years. I came to the realization that it isn't worth it. The role of religion and Christ in my life is part of this. Worrying isn't going to change anything. There is a poem by—I can't remember—but the last line is something like 10 percent is what happens, 90 percent is how we respond. That is the attitude I try to take. Looking too far back and too far ahead is pointless. This attitude, and religion, alters goals and what is really important. I major on the majors and minor on the minors. If you keep what is really important in perspective, the daily grind doesn't get to you that much. Keeping things that matter in focus yields a sense of peace and calm; you don't need to get worked up. That alone isn't it; it is both ideas—a combination of knowing Christ is there and a way of thinking that you have to take on. Maybe I just don't need to understand everything. That is one of the struggles I have. I'm still working on that. It is tough because I like to know why; I'm a fixer, solution kind of guy—I like to know the variables so I can deal with them. If there are no variables, it is tough to deal.

Al's comments reveal that his beliefs about Christ are a part of his self-authorship as they combine with his way of thinking about life. He chose what to believe but still hesitated giving up understanding everything. He authored a way to know even in the absence of the variables he wished were present.

Living with One's Beliefs

Deciding one's beliefs precipitated living them out in every day life. Many participants conveyed that this was not always easy. Heather spoke most directly to the stress of living her beliefs:

It has been a bad time for me to be struggling with things I believe. My strong opinion about responsibilities we have to others has led to my career choice and volunteer work. I still believe it, but it is tougher to hold onto those emotionally. It is easier to just to not live that way. Teaching is a thankless job most days. I had the worst crisis with my little sister this past week. I've known her for six years; intuitively I know I have done some good. It [the crisis] deflated me emotionally this week. This was one of those weeks when I wondered why I left a good paying job [in business] for this heartache. The path you choose for yourself is hard. Bottom line, where I am today, that emotional stress makes me wonder whether I should go back into social isolation, an easier way than what I've chosen. Closing off problems of others would be easier. There have been days when I shut down. I don't know; I never felt like I couldn't keep going.

Heather's commitment to her beliefs remained strong, yet she questioned whether she could continue with the stress they caused. Her stress was heightened by on-going difficulties with her biological sister (mentioned earlier in this chapter) and other family issues. She was able to persist in her goals, primarily by continuing the process of self-authorship.

Others were finding it challenging to live their beliefs as well. Lowell spoke to the issue in the context of his work in the foreign service:

> Standing up for what's right. That is not taught much in school; they teach you *how* to do things. They don't teach you how to balance how to do it technically with what your boss thinks. If you think it's right, you know in your heart it is right, how will your suggestion play out? I have experience with this. Trying to get what you think is the right idea across without angering the boss. Events that have occurred through my last tour . . . disagreements—sometimes you stand up for what you know is right and it can get people in trouble. I'm trying to tell him this isn't good for us. It hasn't been well received, but knew I was 100 percent right; when the boss went to a conference, they talked about people getting into trouble for doing what he wanted to do. He didn't thank me. Even though I was right, and he acknowledged it in an indirect manner, his patience for me was cut short. But I couldn't do anything else; it was right. You learn to understand that if you make a decision to challenge the boss and it becomes apparent that he doesn't want to be challenged, you have to understand going in that it could have negative ramifications.

Lowell understood from experience that his standing up for what he thought was right had negative ramifications, yet he still did it. Maintaining his standards was more important than the external forces brought to bear by his boss. Lowell was implementing insights he had gained from the dissolution of his marriage—not to sacrifice yourself. What he knew "in his heart" was what he had self-authored about what was right.

Barry faced ethical dilemmas in his work too. Barry's work involved creating promotional toys used in fast-food restaurants. He encountered numerous ethical issues in this line of work, as he explained:

> We are dealing with toys for children. We want to make sure it is a safe product, that the standards are being met. We use a manufacturer in China; I'm going back there soon—I was there three years ago. The way things are done there, it is basically going a hundred years back—into a time machine. Ethically, you separate yourself—it is a different culture, they have different needs than our country has. This may be a rationalization, it probably is. You walk into factories, thousands of mostly young women have certificates saying they are over 16, the legal working age. Looking at that and saying my God; then talking to people in Hong Kong, and they tell me their choices. Killing their first-born if female; now they don't do

that because they can work in a factory. If you went back [in time] into Northeastern US, we had child labor, rough conditions, no infrastructure, a huge immigrant workforce. It is the same issues—the early signs of capitalism. Environment is not a high priority either; they want to use resources and get money to get a higher standard of living. The ethics in that is a test; what am I doing here? Yes, I rationalized it; thought about our country and what CNN would say 100 years ago about the exploitation of America. If we didn't do that, where would we be today? You have to look at all this in the context of the growth curve. I'm looking at their own growth curve; not fair to compare them to us. They are doing it exponentially. We can't tell them how do to it, that is hypocritical. Same issue with rain forests; we've never been to South America, how can we tell them not to use their resources? We used ours and that is why we are where we are today. I have deep beliefs on this. There has to be a balance.

Barry speculated that his acceptance of using the Chinese labor force might be rationalization, yet his thinking revealed that he was analyzing it from a contextual point of view. Unwilling to judge other countries in the context of his own country's history, he constructed a view of the role his company played in the lives of other people. His ability to construct his beliefs in context helped him answer the ethical question for himself.

Living with one's beliefs sometimes meant career changes to bring work life into line with self-authored beliefs. The stories told next are in sharp contrast to those in earlier chapters that recounted career decisions. In chapter 3 I recounted Anne's taking a promotion because her boss suggested it and going for her CPA for largely external reasons. In her late twenties, her decisions were very different, as she explained:

I am pursuing my MBA to augment my career. Accounting is great now, but I don't know if I want to do it forever. A lot of things interest me; opening my own business, computers. I've kind of stopped for the moment. I used to stress about what I would be doing in future—now I'm enjoying the moment. We have talked about kids, but we aren't ready. Even that has kind of changed. If I had gotten pregnant earlier, I would have had a fit. If it happened now, it would be okay even though we are not ready. I'm a lot more relaxed about everything. It is nice. I feel like I have this inner peace almost—it is hard to describe— I'm happy with marriage, family, career, house. I have what I want in life. I stopped stressing as much about what I'll be doing. This is pretty recent. It is hard to describe this peaceful feeling.

Anne's becoming the author of her own beliefs led to changes in how she thought about her career. Knowing herself helped her open herself to new interests and to enjoying other aspects of her life. The peacefulness of self-authorship was new to her. She seemed to be describing the makings of the internal home Gwen spoke of in chapter 2.

For some participants self-authorship made taking risks to change jobs possible. Andrew demonstrated this as he bought his own business at age 26:

> The biggest issue was security versus what I wanted to be happy. I could have stayed at my old job, but I made the decision that it wasn't what I wanted out of life. I wanted to be in charge myself, call the shots, try out my ideas. In my own business, I can react to things on a daily basis, and see the outcome of my decisions. Another issue was moving away from family. I had spent my life there; it was not a challenge. I was excited to go somewhere else, to have more things to explore. I'm rational to a point; but I'm more of an intuitive decision-maker than a rational one. If you are completely rational, you can't try new ideas. If you rationalize everything out, the risks outweigh the rewards. When the timing is right for me, I do it. Pursuing my dream of owning my own business may not make sense from rational standpoint. But I knew I could make it work.

Andrew's willingness to take risks was in the service of the dreams he had constructed about what he wanted out of life. He trusted himself to know he could make a business work.

Will also trusted himself that he could change careers and make it work. The change resulted from a change in his personal life:

> Not long after our daughter was born, my wife desired to work less. It wasn't possible; she made $10,000 more than I did. We liked the house we had [recently purchased.] Her desire not to work meant that I had to make more money. Simultaneously an offer for another type of position came in; it was twice as much as I was making. The potential in a year or two would increase beyond what both of us could make. It included an opportunity to get another degree, and met her desire to stay home with the baby. It met the need to make more money. We like to travel and we need to pay for the little one's college. It was interesting talking through how to do me going back to school and trying to do daycare. Our daughter was at daycare for two months while we decided. Once we got comfortable with both doing part-time work for awhile while I went back to school, then we figured out how to do it. If you want to do something badly, you can do it. Taking a big risk doing this; I could fail in this new position, but

I don't think so. We have taken out loans to make this work. If it
didn't work, we would figure out another plan.

Will and his spouse each expressed their desires in the situation and worked
together to develop plans that would meet their collective needs. Will shared
that in his work he was paid to calculate risks. Becoming the author of his own
life, he was willing to calculate risks in both his work and his personal life.

The Inherent Uncertainty in Establishing Beliefs

As is evident in these stories of what to believe and how to live out those
beliefs, authoring one's beliefs was an on-going process. Participants made the
best decisions possible in particular contexts, but were aware of the on-going
uncertainty in a contextual world. Lindsey conveyed this notion in his distinction between being an expert and an authority in his economics work:

> In your career, you have to learn the information; you need to
> know it. I'm being paid to learn and understand this; how these
> relationships work. I get calls all the time asking how accounts
> are put together; these people are smart and pick up quickly. I
> spend a lot of time explaining how I do things. When someone
> calls and I don't have the answer, it is tough to say "I don't
> know." I'm supposed to be an expert. But I am honest, I don't
> know. I consider myself an authority—not an expert. Expert is a
> few years beyond authority. Someone who can tell you every-
> thing about their numbers but also about the numbers used to
> build their numbers. I know how I compile exports of travel, but
> I sometimes don't know how assumptions of the source data
> are made. You couldn't expect to be expert in less than a few
> years. I am pretty confident in what I am doing; I consider
> myself an authority on my numbers.

Lindsey knew what he was doing, but knew there was more to learn. He
would not claim expert status, but he did claim authority.

Al addressed the on-going uncertainty in medical diagnosis in his rotations
through different types of medicine:

> It is a different thought process now than in the first two years
> [of medical school]. In those years it was here is the disease and
> everything you need to know. Now, somebody comes in and
> has symptoms; you have to think of which diseases fit those
> symptoms. It is backwards. People don't come in and say what
> they have; they tell you their symptoms. There are 30 million
> things it can be. You have to come up with a diagnosis; you ask
> the person questions to narrow it down. I'm relearning the

thought process. It is hard to do; I'm still trying to get the hang of it. Still need to be aware of all those diseases to put them into your differential diagnosis.

Al had learned the content of the initial years of medical school and now was learning to think differently about that content. He raised the issue of uncertainty in trying to make judgments about his patients' health:

I'm not that comfortable making judgments; there is always uncertainty. You have to get used to it, you have to do what you know to do and use your best judgment. Right now I don't have confidence in my knowledge base; I'm not to that point yet. I don't know enough. I wouldn't be comfortable with the final decision. Even as a resident, you can be the final decision-maker; others say it is good to get that experience. It forces you to learn more; when you are in that situation you are going to work through it before you make a plan. Now I can take my best shot, and my doc is watching my back. Being in that situation will force me to learn more. I need to start doing that more now.

Al had extensive knowledge at this point but knew he needed more given the seriousness of the decisions he would make as a physician.

Asking the question "what do I really believe?" and sorting through the possible answers led participants to construct internal belief systems. These systems became the driving force of their actions, even when acting on beliefs was difficult. Decisions in all realms of life—career, ethics, spirituality, relationships—hinged on this developing internal belief system. Often experiences were analyzed for how they contributed to the on-going development of the belief system. Becoming the author of their beliefs brought with it the realization that the process is never done and the "answers" are never entirely clear. Participants' growing confidence in the evolving internal belief system made the inherent uncertainty in contextual knowing manageable.

Integrating the Three Dimensions of Self-Authorship

I used stories in this chapter to bring various dimensions of self-authorship to the forefront for closer scrutiny; hearing the details directly from the participants furthers in-depth understanding of the complexities of their journeys to self-authorship. Yet it is clear from the collective journeys that the dimensions are inevitably intertwined. I close the chapter with a story that illustrates the integrated nature of the three dimensions at the juncture of authoring one's own life.

Dawn: Creating Truth in Character

A theater major in college, Dawn accepted an internship in theater upon graduation. She described it as a "development process" and in doing so articulated how she simultaneously authored herself and her work:

> I have had opportunities to play more than one type of charac-
> ter. The thing that's involved in that is exploring different parts
> of yourself, learning about how many different types of people
> you are within yourself and being able to apply that to a script
> that someone has written. And along with your imagination,
> you create these different personas. As far as the character
> aspect—I think there's a lot of self-learning that goes on contin-
> ually. And that's one of the things that I think that always fasci-
> nates me about this business is you never stand still. You're
> always progressing; you're always moving forward, learning
> new things about yourself, learning new ways to present your
> ideas to a group of people. Then that kind of melts into your
> technique. Oftentimes you have to get to a certain emotional
> level that you can't just create. So there's a process that you
> have to go through, self-disclosure, to some extent. You com-
> bine yourself with what you're given, what you interpret about
> a character. The technique comes in as transferring all that is
> within you to this character, your abilities to speak the charac-
> ter's truth from, probably, your truth. There are a lot of tech-
> niques in acting that not everybody can use. You pick and
> choose the ones that are right for you. As far as my technique
> has been concerned this year, it's like getting to emotional
> states that I've never been able to get to before. So working on
> things like that, because this last play that I did was a very pas-
> sionate, a very emotional play. Basically by the end of the play
> I was totally broken down and vulnerable and crying, which is
> not something that I'm accustomed to in my daily life. But just
> finding ways to get to that level of emotion, given what is going
> on in the play, given circumstances where I have been like that
> before, and translating all of that to this character.

Dawn's creation of characters in her acting comes from her on going authoring of herself and translating that to the character. She elaborated further:

> To bring out the truth in a character, I think you have to have an
> immense understanding of all the little truths within yourself.
> So a lot of it comes from you. And that's probably some of the
> scariest work that you have to do in theater because you are
> really exposing yourself. And you have to be willing to say,
> "Within the realm of this character, this is my exposed self,"

and know that the audience isn't going to judge you specifically. They're judging the character, but you have to be willing to put your heart and soul into it. There are outside influences that create a character because you have someone else's opinion, like in the director and the playwright, kind of guiding you. But then you have yourself to kind of give it that life. [You] bring all of the written and spoken ideas about the character to life, which gives it the heartbeat so to speak, and brings this character to life.

Dawn's passion for acting and creating characters, despite the emotional difficulty involved, was clear. The reason for her passion was also related to self-authorship:

Acting has been the one thing that I discovered myself that I could do and wanted to do, not something that someone said, "You should be a doctor because of whatever reason." It's been the one thing that I could latch onto and make my very own. That's a great feeling. I think that's probably why I'm so passionate about it, because it's like, "This is all mine. Nobody can do this for me; nobody can give me the answers. It's all mine to do and to create and be." So that's so exciting and makes it all worth it.

Dawn was equally passionate about the continual self-authorship that acting required. She described it further:

I have really started to open more and more and discover this intense passion I have for whatever it is I do. It's kind of a self-discovery of powers. I'm doing something that I've always dreamt about doing and never thought was possible. But here I am doing it, and it's completely possible. And that is so empowering. It just keeps unfolding and gets more intense and more passionate as I go along. That's remarkable. That just really keeps me going. This has given me such a different outlook than I've ever had in my life before. I think a little bit because it's forced me to discover things about myself that I hadn't really taken time to discover before. It's one continuous process— discovering myself helps my acting and by doing acting I discover myself.

Her continual self-discovery contributed to authoring her sense of self and her ability to know:

The more you discover about yourself, the more you can become secure with it. And that obviously leads to greater self-confidence because you become comfortable with who you really are. My confidence level is so much better than it ever has been. I'm more willing to express my ideas and take chances expressing my ideas. "Who cares what people think?" sort of thing. When you're not as self-confident, you're afraid that people are going to laugh at what you think or you're afraid that they're going to think you're stupid—it's all those petty, little things that inhibit us. Whereas when you're confident, you are more willing to say, "This is my opinion; this is why I hold this opinion. You may agree with it or not, but this is what—with my mind I have formulated this opinion and that's how I think and feel." I'm not as afraid to be willing to say that because of what I am this is how I feel. I try not to step on people's toes with my opinions, be offensive about it, but if someone asks me for my opinion or advice or how I think and feel about something, I will definitely tell them. And I think self-awareness too, because you realize that it doesn't really matter if other people agree with you or not. You can think and formulate ideas for yourself and ultimately that's what's important. You have a mind and you can use it. That's probably the most important thing, regardless of the content of what your thoughts and opinions are. I suppose it's very idealistic to think that everybody can see that. It's the fact that you can form an opinion that's more important than the opinion itself. But I don't think that happens. So it's kind of a self-confidence and self-awareness thing.

Clearly, Dawn's discovery of self also led to viewing herself as a knower. Once she became comfortable with herself, she gained confidence, which in turn led to her ability to think and formulate ideas for herself—in her words "You have a mind and you can use it."

Despite Dawn's enthusiasm for acting, in our eighth-year interview she reported that she needed a respite from it to replenish herself. She had engaged in an intense show in which she and a few colleagues wrote, produced, and performed a play that held personal meaning for them. Subsequently she decided to take a year hiatus from acting and travel to Australia, which she described as an on-going part of her self-discovery:

As far as acting is concerned, this is an "I'm going to go find myself" trip. I was not able to put some things into my work that I felt were necessary. Because I didn't know how to access them. To get to an emotional level, to give, to search out parts of my soul that were needed to give to a role—break down insecurities, trust yourself, trust people you work with. I wasn't able to do that. Traveling seemed like a good way to do that—enjoy myself, see the world, explore myself in a completely different environment—see how I handle things, what my strengths and weaknesses are.

Dawn explained that her trip to Australia would be an attempt to find other aspects of herself that would help her in acting. She hoped her experience would "allow for self-realization and growth and freedom from insecurities I've had before. Getting to know myself so I know I can access things when I'm doing a character, feeling safe doing that." She also believed that this self-exploration would be an on-going part of her life in acting:

> Life is a continual process of self-discovery. Acting is basically a celebration of life in a way—bring life to life on the stage. Any artist worth her or his weight will be on a path of continual self-discovery. To keep your work entertaining and fresh, you need to keep on that path of growing and changing. I'll probably be doing more things like this as I continue in my career.

It came as no surprise to me a few years later that Dawn reported having climbed Mt. Kilimanjaro as another act of self-discovery. Dawn's story articulates the process of authoring herself through authoring her characters. Authoring who she was allowed her to accept that she had a mind and could use it. And she did use it in her continual self-discovery. The confidence emerging from her self-authorship allowed her to be comfortable with herself, avoid letting others' perspectives overshadow hers, express her own knowledge, and face the inherent uncertainty of contextual knowing.

Summary

Participants' particular life circumstances and experiences mediated which of the driving questions emerged as most salient for them. Despite variation in which questions and developmental dimensions were in the foreground, the move toward self-authorship in any dimension brought the other driving questions into play. Just as gaining perspective on the self initiated a revisioning of relationships, making relationship choices often sparked self-reflection. Similarly, deciding what to believe sometimes necessitated self-reflection whereas self-reflection was often essential in living one's beliefs. Living one's beliefs also led to renegotiation of relations with others. Self-authorship became the core of all three dimensions of development. The evolving consistency that came with developing an internal system for making meaning of oneself, relations with others, and knowledge led to an internal foundation for meaning-making, described in the next chapter.

6

THE INTERNAL
FOUNDATION

The continual process of authoring all three dimensions of their lives resulted, for many participants, in an internal foundation from which to guide their lives. As frameworks were constructed to answer the questions about what to believe, who to be, and how to relate to others, the frameworks became solidified and comprehensive systems of belief. The framework for "who I am" solidified into a solid sense of self that made participants feel "personally grounded" and able to be true to themselves in all dimensions of their lives. This sense of self contributed to their ability to choose core beliefs and integrate them into an internal belief system that guided their lives. The security of the internal self and belief system afforded them a new vantage point from which to engage in authentic, mutual relationships with others. The solidifying of the internal self, belief system, and approach to relationships created both a solid foundation and openness to ambiguity and change. Becoming comfortable with the internal voice yielded a security to explore others' perspectives; complex ways of knowing meant ambiguity and uncertainty would always be commonplace. Thus from the internal foundation participants were able to develop their ability to know intuitively and to accept life as it came.

In their late-twenties, some participants described feelings of peace and satisfaction stemming from this internal foundation. Others were still working on building this internal system. Numerous versions of the internal foundation emerged from the stories because participants constructed their unique frameworks from their unique experiences. A return to Evan's and Kelly's stories illustrates the outcome of participants' work on becoming the authors of their own lives.

Evan's solid sense of self—gained from the self-authorship work he described in chapter 5—allowed him to settle in comfortably with various aspects of his life and organize them in ways that were workable to him, yet remain open to change. After three years of working in the city, work had lost its hold on his life even though it was still important. He explained:

> My work role doesn't define me. I take the train in every day, for three years now. Taking the train is a physical separation between work and personal life. I transform from one thing to the other; two separate lives. The train ride is 30 minutes—I sleep through some of it. I wake up a different person, transformed, my game face on, uniform, do what you gotta do. When done, go back on the train, reverse transformation and I'm out. I don't give it another thought. I never dream about work, never discuss it with my wife. I've come to enjoy the activities that define life as how I like to view it. I like work, I would keep working if I won the lottery. I like coming in and being involved. I shut it off, go do my thing. I still play hockey every week—as I've done for 27 years!

Evan had put his work life in perspective with his overall life, based on his ability to "define life as how I like to view it." His internal foundation left him more open than ever to learning new things, as he described in his work:

> I thought I was doing well last year, but I look back, and realize I knew so little. It continues that way each year. I'm glad; it is humbling. My dad used to tell me when I was a kid, "there is always somebody bigger than you that will kick your butt." I keep that in mind. I try to improve what I already know, so I can move on to the next level. At the same time keeping prior responsibility, taking it with me, adding, building onto that.

Evan's ability to define life and himself also led to becoming accustomed to change and expecting it:

> Now we just kind of accept these things; nothing ever stays the same. If you expect it, it is easier. A lot of things I am incredibly inflexible about. As far as other people and other things, I don't try to control. I've gradually gotten that way. The only way is to experience this and to see what happens when you don't take that route. The experience you accumulate can be painful but necessary. It adds to your repertoire of being able to deal with

things in the future; been through it, lived, know what is coming
next. It is less frightening, less mysterious.

Certainly knowing what is coming next helps deal with things, but Evan's
foundation within himself helped him remain comfortable during the major
changes he was experiencing. One was a tragic event involving his father that
he mentioned for the first time in our twelfth interview, although it probably
had been a central part of his earlier shift to expecting things to go wrong. He
explained:

> My dad is still in jail; I visit him once a month. The trial was two
> years ago. At first it was a real drag; it costs me $300 a month to
> support him. That stinks; I'm really the only one that takes care
> of his business. My brother moved away and doesn't participate
> in it. Luckily I make enough money that it doesn't affect me. He
> is appealing, so it will probably be a couple more years. I am not
> gonna fund his appeal; I'll support him in other ways. I buy his
> cigarettes, but I told him I wouldn't throw money away on attor-
> neys. I don't want to be in control of that. Non-productive for me
> to be over involved. My parents divorced before that, so mom
> doesn't have to deal with it.

The other was a more positive change. Evan had resolved not to bring children
into the world given his assessment of overpopulation and society problems.
He did not change this stance, but as he described, he became a father anyway:

> It was not planned! If I had to plan it, it never would have hap-
> pened! It's giving in a little bit to growing up; there's no going
> back after that! I take it seriously—once you are locked into
> something like that, that's it. I'm enjoying it. It took me a little bit
> of time to accept that this was happening—however right or
> wrong that may sound. Once I was able to come to terms with
> that, it really didn't affect my thinking that much—I already had
> a whole bunch of mouths to feed, so it was not that much of an
> adjustment. People who don't have animals might not grasp the
> concept of what I'm trying to say. It is not that far off from rais-
> ing a puppy—on a schedule, responsibility for making sure per-
> son is taken care of. It's a little bit more expensive! It was a mat-
> ter of time for just realizing there is no getting out of this.
> Eventually, in back of my head, I guess, it was exciting. It was
> something that really frightened me for a long time—I don't
> know why. It is such a serious thing—being responsible for
> somebody forever. It was different than getting married, if that
> was not right, you could get out of it if push came to shove.
> Only a semi-permanent thing, realistically. Once this went into

effect, you can't undo it. Once a child is born, you are attached to another person through the child. Permanence, responsibility, always played a part in my willingness to go through with it. I knew if my wife didn't just force me, I would never do it. I needed that shove. She just did it—I don't ask, I don't even want to know!

Evan's internal belief system did not lead him to actively seek to become a parent; yet when his wife became pregnant, his internal belief system helped him come to terms with the idea of parenthood. His foundation also mediated how his differences with his wife were playing out. That, too, seemed more settled, as Evan described:

We still have a lot of differences. Yes, it used to cause a lot of problems, but now it doesn't. We came close to calling it quits a couple times, but not that close. She does her part; works hard. I don't know too many other people who would put up with hockey and my family. I am not the easiest person to live with. We do our own things and don't get worked up about it.

Evan was comfortable with his life circumstances, with himself, and with his never-ending capacity to keep growing.

When you're a kid, you think you are developed but you aren't. At this age you realize you aren't. Experience level helps you to become comfortable with yourself—realize you have lived through certain events and either have taken it on the chin or given in, but you're still here and still going. You realize you can live through certain things. When Kristy was having the baby, she dilated to 10 centimeters before taking pain medication— she was freaking out! I was like, I know you are in a lot of pain and this sounds schmucky, but lots of people live through this. I open my mind to learn, you never know what is coming down. I call it floating on the waves. I kind of imagine myself in the water, a Cancerian thing to do, going with the direction of the ocean, going up and down with the waves. Knowing that there are times at the top, other times the waves are above your head. I don't try to control it, it is impossible. Taking that into account allows me to relax and deal with things. You can't control things that happen to you, but there is no reason why I shouldn't control what I can. I'm not ashamed to organize. Why shouldn't your house look the way you want it?

The threads of Evan's journey are consistent—his love of learning, his willingness to reflect on his growth, his love of organizing his life! Yet the shift from being a superhero (chapter 3) to floating on the waves is dramatic. It is the shift from external sources of success to his internal mind, voice and self. Floating on the waves and controlling less is possible because his internal foundation grounds him.

As participants worked to solidify and strengthen their ways of making meaning, they became simultaneously more flexible and more grounded. Kelly continued to place her faith at the center of how she made meaning. She shared:

> My faith is the most important thing in my life, the center of everything. It has made me more patient and understanding, slower to be accusatory, slower to judge. I am quicker to find out why. Those characteristics affect every aspect of my life. I am more at peace, know who I am more now. I feel like every year I come more into myself. I thought I'd have it all together by now! Every year, I wonder if I'll ever figure it out. When I master something, something else crops up. Faith is at the center and belongs there.

Kelly's faith helped her deal with a situation in which she felt betrayed. She bought a house from a couple her family knew and shortly after moving in discovered that it needed a new roof. She was angry that this had not been disclosed to her. Yet she was determined to do what she felt was right in the situation. She explained:

> I have a better self-image than I have ever had in life. People are going to have their perceptions, but I have to be firm in my convictions and do what I know is right. My family philosophy is don't do something halfway; do it right. I found out not everyone is like that. I have to be flexible. I held a grudge against this couple who owned the house until two weeks ago. She is a good friend of my aunt who I am close to. I felt like they misrepresented themselves; they knew how bad the roof was. But society today is too sue happy; I'm not going to do it. Take what life gives you and take it as learning experience. The owners are nice Christian people, their opinion of quality work is not mine. I can't hold that against them. The town is to too small so I'm going to let it go. When I was on the Deacon's board, I learned that people perceive actions all different ways and react in all different ways. I might not always understand why they are doing something but I'm in a responsible position, have to deal with it, come to a solution or conclusion. Have to be flexible. Being a kindergarten teacher has really helped me be flexible! You can't work with small kids and not be willing to shift the lesson. It really hasn't shaken my self-image at all.

The fact that this situation, which was financially costly, did not shake Kelly's self-image conveys the strength of the internal foundation in young adults' meaning making. Kelly elaborated on being comfortable with who she is, saying:

> My values are the same, but I think every year I get more of a sense of self-worth. It has been a struggle, in high school I was extremely shy. Through four years at college I experimented with a lot I shouldn't have, it continued after college. Through all that I found out who I was and was not. It culminated in me turning the corner with my faith. I am extremely comfortable with who I am—not as worried about what people think of me as of what I think of myself—an important realization. Faith was a significant event in knowing myself. It created a comfort zone and a sense of purpose, from there everything else fell into place around that. The puzzle is not done, but the pieces are falling into place. The puzzle won't ever be done. All different situations can cause a person to turn a corner.

Kelly acknowledged that being comfortable with herself and centered around her faith did not mean there were no struggles. She struggled to deal with the betrayal she perceived and the feelings it sparked for her:

> I am still dealing with the betrayal part—to let go of the burning anger. I just had to simmer on it for awhile—the longer time went by, I was seeing this as not a positive part of my life. I am definitely a person who says the glass is half full rather than half empty. It was bringing me down—nothing constructive was coming from this anger. Once I decided not to use the justice system, I just thought, "I've got to figure out a way to let things go." I read the Bible a lot about forgiveness, turning other cheek; turned to that as an example to help me. See the words, try to say the words, it is easier to say the words than to feel it! Easy to say forgive and forget—I'm still dealing with forgetting. I prayed about it, try to be positive toward her, but it is still stilted. I don't want to say I hold grudges, but I think I am! It is hard for me to deal with that side of my personality, especially when I feel I've been wronged. I had to deal with that—don't want to be that way if I have a choice. I try to teach myself, force myself to not think this way; yet these little nasty thoughts just keep coming inside!

Kelly continued to explore these issues, saying that there was always room to grow:

> I will never be satisfied, there is something more out there—I am not through growing and learning. I've not reached my

capacity at all—I hope I still feel like this when I'm 60. The world is an infinite source of knowledge, experience. I'm having a great time watching my parents—they are three years from retirement. They want to take a boat up the Amazon River. It is neat to see how they want to expand their world, expand their knowledge. There is so much out there. Life is a journey. Some of the big hurdles have been achieved. I am learning who I am and what I want to be with myself. Part of me is kind of upset at not having family yet, part of me is thankful that I've had this time.

Kelly's comfort with herself not only allowed her to continue to explore, but to understand her strengths and weaknesses more clearly:

I see myself as more of a realist regarding who I am and my strengths and weaknesses than I did two years ago. I always want to think of myself as being the best. I think I'm becoming better at dealing with weaknesses—learning how to overcome those more than I used to. Rather than seeing self as all positive, I'm seeing myself as a good person, but I still need to work on things. I never dealt with that as much; I was quicker to put weaknesses on others. This shift is due to issues I'm dealing with now—being a homeowner, my experience as a teacher—they are a lot more—what is the word I am searching for? Bigger issues than where do we go on Friday night. Decisions I'm making these days are much more serious and life changing than they were five years ago.

Encountering the difficult realities of life, and needing to face them as a responsible person, helped Kelly continue to strengthen the foundation of her inner meaning making. She was able to reflect on how she thought about herself and take responsibility for her own need for improvement. The stronger her sense of faith and her sense of self became, the more open she remained to learning more and analyzing herself more closely. The solid sense of self that came from internal meaning making left her secure to face the uncertainty, disappointment, and complexity of adult life.

Evan and Kelly described core beliefs about life they had constructed and actively used to make meaning of all aspects of their lives. These core beliefs were self-authored and came to define an internal belief system. That system had a consistent core, yet was open to expansion. Kelly, Evan, and others who had arrived at a foundation were open to growing and new experiences, in part because their internal belief system offered security. It also offered a solid, internal sense of self that was not threatened by new experience. This made participation in mutual relationships possible. Mark's (chapter 2) phrase "To thine own self be true" became the mantra in the late twenties. The internal voice won the long, arduous battle between external control and self-authorship and participants rejoiced in the peace the internal voice brought to the complexities of adult life. Many participants described having an internal belief system as "coming home."

The combination of dynamics across dimensions left participants feeling "grounded." Their stories reveal that they were grounded in their internal belief systems and the internal self-definitions that accompanied those belief systems. This grounding afforded them the opportunity to construct mutual relationships in which they could function interdependently with others. These connections were strengthened by the clarity of the self they brought to the relationship and their consistency in acting according to that internal self. Unlike in previous phases of the journey where a particular dimension of development could be pulled apart from the others for in-depth exploration, the three dimensions were tightly interwoven by the internal foundation phase of the journey. Thus the stories that follow are organized around key characteristics of the internal foundation rather than the three dimensions.

Personally Grounded

Some participants used the phrase "inner strength" to convey how they felt in their late-twenties. The phrase captures the essence of the internal foundation, an entity that had solidified beyond the evolving internal self-definition that had been growing in previous years. The difference is subtle but listening carefully to their stories revealed a qualitatively different place in the self-authorship journey. As was to be expected, it came from different directions for different people.

Celebrating the Self: Intrapersonally Grounded

Dawn's foundation solidified as a result of her self-discovery trip to Australia. She explained how it affected her:

> I spent two months on my own backpacking around the country. It was a great experience for me on a multitude of levels. On a personal level it was an incredible journey. I was going to explore myself and I accomplished that. I did things I never thought I would do. I camped in the mountains by myself in the middle of desert. I traveled by myself, and I spent four weeks on a sheep farm, working for a family in exchange for room and board. It is an experience I'll never forget. I can be very independent if I have to be. I noticed that if you listen to the world

around you, you can learn a great deal about where you are and what you are doing. It gave me a chance to develop my intuitive nature; I never planned ahead for anything—just wake up and decide each day. It was a tremendous feeling of freedom, a sense of doing it on my own. I came back, felt more self confident, at peace with who I was and reasons why I did things. I had a much clearer sense of self. When you put yourself in a foreign environment you quickly learn how to make the decisions that are the best. In daily life we make a lot of decisions on things that aren't as important. There is a lot of noise in our daily lives—doing your job, thinking about bills, feeding the cat. When you take yourself away from that you realize your existence is all that matters. There is a clarity that almost instantly happens.

The clarity Dawn sensed when the routine noise of her life was absent helped her solidify who she was. She had self-authored her identity prior to this trip but was intentionally seeking further self-discovery. Upon her return she felt at peace with who she was.

Cara was experiencing the same inner strength; it came from different sources, however, than the ones Dawn described. In her late-twenties Cara completed her dissertation, married, and took up kick-boxing. She explained the ways in which these events helped set her foundation:

I feel like a somewhat different person than I did in my twenties. In high school, I was somewhat confident; in my twenties this took a downward swing, and now I'm back to how I used to be. [There were] different pieces up in air—they've come together now. Finishing my dissertation was great—some say it was a let down; it was huge to me. Part of it was getting rid of the negative, getting it off my back; and feeling like, "I did this." It was not the dissertation itself, but just to finish it. I was visualizing myself as—not fragmented as in schizophrenia—just not grounded. I felt like every external event, I was swaying with it. I don't feel that way anymore. I'm not impervious to external events, but I don't feel that way.

Finishing the dissertation was only one part of what helped Cara feel grounded. Her marriage, and some battles that came with it, also contributed:

One thing is like when you marry someone—he is so grounded and stable—when someone loves you despite your flaws—it is an amazing thing. That is how he is. [Our relationship] isn't without problems, but when someone loves you unconditionally, it is healing. It changed my perception of myself. How I see that he sees me, has changed how I see me. Isn't there a theory of social reflection? See yourself mirrored in other people. He came from a fundamental Christian background; I was Catholic. His family liked me, but was not happy. The process of choosing where to get married, how to run our lives—that was another big battle that was going on during my doctoral program. He had to go through a lot to separate from his parents; he hadn't to that point. Going through those battles strengthened me; I could see my values, convictions—this is my life, not run by in-laws. It made me closer to my parents—my parents were ready to say you're an adult. All these little battles really shaped me now, but not for the worst. Helped me to find how I see myself and who I am. That caused initial problems in us—I was horrified when I went to church with them. I was attacking people he loved; we had to work through that. It is settled with us, not with them. If we ever have children, that will be another road. I used to get all wound up—and [his mother] still makes me mad. I used to go around the truth; now I don't care—I just tell her. She was an external event I swayed to; not now.

At the outset of this conversation, it sounded like Cara was defining herself through her husband. And, in fact, his perception of her did alter her perception of herself. However, it becomes apparent that her self-authored values and convictions came to the forefront when controversy arose. She expressed and stayed true to her convictions; she and her husband worked through the problems this caused. Cara's grounding in her internal self-definition helped her express herself in these controversies and the process helped her see even more clearly who she was. Her grounding also made these controversies less traumatic, primarily because she no longer swayed to external events. Cara's story raises an important point about the role of external influence. In becoming the author of their lives, participants' internal voices took precedence over external influence, yet it was still present and they were still pulled by it. Once the foundation was in place, external influence receded even further from their concern. It remained, they acknowledged it, but they refused to get worked up about it. Instead, they made meaning of it in a manner consistent with their internal sense of self.

Finally, Cara's venturing into kick-boxing resolved some issues she had faced for most of her twenties. She described what this was all about:

I started kick-boxing—martial arts. I have always run and jogged—but this made me feel like a stronger person. It's a mix of karate and boxing. I take a class where we do strength training, then drills—punching and kicking—then get a partner to punch and kick, but you are not supposed to hurt people. The great thing is there are men in class; I've been there longer, so I'm paired up with men because they try to keep people at similar levels. I am smaller, so I'm allowed to hit and kick. It has given me better self-confidence and presence—all my life people have commented on my height. "You're small," etc. This related to the whole "I'm weak, not professional enough" aura. That has helped me feel more confident. I carried a 150-pound woman around the gym; I weigh 110. Others at work joke about it—have Cara walk me to the parking lot. That must have been some issue I must have been worried about. People pat me on the head! The other night I was walking to car by myself, and a man said I shouldn't be doing it. He was looking at me as a potential victim. Kick-boxing has helped me. I'm not as weak as people make me out to be. Apparently I had a ton of aggression I didn't realize.

Cara's doubts about herself had been receding slowly as she authored aspects of her life. The kick-boxing seemed to be the final piece of ridding herself of perceived weakness and honoring her competence and confidence.

Although some, like Dawn and Cara, were feeling a sense of peace from their internal foundation, others still encountered dilemmas. Lydia's story is a good example of trying to juggle multiple roles based on the internal foundation. Her comments reveal that the struggle, however, is internal this time:

I've had a lot of struggle since starting my graduate degree—time management, where are priorities, focus, how to spend my time. Where I want to or on activities that in the long run don't match my priority system. I read the seven habits book— here are roles, priorities, time—it should match. I looked at mine—they didn't match. What is the higher priority, grading 150 papers or writing my paper? That is where I struggle. My classes are Saturday and Sunday, ten hours each day, one weekend a month. Get up Monday morning and keep working—no down time. It's a 12-day week. On the second week, my students don't get my best. At first I thought one weekend a month, no big deal. But then all the work that goes along with it—how to fit in a schedule that is already packed. Some part of my life is different from other parts; military people don't know work people, two separate social groups that don't mix—how do you split your time? Then class people, another chunk that doesn't know the other circles. Maintaining circles, I don't know if I'm doing a good job at any of them—there are so many. Which to let go? There are really none to let go. Especially in last three months since my husband left [for military tour], it is a huge problem because everyone thinks I have nothing to do. My schedule is so packed, I have no time to recover before the next day is up and running. It is the biggest inner turmoil. I became a teacher to help other students—that is the core of why I teach. If I've lost that, then what difference does anything else make as far as the profession? The degree is a professional step—am I taking away from part of the profession because I am trying to grow professionally? The principal has put me on district committees because he thinks I have good ideas on math curriculum; I have that due to different district experiences. He is trying to utilize that; it is just another professional strain. Yes I want to do it, grow and learn and carry things on with me; at the same time, how much can one person do? And still do things well? Too many irons in the fire—some are burning and some are underdone. I'm not doing anything well because I'm doing everything. It is coming to a head—I'm pregnant, so what good am I doing myself and child—exhausted and not taking care of myself. Where are my priorities? What to accomplish this year? I don't know that there is any answer to time and priority questions. I'm due in June—we are moving in June. Full plate! It has been a huge inner battle. I feel it because I see light at the end of the tunnel—sometimes an oncoming train, sometimes the sun.

The essence of Lydia's struggle was conflicts within her own priorities. She valued teaching and learning to be a better teacher and these two values conflicted. She valued her circles of friends but spending time with them conflicted with other priorities. She described her battle as internal; this is what distinguishes it from struggles that existed prior to self-authorship. Her story carries no hint of external influence; her struggles are totally within herself. So, despite being in a period of struggle, Lydia still exhibited a strong internal foundation. Lydia's story suggests that constructing an internal foundation does not solve all of life's dilemmas. Perhaps hearing her continued story in the coming years will reveal another phase of development within the internal foundation.

The internal foundation stood at the basis of life decisions and altered the role of career for some participants. Sandra articulated this succinctly:

I have a clearer vision of what I really want to do. I have a stronger image of who I am. I'm not so wrapped up in being a counselor, I'm being Sandra. I have a clearer vision of Sandra and the different things that make up who I am. I went from "I am a counselor" to "I do some social work."

Sandra's "I am a counselor" implied that her work defined her. Her shift to "I do some social work" indicates that her work is now an aspect of a larger entity—her stronger image of who she is.

Alice was rethinking the role of her career as well. Earlier in her twenties she reported frustration that she would have to juggle her career with her desire to have children. Her strong internal foundation, however, made it possible for her to be open to new feelings that emerged after the birth of her first child. A year after her daughter was born, Alice reported that she planned to give up her supervisory position and work part-time as a counselor in a few months. She explained:

> If someone had told me two years ago that I would make this decision, I would have said they were crazy. It really wasn't a struggle. It was a matter of "Wow, I never thought *I'd* feel this way." I certainly respected people who did think this way, but I just didn't think I would. But it wasn't like I was trying to change my mind. It was "Now I have these feelings, I know what they are; I trust that, now what do I do about it?" Then it was thinking about how would this change things financially. My primary source of satisfaction is motherhood. I still find work very interesting, and maybe I'll eat these words next time we talk, I don't know! It is a big change. But now it's been a steady feeling and over time it hasn't changed.

Despite her surprise at how she felt, Alice knew her feelings and trusted them. She acknowledged that her feelings might change, but trusted them enough to act on them. Her internal foundation made it possible to accept this major life change and it emerged from her knowing herself.

These stories of celebrating the self reveal the authentic self that was constructed in the self-authorship process. Maintaining connection to this authentic self was central to self-authorship and building the internal foundation. The strength of the authentic self also made mutual connections possible with others. These connections were evident in participants' balancing self-chosen responsibilities to others and their own internal voices.

Self-Chosen Responsibilities to Others: Interpersonally Grounded

Being grounded in the internal foundation also included considering one's responsibility to others in making decisions, making clear that self-authorship is not the equivalent of self-absorption. This differed from considering what others wanted in earlier years; it was now focused on internal judgments about what one believed one's responsibility to others to be. Mutual relationships with coworkers and clients were evident in participants' stories about managing their responsibilities. Alice's choice to resign her supervisory position affected her colleagues and the agency's clients. Alice took this responsibility seriously and considered it in implementing her change of priorities. She explained that she did not immediately act on her feelings because she had to entertain important questions first:

> "How can I prepare to do that in a way that is responsible to other people?" I have chosen to take on responsibility, and there are lots of people who trust the decisions I am going to make. Knowing that, respecting that, I'm not going to rush— there is going to be a transition period, room to explore how all this fits and how do we make this smooth. I'll probably end up doing this in four or five months while the feelings at that point will have been here for a year. I guess the gut leads me and the rational thinking sorts out the details.

What was right for Alice was at center stage, yet it did not totally eclipse what was right for others. She honored her internal voice but avoided making rash decisions.

Balancing self and professional responsibility to others was also salient in Sandra's experience, as she described her ability to do so in her work:

> I am not afraid to say what I believe in and stand for it. I don't make reckless decisions that hurt my lifestyle or self—like quitting my job—but I am able to say, "this is how it is." Like I told our regional representatives that I felt their billing plan was unethical and would break our relationship with patients. I was able to articulate that and stand behind it; I've never been one to be pushed around. To help others, you have to maintain self. Now that I'm out of my old job, I recognize the point where I began to lose myself. If it happens again, I see it and don't do it. I don't worry much. I'm confident that I do a good job; I know this. If others disagree, they can find someone else. I have a lot of feedback that I trust is the truth. I've taken charge and get things done. I am more confident. I am able to recognize signs more quickly now. It sounds nonchalant, but that is how I feel. Some of that was blurry in my old job. I knew some things I wouldn't do, but as we were speeding towards them, I couldn't tell how many I would do. Now I can see the line, and know what I won't do.

Sandra's patients were a priority for her yet maintaining herself was an equal priority. Her foundation, evident in her confidence and what she trusted as the truth, helped her see the boundary beyond which she would not go. The foundation yielded integrity that would prompt her to change jobs rather than cross that boundary. Her labeling her attitude as nonchalant conveyed to me that it had become so internalized that it had become a given for her. Her statement that she did not make reckless decisions conveyed that she considered consequences but would not allow external pressures to override her internal foundation.

Lydia's struggle, mentioned earlier, between doing something for her students and doing her own graduate school work also speaks to the issue of responsibility to others, as does her concern about remaining healthy for her unborn child. Like Alice and Sandra, Lydia consciously chose these responsibilities from the vantage point of her internal foundation. Her balancing act was more complicated because her immediate circumstances did not yield any workable solutions. To live out her priorities, she needed to complete her teaching contract, complete her graduate degree prior to moving away, carry her child to term, and prepare to move. In the long term, however, she had already made some choices about how to manage her responsibilities to others:

Next year will be a huge personal life adjustment—I know I won't work next year. I'm getting a master's degree but not going to work next year—crazy. I'm going from a place where I know so many people, so engrossed, then have a baby and move across the country and know no one. It will be a complete switch of what defines me and who I am. My husband will be home all the time, which is good, but an adjustment—a huge life swing. I have felt I was who I was through success at work. Who are you? A teacher. Now I'm going to be a parent. It will be a different focus on who I am and what my purpose is. Lydia the wife, with a daughter, but my independence will still be there. I know that will still be part of me. I will still be so organized that it will drive people crazy. Those things are still the same. I don't want to be defined as so and so's mom, or so and so's wife; I need my own identity. Getting my Master's degree is rolled in there—I need to do something for myself. That's why I waited to have children; I wanted to teach and didn't want to give that up. I can't do both well. I don't know that I'll teach for several years, or ever full-time again—that is a real possibility. I'll also adjust pretty well to new situations. I haven't had a bad job since graduating from college, except one. I could pick good jobs, sense if I belong there, if it is a place I can give something. I think that will stick with me, I'll do that when I go back.

Lydia initially sounded like she was losing her sense of self in this pending transition, but as she continued it became clear that she was not. Although her primary role would change from teacher to mother, she was taking the internal foundation of who she was along through the transition. She recognized the challenges that lie ahead, knew she needed to maintain her own identity, and was flexible in thinking about the future. Her sense of responsibility to her child and to herself remained strong. Again, there was no hint of external control regarding what she should do in the decision regarding career and parenthood.

Al was also working on balancing responsibility to himself and responsibility to others, in his case his patients while he was doing his residency for medical school. He described how it was going early on in the experience:

> The hard part is making decisions and being responsible for them. I still have a backup resident and attending physician; once I'm done with residency there will be no final stop. If I call backup every time, it won't be looked upon favorably—you use your resources and just do it. You hear about it the next morning if you screw up. We do rounds every day—where we talk with the upper level resident and attending physician about patients—things are processed every day. You can make mistakes. You can't call backup every time or you won't get very far. I get tests before calling. At least you need to get things started. It is hard getting comfortable with being responsible. If a life is on the line, and you have any doubt, you are responsible for getting help. I'm not going to put somebody's life on the line for [fear of] waking someone up. But I need to decide when life is on the line. I tend to err on trying to do too much myself; sometimes I should call when I don't. If I am ever to a point [where] I feel it is dangerous, I'll get help. Sometimes I take care of it, and they say I should have called. If anything, I've got to go the other way. I'm still new at interning—in a few months I might be okay.

Al was trying to balance his responsibility to his patients with his responsibility to learn how to make good decisions when he becomes the "final stop" in decision-making. His boundary was not putting patients' lives on the line, but even that called for a judgment on his part. Al's internal foundation led him to act too independently sometimes. At the same time it made him open to the feedback that he might need to "go the other way."

The salient characteristic of these stories about responsibility to others is that the responsibility was internally chosen instead of accepted from the outside. Whether it was responsibility to people, as in the case of the stories recounted here, or responsibility to the financial stability of a company as was the case for some participants, responsibility was freely adopted from an internal construction of one's role, based on one's values. Thus this responsibility reflected how participants chose to construct their relations with others rather than how others expected these relations to be. The minimal—or complete lack of—discussion about others' expectations is consistent with the notion that the internal foundation ran so deep that it became the main focus of discussion about particular decisions and how to conduct one's life in general.

Knowing Intuitively

The epistemological dimension of the internal foundation was also so deeply ingrained in participants' meaning-making at the late-twenties that it sounded less complex initially than the meaning-making articulated as they became authors of their lives. As they mastered the processes of constructing their own beliefs, the beliefs became so ingrained that participants began to describe knowing as intuitive. Upon closer examination, the contextual processes of evaluating evidence were still there, but the role of the self as one of the variables came to center stage. Listening to their descriptions also revealed the blend of styles—relational and impersonal—in this complex form of knowing.

In a conversation that took place two weeks before the birth of her first child, Lauren described how she knew she was "as ready as I'll be" to be a parent:

> I am very much looking forward to it, but I would be lying if I said I wasn't totally scared! I know I'll never be 100 percent ready, but where I am in life right now, I'm probably the most ready as I'll be. At first I felt I was too young. As time has gone on, I feel ready to be a parent and discovering what it is all about. I always wanted this, but I didn't know when the right time would be. One thing I have definitely learned; I try to be a big planner and control person. This is one thing you can't plan! I'm learning to be flexible. I can't say I'm good at it yet, but I'm trying. Being around kids, I would think to myself, "I can do this, I am ready for this." Whereas before, I didn't feel that way. Having an experience and getting comfortable with it—growing into it. It was the same in the marriage and child decision. I could tell—it is hard to describe.

As was the case with her marriage decision, Lauren gave herself time to process experiences and grow comfortable with decisions about her life. Although she describes "knowing" as when it feels right, this feeling stemmed from processing experiences she had and listening to her reaction to them.

Dawn was able to describe "when the feeling is right" in a little more detail. Taking a position as a cook in a French restaurant primarily for financial reasons, she became fascinated with the creativity involved in cooking. She reported that they did not use measuring cups when cooking, but rather "you pour salt in your hand, it looks about right, and you throw it in. It's an intuitive process." After eight years of interviews Dawn asked my next question before I got the chance:

> How you acquire that? I have no idea. You look at a square, someone says it is a square, and you know it is. Me taking salt,

> pouring it into my hand, check it once, then I know by looking at that shape in my hand that it will be a tablespoon. It's a sensory thing too. You constantly taste, when you add ingredients, especially without a recipe, to see if it balances out right. Recipes aren't always right so you start to create.

Pursuing the question, "How do you know things?" further, she continued:

> That's a question I've pondered a lot. Sometimes the only answer is you just know—a feeling, an intuitive thing. Something in your body or mind says it is right—a feeling to go on. If you go on it, you apply more technical [ways of knowing]—act on it, test it out—if the results are right, the feeling is right. This is a whole other can of worms. I trust what I feel as far as knowing things, or thinking things. Knowing they are right or wrong—I have a physical response—my stomach twinges, or a satisfied feeling comes over me. It goes beyond the realm of factual information.

Dawn focused on the intuitive dimension, the feeling to go on, in how she knew something. Yet she indicated that there were more technical aspects of testing it out. Her statement that it "goes beyond the realm of factual information" indicated that she did not deny factual information; rather it was not enough for her to complete the knowing process. She used both a relational style that centered on the feeling and an impersonal style that focused on analysis of the more technical aspects.

Kurt elaborated on this concept even further in talking about decisions he was trying to resolve in his work and personal life. Kurt had changed jobs, was more satisfied with his current work, and was involved in a serious relationship. A number of things were still up in the air, however, as he explained:

> I'm not as far as I want to be in identifying my values, goals, and then the actual things to achieve them. The thing about being of service is one of those values. At church, I can put that into me fulfilling my lifelong values; it is not just an action. That is cool! It is not noble, but it feels good to do something for myself. That definitely comes from inside. [At work] we were thinking about posting another supervisor position for the day shift. Working on the sunrise shift is difficult. I always feel tired, so I thought about trying to get the day shift position. But then something is not right there for me. It doesn't feel right—not where I am needed right now. One thought is, "This is my chance, the others aren't applying, I'd like to think I would be a shoo-in." I don't know if I feel there are greater things to do on the sunrise shift?

> I'm trying to get inside that a bit to.figure out what isn't right. I
> don't want to abandon my shift, so part of it is what I can com-
> mit to people. For me it goes back to the head and heart thing.
> In my head it makes sense; in my heart I'm not quite there—I
> don't know what is there—have to honor that. I couldn't, being
> true to myself, couldn't go into [the new position]. I could suc-
> ceed, enjoy it, but it would be making a mistake.

Kurt did not apply for the day shift position because he vowed to honor what
was in his heart (representative of the relational style and his trust of his
authentic self). Yet he made it clear that part of the consideration was what
was in his head, and trying to get inside of what was bothering him. He was
using the evidence he had to help with this decision (an impersonal style) but
was not stopping at what made sense in his head. His internal foundation
required using both his head and heart to know. Although Kurt couldn't put
his finger on what the problem was with applying for the day shift position,
he was certain that it was a mistake. He was also fairly sure that his current
significant relationship wasn't right, either. He said:

> This relationship is deteriorating. I wanted to hold onto it. What
> to do? Then it didn't feel right—maybe it isn't the relationship I
> should be holding onto. One thing I recognize in myself is that I
> have a tendency to over commit myself to things. I go around
> committing to everyone who needs something, then see what
> is left for Kurt. Sometimes there is something left, sometimes
> not. I have to start cutting out some before I can give to Kurt. For
> me, balance is not a conscious thing—it just happens when I am
> following what feels right and what doesn't. If I go out to try to
> get balance, you can bet I won't get it. The act of consciously
> trying to do it eliminates the possibility of achieving it. I don't
> know why that is. For me, if I want balance, I have to be bal-
> anced. If I want peace, I have to be [at] peace. If I go out and look
> for it, it is elusive—it's outside. I have stopped looking for it out-
> side myself.

Again, Kurt's way of knowing in this context combines his understanding of himself and the world around him. Achieving what he calls balance requires more
than just seeking it; it requires acting on what is in his heart. In many ways, Kurt's
approach is similar to the one Lauren used—listening to his internal voice and
allowing it to guide him. The only difference is that Kurt's voice thus far has given
him insight about what he doesn't want and has stopped short of determining
what he does want. Despite that, he did not allow others in his personal life or
work life to influence him to do what he felt was not right for him.

Alice clearly articulated that knowing intuitively required a rational component. Talking about her change of heart regarding motherhood and career, she clarified that she did not immediately act on her new feelings. She described using her instinct (the relational style), but also rationality (the impersonal style) in deciding to how to act on her internal voice:

> I think there has always been a rational component. But ultimately it has to feel right in the gut. My main approach as a counselor is a strong cognitive, rational piece to my therapy. I constantly tell clients just because we feel a certain way doesn't mean we have to act on it. There is a rational process that needs to be there—I didn't quit my job the first day I had this feeling! But I have always had access to that gut awareness and probably some of that is spiritual. My prayer life and spiritual life has always been there. That is very interrelated to that gut feeling— what is the right thing for me? I don't act immediately on this gut feeling, I sort through that with rational processes "Why do I feel this way?" and "What does it mean financially?"

Alice summed up the notion of knowing intuitively described by participants who had constructed and solidified an internal foundation. As described by Lauren, Dawn, and Kurt in varying levels of detail, participants with an internal foundation trusted their feelings, pursued the implications of those feelings rationally, and acted on them only when all dimensions were in place. Alice's comment about some of her access to gut awareness being spiritual introduces a topic that was increasingly prevalent in how to know from the internal foundation.

Spirituality

Many participants introduced the notion of spirituality in our conversations in their late twenties. It took on many forms; some specified it as religion or faith (as did Kelly at the outset of this chapter) whereas others specified that it was not a religious idea (as did Mark in chapter 2). For Al, it was related to religious beliefs. He described a growing interest in religious faith within a couple of years after graduation. His dissatisfaction with the meaning of his work in computer consulting, and his analysis of the meaning he derived from volunteer activities, led him back to church involvement. By his late twenties he had settled on the meaning of religious beliefs in his life and his work:

> Becoming a Christian—I grew up in Christian home, but wasn't feeling or living being a Christian. I don't want to say I was born

again, there was no radical event, but over a year or so, I refocused on what I think is important. I started to get back involved in church and reading the Bible and liking it, doing it because I wanted to. In the long run, that is where it's at, at least that is what I think. I'm not going to live forever, so I need to get this figured out sooner than later. Spiritual can mean a lot of things; for me it means Jesus Christ and the Bible. Reading it and trying to learn it, understand it, attending church, praying. I am not real outspoken about it, I don't bring it up unless people want to talk about it. I'm not a preacher—I'm happy to talk about it if somebody wants to know what I think, if they bring it up. I don't shout it from the mountaintop. I'm a firm believer that action speaks louder than words; you can do a lot more good and people can be changed a lot by seeing your actions than by you telling them anything. I don't know who said it—some Christian person said "spread the gospel, and if necessary, use words"— that is just about right. That's how I look at it, how I represent myself, how I display my spirituality.

Al's return to church involvement and studying the Bible increased his satisfaction with how he made meaning of his life but he did not impose it on others. This was true in his work with patients as well:

I have a lot of conflict with the abortion issue. Typically I don't share my personal convictions, unless someone asks me. I give them options and let them decide. I don't try to offer my bias; some may come through, I can't avoid that. I tell them what is currently acceptable in medicine. I wouldn't do an abortion myself, but I wouldn't judge someone who had one. There is a test for every pregnant female—indicator for downs syndrome or defects. If the results are abnormal they could have an abortion. When you get them to consent for the test, you have to talk through that. I try to keep my personal views about it out; just present the facts. If patients ask me about religious beliefs, I tell them, but otherwise I don't. In making my own decisions, it does have an impact in how I deal with people. I decided not to get abortion training. I think [my being Christian] has allowed me to be more open; it is weird because people view Christians as close-minded and judgmental. For me, it has been the opposite experience—realize how heathen we all are, prone to mistakes. I was more judgmental before. Ideally I am not the person to be making those judgments.

Al's bringing Jesus Christ into his life was one component of how he authored his own beliefs, sense of self, and relations with others. He acted on this part of his foundation by "doing good" as he saw it, for example, deciding not to

learn how to or to perform abortions. His foundation also opened his thinking, as was described by many with an internal foundation, to refrain from
judgment about others' choices.

Rosa shared Al's experience of straying from her religious faith and
returning to it but there were particular events in her life that affected her journey. The first was her sister's bout with cancer:

> My sister has breast cancer. She is doing okay; it's been five
> years now. She has spots in her shoulder, hip, and lungs. She
> went through a phase where her hip bothered her and she
> couldn't move. She thought she might beat it but then she had
> tumors growing on her spine. She thought it was out of remis-
> sion. I helped her because she couldn't do anything. It was a
> struggle to walk to the bathroom. She talked over funeral
> arrangements with me when she was 32; she had things written
> down. She has become very religious. It has drawn us all closer
> to God. We were raised Catholic; my mom had us pray the
> rosary. I pray more; when I pray I am more involved. I used to
> just recite prayers; now I really pray. I've become much more
> spiritual. I got away from that in college. I go to church some-
> times during the week for my sister. She has made me a much
> more spiritual person. She is still here because of her prayers.
> She gets angry when she has bad spells but always comes
> back a little stronger. She has gone through every treatment—
> chemo, radiation, hormones in increasingly strong doses—she
> has done all of them. Now she is in a clinical study; they inject
> a drug that kills capillaries around cancer tumors. Of a small
> group of women in this study; she is the only one still on it. She
> is doing fine. Her tumors haven't changed at all. She must be
> doing something good. Prayer had a lot to do with this. I think I
> pray more intensely. In college I questioned, "Is there really a
> Jesus? What kind of proof is there really?" The professors make
> you think. You do question your faith, I went through that; with
> [my sister] it brought me back. I still don't believe everything the
> Catholic Church does, but I do still have a strong faith.

Trying to make sense of her sister's illness and continued survival against the
odds, Rosa turned to her faith. Having set it aside during college due to lack
of proof for Jesus' existence, she reconsidered in light of her sister's situation.
Although Rosa's story could initially be interpreted as falling back on some
authority to handle the trauma of her sister's disease, it can also be interpreted
as considering her sister's survival as new proof that Jesus does exist and
responds to prayers. Another tragedy in Rosa's life helped me choose the latter interpretation. She had shared with me in an earlier conversation that a

stranger murdered her cousin. Her aunt and uncle were able to forgive the perpetrator, a concept Rosa could not initially understand. In our discussion about her renewed faith, Rosa talked about how experiences related to her cousin's death have shaped her belief that "there is a heaven and good people will get there." She told this story to explain:

> I really feel there is an afterlife. Some weird things have happened in the family that related to my cousin. My uncle had a dream two years after her death. He dreamed she was in her red sports car; she stopped and he got in the car with her. She told him she was fine, busy, and doing okay. He woke up, told his wife the dream, and told her he felt better. He felt like the dream was really happening. He has another daughter and four sons. He told them about the dream—they had had the same dream that same weekend! It gives you the chills. They all live in different areas. My sister had a similar dream before she heard the story. A month or two later, we were at another uncle's funeral and we realized they had the same dream. It made me a stronger believer; there are angels, there are people watching down on us.

Although some readers may scoff at Rosa's story, it demonstrates that she used her experience and that of others to construct a way to make meaning of life. This believing was a component of her internal foundation.

Dawn defined spirituality as "not religion" in our tenth interview, saying, "I have a very intense spiritually about myself and live my life very much in that way. It is not religion, but a definite spiritual self within me." We talked about it in considerable depth two years later. She still had trouble defining what she meant; as a result the story that follows was punctuated with long pauses and sighs:

> How do I define this? I know what it is, but how do I put into words what this is? I guess, for me, what spiritual is—is what some would consider their religion, although I think they are two very different things. I think a greater knowing of the self, knowing of the self in a greater grand scheme of things, knowing that there are forces greater than me that are at work in the universe. Um, I think that is what I consider to be my spirituality—knowing there are greater forces at work and accepting a certain understanding of them, or trying to gain an understanding of what exactly they are and how they have worked in my life. Honoring myself and other beings, things, forces at work —taking, um, I see that look on your face—you want to know more! Let's see. All right, let's just cut to the chase then. I would not

consider myself to be a religious person, but consider myself to be a very spiritual person. Having said that, um, I believe that there are forces in this world that are more powerful than we are, and there are some we can readily acknowledge and others that I think we cultivate over time. It's, I mean, I would say one of those [that we cultivate] would be intuition—well actually it could fall into both [categories]. It is readily available, but it takes time to cultivate as far as trusting your intuition and trusting that voice that says, "This is where I need to be." To the point where I think it almost takes on psychic proportions. That is all part of spirituality—mine anyway—knowing that there is a purpose for me in this world. It is a journey—my life is a journey to discover or get closer to what my purpose is. And I think acknowledging that perhaps there is not necessarily one, but there is a higher power, and how that is broken down differs for everybody. Does that answer the question?

The relationship between higher power and cultivating one's intuition and inner voice still escaped me, so I asked Dawn to talk further about trying to understand these forces. Her response was:

Okay. Explain that—hmm. That is huge. [after a long pause] What do you want me to explain? It all ties in, coming back to that intuition thing and listening to the voice inside of you. Um—hmm. I'm trying to think about what Australia was for me, and even Africa, well gosh—this is complicated. It all does come back to being able to listen to yourself, and understanding, for me personally it is all based in energy. We receive energy and give off energy That energy takes the form of whatever—be it like, dislike, positive, negative—allowing yourself, physically or spiritually, to process that—there is information there that allows you to act. Your intuition is the central processing unit. This may be complete garbage that I'm telling right now—you really pinned me on that question. That is how I felt when I went to Australia—being thrown into this completely foreign environment. It really awakened something in me that I felt like I could tap into—almost supernatural powers of the world. And whether that is one of the higher powers, I tend to think in a way it is all related, just the way things happened when I was there. I would feel stuck, I needed to figure out where I was going to go, I would forget about it for a minute, then I would meet someone that would point me in a direction. That weird little synchronicity that happens that I think if you will things into your life, they come to you. That's all part of that bigger picture as I see it. Don't know if I am getting anywhere on this question.

I was still confused about the notions of stepping back and not trying to force things versus willing something into one's life. I asked about the difference and Dawn said:

> It is a real fine line. To find that balancing point, but like that ability of saying I really want to do this. Put the thought out in the universe that I can bring this into my life, somehow I will make this happen. Doing that, and allowing the universe to work its magic and bring it to you. It happens, I've done it! I'm trying to understand how that works, I don't think the linear mind, the brain cannot process that on a linear level, but the heart and soul can, because it knows what's going on. That is the big clarity that happens when I travel. I get myself to a point—and I'm trying to figure out how to translate this into my daily life —I get myself to a point where I can just strip away—oh, balance my checkbook, the time clock, fight traffic—you lose all of that. It is a complete simplification of what your reality is at the very moment. Like climbing the mountain. So in the moment, what is past and ahead doesn't matter, because you are so consumed by what is going on at that time. That, too, is clarity. If that makes any sense. Then again, as time goes by, the noise filters back in. Something I am having to learn how to do—coming back to the whole spiritual self thing, maybe I've gathered enough insight, that I'll know what to do. Whether it is stare out the window for 15 minutes a day, or live in the moment. Because, barring deciding to take every day off for life and travel, I have to find a way to function in the noise.

Dawn's story sounded very much like the conversation I had had with Mark about stepping behind the waterfall (see chapter 2). I described part of his notion to her and asked if it was related to her thinking. She responded:

> Yes! To be able to let it flow by—yes, that is ultimately what I am working toward. I am trying to figure out how I can do that. Especially with my job now, it can be stressful and frustrating because not everything always goes according to plan. Instead of letting that take charge of what is going on in my life, letting the chaos control me, I'm learning to step away. I'm allowing the chaos to happen, because it will happen no matter what, but not letting it rope me in to the point that I get exhausted, angry or beaten up by it.

It did seem that Dawn and Mark were on the same plane in their thinking about spirituality. Both explained it as something beyond themselves, yet intricately related to their own souls. Both acknowledged that life was beyond their control, yet both believed that they could step away from the chaos and noise to make meaning of their existence themselves. The internal voice stood at the core of this ability but each expressed the notion that the internal voice was something beyond what they had constructed. Mark explicitly said he did not construct it, but rather discovered it inside where it had been all along. Dawn spoke to cultivating it but simultaneously acknowledged that it could fall in the category of "forces more powerful than us."

What is consistent across the various descriptions of spirituality is an internal foundation that makes facing everything from everyday "noise" to tragedy possible. For some the story had the dynamic of powers beyond the self; for others the self seems to be the power. The stories I have recounted here are the beginning of this spiritual journey in these young adults' lives and I do not profess to understand them at this point. Hopefully these dimensions of their self-authorship will become increasingly clear as we continue our work together.

Accepting Life

One of the distinct outcomes of the solidified sense of self and the integration of self and external reality in knowing was an overall acceptance of life as it unfolded. This notion is apparent in some of the discussion of spirituality in terms of accepting the chaos of the world, but it also appeared in discussions in which spirituality was not a factor. A few examples convey this acceptance and how it stemmed from the internal foundation.

Rosa reported that her life had become stable, although she did not expect it to remain static. Rosa had twins recently and with four children there was no question that she would remain the primary caregiver for the next few years. She shared:

> Everything is very stable and things will change after the next five years. I'm a little more confident in what I'm doing. I know we aren't wondering about more kids; we're done! I know I'm not going back to work. My job is mom, taking care of the kids. I'm at a stable point right now. Sometimes you wish things were calm and it is right now.

Calm in the context of having four young children speaks to the power of the internal foundation! Rosa knew what was on the immediate horizon, accepted it, and knew it would change eventually.

Phillip was accepting the realities of his life as well. Recently turning 30, he reflected:

Since turning 30, and with the recent breakup, I've had a little maudlin period. That is surprising for me; I'm trying to come out of that. What am I doing? It hit me really hard. In the next ten years, some things have got to happen. I guess they really don't. I could marry at 45, have children at 47, buy my first house at 50. If I had my druthers I would be married by now, and have plans to start a family. I can't control that. I'm of the ilk that I want to [marry] once, I'll wait until that happens. I make these choices with people I date; I could have convinced this woman to marry me, but it was not a good choice. I resign myself that these were good choices, even if they are painful. I made the choice to stay in [this city], it has had its problems, but I have toughened up. I'm glad I have chosen to live the way I do, so I have a reserve of money. Part of that comes from my upbringing—dad hounded me to stay out of debt. I thank him for that. . . . As positive as I am, this has been a rough year. I have had two breakups. My boss is dying. My aunt died of cancer in May. My favorite aunt, the one who got me into a positive attitude, is ill and may die. This year has been a washout. Put bets on next year. It hasn't been bad, but things happened that made me more cynical. I'll continue to date; I won't get a thrill out of it like I did when I was 25, but what is the alternative? Computer solitaire? I'm a social creature, I need people. I'm continuing what I set out to do. Things shake me up, and there will be more—don't get any release from it. Best thing you can do is to make lemonade out of lemons. Until the big break comes, that's what I gotta do. Some say, "you are such an optimist." Maybe I am, but what is the alternative? I've been there—life is miserable, yaddi, yadda. But it doesn't get any easier. I have chosen to just not let—even though it is hard, and sometimes I need to recoup—but try to show the world that I can rise above. I'm not going to buckle or equivocate or succumb. I do the best I can with what I have. I find that some folks my age tune out problems they face. For me, I'd just rather face them head on and work on them. They aren't going away.

Phillip was facing what life offered him. Even though it was not all that he wanted, and some events were traumatic, he resolved to make the best of it. His internal foundation guided him in making difficult decisions, in staying positive, and in being hopeful that some of his dreams would be realized in the future.

Like Phillip, Kurt also acknowledged that he had hoped to be further along in various aspects of his life, but he also conveyed that he was content with his approach to life. He clarified:

It is not that you get to control the circumstances of events happening to you; I've tried to stop that and [instead] control how I think about it. I had hoped I would have a family by age 31—but I'm not dwelling on it. I couldn't work the hours I work right now if I had that. It is nice to have the flexibility to do that. I try to control events less, and control my perception of them more. What other people think is still a motivating thing for me. There are times when I am extremely confident, and then what people think doesn't matter. It is the power of my conviction. At that time, I am going to do it, it is going to happen. In the mode I am in right now, I am concerned about what other people think, but not to gain approval for myself. It is more where I am in a whole learning process. I have a great relationship with my boss. A lot of times I'll ask him how he'd play something. I want to know what he thinks. But it's not who I am, I'm not basing my identity off it. It is not for gaining self-worth, just for getting resources. What makes our relationship solid is that we have an understanding— he'll come to me with the same thing. We ask what each other thinks. It is a positive mutual understanding. We aren't looking for each other's approval. My boss is not concerned about what other people think—he doesn't define his worth on that. I take a lot of that from him—he's a positive role model.

Kurt's internal foundation prompted his acceptance of his current circumstances even though he would like to see some of them change. It also changed his earlier struggle with others' influence. He had achieved the power of choice he had imagined years earlier and could now access what others thought as resources for learning rather than for defining who he was.

Getting totally past what others think was salient for Dawn's acceptance of her sexual orientation, which she introduced for the first time in our tenth interview:

One of the biggest things—it hasn't come up in any of our conversations before—was accepting the fact that my sexual orientation is out of the mainstream. It was a big thing for me. It started for me when I was in school. You finally getting to a point where you can feel comfortable enough that you don't care what people think about you. The turning point was in the last couple of years. It brought out interesting things in me. It has taken me probably five years to feel solid. Now, I don't care if you know if I'm gay and what you think. It doesn't matter and this is who I am. Dealing with that with family; I told my parents three years ago. That's been an interesting process.

Dawn's comment on taking five years to feel solid about this suggests the arduous process of solidifying one's foundation. We talked about why this had not entered our previous conversations. Dawn said:

It wasn't that I couldn't talk about it; becomes a personal thing. Now I am at that point that I am comfortable—it doesn't bother me. A big thing in the last couple years in my life. That has contributed a great deal to how I see things and how I think. Getting to where I am now, the confidence thing; you know you have the inner strength to stand apart from the mainstream. I don't have to be a duck in a row, following what everyone else is doing. Whether it has to do with being gay or not. The best way I can explain it is learning to walk. You get stronger and finally run. It is a release, where you are willing to let go of clutter that people throw at you.

The inner strength to stand apart from the mainstream is the internal foundation. Participants who solidified the foundation of how they knew, who they were and how they related to others were able to run—to let go of the clutter everyone had thrown at them for nearly 30 years.

The Nature of the Internal Foundation

The solidification of inner strength – the combination of an internal sense of self and internal belief system—led to greater openness and flexibility in approaching life. Rather than working toward answers or a "finished product," as was the case in the earlier portions of the journey, participants in the latter portions of the journey were working toward increasingly satisfying definitions of themselves. In doing so they welcomed new experiences for their contributions to the evolving definition. Because participants had solidified an internal sense of self and belief, their sense of self was no longer threatened by new experience. Evan's ability to "float on the waves" or Kelly's comfort with the puzzle never being complete are examples of this flexibility, made possible by the internal foundation.

A closely related dynamic of the internal foundation was participants' giving up the notion of control in exchange for the ability to manage their lives. In the process of becoming authors of their own lives, participants realized that they could not control the external world; rather they could control how they made meaning of the external world. Their ability to make meaning of the external world stemmed from their ability to make meaning of their internal world—the achievement of becoming the authors of their own lives. The internal self-authorship of who they were, how they related to others, and what to believe formed boundaries that defined both their internal lives and their interpretation of the external world around them. Their increased sophistication at self-reflection made this internal definition dynamic because it would continue to develop as they continued to make meaning of their experiences.

Participants who had moved into the internal foundation portion of the journey took responsibility for making meaning of both their internal and external worlds. They actively used their internal foundations to approach the world, react to events beyond their control, and mediate their interactions with external circumstances. The internal sense of self and belief was central, yet hard to describe. Kurt called it listening to his heart, in addition to his head, in making decisions. Others spoke to it as being heart or soul. Some labeled it spiritual. Dawn called it intuitive, noting that it almost took on "psychic proportions." Regardless of its label, the internal sense of self and belief became central to life decisions. Even when a decision seemed rational, for example Kurt's application for the day shift, the internal self and voice mediated it. The self became a crucial part of knowing. When participants were overwhelmed by the "noise" in their everyday lives they actively sought out the internal foundation to regain their grounding. For Mark this took the form of meditation; for Dawn it was getting out of the everyday routine; for Rosa, Alice, and others it was praying.

Getting in touch with the internal foundation helped participants simultaneously guide and accept their lives. The acceptance of unfulfilled dreams, tragic events, and general disappointments in life was made possible by taking responsibility for making meaning of one's self, relationships and beliefs. A sense of agency was evident at this point in the journey to direct one's life, choose priorities, and act consistently with self-defined boundaries. Simultaneously, a sense of communion was evident in the ability to connect meaningfully and mutually with others while maintaining an authentic self. Thus being "at home" with the internal foundation yielded a combination of comfort with ambiguity, confidence to shape one's life in positive ways, and the capacity for interdependence with others.

Toward the Evolution of the Internal Foundation: The Journey Continues

Participants' stories of the internal foundation reveal a "settling into" their internal homes that simultaneously brings an openness to new experience and further growth. Although journeying toward self-authorship was the major focus of their twenties, establishing the internal foundation did not solve everything. Participants spent their adolescence and their early twenties responding to external demands (swaying to them as Cara described earlier). Moving through the crossroads to become the authors of their own lives did not bring an end to external demands; rather it meant establishing an internal foundation from which to manage external demands. In fact, as the internal foundation formed, internal demands and priorities became the focus of participants' attention as well. Lydia's story of trying to choose among priorities she had established for herself illustrates this dynamic. Arriving at the internal foundation helped participants establish their priorities internally, but they still had to manage them in the context of the external world.

Sharon Daloz Parks, writing about adult faith development, noted that one's psychological home "is constituted by the patterns of connection and interaction between the person and his or her environment" (1986, p. 61). It is these patterns of connection and interaction that participants are reconstructing from their internal foundations. They are making peace with constraints and acknowledging that sometimes the waves will be over their heads. They are learning to be adaptive—being able to read and navigate external environments to make choices in context. They are able to do so because they are beginning to use their internal foundations to make sense of their experience and influence their lives. For most this is new territory marked by the recognition of internal authority more than by its sustained practice. As such, self-authorship can be viewed as the beginning of another phase of development—the evolution of the internal foundation and the renegotiation of self and other toward mutuality. As the participants move through their thirties the dynamics of this new phase of the journey will no doubt emerge in our continued study of adult development.

PART TWO

PROMOTING SELF-AUTHORSHIP IN HIGHER EDUCATION

The participants' stories in Part 1 convey their evolution from formula to foundation across their twenties. Inherent in the stories are multiple circumstances in which participants needed an internal definition to function effectively. To conduct their professional and personal lives productively, they really needed to achieve self-authorship earlier than most of them did. In addition to articulating the evolution of self-authorship, their stories do contain the conditions that promoted this evolution. Part 2 of the book brings those conditions to the forefront. Participants' experiences in graduate and professional schools, employment, community leadership and their personal lives identify the conditions that helped them leave external formulas, traverse the crossroads, and achieve self-authorship.

Part 2 organizes the collective conditions that promoted self-authorship into a framework consisting of three core assumptions and three principles for educational practice to connect the assumptions to students' development, or their place along the phases of the journey toward self-authorship. The three core assumptions demanded self-authorship in the epistemological, intrapersonal, and interpersonal dimensions; the three principles for educational practice offered a means of matching educational practice to participants' ability to meet those demands. Connecting the demands to participants' current development gave participants' the support and guidance they needed to shift from external to internal self-definition. Figure II.1 depicts this framework for promoting self-authorship.

Three Core Assumptions: The Demand for Self-Authorship

The three core assumptions reflected the need for self-authorship on each dimension of development. The first assumption—*knowledge is complex and socially constructed*—reflected complex epistemological development. The epistemic assumptions of contextual knowing best matched this assumption. Similarly, the second assumption—*self is central to knowledge construction*—reflected complex intrapersonal development. In order to bring the self into the knowledge construction process, participants had to have an internally defined sense of self. Essentially they had to have left the crossroads and entered into becoming the authors of their own lives. The third assumption—*authority and expertise are shared in the mutual construction of knowledge among peers*—reflected complex interpersonal development. Mutuality and interdependence were necessary for genuine participation in mutual construction in which parties listened carefully, considered others' perspectives, and authentically shared their own perspectives.

FIGURE II.1 A Framework to Promote Self-Authorship

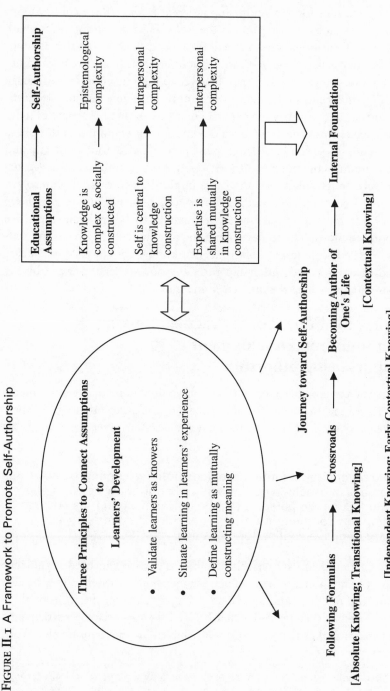

The expectations for self-authorship inherent in these three core assumptions were a stretch for participants in the *following external formulas* phase of the journey. Transitional knowers had the most difficulty with this assumption because they believed that authorities would be able to resolve uncertainty through continued research and they had yet to see their role in knowledge construction. Independent knowers were more amenable to knowledge as complex and socially constructed but were unaware of the complexity of judging knowledge claims. The dominance of external self-definition in this phase made including the self in knowledge construction and sharing authority and expertise in mutual construction difficult. After arriving at the *crossroads*, participants were better able to see the value in all three core assumptions even though they were still limited in their ability to live them. Entering *becoming the authors of their own lives* made it possible to begin living the three assumptions comfortably and developing the internal belief systems and self-definition needed to mutually join others in knowledge construction. Being supported to develop self-authorship through contexts characterized by the three assumptions yielded the *internal foundation.*

Principles for Educational Practice: Linking Assumptions and Development to Support Self-Authorship

Helping participants achieve self-authorship required more than environments that adhered to the three assumptions. Robert Kegan argued that when expectations demand ways of making meaning learners have yet to develop, we must create:

> a holding environment that provides both welcoming acknowledgement to exactly who the person is right now as he or she is, and fosters the person's psychological evolution. As such, a holding environment is a tricky, transitional culture, an evolutionary bridge, a context for crossing over. (1994, p. 43)

To stretch beyond their external self-definitions, participants needed guidance and support to develop new ways of making meaning—in essence, they needed good company for their journey. Good company came in the form of three principles for educational practice that bridged the gap between participants' development and the goal of self-authorship.[1] The three principles work

---

[1] These principles were initially identified in the college phase of this study (Baxter Magolda, 1992) and were further refined through a course observation study (Baxter Magolda, 1999b). They are further refined in Part 2 on the basis of the participants' post-college experiences.

together but each one makes an important contribution as well. The first principle—*validating learners as knowers*—conveyed to participants that they were capable of creating knowledge and making knowledge claims. For those in the external formula phase, this contradicted the notion the transitional knowers had that they should follow authority's lead. Simultaneously, it gave independent knowers confirmation that they should be working on what they believed. As participants entered the crossroads, validating them as knowers supported their awareness of their internal voices. Continued validation once they left the crossroads helped them build their own belief systems and internal self-definitions and arrive at the internal foundation. Validation as knowers, regardless of where they were in the journey, supported that knowledge was complex and socially constructed, invited participants to view self as central to knowledge construction, and increased their confidence in their ability to participate in mutual construction of knowledge.

The second principle—*situating learning in learners' experience*—offered good company by starting with the learners' location on the journey. Using what participants did know or had experienced as a starting point conveyed that their experience was important, another means of inviting the self into the learning process. Respect for learners' experience contradicted external definition and encouraged learners to analyze their own experience. Focusing on their experience helped those in the crossroads value their voices as well as those of others and to strengthen their own voices sufficiently to leave the crossroads. Using their own experience in becoming authors of their own lives helped them reflect on what they had experienced and actively make sense of it to contribute to their evolving belief systems and internal sense of self. Situating learning in learners' experience supported the social construction and complexity of knowledge, kept the self central to the knowledge construction process, and offered a foundation from which to join others in mutual construction.

The third principle—*defining learning as mutually constructing meaning*—directly invited participants into sharing authority and expertise in mutually constructing knowledge with knowledgeable peers. Doing so helped followers of external formulas to see that they needed to participate in determining their direction. For those in the crossroads, the invitation to join in mutual construction conveyed a respect for the internal voice, thus pulling it closer to the foreground. Once the internal voice emerged in the process of becoming the author of one's life, the invitation for mutual construction offered opportunities to explore and determine belief systems and internal self-definition. Finally, the invitation for mutual construction aided those at the internal foundation in their interest in others' perspectives and their capacity for mutuality.

The three principles obviously compliment one another. Situating learning in learners' experience is also a form of validation of their capacity to know and a foundation for their participation in mutual construction. Defining learning as mutual construction also validates them as knowers and situates learning in their experience. Validating learners as knowers helps them participate in mutual construction. Together the three principles helped educators, employers, and other adults in these participants' lives stay connected to their current phase of the journey in order to provide good company on the way to self-authorship.

Using the Assumptions and Principles in Higher Education

The next three chapters use participants' experiences during their twenties to illustrate how the framework of the three assumptions and principles can be used to promote self-authorship in multiple higher education contexts. Pedagogy and faculty-student interactions built on this framework are culled from participants' stories about advanced educational settings (chapter 7). Using the framework to conceptualize campus work roles in academic affairs, student affairs, and campus services is demonstrated through participants' employment experiences (chapter 8). Finally, stories about volunteer, leadership and family roles help frame the cocurriculum to promote self-authorship (chapter 9).

7

CREATING CONTEXTS FOR SELF-AUTHORSHIP IN ACADEMIC AFFAIRS

I wish teachers wouldn't do so many multiple-choice questions and have some more thinking type things because life is not multiple choice. I've been realizing out here, I mean, there's so many things I have to think about and look up and research and think about more. It seems like in college and high school everything is just so multiple choice, "Memorize this and spit it out." And that's mostly all I ever did, memorize, memorize, memorize, and learn facts and just spit it out to someone and circle answers and that was it. I wish we'd done—I don't know—more thinking things or stuff like that.

Anne

Anne spoke for the collective group of longitudinal participants when she reflected that "life is not multiple choice." Fortunately for the majority of those participants continuing their education after college, the notions of thinking about knowledge, researching it, and thinking about it more superceded memorizing, spitting it out, and circling answers. Their stories reveal how undergraduate education could—and should—be redesigned to focus on thinking and self-authorship. Of the 39 longitudinal participants who currently remain in the study, 24 pursued some form of graduate or professional education. In addition, seven others who are no longer in the study but participated in the early years after college pursued graduate or professional study. The participants collectively attended a wide range of institutions from small, private colleges to major research universities. Twelve participants completed their degrees part-time while working full-time. The majority worked for one to three years prior to pursuing graduate degrees, whereas those going into law, medicine and the seminary did so immediately after college graduation. The pursuit of advanced education was equally prevalent among women (16) and men (15). A summary of the types of graduate and professional degrees participants pursued appears in figure 7.1. Based on these collective stories, this chapter describes the three core assumptions of learning environments that required thinking and thus promoted self-authorship and learning. The stories show how the three principles for educational practice linked participants' developmental journeys to the demands for self-authorship.

FIGURE 7.1 Longitudinal Participants' Advanced Education and Degrees

	Disciplines	Women	Men
Business			
	Masters of Business Administration	2	4
	Masters of Economics		1
	Masters in International Affairs		1
Education			
	Masters in Teaching	3	1
	Masters in Supervision		1
	Masters in Educational Technology	1	
Social Sciences			
	Masters in Psychology	3	
	Masters in Social Work	2	
	Ph.D in Organizational Behavior	1	
Professional Schools			
	Medicine[1]	1	1
	Law[2]	1	2
	Seminary		2
	Culinary Arts	1	
Continuing Education			
	Teacher licensure	1	
	Computer technology		1
	Mathematics education		1
	Art history	1	

[1]One participant is in residency; the other dropped out of the study.
[2]One participant dropped out of the study.

Core Assumptions and the Principles Used to Implement Them

Despite the diversity of these educational settings, three core assumptions characterized contexts that promoted self-authorship. Forms of educational practice via the three principles assisted learners to meet these demands. The first core assumption—*that knowledge is complex, ambiguous, and socially constructed in a context*—undergirded the others. Using this assumption about knowledge, educators conveyed to their students that learners have to learn how to construct knowledge and have to decide what they personally believe in a particular context. Validating their students as knowers, educators extended this process beyond the undergraduate focus on learning the process anyone uses for constructing knowledge to how participants personally constructed knowledge. Thus while this was a demand for self-authorship in the epistemological realm, it was simultaneously a demand for self-authorship in the intrapersonal dimension. Contextual knowing was conveyed as a process that centrally involved, in fact hinged on, an internal sense of self to guide knowledge claims.

The incorporation of the sense of self into the process of knowing was evident in a second core assumption: *an internal sense of self is central to effective participation in the social construction of knowledge.* Educators operating from this assumption viewed learners as capable of learning and trusted them to personally construct knowledge. Educators acted on this assumption by inviting participants' minds, voices and selves into the learning process (thereby validating them as knowers and situating learning in their experience), expecting them to function autonomously, and express their perspectives (again validating them as knowers). This view of and approach to learners represented a demand for self-authorship in all three dimensions. It brought the intrapersonal dimension to the forefront in asking learners to reflect on how the "who am I" question informed their decisions about what to believe. At the same time expressing one's thoughts required addressing the effect of others' perspectives on one's own—the interpersonal dimension. Both dimensions were brought to bear on the epistemological dimension of deciding knowledge claims.

The third core assumption—*expertise or authority is shared among learners and teachers as they mutually construct knowledge*—compliments the first two assumptions. The social construction of knowledge and the central role of the self in that construction lead to learning as a process of mutually constructing meaning. Educators conveyed this assumption through the principle of mutually constructing meaning—emphasizing collaboration, exchanging

and critiquing multiple perspectives, and joint thinking in the process of deciding which perspectives to personally endorse. This mutual process took place
among learners as well as between learners and educators. This brought the
interpersonal dimension of self-authorship to the forefront as learners engaged
others' perspectives, yet maintained the intrapersonal dimension in stressing
the importance of deciding one's own internal beliefs. Both the "who am I"
and the "what kind of relationships do I want to construct with others" questions were central to the "how do I know" question.

The stories that follow illustrate how the three core assumptions and principles for educational practice helped participants make this shift. The three
assumptions are tightly interwoven, as are the three principles for practice. I
have organized the stories around the three assumptions to bring them to the
forefront for detailed analysis. Within each, the three principles are inter-
spersed to demonstrate how a particular assumption is implemented. Good
company requires integrating the three assumptions into educational practice
and using the three principles as a set to connect the demand for self-authorship to
learners' progress on the journey.

The Social Construction of Knowledge

The view of knowledge as complex, ambiguous, and socially constructed in a
context surfaced in multiple educational contexts. The ambiguity of knowledge was consistent with participants' everyday lives, as Kurt succinctly noted
in comparing to continuing education courses and his everyday work life:

> I'm taking two upper level math courses. They involve abstract
> problems. They do not have an answer to them; it is a subjec-
> tive thing. It is only natural that I have abstract problems in life
> which don't seem to have an answer to them.

The ambiguous nature of everyday life heightened participants' interest in
multiple perspectives and the process through which one chose among them.

Developing and Defending Beliefs. Bombarded with ambiguity and
complexity in both their everyday lives and educational experiences, participants learned how to construct what they believed in light of identifying multiple perspectives and how those perspectives related to particular contexts.
Learning was facilitated when it involved complexity, acknowledging multiple
perspectives, and questioning why things worked in a particular way. Andrew's
MBA program, in which he enrolled after working in business for a year, mod-

eled the three principles for helping students establish and defend their perspectives. He reported:

> In graduate school there was a lot more taking a position and defending it. There were a lot of things where there wasn't exactly a right answer. But you could come up with better answers and explain why you got to them. I had a management class where we were in essence running a business. We ran a simulated airline. There was no one right answer because we had nine groups and nine airlines in the class and all of them chose different philosophies in how they wanted to run their business. And three completely different airlines finished up at the top. In fact, the way our airline did it was different, the teacher said, than any other class had ever done. We just took a completely different approach, yet it was still successful. He even said in the grading of our report that he completely disagreed with it, but it was well argued and reasoned out, and he still gave us an A. I guess I kind of respected that aspect of—you know, "We agree to disagree." I like not always thinking there was one right answer because when you go out and try to deal with a lot of things, there isn't always one right answer. I think too much as an undergraduate we're taught to believe in black and white and there is no gray. And I think there's a lot more gray than there is black and white.

Andrew found the complexity of knowledge and the lack of one right answer appropriate and stimulating. The simulation situated learning in students' experience, giving them an opportunity to explore multiple ways of doing things. Andrew appreciated the freedom the instructor afforded his group to explore and support a unique approach to running their simulated airline. The instructor validated Andrew and his group as knowers by respecting their work and rewarding them for supporting their arguments even though he disagreed with their approach.

Publicly declaring and defending their positions contributed to learners' construction of their own views because it helped them clarify why they held particular views. Andrew explained how this worked for him:

> We had to pick a topic and kind of take a position—we had to use economic tools, supply and demand charts, and explain why we thought is was correct or incorrect. Which was something I had *never* done in economics. Someone had to explain why supply side economics would reduce the federal deficit or would not. You had to argue it. And we weren't told what topic

> to choose—it was our own decision. . . . Defending your point
> and getting your point across is important. You are presented
> with a lot—you have to defend your position and why you
> chose something . . . people asking questions 'why?' You have
> to reason why you did something. Every time I do something I
> think through it a little more. Asking that why question a lot
> more.

These activities emphasized developing reasons for one's perspectives and integrating them into a rationale to express and defend one's position. Instructors validated students as knowers by providing students freedom to choose their own topics and trusting them to work through arguments. Learning was situated in students' experience through their choice of topic and their use of the economic tools in that context. Other students asking "why" questions about his position prompted Andrew to ask himself "why" questions both in his classes and later in his work. This mutual construction with others and the instructor helped hone Andrew's perspective and rationale for it.

Lowell's masters program in international affairs (which he entered immediately upon college graduation) also emphasized complexity, valued multiple perspectives, and embraced analyzing why things worked in the social construction of knowledge. His experience demonstrates developing a framework from which to decide what to believe. He used his national security course as an example to explain how the content of the program was addressed:

> It's the sort of class that builds upon itself, . . . it doesn't repeat
> itself but it shows its face in different ways. It is like building a
> brick wall; you need all of it to make intelligent statements and
> to think about the things that happen.

Lowell conveyed that the content was additive and that multiple perspectives appeared as the term proceeded. Keeping track of earlier ideas and how they appeared in different ways later was necessary to integrate the content to analyze ideas and "make intelligent statements." The course content yielded basic models and tools the class then used to analyze various national security situations. Lowell described how short papers were used as a way to think about these situations:

> They [the papers] all go back to take the basic model or different
> tools to look at a situation, and compare it to different situations—
> we talked about the Iran Contra affairs and the Marines in
> Lebanon. Different issues that have come up in our national security, and can you explain them. You've got the basic tools and you

> try to manipulate them and see if they work. And if they don't,
> why, and if they do, why? So you really have to be thinking; you
> have to be on your toes. So it's not by any means easy.

The basic model built in the class created a context from which students could
operate, a version of situating learning in students' experience. Lowell and his
peers were validated as knowers because the instructor trusted them to use the
basic model and tools to ascertain how to explain national security situations.
Lowell described using the tools to ask why things work as "really thinking."
He distinguished this from his earlier education:

> I am more thoughtful. I guess before it was getting a lot of the
> facts down. And now it's, like with the national security, you
> truly try to analyze, try to really think. We're taking facts that
> we've hopefully learned and applying them and always open to
> new facts if we find them. That doesn't mean closing our mind
> to facts.

Analysis and thinking mean taking existing knowledge (facts) into account,
applying them to various contexts, yet remaining open to new facts or knowledge. This mutual construction of meaning enhanced learners' understanding
of current situations and helped them remain open to new facts. This openness
was important as Lowell made it clear that his program did not yield one right
answer to these complex national security situations:

> Sometimes it's hard to come to a conclusion because there
> aren't really any good answers. Otherwise we'd be sitting in the
> White House or in Congress. I think it's good the way it is. I don't
> think it's bad not to have the answers. If a decision has to be
> made, you're going to have to make it, if it really, truly has to be
> made. Someday something will come your way and you'll have
> more of an opinion about something or a belief that what you
> now believe is really the truth or whatever. I don't think it has
> to—you know, there is no one truth. So I don't believe that you
> have to come to a decision.

Expressing what he hoped for as a result of this program, Lowell said:

> The program [is based on] your thought processes and how
> well you back up your argument. So for me personally I like to
> get as much of a cohesive view at the end, not that it's the final
> one, but just a better-informed opinion or conclusion than I had
> at the beginning of the class.

Lowell's program validated his ability as a knower to develop his own thought processes. He expected the mutual construction he experienced to yield a more cohesive view, but was prepared to continue his learning beyond the program. Lowell's program emphasized the complexity of knowledge, how facts could be coordinated and applied in the analysis of complex situations, and how this analysis could lead to construction of a cohesive view from which to back up your perspective. Lowell learned a process for becoming a life-long learner.

The Role of Multiple Perspectives.   Another important dynamic of choosing and defending particular beliefs was exposure to multiple perspectives. Encountering new ideas raised new possibilities for what to believe and opportunities to hone one's views. Andrew offered an example:

> For graduate school, something that added a lot was dealing with the different cultures and the people from different countries and backgrounds. Graduate school was very heterogeneous, very mixed, very unlike my undergraduate. And I think it was much better just because of that. You had people who came from different backgrounds with different opinions. And I think when you're put in a class where too many are exactly the same, a lot of things are not brought out just because you don't have anybody that's being a devil's advocate. I think a little bit of antagonism is good for learning because it forces you to think why you believe what you believe and all that. It's not just a bunch of robots taking stuff in.

Andrew liked the challenge to consider diverse perspectives because it forced him to explore why he believed what he believed. The opportunity to engage in mutual construction of meaning with people whose views differed from his contributed to his progress toward self-authorship. It also called into question some of what he had been taught to believe was the norm, as is evident in these comments:

> I mean, just a lot of things we're taught in business are from an American perspective and American approach. Well, that's not necessarily the best and most correct way. In fact, at least in the manufacturing environment, we're getting our rear ends kicked. The Japanese have a much better approach that seems to be working. They challenged a lot of what we took as standard. They even argued with some of the financial theories, which supposedly aren't one of the things that you debate. But it was really good. We had people from communist countries that just had a very different perspective. And a lot of what they said made sense from the type of situations they were dealing with.

Mutual construction with learners who worked in diverse contexts helped Andrew and his peers analyze why something would work in a particular context and to question the validity of ideas accepted as "standard."

Anita, studying for her masters in social work after eight years in business, encountered questioning what she had come to believe as standard as well:

> [My classmates] think the focus should be on groups, and societies, not individuals. Discussions we get into in policy classes are the complete reverse of [my undergraduate school], which is a conservative republican environment. This group is so liberal; they almost lost a sense of reality. I can see both perspectives. It definitely opened up my eyes and made me think differently about things and more critically. Things we talk about in classes I have dealt with second hand or not at all—just theoretical concepts like poverty, homelessness, various social problems. I can't say that I understand them first hand. I talk to my friends or husband, their perspectives go along with the stereotypical views—like, why doesn't an African-American male go out and get a job. They can't see anything beyond that. Maybe because of environment they grew up in, were abused, etc.—you have to go further back, you can't just look at the current situation. It is more depressing; I see a wider scope of issues.

Mutual construction with classmates who held different perspectives on complex issues introduced Anita to new ideas that complicated her original views. Discussion of social issues like poverty and homelessness with her more liberal peers broadened her perspective beyond that of her friends and spouse. Her comments suggest that she was analyzing experience in her own life and the lives of others around her to figure out where she stood on complex social issues.

Whereas Anita focused on exploring issues new to her experience, Sandra offered an example of honing views already established. Despite entering her social work studies soon after college graduation, Sandra already had significant work experience in her field through internships; yet she wanted to expand her perspective:

> I like to hear, especially people with business backgrounds, I like to hear their viewpoints because they're a lot of times very different from mine. How do I decide what I agree with? From experience that I've brought with me, I already have a pretty solid idea of how I think it should be. . . . I guess I kind of go with a gut feeling. . . . I still have to prove it; definitely, if there is no proof, forget it. I won't take it in. But I guess that you really

have to work harder if it felt uncomfortable to me or if it was different from a basic knowledge that I had or a basic foundation
for what I believed in.

Based on prior experience, Sandra had already constructed some of her beliefs
into a framework that she described as a basic foundation. She actively sought
multiple perspectives but made judgments about them based on their consistency to beliefs she had already established. Her comments illuminate using
multiple perspectives to hone one's views after the core framework of belief is
already established.

Dilemmas in the Social Construction of Knowledge.   Not all educational contexts used the three principles to help students construct knowledge in the face of complexity. This resulted in difficulties for learners trying
to answer the "how do I know" question. Al, for example, entered medical
school in his mid-twenties with the idea that knowledge is complex and
knowledge claims are made in context. Talking about his initial understanding
of medicine, he said:

> . . . it's not a perfect science. There is not always a right
> answer. You make the best choice. Even in what little I know
> now, you read a case and you think it could be any of a mil-
> lion things. Different kinds of infections look like each other.
> How to wade through it all? Hopefully I will learn. It will be a
> challenge! In primary care it is usually not life and death but
> could have long range outcomes. [I] could endanger people.
> How do you know what to do? Use your best judgment I
> guess.

Al's expectations regarding learning how to make the best judgments were
not realized during his first year of medical school, which he described like
this:

> The material isn't hard—anybody could learn it. The volume is
> difficult. You learn what you can. It's like trying to drink out of a
> fire hose; sheer volume. I started off really wanting to learn as
> opposed to figuring out what I needed for a certain score. This
> is my life now; I need to know it. [But it is] almost impossible to
> do that. I had to shift back to efficiency mode—figure out what
> I'll be tested on as opposed to really learn and understand. . . .
> Had good intentions when I started. I'm dealing with people's
> lives. Get to a point where you don't have much choice. Do what
> you need to do to pass. It's doable.

Al felt that the volume of information restricted his ability to really learn and understand it, his goal for becoming a good physician. The need to pass the tests led him to shift to the efficiency mode out of necessity. There is no evidence of any of the three principles in his report. He did augment his education, however, with other opportunities to learn such as shadowing a doctor and helping with a student health clinic—settings in which learning was situated in his experience. He reported, "It would make me crazy if I didn't do these."

Al's reflection about his second year of medical school suggests that the principles were useful in this context:

> The second year is the same amount of material if not more, but more thinking, applied knowledge type of learning. I still have to memorize a lot, but what they expect you to learn is different; mostly apply your knowledge. The tests have cases—you begin to apply what you know to the case. It is more interesting to me to learn something I know I am going to use; the first year I didn't see the point. The second year I realized I had to understand how the diseases work. I did much better because I liked it more and because the testing was oriented toward application.

Understanding how diseases work and ascertaining how to apply knowledge to particular cases situated learning in Al's experience and validated his ability to make judgments. Once the content was presented and knowledge evaluated in an applied format, he was able to focus on constructing knowledge in context despite the volume of information. This approach was consistent with his belief that he needed to understand these things to be an effective physician.

Heather encountered a similar dilemma in her quest to acquire licensure to teach after working in business for three years. Although the assumption about complex, socially constructed knowledge was evident, the principles to connect it to her goals were not:

> I was frustrated with it; I didn't gain a lot. The main thing—it was too much theory. It's very important to push the envelope and think creatively—the current educational system is not ideal, so those discussions are important. However, we still have to survive in current institutions. We were taught more about how we should change current institutions. We didn't learn what we would have to do to be effective in this environment. The other thing for me is that I did student teaching in the inner city. I want to get back to that. The school I went to portrays itself as educating urban educators, but we didn't focus on issues in urban

education. I did not feel that the suggestions they put forth were workable in an urban institution or dealt with the core issues kids there are dealing with. I went into this profession with very strong principles, what I felt kids needed to be good learners—it seems to be working so far. I could be wrong; maybe I gained more than I realized. A lot of what makes me effective now is ideas I had before. I don't think I got it from education, but it might have been reinforced by those conversations.

This program's focus on theory and changing the institution of education implies that it also operated on the assumption that knowledge is socially constructed. Although Heather desired multiple perspectives, her frustration demonstrates that she also wanted some guidance on what to do with them and how to decide effective teaching practices for herself in the settings in which she would teach. She also found perspectives on urban education wanting given her student teaching experience. There is no evidence in her story that she explored how those perspectives and her original ideas related to form a more complex view; rather she reported discarding the new perspectives in favor of her original thoughts. Heather's story suggests that her program did not situate learning in her or her peers' experience (e.g., her student teaching), or validate them as knowers (e.g., by bringing her views into the discussion for reconsideration and transformation). Whereas instructors encouraged Lowell and Andrew to incorporate their experience with the class material to construct more complex perspectives, Heather was unable to incorporate her experience and thus chose between the two.

Translation to Educational Practice.   Contexts that helped learners construct what they believed among complex knowledge claims used the three core assumptions and three principles to help learners analyze multiple perspectives, establish and defend their own positions, and develop frameworks for authoring their own views. Instructors introduced multiple perspectives through course content and inviting learners' diverse experiences into learning. Instructors valued learners' previous experience yet invited learners to expand previous knowledge through mutual construction with instructors and peers in the face of new perspectives and knowledge. Activities and assignments that demanded establishing and defining one's own position offered both the invitation and the challenge to establish one's own beliefs. Instructors who facilitated exploration of positions and mutually constructed with students how to defend positions provided the support learners needed to author their own views. Introducing learners to frameworks for knowing in particular fields and how to apply those frameworks to the objects to be known (i.e., national security, economics, and medicine) helped learners develop on-going processes for authoring their beliefs and increasing their sophistication in their fields.

To create these conditions, pedagogy must move beyond knowledge acquisition to active knowledge construction. Acquiring basic knowledge is a necessary but insufficient layer of learning in every discipline. Learners cannot become experts in their field of study without acquiring the requisite knowledge, yet they cannot think critically and participate in the evolving development of their fields unless they know how to construct new knowledge to extend existing knowledge. Andrew and his peers needed requisite knowledge to simulate their airline, yet providing them with knowledge about how to run a business would have been insufficient. They needed the opportunity to apply existing knowledge to extend their ability to use business knowledge in actual work settings. Although knowledge acquisition may have been sufficient preparation for adult work roles in earlier times, the complexity and rapid change inherent in contemporary society require that higher education add the ability to actively construct knowledge to its list of goals for graduates.

Helping learners both acquire requisite knowledge and learn to actively construct knowledge can occur through simulations like Andrew's instructor used or actual projects such as marketing campaigns for local businesses. Simulations or "real-life" projects situate learning in students' experience; they must offer opportunities for mutual construction of a quality product and trust students to perform. A science course I observed used a simulation in zoology in which students chose a topic of interest to them and relevant to the course, synthesized the primary literature on that topic to identify the next step in the research, then wrote a grant proposal to justify funding for that step (Baxter Magolda, 1999b). They acquired the requisite knowledge by synthesizing the primary literature, learned the basics of the research process, and learned to actively construct knowledge all at once. Active knowledge construction can also be achieved through projects to explain particular phenomenon like Andrew's economics class and Lowell's national security course. Using existing knowledge to explain the phenomenon gives students an opportunity to interact with it and at the same time validates their capacity to defend their arguments and engages them in mutually constructing meaning. Similarly, projects, discussions, or examinations that offer opportunities to apply knowledge to various contexts, like Al's second-year medical school experience or Sandra and Anita's social work studies, help students learn existing knowledge and the process for deciding what to believe in the context of existing knowledge.

Inherent in these examples are key factors that help students learn to participate in the social construction of knowledge, including respecting students' epistemological assumptions, discussing ill-structured issues, offering opportunities to analyze others' views and defend one's own, teaching students how to gather, analyze, and make judgments about data, and helping students struggle with uncertainty (King & Kitchener, in press).

The key component that made these approaches work was not simply the technique of a simulation, project, or discussion but rather use of the framework of the three core assumptions and three principles. The beliefs about knowledge, learning, authority and learners inherent in this framework are a significant departure from the traditional view of authorities depositing knowledge in learners' brains. The vision of learning inherent in the framework to promote self-authorship resonates instead with contemporary approaches such as constructivist pedagogy. Constructivist pedagogy is based on viewing learning as:

> a self-regulatory process of struggling with the conflict between existing personal models of the world and discrepant new insights, constructing new representations and models of reality as a human meaning-making venture with culturally developed tools and symbols, and further negotiating such meaning through cooperative social activity, discourse, and debate. (Twomey-Fosnot, 1996, p. ix)

Constructivist pedagogy, which is gaining ground in science and mathematics educational reform efforts, endorses both the social construction of knowledge and mutual construction among learners and educators. Constructivist pedagogy certainly implies that the self is central to knowledge construction in its involvement of the learner in the knowledge construction process. Dewey Dykstra, a physicist, asked the question, "How can one come to know the nature of knowledge as something constructed and tentative if one never makes some of it oneself?" (1996, p. 200). Use of the three core assumptions and three principles to help students work with the complexity and social construction of knowledge conveyed the notion that self was central in knowledge construction. This second core assumption is taken up next.

The Central Role of the Self in Knowledge Construction

When educators encouraged participants to establish and defend their own positions in their graduate and professional education, they were encouraged to bring their own identities—their minds, voices, and selves—to learning.

Educators in these contexts emphasized that an internal sense of self is central to effective participation in the social construction of knowledge and offered opportunities for that internal sense of self to develop in the context of authoring one's beliefs.

Developing One's Own Beliefs. Reginald found support for developing his own sense of self in relation to his beliefs during his seminary education, which he embarked upon immediately after college graduation. Reginald's story begins with a struggle to express his own ideas and leads to claiming his own authority because his instructors' use of the three assumptions and principles offered him the support he needed for this crucial shift in the journey. His seminary education emphasized developing his own ideas, deciding what he believed, and integrating that with his own pastoral practice. The integration of the "who am I" question throughout his education helped him define his identity as a crucial part of deciding on his belief system. He described the beginning of the journey:

> There's another professor that allows creating your own ideas . . . he offers creative choices. You can do a regular paper or you can do something like a poem or a short story or a painting. And then also their doors are open to come in . . . or to hand something in and say, "I've struggled with this," or I might have had to hand in something a week later because I had started off in one direction and realized I was just spitting back someone else's words. But I've struggled with this and now I've done something that I need to write it for myself. And they present the grace of saying, "Yes, do that. That's what I expect. That's what I'd like you to do."

The faculty situated learning in Reginald's experience by encouraging him to create his own ideas through the format of assignments and the freedom to choose his approach. Reginald's instructors validated him as a knower by acknowledging the struggle involved in developing his own ideas and being flexible with deadlines to accommodate his struggle. As Reginald proceeded in seminary, the notion of developing his own beliefs expanded from expressing his own ideas to what he believed:

> What's going to start to happen [is] . . . What does this theory mean to me? What does it mean to live it? What does it mean to live what you believe? And very soon, I think it will continue throughout the year . . . the sense of systematic theology. Here's what other people believe. What is it that you believe?

> What is it that we believe as a community or at least profess
> that we believe? And what is the moral context and ethical
> nature of things?

This context asked Reginald to internalize his ideas into a larger framework of belief, to form a position that would enable him to live out his beliefs. He gathered more experience in this knowledge construction process through clinical work:

> We had a clinical pastoral education . . . doing a lot of what was
> being taught and starting to define identity along with what you
> were learning. That was probably a very big step in terms of
> learning, developing the sense of what it is that I'm doing, what
> it is that I'm learning, putting that into action. And also seeing
> that when you do put it into action, what part of yourself is that
> unique part that you bring to that role. . . . I felt there was a lot
> more independence given, that I could just help my own sense
> of authority—and claiming that.

Learning situated in his experience (the clinical pastoral work) helped Reginald connect his identity with what he had been taught. This enabled him to envision how *he* would do pastoral work, rather than how anyone would do it, further validating his ability to know. The independence he was offered helped him claim his own authority.

Alice's masters program in counseling also used the three principles to help students develop their own theoretical perspectives. She described the process:

> We did a lot of videotaping and audiotaping that were reviewed
> with the professor and kind of critiqued with different counsel-
> ing styles. And I thought that was real helpful. I guess just mem-
> orizing the concepts and writing them down is one thing, but
> then practicing them is a whole different ball game. And it
> helped me to find out which styles felt more natural for me, and
> it has kind of helped me evolve into what theoretical back-
> ground that I adhere most strongly to. By doing it some of them
> really feel better, seem to fit better than others. And the actual
> doing them on tape really helped in that process, I think.

Instructors situated learning various counseling styles in Alice's experience with clients, particularly useful because Alice entered her program immediately after college graduation. Alice explained why this was so important:

> Well, you read all these hundreds of different counseling theo-
> ries and it's just real overwhelming and confusing. They tell you

that they want you to work with it and develop your own—not that you have to pick one theory and say, "I'm this," and never do anything else. But they kind of want you to have in the back of your mind that you should be trying to evolve and select one that you feel is going to work best for you. You know, just try them on and see which ones fit your own personal philosophy and things like that. And by actually doing them and seeing them on tape, that helped me to do that process.

These comments suggest that in addition to helping students learn various counseling techniques, Alice's program focused on validating students as knowers through asking them to work with theoretical perspectives to identify ones that work best for individual students. Alice took her professors' invitations to experiment with various theories and to judge their fit with her personal philosophy. Actually using them made them more real and helped her determine what felt natural to her, contributing to her ability to self-author her counseling approach. She also learned from her professors that good therapists choose multiple approaches in the evolution of their approach. She acted on their advice in making choices about her own evolving therapeutic style:

I guess it just went with my personal philosophy, the way that I kind of view the world or people anyway. Like I said, it just felt better. I felt like I was able to be more genuine using that group of techniques and that type and style of counseling.

Alice had more extensive opportunities to experiment with counseling styles through internships. This experience further reinforced the necessity of clarifying her own thinking:

The hands-on experience through my practicum and internship has made me realize nobody else is in this room with me when I'm doing this counseling session. And so, for me to be clear on these issues, I need to figure them out for myself. Not to say that I'm ever going to figure them out, but to know where I stand on them and to think them through. And I think that's kind of encouraged that process. It's you and your client sitting there. I feel like if I'm not sure where I stand or I'm not clear on what the issues are and what the arguments are both ways and process that myself, then I don't see how I can be of any help at all to this client. So I think that's really encouraged me to do that.

Realizing that she needed to ascertain where she stood on issues stemmed from her instructors validating her capacity to develop a counseling style and theoretical perspective. Learning situated in her experience and mutual construction through critique of her work helped her move toward self-authorship. She described the outcome of her program:

> I think that I'm more independent. I'm more of a self-thinker, if that makes sense. I'm questioning things more, and I'm not taking—just because I take notes and then that's the way it is and that's all that's been written and that's law. I'm finding that I'm really questioning things and issues. Like with the dual diagnosis. I'm really sorting stuff out for myself instead of just taking notes about everybody else's opinion. In that way I think I'm a lot different.

Alice's professors expected students to learn counseling theories, yet they expected more than that. They expected Alice to bring her own sense of self to the process of constructing what she believed and how she would counsel her clients. Their guidance through the three principles helped Alice incorporate her sense of self into knowledge construction and achieve self-authorship.

Bringing the self to knowledge construction was not limited to the helping professions. Mark, who entered law school upon college graduation, described a similar emphasis there:

> One of the best ways I learned during law school [to function effectively as an attorney] was to talk to experienced practitioners. I took classes that would bring in a parade of trial lawyers each week. And we'd view various techniques. You'd use cross-examination, direct examination, opening and closing statements. We would prepare our own and then the practitioner would critique and tell us how he or she would approach it. That isn't rote memorization because part of being a good trial attorney is you have to be true to your own personal style.

Instructors validated Mark as a knower by allowing him the freedom to prepare his own examinations or statements. Instructors situated learning in students' experience as students' presented what they had prepared. Mutual construction took place with the expert practitioner sharing her or his approach and offering feedback.

Refining One's Belief System.   Making the self central to knowledge construction is not the same as letting students think anything they wish. Reginald, Alice, and Mark did not choose a personal style bereft of existing knowledge. The invitation their educational programs offered to bring the self to learning was not an invitation for independent knowing or choosing whatever one felt best without regard to existing knowledge and persuasive evidence. Critique, feedback, and on-going evolution of perspectives were mainstays in their experiences. Instructors encouraged them, primarily through mutual construction of meaning with experts, to choose their beliefs and practices in the context of existing knowledge. Instructors engaged them in the process of on-going learning and evolution. Participants clearly articulated their awareness of the contextual nature of their beliefs and the need for continued evolution to refine belief systems. For example, Andrew explained:

> The big thing is to see both views on a thing, and there may be more than just two. There may be several approaches to something. It's just a process of where you're coming from. And there are a lot of other views outside of your major that come into play, especially when it comes to economics. What you think is right as far as politically sometimes comes into the economic view that you support—whether you think the government should be bailing somebody out, whether the model that you use includes lots of government spending—it's going to be so different than somebody else that thinks the government shouldn't be involved.

Andrew was aware that his beliefs in one arena mediated his beliefs in another. This awareness helped him look more carefully at his own views and other views he might encounter. Sandra described a similar awareness of how self and beliefs mediated learning in her graduate social work classes:

> There will be different viewpoints . . . Some of the class will say, 'This is confidential and unless it fits under those specific legal guidelines of they're going to hurt themselves or somebody else, then you don't report that.' And then we'll make different cases for, 'Yes, you should,' or 'no, you shouldn't.' And I guess if somebody could come up with some pretty good reasons as to why you should or shouldn't, then if it's consistent with how I feel I will take that. But if I don't feel that way on a gut level, then they're going to have to come up with a lot more to be able to convince me that you shouldn't report it.

Sandra's own gut level feeling (which I interpret as her sense of self and knowledge she had previously constructed) mediated her reaction to the rationale her peers offer. If their rationale was consistent with her current view she accepted it. If their reasoning differed from her current view, it would take more evidence to change her mind. Yet she valued the mutual construction with peers to refine her thinking.

Ross was attuned to his own biases and the need to monitor them to expand his views. Describing this dynamic in his seminary studies, he said:

Most of the time I try to, I would hope I'm being objective. That's what our professors harp on, being objective when you come. But I've found it near impossible to do, in coming with so many experiences and knowing to a certain degree what God has done in my life and the different things and people I've seen changed. And to forget all that and let's be totally neutral and see what these different people say—it's been real difficult, to take that neutral stand. . . . One of the most important things is recognizing what you come to questions with—this bias, or this experience—recognize it and try to not look from just that experience, but from this other person's point of view. . . . It's too easy to come to questions and say this is the answer based on what we've heard or experienced rather than looking at all sides.

Ross made it clear that his own experience was a powerful force that shaped how he approached knowledge construction yet he realized the importance of looking beyond his experience to examine many sides. He judged relying on his experience for deciding as "too easy" and worked instead to hear other perspectives before deciding what to believe. Ross conveyed a comfort with his own sense of self that allowed him to open his mind to other perspectives, a concept that will be taken up in more detail in the next section on learning as mutually constructing meaning. Having encountered learning situated in their own experience coupled with the expectation for mutual construction, Andrew, Sandra, and Ross learned to blend their experience with existing knowledge and others' perspectives to refine their belief systems.

Dilemmas with the Self as Central.   Not all educational experiences welcomed the self into the knowledge construction process. Some of the stories told earlier conveyed contexts in which instructors did not invite students to establish their own beliefs (see Dilemmas with Social Construction of Knowledge earlier in this chapter). Sometimes instructors explicitly excluded the self, as Cara shared from one of her graduate psychology courses in which the instructor told the students they would exclusively use his perspective. More often the lack of invitation to bring the self to learning was indirect, as Laura's story about her graduate work shows:

When you're taking all economics, a lot of mathematics, they're shaping the way you think about things. I really am fearful of that. And I sometimes fear that I'm losing creativity over this logical process of thinking in economics. A large part of myself is very creative. I play the piano; I can draw. And the more I go in this logical direction, the more I seem to lose my creative side.

Laura's instructors did not value creativity in the logical bent of her classes thus she feared losing it (Laura entered her MBA program immediately after college graduation). Andrew's earlier story about economics suggests that it could be taught in ways that invited the self as central and involved creativity in approaching how to run a business.

Another dilemma arose for some participants who had not yet developed a sense of self to use in knowledge construction. Amy, pursuing continuing education courses two years after graduation, offered an example:

We would have [to] give our own opinions on artists—were they pop artists or pre-pop? And I would just be like ugh . . . What in the world could I have to say? It had probably already been hashed out. Different people have different opinions and it's so hard for me to say 'this is *my* opinion. 'It was easier for me to say these are the pros and cons of different people.

Amy was comfortable summarizing what other people thought but had a hard time imagining what she could contribute to the conversation. She noted that part of why it was hard for her to say "this is *my* opinion" was being "scared of showing my own ideas, being completely off." Amy did not yet have the sense of self that allowed her to have confidence in developing her own opinions, let alone sharing them with others.

Gavin spoke to this same dilemma in retrospect as he described how a personal change in himself changed his approach to learning when he returned to school after four years in the insurance business to acquire a master's degree in education:

Last time I was in school, I preferred to be very quiet, get notes and leave. I was extremely apprehensive about interaction—I didn't like group work, etc. I've done the full 360. Exactly opposite now. I don't mind that environment, but love interaction now. It's a combination of life experience selling insurance— prospecting for business you gain humility and confidence. The feeling of learning how to get a prospect, get one, close it—that type of learning curve is carried over to academics. I'm taking one graduate course now, European historiography. There are no notes, no tests. Sixteen of us; we sit in a circle and read two or three documents, come in and discuss and analyze. We give presentations—I would have dropped this five years ago. Now I've gained confidence that I lacked.

Gavin explained that the confidence stemmed from his increased understanding of himself and his purpose:

> I'm going after what I want to do. At Miami it was just to get degree to do who knows what? I didn't care before. I just wanted to get on with life. Now its "What am I going to use this for when I get my own class?" because I found what I want to do. That gives me a lot of confidence and direction. When I get to class, it is an environment I'm comfortable in, more confident in there than any other aspect of my life. It's amazing when you actually figure out what you want to do—it changes you, gives you a confidence. I touch base with a couple of people I've worked with and they say they can tell a difference in the way that I act. When I talk, I talk about what I'm doing. I'm excited about it.

Gavin's graduate courses advocated the social construction of knowledge and the central role of self in that process. However, his story illustrates that he needed to develop some sense of self in the form of career purpose to be able to engage in this knowledge construction opportunity. He apparently did not encounter sufficient emphasis on or support for incorporating the self in his undergraduate education. Additional guidance is needed for those who are beginning to develop a sense of self as part of knowledge construction, a topic that resurfaces in the next portion of the chapter.

Translation to Educational Practice.   Contexts that helped participants develop the sense of self needed for knowledge construction used the three principles to guide learners in developing their own belief systems. Educators validated learners' ability to form their own beliefs and doing so was conveyed as an important part of becoming a professional in their fields. Educators situated learning in students' own experience as learners practiced various theoretical perspectives or practical approaches; yet learning was simultaneously grounded in the existing knowledge of learners' respective fields. Mutually constructing meaning with experts and peers to refine their belief systems taught them a continual process of learning and incorporating new knowledge.

Self as central to knowledge construction is not a new concept. Feminist pedagogy, described by writers like Belenky et al. (1986), bell hooks (1994), Gloria Ladson-Billings (1994) and Nel Noddings (1984), entails an explicit focus on the role of self in its emphasis on respecting and caring for students to empower them to find their own voices, learn from their experience, and learn in connection with others. Forms of critical, liberatory, and empowering education (Shor, 1992, 1996) also emphasize the role of the self in their invitation to learners to critique existing knowledge and form their own beliefs. Proponents of using narrative in education also regard self as central to knowledge construction. For example, Richard Hopkins wrote, "Our narratives are the means through which we imagine ourselves into the persons we become" (1994, p. xvii). Similarly, Maher and Tetreault argued that students "bring their own questions and perspectives to the material, they use relevant personal experiences to shape a narrative of an emerging self" (1994, p. 18).

Implementing the assumption that self is central to knowledge construction is undoubtedly the most significant challenge to reforming higher education to promote self-authorship. Helping students establish their own belief systems, determine how to implement them in their professional practice, and refine them as knowledge and they as professionals evolve again calls for a layer of education beyond knowledge acquisition. It requires conveying information in a way that links existing knowledge to students' experience and development, engaging the messiness of working through knowledge claims, and engaging in genuine mutual construction with learners. It is hard to translate into concrete techniques because it is a matter of sharing authority and mutual engagement in thinking and learning. It is possible, however, and yields major rewards. The self-authorship Reginald and Alice describe is clearly a result of this multi-layered practice and their stories exemplify how educators implemented this assumption. I observed this pedagogical approach in a college mathematics course that emphasized students' personal construction of mathematics. Class time was spent on students investigating some aspect of mathematical structure, sharing their conjectures about it, and mutually constructing meaning about the topic at hand. Students in the course, most of whom were juniors and seniors, reported understanding mathematics for the first time and felt that they could construct mathematical ideas at the end of the course (Baxter Magolda, 1999b).

Implementing this assumption involves transforming traditional perspectives about teaching, learning, learners and authority. Blythe Clinchy (2000) argued that this means making education "more connected" by giving students permission to reflect, develop and defend positions, enter the perspectives of their peers, and build on each others' ideas as well as teachers who will share the process of their thinking and think out loud. These recommendations invite self as central both on the part of students and educators. Similarly, Mary Howard-Hamilton (2000) advocated inviting students' selves into learning.

Encouraging students to engage in self-reflection and empowering them to express themselves are crucial components of her vision of a culturally responsive learning environment that simultaneously promotes students' racial identity. Inviting the self into a central role also requires the third core assumption, learning as mutual construction of meaning.

Learning as Mutual Construction of Meaning

Assuming knowledge is socially constructed and that self plays a central role in that construction leads to the assumption that learning involves mutual construction of meaning. In this view of learning expertise and authority are shared among learners and educators as they mutually construct knowledge. Educators bring their expertise to the dialogue and invite students to do the same. Working collaboratively, educators and learners reflect on their experience, analyze existing knowledge, explore connections between experience and knowledge, and exchange insights to arrive at their own beliefs. The dynamics of mutual construction of meaning helped participants develop their own views and move toward self-authorship. Although the principle of defining learning as mutually constructing meaning is the most closely related to this assumption, validating learners as knowers and situating learning in their experiences were central to engaging them in this mutual endeavor.

The Role of Respect and Shared Authority.   An important characteristic that helped participants develop the sense of self so necessary for authoring their own beliefs and participating in mutual construction was respectful professors. Deirdre, getting her masters in teaching the year after college graduation, summarized it like this:

> We're not treated like kids; we don't act like kids. Some people don't work in the class and the teacher accepts that but doesn't take it like a personal thing. . . . We're all adults in there. And there's that kind of respect and listening to each other and it's less master-slave.

Her comparison to master-slave speaks to her sense of the traditional role of teacher and student in which students are not validated as knowers. Deirdre appreciated being validated as an adult capable of sound decision-making. Sandra offered an example of how this respect played out in her graduate classes:

> If you have a question they're going to explain it and they're not going to go, 'Well, it's in your notes.' They're really good about explaining, and if you have an example that you just don't

understand where it would fit, they'll tell you. Or they'll help you figure it out. And that's kind of how I think it should be. . . . if she didn't know, she said, 'I don't know. Let me look that up or check that with the agency that you work at to see who's going to be liable'. . . . and told us where to find state law if we'd like to look it up.

Sandra appreciated professors joining her in exploring how knowledge applied in her work setting rather than implying that she should simply consult her notes. This attitude—validation of learners as knowers—is a key ingredient of learning settings in which learners are regarded as professionals. Kelly spoke explicitly to the importance of her graduate professors accepting her as a professional:

The professors use more of our knowledge. The feeling that I get from the professors is that they accept me as a professional. They expect me to come to the class with all this knowledge. And they're going to take that knowledge and maybe expand on a part of it and make me maybe see a different avenue of a part of my knowledge. I feel like they'll use the knowledge that's in the class, they'll use all the different areas in the class. Like just last night, only five out of fifteen of us showed up because we had ice storms. But just with the five of us we had one person working for IBM in the Writing to Read program, we had another Chapter 1 teacher, a media specialist of a school district, a plain old graduate student, and me, the kindergarten teacher. Just within the five of us there was a vast amount of different types of knowledge. He was pulling things out of each one of us differently and actually tying it all together to make us see a point. And I felt like the level of respect was there. Because, I mean, I consider myself a professional. And that professionalism doesn't leave me just because I walk in a classroom door. And it's nice to be treated like I've got knowledge. . . . It makes me feel more confident. The respect that I feel from the professors makes me more comfortable to maybe go out on a limb and say something that I might not be so sure of. Their respect helps me to get more out of the class because I'm going to feel better about contributing. And I'm going to contribute more. So ultimately I get more out of the class.

Integrating the knowledge and experience of learners in the class demonstrated to Kelly that the professor valued her knowledge, an important dynamic because Kelly taught full-time while pursuing her masters in the summers. Because she was welcomed as a knowledgeable professional, she felt more confident to actively engage in learning. She joined in mutual construction of knowledge because instructors situated learning in her experience and validated her as a knower.

Andrew reported that his graduate professors incorporated more of students' thinking about both content and process into the classes:

> I find in economics, we talk about what's going on in the *Wall Street Journal* or articles all the time. The same thing in finance; we pull a lot more in and it's a lot more open discussion. The teacher asks, "When's the best day for the test for you? Let's look at our schedules. Do you want to take it at night so we can have a longer time frame? Do more of an essay test?" There's a lot more of that going on. A lot less, "This is the way it is.". . . When we have (exams) we sat down and discussed, depending on when would be a good break as far as what we're going to be studying and whether we did cases in classes. Do we want to do more than one team project? So a lot of that was a lot more flexible and it wasn't set for you right away. . . . A lot more of your thinking is put into class.

These educators not only respected Kelly and Andrew, they invited them to share authority. In Kelly's case the instructor advocated sharing expertise among the professor and members of the class; in Andrew's case the instructor invited sharing expertise and decisions about class process. These conditions helped learners explore and develop their internal beliefs about both the content and process of their learning.

In some cases respect took the form of acknowledgement and empathy for learners' perspectives. Cara described an awkward situation in which two male students in the class she was teaching as part of her doctoral assistantship asked her for a date. Her advisors, one woman and one man, interpreted the situation differently. She explained:

> [My female advisor] really helped, being a woman. I felt like she understood things I was saying that [my male advisor] couldn't relate to. After these students asked me out, I was asking myself "What am I doing?" [My male advisor] thought it was a compliment. [My female advisor] understood—she would say I was internalizing this and shouldn't. He never got it. She understood my experience better and had more empathy. [Then] I had more confidence—she gave me good direction; was a good role model. Watching how she handled herself was good for me to see.

Cara's female advisor accepted Cara's concern about this situation (validating her as a knower) and mutually constructed meaning of it with her. Cara found this more affirming, both in handling this situation and her teaching role in general, than her male advisor's response to not worry about it. His response dismissed her concern, offering little respect for her way of making meaning of the situation. Respect for learners' perspectives was a key component of learners' ability to participate in mutual construction to develop their own views.

The Role of Mutual Exchange of Knowledge. Mutual exchange of knowledge with others led to active engagement in learning, useful frameworks for discussion and analysis, new insights from peers, and learning to discern and defend one's position. Justin described active engagement in the education classes he started in his mid-twenties to change careers:

> People talk a lot more. There's a lot more questions and answers and discussion. It's a lot more of an open classroom. It's a lot better learning experience, instead of the lecture, take notes, and leave when the time's up. The professors are able to generate interest in the subject matter because they are into it, they believe it. It really sparks interest, sparks discussion, and you get a lot more out of it because people are talking. You really can clarify your beliefs, you can really identify what you think is right or wrong or will or won't work because you've got all this verbal interaction as opposed to a lecture setting where you just get the material and that's it. If you are not involved in it, who cares? If you're not sparking any thought, if you're just not thinking about it, if your wheels aren't turning in your head then it's not doing you much good.

For Justin, verbal interaction was an opportunity to exchange ideas with his peers about what might work in teaching or help clarify his own beliefs. Talking with peers prompted him to think in ways that "taking notes" did not. Although Justin emphasized verbal interaction, the crucial insight in his comments relates to the wheels turning to clarify beliefs rather than "take notes and leave."[1]

Lowell's story recounts more details about how active engagement through mutual exchange with educators and peers merged to promote his own knowledge construction. He said:

---

[1]Educators and students often believe that getting the wheels turning requires verbal interaction. Richard Hake (1998) notes that learning requires active engagement, what he calls "heads-on" activity. This may also include "hands-on" activity, but hands-on activity can also be devoid of having students' heads on. In my course observation study I witnessed an interactive lecture approach that actively engaged students in mutual construction of meaning (see Baxter Magolda, 1999b for an extensive description of the class). This experience dispels the myth that lecture cannot spark thinking and self-authorship. The key issue is that passive lecture, the kind Justin describes as taking notes and leaving, does not promote self-authorship.

> Our professor starts off the class with some anecdote about his experiences. They're often funny, but that initiates discussion. And he sort of acts as referee, and we kind of throw arguments back and forth at each other. He'll summarize things and say "Okay, here's this, this and this," or he'll tell us a fact that he's seen because he's worked so closely with it. And then we discuss it and say, "Ah, well you know, that's wrong," or "they shouldn't have done that." It is a different type of learning.

Lowell's depiction of the instructor as referee reiterates that the instructor plays an important role in mutual construction. Here, Lowell's instructor framed the discussion, guided the students' progress, and inserted existing knowledge in ways that moved the conversation forward and enriched the mutual construction of knowledge. Although the instructor validated students' ability to know by giving them freedom to explore, and simultaneously situated learning in their experience, he still brought his expertise to the discussion. Lowell enjoyed this type of learning because it provided him with multiple perspectives:

> I enjoy taking the argumentative side if there is one; if someone is speaking conservatively, then I take a liberal view. I enjoy, not arguing, but discussing. If they come to arguments, then we've failed. Mulling over an issue or a topic and trying to get all perspectives that are possible. . . . There are a number of people like myself who work in the federal government and for business who have a lot of experience. So they can bring a lot of their own experiences . . . into the classroom situation. Many people are interns at the World Bank or the International Monetary Fund or State Department. . . . So the professor starts off, and everybody can put their input in. And it's pretty relevant since most people are really tightly involved in what's going on.

Situating learning in this group's experience gave Lowell access to others' expertise and validated his own. The range of expertise enriched the mutual exchange of knowledge. Lowell's enjoyment of this type of learning stemmed from debates it created within himself about ways to think and what to think:

> Especially when people bring up facts that I didn't know. You are going to have a theoretical opinion and that hopefully is based on facts that you have learned. In the Soviet Union class there are a lot of things now that I'm learning that I didn't know and that changes what my answers would be. My beliefs or values haven't changed, but if you know something to be a fact and it is different from what you believed, if you don't change, if you

are not pragmatic, then you're just going to sink. And if you close your eyes to the truth, or what other people see as truth, then you're going to fail. That's when arguments happen [when people don't consider other perspectives].

These comments reveal that Lowell's beliefs evolved through mutual construction of knowledge with others who have expertise in the topic. Describing the effects of this type of learning at the end of his first year of graduate school, Lowell said:

I think I'm more patient. I'm more willing to open myself up to other sorts of experiences, other people's points of view, more open-minded I think. I don't want to give the impression that it's wishy-washy, just more open-minded. I still like, as I say, to discuss. And I do enjoy taking a position and sticking by it or trying to. And perhaps I learn more when I'm forced not to stick by it, hopefully.

Lowell's instructor set the stage for mutual construction of knowledge. He gave the class a context for discussion and refereed as they shared their experience and opinions. Students explored multiple perspectives and the instructor encouraged them to listen to and debate those perspectives. The instructor added ideas from his own experience as appropriate to extend the conversation. Lowell enjoyed advancing his own views and challenging himself to support them. Yet he also valued the experience of his peers who were in meaningful work roles. The emphasis on deciding what to believe supported Lowell's intrapersonal growth in incorporating himself into the knowledge construction process. The emphasis on exchanging expertise facilitated Lowell's interpersonal growth. The combination of these two dimensions of his development led to Lowell's increased openness to new perspectives and his ability to mutually construct knowledge with others without automatically accepting their views or automatically sticking to his own. Lowell's graduate program offered good company and helped him achieve self-authorship.

Mutual exchange to discern and defend one's own position occurred in individual faculty-student interactions, as Alice described in her counseling internship:

I have a site supervisor who I review all my cases with a couple of times a week. And then once a week I meet with my adviser, who also supervises me as far as going over my cases. It's real tight supervision. I'm glad it is. I would feel like I was floundering without it. They can give me some insights or different

> strategies that they feel might be effective. And a lot of times what they're doing is just kind of letting me flounder through it and go through the process myself. And while that's hard, I remember it and use it better if it's something that I came up with than if they just told me, "Use this technique; this works best for this."

Alice appreciated the high quality supervision yet valued working through strategies and techniques alone. Her supervisor and advisor both shared insights with her but emphasized her self-authorship as they discussed her cases. Thus they modeled all three principles in their interactions with her.

The Role of Trust.   Mutual exchange and developing one's own beliefs in this collaborative context required trust among learners and between learners and educators. Alice articulated this dynamic:

> I'm taking a counseling techniques class. It's hands-on, they throw you in the video booth and just do it. . . . There's a group of four of us and two supervisors. We view them as a group of six. We each point out what we think are the strengths and weaknesses of that session, what we think needs improvement, what was good. You get a lot of feedback from different sources. So I think that's been real helpful. . . . You learn to trust those people real quick.

Mutual construction about their performance made Alice and her peers vulnerable as the group watched their tapes and critiqued their counseling skill. Trust was important to both accepting and giving feedback in the group.

Exploring what to believe also required trust among peers. Deirdre described its effect in one of her classes:

> It's a really dynamic kind of environment. The class is so close now. I mean, I know everybody in there; I could talk to them about anything. It's very close and we work well with the teacher. And I think we all see each other as very different in terms of what we'll choose to read for each other. And that's a whole good thing. You can look at them and really appreciate what they have to offer. And the class seems really rich because there are some really different people in there.

Reginald had a similar experience in seminary:

> This year is the first time I did a study group, I used to do things individually. I had a good study group of people I trusted, and

some interesting things came out of that group in terms of what people were believing—it was a biblical class on the prophets. A critical analysis of it, learning different people's views of how they went about biblical interpretation. Where they drew the line in terms of critical analysis and scripture, holy piety kind of thing. We were very close—we knew how to laugh together—but had differences in beliefs.

Reginald and Deirdre conveyed that trust among learners led to a closeness that supported exploration of varying beliefs. Trust supported individual learners to take risks to share their evolving beliefs, entertain the beliefs of others, and work toward self-authorship.

Trust between educator and learner was equally important. Instructors made Sandra's struggle with how to handle particular mental health dilemmas easier by sharing their own struggles. She experienced a trust with instructors who would say:

'Well, gosh, that really bothers me too.' So that's probably the biggest help, especially when the professor says so, too, 'Well, yeah. I've been in this field for however long, and that still really bothers me too.' Or, 'It's still a really difficult decision to know what to do.'

Educators' vulnerability helped learners put their own struggles into perspective and created a sense of reciprocity and rapport. The lack of this mutual trust and empathy interfered with the knowledge construction process as is evident in the next set of stories.

Complications with Mutual Construction.   Some educational environments attempted mutual construction but failed due to the absence of the principles to bridge the gap between expectations and learners' development. Pamela's experience in a graduate education course illustrates what happens when insufficient guidance and respect exists:

They tried to teach us by inquiry. And they kind of went a little overboard in it, pushing too many things too fast with not enough guidance. This was total unguided, free inquiry. 'Here's something, figure it out.' And I felt like I was spinning my wheels a lot, trying to do these activities. I did learn a little bit more about the inquiry approach to teaching, and I think it was good—you really have to learn in a certain way in order to teach that way. But I think they needed to give us a little bit more guidance. Some of the activities were so unstructured that you would do something and then when you'd finally go to have it checked—they would have a checkpoint and the instructor would come along and ask you questions about things and then you'd move on. Well, some of those steps took a full day to do and then you'd go to the checkpoint and you found out that everything you had been doing was on the wrong track. And so you had to go back and start all over again. I felt like we had to do that too many times. And any time you asked a question it was answered with a question. After a while it got to be really, really annoying. Sometimes after thinking so hard for eight hours you just want an answer. 'Will you answer my question, please? Don't give me another question. I'm tired of thinking.' Also, just kind of the attitude of the instructors. I felt they were a little condescending at times. And here we are, a group of teachers taking time out of our summer to learn about this because we want to, yet when you go there they make you feel stupid. It made me feel like I was a really bad teacher. It destroyed any self-esteem I had or any self-confidence I had in the classroom.

This approach to mutual construction was too challenging for Pamela given her confidence level, despite her having two years teaching experience. Although learning was clearly situated in learners' experience, and it seemed that they were validated as knowers when they were given the freedom to pursue the tasks, Pamela's reactions suggest that there was insufficient validation because of instructors' condescending comments and failure to adjust when the learners needed more guidance. The frustration of failed attempts overshadowed whatever learning took place in those attempts. The lack of respect Pamela perceived from the instructors interfered with her ability to stay engaged with the tasks because she felt stupid. This shook her self-confidence, the exact opposite outcome espoused by inquiry courses. Despite these negative feelings, Pamela reported that she learned in the course:

I did learn a lot. It did get me to rethink ideas that I had in the past. And I realize that some of the things that I thought I knew and had a strong content knowledge of and good understanding I really didn't because of the class. And it made me think deeper into things rather than just looking right on the surface. So that's one thing I did learn from it. And one topic that a lot of people struggled with was growth because as we dug deeper and deeper into questioning about growth and just talking about it, most of us realized that we really didn't know what growth was.

Digging deeper into topics revealed to Pamela and her classmates that their understanding was insufficient. Her dedication to teaching, rather than the encouragement of her instructors, prompted her to acknowledge this short-coming in her knowledge. Due to the insufficient participation of the instructors in the mutual construction of knowledge, however, what Pamela gained was a realization of something she did not know; she did not move closer to self-authorship from this experience. Use of the three principles in the follow-up session during the academic year did promote her self-authorship, as she reported a year later:

> We had academic year follow-up sessions throughout the course of the year, and things were much better in the follow-up sessions. A lot of the bad feelings were made better. And it was nice to get to meet with professionals. We met six times during the school year, spent a whole day together. We had time to share ideas—what's working, what did we try from the institute or what did we develop ourselves to share ideas. I feel like I have a nice network of teachers around the state that if I need an idea I can call these people up.

Professionals meeting together who mutually respected each other assuaged the "bad feelings." Pamela appreciated having a network of professionals with whom to explore her ideas and plans. The major distinction between the course and the follow-up sessions was the degree of respect and empathy learners perceived to support taking new risks. Had support in the form of increased respect as well as guidance been prevalent in the course, it would have taken on the same dynamics as the follow-up sessions.

Mutual construction was also complicated by the gender-related styles learners used to interact with each other. Cara explained this issue in describing her struggle with her doctoral peers despite the nature of her seminars, which emphasized discussion and equality among learners:

> Some people like competitiveness to make them work harder. I am mildly competitive, but more into doing for myself. I don't like the feeling—what did you get? [or] not helping each other; that makes me tense, and interferes with my learning. I am clicking with some, but there are no women [in the program]. I would be more comfortable if there were more women.

Cara's desire for more women in the program related to how she perceived the men interacting with each other and the fact that men's style of interaction dominated the seminars:

Socially I wasn't prepared to be a good interacter in these classes. I knew I was smart enough. I would wait, didn't want to cut others off, felt unsure, and my thoughts were not completely formulated. Others didn't [hesitate]—men in particular. People said I needed to participate. Ph.D. seminars were totally different than what I had experienced and I struggled with the lack of direction. It was hard until I got comfortable with people, then I could get in more. I am still less vocal; this has to do with being female. Men cut people off; they don't care. They want to tell what they know. Some are from MBA backgrounds; they are not introspective. I wasn't fitting in with this Ph.D. environment, but was just as knowledgeable; I wasn't expressing it their way. I have made an effort to move toward this. I noticed I cut people off more; it is not a conscious choice, I just jump in. Before I would have said "I'm sorry." I don't state the obvious [because] I feel like that is boasting. Why would I tell someone what they already know?

Cara viewed this style of interaction as competitive because it encouraged students to showcase their knowledge. Cara struggled with this atmosphere initially because she was unsure of her thoughts, inexperienced in discussion, and needed to connect with her peers before substantively participating. Yet even when she was sure of her thoughts, her style of expression varied from that of her peers. This difference became apparent in a group project:

I worked with a guy on a project in a statistics course. I had already had a lot of it, and he hadn't. We had a computer project. I knew the package and he wanted to practice. I would say "why don't you try this?" the translation being "this would work." Sometimes he would and sometimes he wouldn't. When it worked, he would act surprised. I said to him that he didn't trust that I knew this. He got upset! He said he couldn't tell from my tone of voice if I knew it. I hadn't thought of it that way. It was eye opening. Wow! He is one of first people I questioned about it, and he was honest and told me.

This interaction made Cara aware that her peers did not value her opinion because of her tone of voice. Because she invited him to try a particular approach rather than telling him it would work, her classmate doubted her knowledge. Because Cara's style was the exception in this program, she had to adjust. The implication of her story is that effective mutual construction requires teaching students various styles through which to mutually construct knowledge. The gender-related patterns that emerged from the college phase of this study (Baxter Magolda, 1992) are consistent with Cara's portrayal of styles in her program. The men in her program used a separate pattern of knowing in which they focused on refining their own knowledge and their opportunity to share it with others. Cara, in contrast, used a connected pattern of knowing in which she linked her ideas to those of others and waited patiently to be included in the conversation. Because these styles have surfaced in numerous studies (e.g., Belenky, Clinchy, Goldberger, and Tarule, 1986; Gilligan, 1982; Kegan, 1994), teaching learners about these styles and their effect on interaction is necessary to effectively implement mutual construction of knowledge. Validating both styles in crucial to creating an inclusive learning environment.

Learners' Reactions to the Lack of Mutual Construction. To some degree, Cara's struggle in her doctoral work stemmed from experiences in her master's program, which she enrolled in upon college graduation. That program did not value mutual construction of knowledge, leaving Cara dissatisfied with what she learned:

> I thought [the program] would be a little more intellectual and kind of like group studying and people sharing ideas. It's much more competitive. Everybody wants to get the A. If you know something, you only share it with a few people because you don't want anyone else to do better than you. You pretty much walk in and you take a lot of notes and you leave. And it's run like a drill sergeant; he's like 'We're going to do this, this and this.' I thought we'd be more on the same level. In the Ph.D. program at [another school] I know that they are treated more adultlike in their classes. And their views are—I mean, they sit around and talk. They study and learn. I personally learn better when I am able to just understand everything and when I know all the whys in understanding it. This atmosphere is the "what." 'Can you memorize everything in your chapters? You don't need to understand it.' I don't think that is right at this level. It's like a cow; I'm chewing up information and then spitting it back. That's all I'm doing. But I do know it.

Cara articulated that she "knew" the material but did not understand it. She also acquired no experience in talking with peers to further her understanding. She was not treated as an adult or encouraged to self-author her beliefs. Thus she completed her master's program with memorized content and minimal readiness for the seminar discussions she would encounter in her doctoral work.

Lindsey shared a similar experience in his economics masters program, which he started on a part-time basis a year after his college graduation:

To be honest with you, I haven't had too many graduate-level classes that I actually looked forward to going to. Maybe it's because it's night school and you're tired already. But so far there have been very few conversational classes. All four of them that I've had have all been one sided: teacher talks, you listen. I don't have a problem with that per se. I mean, there are some things that have to be achieved that way. But after a while that'll drive you nuts. I'm only taking one class right now at a time. But if I were to take all five of these classes at once and sit through a lecture day after day after day, I think I'd want to blow my brains out after a while. I've taken the econometrics class, which is very technical, and I've taken the macroeconomics and the microeconomics, and another sort of mathematically oriented class. I think it depends on the teacher because you could make the macro or the micro more of a discussion-oriented class if you were good, I think.

Although Lindsey acknowledged that part of his dissatisfaction could stem from fatigue, it is clear that his classes did not focus on mutual construction. Lindsey accepted that the "teacher talks, you listen" approach might be necessary at times yet he believed that a good teacher could educate through discussion. The nature of his classes led to lack of enjoyment; Lindsey made it clear that he would not be able to handle this on a fulltime basis.

Barb's law school classes (which she started part-time a year after college graduation) mimicked Cara's and Lindsey's programs, but she simultaneously experienced a different learning environment in her work as a law clerk:

A recent sort of revelation that I had is the different kinds of learning that I've had in school as opposed to work. In law school, all you really have to do really is a lot of memorization; it's a lot of information. The actual principles aren't really that hard to understand themselves. It's just all new and you just have to spend the time to get it all organized in your mind. At work it is more of correlation, trying to find facts and apply them to a certain case, which is more difficult to me that memorizing facts and just learning a bunch of information. . . . I guess the thing I find challenging at work is they'll give me a problem and I'll have to go and find an answer to it. But I'm reading so many different things that could apply or you try to twist the facts to make it apply, that you lose sight of what you're looking for in the first place. You have to keep going back and reading what you initially set out to find. Law school helps because you know what to look for and you know the rules behind it. But as far as making arguments or trying to find things that would apply to your situation, it's correlation type things. I wouldn't be able to do what I'm doing if I didn't have [the basis of] law school. It leads you right—if you know this problem's going to be on constitutional law of something, you know where to go for that and you know the basic principles behind it. But I think it's much more challenging than actual law school.

Barb's law school classes contributed to her ability to perform her clerk work yet they did not really prepare her for law practice. This exemplifies the insufficient nature of education as knowledge acquisition alone. She found the nature of her work more challenging because she was able to use information in problem solving and application to a context. Her law school classes could have used cases to offer her the same kind of challenge she experienced in her work—a challenge that validated her as a knower and situated learning in her experience. Fortunately she became aware of the nature of law work through her clerkship; without that experience she would have entered practice without the skills to apply what she knew to particular cases. Collectively, the learning environments that focused on memorization, listening to the instructor, and repeating knowledge did not contribute to the continued educational or work environments in which participants would find themselves because at best they focused on knowledge acquisition rather than the additional layer of active knowledge construction. Learners viewed these programs as processes to survive rather than productive learning environments.

Translation to Educational Practice. Contexts that successfully engaged learners in mutual construction of knowledge respected students, shared authority with students, guided the exchange of knowledge among learners, engendered trust among learners and educators, and included diverse styles of participating in mutual construction of meaning. Validating learners as knowers through respect and shared authority strengthened their confidence to bring their knowledge and experience to the mutual exchange of knowledge. This validation also made it possible to accept critical feedback and challenge their own beliefs. Having learning situated in their own experience, either through class discussions that invited their experience or activities in which they could practice what they were learning, heightened its meaning and got the wheels turning in their heads. When educators used the three principles to create bridges between learners' current development and self-authorship, trust developed that enabled authentic participation in mutual exchange of knowledge.

As was the case with the first two core assumptions, the stories reveal more about a vision of learning and pedagogy than they do concrete techniques.

Some concrete forms of implementing this framework are obvious in the stories. Sandra, Kelly, Andrew, and Cara shared various ways instructors treated them that promoted their ability to join in mutual construction. Sharon Fries-Britt (2000) cited faculty members assuming students were capable as a significant factor in engaging African-American students in mutual construction. Justin and Lowell described how class discussion can create mutual construction to promote learning and self-authorship. Alice described how feedback could be shared in ways that promoted self-authorship. Their stories support Michael Ignelzi's (2000) recommendations for promoting self-authorship, which include among others, critical thinking exercises, ethical dilemma discussions, journal writing, and group work as means to provide structure, guidance, support and feedback for evolving self-authorship. Deirdre and Reginald spoke to the value of helping students get to know each other for mutual construction to succeed. Similarly, Anna Ortiz (2000) emphasized the value of building a sense of community in which students feel free to participate, take risks, and begin to trust their own meaning-making. She recommended this community building in the context of helping learners develop intercultural competence. Even the stories about complications offer suggestions, such as Barb's opportunities to apply knowledge to cases. These examples, however, are not successful because they are discussion-oriented, constructive feedback, or interesting cases. They are successful in promoting self-authorship because they implement the framework of the three core assumptions connected to students' development through the three principles. Implementing that framework stemmed from a belief in empowering learners to construct knowledge, beliefs inherent in the critical, liberatory, feminist and constructivist contemporary pedagogical approaches noted earlier in this chapter.

Transforming Higher Education to Promote Self-Authorship

Although I separated the three assumptions to highlight each one, the stories demonstrate that contexts that promote self-authorship integrate all three. I now offer a synthesis of pedagogy that integrates all three and address the promise and challenges of transforming higher education toward this form of pedagogy.

Pedagogy that Promotes Self-Authorship

The collective stories yield a vision of pedagogy that actively engages learners in analyzing multiple perspectives and applying existing knowledge within contexts to establish and defend their own perspectives. This vision of pedagogy guides learners in developing a framework for knowing so that they can develop their own beliefs, implement them in their professional practice, and refine them as their experience and knowledge evolves. Respecting learners' experience, concerns, and capacity to learn, sharing authority with learners, building trust, and engaging in mutual construction of meaning with learners supports these expectations. This vision of pedagogy is an implementation of the three core assumptions connected to learners' development via the three principles.

The vision of pedagogy that emerges from the participants' stories enhances an already existing form of pedagogy. The concept of constructive-developmental pedagogy is rooted in John Dewey's (1916) conceptualization of education as the reorganization and reconstruction of experience and Jean Piaget's concept of equilibration (1970, 1977) which prompted learners to remake meaning of their experiences. Both of these pioneers advocated forms of pedagogy that embodied the three core assumptions evident here. William Perry's scheme of college students' intellectual development led him to advocate teaching in ways that connected to students' assumptions about knowledge (1970). Similarly, Belenky, Clinchy, Goldberger and Tarule's research on women's intellectual development led them to espouse connected teaching in which pedagogy linked to students' ways of knowing (1986). Robert Kegan (1982, 1994) labeled this approach constructive-developmental because of its dual focus on individuals constructing meaning and their doing so being grounded in their evolving ways of making meaning.

The longitudinal participants' college stories led me to the initial identification of the three principles for practice described here. Further observation of these principles in action in three undergraduate courses as well as implementing them in my own teaching led me to advance the three principles as the *structure* of constructive-developmental pedagogy (Baxter Magolda, 1999b). The observation study also allowed me to sketch three distinct *processes* for constructive-developmental pedagogy that represent diverse approaches to using the three principles as structure. The interactive lecture introduced a phenomenon, engaged learners in interpreting data related to the phenomenon, and guided learners in making knowledge claims as a result of those interpretations. A second process, investigating together, provided an investigation topic to spark learners' thinking, allowed them time to explore aspects of the topic, engaged them in sharing their insights and hypotheses, and concluded with their mutual construction of knowledge claims about the topic. The use of narrative, a third process, used narratives to introduce a topic, invited learners to bring their own narratives on the topic to bear on their understanding, engaged learners in interpreting the narratives in the context of the issue being studied, and concluded with mutual construction of knowledge claims. These three processes demonstrated that use of the principles could take various forms. All three processes resulted in moving learners toward self-authorship. The complete stories of these processes and their underlying structure in the three principles are included in *Creating Contexts for Learning and Self-Authorship: Constructive-Developmental Pedagogy* (Baxter Magolda, 1999b).

The longitudinal participants' post-college stories shared here expand the structure of constructive-developmental pedagogy beyond the three principles. These stories reveal that the three core assumptions are a central part of the structure because they reflect the goals of epistemological, intrapersonal, and interpersonal self-authorship. Knowledge as complex and socially constructed represents contextual knowing or self-authorship in the epistemological dimension. Self as central to knowledge construction represents the internal sense of self required for self-authorship, or the intrapersonal dimension. Sharing expertise and authority in the mutual construction of knowledge represents the interpersonal dimension of self-authorship in which the internal voice is strong enough to participate in mutuality. The three principles for educational practice are then essential to bridge these expectations for self-authorship with learners' locations along the four phases of the journey toward self-authorship. Together the three core assumptions and three principles form a vision, or philosophy, of pedagogy.

This vision of pedagogy is multi-layered because it engages learners in understanding the necessary knowledge for their field and simultaneously engages them in actively constructing knowledge within their field. Research on educational practice (e.g., Barr & Tagg, 1995; Pascarella & Terenzini, 1991) and on students' ways of knowing (e.g., Baxter Magolda, 1992, 1999e; King & Kitchener, 1994) suggests that education typically focuses on the first of these two layers—knowledge acquisition—more than on the second layer of active knowledge construction. National educational reform efforts support this multi-layered approach. For example, the Association of American Colleges advocated that:

> Faculty members must take seriously what students believe about a given subject and engage their prior knowledge so that new learning restructures the old, complicating and correcting it rather than merely living side by side with it. (1990, p. 12–13)

The notion of "restructuring the old" relates to both restructuring the content of what learners know and the way they know. If the learning environment fails to engage students' current beliefs and experience, it will result in transmission of knowledge that simply sits beside current beliefs, as Pamela's story earlier conveyed. This potential outcome is unacceptable according to the National Research Council which argued that "Absent a conscious effort to set mathematics in the context of learners' experiences, mastery of skills (including vocabulary, notation, and procedures) serves no legitimate educational purpose" (1991, p. 25). Their report argued that courses which failed to engage students in their own learning resulted in a "very misleading impression of mathematics—as a collection of skills with no connection to critical reasoning" (p. 24). Similarly, the National Science Foundation's recent report "Shaping the Future: New Expectations in Undergraduate Education in Science, Mathematics, Engineering, and Technology" recommends that science, mathematics, engineering and technology faculty:

> Believe and affirm that every student can learn, and model good practices that increase learning; start with the student's experience, but have high expectations within a supportive climate; and build inquiry, a sense of wonder and the excitement of discovery, plus communication and teamwork, critical thinking, and life-long learning skills into learning experiences. (1996, p. 4)

Constructive-developmental pedagogy is essential for a multi-layered approach that prepares college graduates to be lifelong learners who can keep pace with the evolution of knowledge.

The Promise of Constructive-Developmental Pedagogy

The primary promise of this vision of pedagogy is that it helps young adults achieve the self-authorship of knowledge, themselves, and their relations with others that is demanded of them in contemporary life. It does so because it connects to their epistemological, intrapersonal and interpersonal development along the journey toward self-authorship. It also connects to their previous knowledge and experience. Stories throughout the chapter reveal how these connections contributed to the journey toward self-authorship. Progress toward self-authorship contributed to participants' success in advanced academic settings, their work and their personal lives.

A crucial dynamic of the primary promise of promoting self-authorship is that constructive-developmental pedagogy can promote self-authorship for *all* students. Because the assumptions and principles mean connecting to and respecting learners' experiences and perspectives, constructive-developmental pedagogy includes students who have traditionally been marginalized. Frances Maher and Mary Kay Tetreault noted that:

> Until recently, the content and pedagogy of American education, although projecting the "illusion" that it spoke to everyone, ignored the needs, experiences, and perspectives of the majority of people in this country—women of all backgrounds, people of color, and all women and men who perceive their education as not made for them. (1994, p. 1)

Students perceive education as "not made for them" when it does not acknowledge, respect, and connect to their experience and perspectives. Hostile learning environments created by marginalization of particular students interfere with learning. Nancy Evans (2000) emphasized a learning environment characterized by explicit centralization, or active support for gay, lesbian and bisexual students, as crucial to providing opportunities for centralization and thus connection. Using the three core assumptions and principles tailors education to the particular students involved. Pedagogy advanced as "culturally relevant" (Ladson-Billings, 1994, 1995) endorses these three assumptions and principles. Gloria Ladson-Billings articulates how such pedagogy is culturally relevant:

> Teachers who practice culturally relevant methods can be identified by the way they see themselves and others. They see their teaching as an art rather than as a technical skill. They believe that all of their students can succeed rather than that failure is inevitable for some. They see themselves as a part of the community and they see teaching as giving back to the community. They help students make connections between their local, national, racial, cultural, and global identities. Such teachers can also be identified by the ways in which they structure their social interactions. Their relationships with students are fluid and equitable and extend beyond the classroom. They demonstrate a connectedness with all of their students and encourage that same connectedness between the students. They encourage a community of learners; they encourage their students to learn collaboratively. Finally, such teachers are identified by their notions of knowledge. They believe that knowledge is continuously re-created, recycled, and shared by teachers and students alike. They view the content of the curriculum critically and are passionate about it. Rather than expecting students to demonstrate prior knowledge and skills they help students develop that knowledge by building bridges and scaffolding for learning. (1994, p. 25)

Ladson-Billings' notion of teaching as an art conveys that it is the assumptions—the same core assumptions I advocate—that are central to making pedagogy culturally relevant. Thus how educators envision learning, teaching, students and authority is what makes constructive-developmental pedagogy promising.

Dilemmas in Transformation to Constructive-Developmental Pedagogy

The stories of participants whose educational settings promoted self-authorship demonstrate that all three assumptions—knowledge as socially constructed and complex, self as central to knowledge construction, and mutual knowledge construction—must be present if self-authorship is to be achieved. Most educators agree with the assumption that knowledge is socially constructed. Even professors who present the existing knowledge of their disciplines as "fact" recognize that these facts are knowledge claims substantiated by a community of knowledgeable peers whose research has led to commonly accepted beliefs. Ken Bruffee conveyed this notion when he wrote, "knowledge is a consensus among the members of a community of knowledgeable peers—something people construct by talking together and reaching agreement" (1993, p. 3). Educators also recognize that these knowledge claims are always open to revision on the basis of new research. Despite acceptance of this assumption, the notion of social construction of knowledge does not explicitly play out in many educational contexts because educators diverge on the other two assumptions, often questioning learners' ability to participate in knowledge construction.

One possible reason for the long-standing dominance of knowledge acquisition instead of active knowledge construction is the belief that students learn to construct knowledge by learning disciplinary content. A substantial body of research suggests that this is myth. For example, Arnold Arons, a scientist, argued that students emerge from conventional college physical science courses "understanding nothing whatsoever and possessing only strings of memorized technical jargon that help them recognize enough juxtapositions of words on a multiple choice test to get an A or B in the course. The jargon is then quickly forgotten" (1989, p. 15). If knowledge construction and thinking is not modeled in the exploration of content, students end up, at best, with what Cara called "knowing it but not understanding it;" at worst they end up with material they quickly forget after the course. Similarly, some educators fear that focusing on mutual construction will reduce both the time available and the quality with which content is covered. This, too, has been shown to be a myth (Nelson, 1989, 2000) as the covering the content without mutual construction does not result in learning.

Perhaps a more deep-seated reason for the dominance of teaching-centered pedagogy is educators' lack of trust in students' ability to learn and know. The assumption that students cannot engage in knowledge construction until they have memorized all the foundational content of the discipline suggests that learners have no relevant experience or knowledge to bring to the learning enterprise. It also suggests that they will not be able to construct knowledge effectively. Because students have often been taught to depend on authority for the truth, they often do not exhibit the capacity for knowledge construction, leading educators to perceive that it is not present. These perceptions of learners lead to hesitation or fear of implementing the second assumption described here—acknowledging the self as central to knowledge construction—because to implement this assumption means to invite the self into the learning environment. Doing so means exploration of learners' experiences and perspectives, integration of views among learners, analysis of existing knowledge from new perspectives, and sharing authority—all dynamics that make pedagogy far more complicated than it has traditionally been.

Mutual construction of knowledge is further complicated by educators' hesitancy to share authority with learners. Some educators prefer to organize their teaching and implement it as planned rather than using a flexible approach that adapts to the changing needs of students in a particular course. Changing the course schedule or discussion content to connect existing knowledge to students' previous knowledge is a more fluid and difficult process than presenting existing knowledge and entertaining questions about it. Some educators view responsibilities such as class structure, activities, assignments and evaluation as their sole purview rather than shared responsibilities with learners. Joint decision-making about class process and content is more time-consuming than individual decision-making about these matters. Educators often perceive that they will be shirking their responsibility or downplaying their expertise by sharing authority with students. Yet the stories here illustrate the powerful effect of mutual construction of meaning on students' learning and self-authorship. This is another arena in which transformation of assumptions about educators and learners is warranted.

Of course the larger institutional context in which educators work mediates the implementation of these assumptions and principles as well. Adding the layer of active knowledge construction and the goal of self-authorship make teaching more complicated. Connecting with learners takes time and energy. Genuine partnerships with learners make class time more intense, out-of-class time more necessary, and interactions in evaluation more time-consuming. The standard class schedule, class sizes, and facilities all mediate educators' ability to enact constructive-developmental pedagogy. The faculty workload and reward system also mediate the amount of energy faculty can devote to teaching. I do not mean to convey that these dynamics make constructive-developmental pedagogy impossible; they do not. It can be used effectively in large classes (see Baxter Magolda, 1999b) and in the current educational landscape. More faculty would be amenable to transforming their assumptions and pedagogical visions, however, if their educational contexts provided more support than obstacles.

The Urgency of Transformation

Constructive-developmental pedagogy, complicated as it is, is necessary if educators are committed to learning and self-authorship. This vision of constructive-developmental pedagogy emphasizes inviting the self to be a central component in learning. Parker Palmer, an eloquent advocate of including the self in knowing, calls this using the heart's eye as well as the mind's eye (1993). Teaching students the epistemic assumptions of contextual knowing—that one analyzes relevant evidence and makes a reasonable judgment in context—is insufficient for self-authorship. In order to act out this form of knowing, learners must also traverse the crossroads in both the intrapersonal and interpersonal dimensions of development. The "who am I" question must be answered internally and that sense of self must stand as equal to others in relationships. Others' perspectives remain central, as is evident in the stories here, but they are used in conjunction with the internal sense of self to choose knowledge claims. Inviting the self into the knowledge construction process moves beyond a self-reflection paper here and there, or a seminar format in which students share perspectives. "Teaching beyond technique" is a phrase Palmer uses to capture this notion (1998). Acting on the assumption that self is central to knowledge construction means changing the core assumptions many educators take for granted about the educational process, a few of which I have highlighted here (for further discussion of these issues see Baxter Magolda, 1999b, 1999d).

Transforming pedagogy and student-educator relations is crucial to assisting young adults in their journeys toward self-authorship. However, there are additional components of higher education beyond academic affairs that are central to this transformation. The role of campus work settings is one such component taken up in the next chapter. Participants' experiences in professional employment are used to suggest how this dimension of higher education might contribute to the journey toward self-authorship.

8

CREATING CONTEXTS
FOR SELF-AUTHORSHIP
IN CAMPUS WORK SETTINGS

My company is saying, "Here's your desk; here's your office; here's your phone; here's the mailbox. Here's a little bit of clientele to get started. Start your own business. Here's some suggested ways to do it. Here's people who have done it and been successful. But this isn't necessarily the way you have to do it. See if you can build yourself a business."

Gavin

The autonomy Gavin experienced in his first job after graduation was typical of what most participants encountered in the world of work. Although guidance and mentoring varied across contexts, most supervisors expected participants to function independently, sort through complex information, and make decisions themselves or in conjunction with coworkers. Their experience, particularly in business and industry, mirrors complex portraits of contemporary organizational life. To keep pace with rapid change and globalization, organizations are increasingly flexible, focused on identifying and solving problems, rely on team collaboration over individual performance, and emphasize the necessity of continuous learning (Gardner, 1997; Oblinger & Verville, 1998). The skills needed for this environment—flexibility, the ability to cope with ambiguity, the capacity to learn quickly—go beyond particular knowledge and skill to what Senge (1990) calls personal mastery, or the capacity for continuous learning. According to Oblinger and Verville, "this personal development is considered at least as important as the intellectual benefits of a degree and often more important than the development of a specific knowledge base" (1998, p. 21). Gardner (1997) noted that employers identified teamwork, interpersonal communication, flexibility and innovation, to name a few, as skills required for success in the workplace. These dynamics indicate that success in contemporary work settings requires complex epistemological, intrapersonal, and interpersonal development.

Because most participants' undergraduate experiences lacked this level of complexity and autonomy, many struggled to respond effectively. Their reliance on externally acquired formulas for success led them to expect those formulas in their work settings. Although some formulas helped them get started, most found these formulas inadequate; they had to bring their own minds and voices to their work. Gwen's story in chapter 2 exemplifies this discovery. The complexity of their work, the trust their employers conveyed in their capability to author their own work, and the opportunity to mutually construct knowledge related to their work with supervisors and coworkers guided them through the crossroads into internal self-authorship. Their level of preparation for these roles, however, could have been enhanced had more of this journey taken place during college. To accomplish higher education's mission of preparing graduates for work roles in society, I advocate the promotion of self-authorship throughout the college experience.

Participants entered the work force in numerous occupations in diverse settings. Some followed the same career path from college graduation to their thirties whereas others changed paths. Although some stayed with the same institution or company for this span of time, most moved to new institutions or companies at least once or twice over these years. Figure 8.1 includes a summary of work settings for the 39 participants remaining in the study.

Similar to the graduate and professional educational settings described in the previous chapter, the diverse employment contexts participants entered after college graduation contributed to their journey toward self-authorship. It is apparent, however, how participants' external self-definition or experience at the crossroads mediated their success in their work and accounted for their struggles. Those who had good company fared far better than those who were left to shift from external to internal self-definition on their own. Exploration of these work settings reveals how the framework of the three assumptions and principles translates to campus work settings to assist college students with the journey to self-authorship.

Core Assumptions and the Principles Used to Implement Them

The complexity and social construction of knowledge was evident in the significant responsibility within participants' work roles. Their decisions

FIGURE 8.1   Longtudinal Participants Post-College Occupations

Occupation		Women	Men
Education			
	K through 12[1]	8	2
	University	1	
Business			
Business: Financial Specialists		1	2
Business: Service/Sales			
	Insurance		1
	Computer Training	1	2
	Pharmaceutical or Medical Equipment	2	
	Advertising/Marketing	2	1
	Real Estate		1
	Automobile Financing		1
	Paper Chemicals		1
	Other	1	1
Business: Retail Sales[2]			
	Clothing	2	
	Music		1
	Furniture		1
	General		1
Federal Government			
	Economist		1
	Security		1
	Foreign Service		1
Human Services[3]			
	Counseling	1	1
	Social Work	1	
	Pastor		1
General Services			
	Airlines	1	
	Restaurants	1	
	Services for the Blind		1
	Attorneys	1	1

[1]Seven participants took teaching positions upon graduation. Six of those continue to teach and one is a stay-at-home mother. Three additional participants left careers in business and human services to become teachers.

[2]Of these five participants, one became a clothing store manager, one moved to selling services, one became a stock-broker, and one left business to purchase his own furniture store.

[3]One of these four moved to teaching.

affected people's lives, their company or agency's effectiveness, and the financial health of their clients. Despite the importance of their roles, supervisors offered participants extensive autonomy in learning and implementing their work. Supervisors conveyed that the knowledge needed in their work was complex, dependent on multiple factors in particular contexts, and socially constructed among the constituents in each context. Working in this context demanded that participants develop complex epistemic assumptions and an internal sense of self to guide their decisions. The autonomy to conduct their work situated learning in participants' experience. Supervisors further situated learning in participants' experience by soliciting input in problem-solving or decision-making interactions. This simultaneously validated employees as knowers and engaged them in mutual construction of meaning in their work.

Although the notion of the self as central to knowledge construction, and thus to effective work performance, was not explicit in most work settings, it was evident in the way employers approached their employees. Participants were trusted to engage in complex tasks independently and viewed as capable of performing effectively, thus they were validated as knowers. Supervisors were available for consultation and guidance (thus offering opportunities for mutual construction) but rarely meddled with participants' work without being invited. Supervisors gave participants authority to make important decisions and autonomy in carrying out their assignments, which validated them as knowers and situated learning in their experience. Freedom to develop their own style and philosophy to guide their work encouraged them to develop their identities through their work.

The third assumption that knowledge is mutually constructed permeated work settings. Mutual construction of knowledge occurred between employees and supervisors, among coworkers, and with the constituents affected by the work role. Supervisors asked employees to identify questions to ask, synthesize information, and weigh alternatives in deciding what to believe. Supervisors did not simply give this information to employees, but rather developed it collaboratively. These interactions incorporated all three principles. Many work settings valued collaboration among employees to generate information, share expertise across functions, and share decision-making to accomplish their tasks. Collaboration and mutual construction of meaning with constituents was a mainstay across employment settings. Because the interests of collaborators often conflicted, employees were expected to manage these differences, use others' ideas effectively, and yet not allow others' views to overrun their ability to meet their responsibilities. Thus the prevalence of mutual construction in work settings demanded intrapersonal, interpersonal, and epistemological growth. The stories in this chapter detail how these expectations materialized across diverse work settings.

Work-Related Knowledge is Socially Constructed and Complex

Participants found their work more complicated than the external formulas or content knowledge they learned in college. The complexity of their work and the degree to which it was socially constructed with multiple others interrupted their external formulas. This dynamic crossed contexts, including professional and technical occupations, managerial roles, human services, and government settings. They were faced with understanding the complexities of their work and developing frameworks for functioning effectively within this complexity.

Developing an Understanding of Complexity.   The process of learning the complexity of participants' work generally took place as they were carrying out their responsibilities. Anne's responsibilities as an accountant in a paper mill were to manage debt and help mill managers control costs. Learning how to do this in the midst of doing it was not always comfortable, as Anne reported:

> I guess you just do it because you have to. You have to come up with some answers. Just kind of bumble through it, try to rationalize things out. I wrote down some solutions and pluses of the solutions. Then I'd try to think of what kind of questions my boss would ask, like "What would happen if we did this?" and "Where did you get these numbers?" It makes me think of "Is this the best solution? Have I explored my options?" I guess that's one thing I've learned working over the past two years. Before I would make a decision and take it into my boss. But now I've learned to say to myself, "What's he going to want to know? Have you thought of everything?" And it's made me go back and rethink everything and come up with some other alternatives and just make sure what I'm thinking is good. . . . They'd ask questions and sometimes I'd be like, "Oh, I don't know. I didn't think about that. I'll get back with you." I'd feel kind of stupid. I didn't want that to happen. You kind of learn what they're going to ask I guess.

Anne's supervisor situated learning in her experience in giving her autonomy to work with the complexity of generating solutions. He then guided her thinking by asking appropriate questions. Listening to his questions over time, as well as her interest in appearing knowledgeable to her colleagues, helped Anne anticipate the questions. Once Anne learned how to ask the questions herself, she developed perspectives on what should be done and how it should be done.

Megan and Scott developed an understanding of the complexity of their work through studying written materials and interacting with colleagues as they performed their duties. Megan worked in the internal marketing department for an insurance company and was responsible for designing publications to market the company's insurance products. She had to constantly learn new insurance products given the rapid change that occurred in investments and she did so by reading materials the company produced and asking her colleagues to explain their product or investment strategy. Her company relied on her to produce accurate marketing and validated her ability to do so. Mutual construction with her colleagues helped her succeed in areas that were new for her. Scott approached his work as a government security specialist similarly. Asked how he learned to organize the lock system for which he was responsible, he replied: "The job demanded it. I just had to sit down and just poke through manuals, listen to people, and just listen to the professionals who work at it every day." Learning situated in his daily experience and mutually constructing meaning with the other security specialists in his office helped Scott gain knowledge and confidence in his work. He reported substantial autonomy yet found his work mediated by politics. His ability to work with political disagreements improved as his basic knowledge grew. He reported:

> I have no fear anymore of just saying, "Hey, this isn't going to work." But I've now learned to be much more, well, sometimes because still I'm pretty much a brutally honest person, and it gets me into trouble. I'm usually prepared to take it. I've learned how to recommend things in a little bit more soothing fashion. And that just came with experience on the job.

Mastering both the technical and interpersonal complexity of his work helped Scott speak up for his own ideas.

The combination of ambiguity, social construction of knowledge, and access to role models helped participants move toward self-authorship in very disparate contexts. For example, Dawn experienced these dynamics working in a restaurant kitchen:

> I'm one of the line cooks. I'm working with a certified chef—a brilliant woman—food is second nature to her. When you are cooking food, it's easiest to just watch. I've learned so much in five months that I never knew before. I pick up things in con-

versation, but the easiest way to pick up this skill is to watch someone who knows how to do it. Also experimentation—make this, taste it, have chef taste it, and she knows what to do with it. I thought of myself as one who learns by doing or watching rather than actively pursuing knowledge by questioning. I notice now that I ask questions. There is a wealth of information at my fingertips and I want to learn as much as I can while I have this opportunity. I never had a job like this—outside of theater—where I can actively pursue an art or craft. Acting is more of an exploratory thing—no right and wrong. That is true to some extent in culinary arts. But there are rights and wrongs—four tablespoons rather than two. But you taste, create, explore putting flavors together to come up with a final product that you present. It is experimentation like in theater. It is set up very much like theater is set up—work with a group of people, creating a product, give it out to the masses. Every night we look at elements we have, and we have to make something. The job appeals to my frame of mind.

Dawn's theater background predisposed her to value ambiguity, complexity and creativity. She enjoyed the ambiguity involved in creating something from the available elements, yet appreciated the training she received from an expert cook. It is clear from her description that beyond a few basics, creating the day's menu was a complex and socially constructed task. Learning was situated in the everyday experience of creating the product and experimentation; Dawn and her colleagues mutually constructed their work with the guidance of the expert chef.

Barb, a new attorney, also valued creating her work although she emphasized the importance of resources in fashioning reasonable arguments. She explained how she was learning her role:

People are understanding. They know we are just starting out. They give samples and point you in the right direction to get started. With corporate work, I like it because it is new. You are drafting things you have no idea how do to, so you use samples. A lot of times, I'll be confident enough to know it is common sense. If there is no sample, I have friends that have worked on it so I ask them. Or look it up in reference books. Confidence is key. There is no right answer; with law you can argue both sides. You have to state your position with authority so people perceive you as knowing what you are talking about, to put clients at ease. Sometimes I tell clients both sides, but then you say which way we should go. This is all new; you don't learn everything in law school. Practicing law is doing it off-the-cuff; I have no idea how to wing it.

There were no "right" answers in Barb's work, although she had samples, peers and common sense to use to determine her arguments. Putting what she learned in law school into practice required these resources as she learned the complexity of her work.

Even in highly technical fields, ambiguity, complexity, and social construction of knowledge were commonplace. Ned's job selling chemicals to paper mills involved analyzing extensive technical data to make subjective decisions. He explained:

> There are probably several hundred people working at a mill, making thousands of tons of paper a day using millions of gallons of water. So within that system there are many things that can go wrong on a day-to-day basis. So when I go into a mill, I never know what to expect. I start with a process engineer, and say, "What are the problems that you're encountering?" Then the problem-solving process starts really by asking lots of questions and just getting the feel for what their process is like. A lot of it is by drawing simple diagrams at first and just getting comfortable with "What are they doing from start to finish there?" From that point I have to, on a rough scale, judge whether we can make a change or not with my chemicals.

Ned had to understand the complexity of the mill operations before he could even offer a preliminary judgment about whether his chemicals could help the mill. This preliminary judgment was made in the context of his experience learning that particular mill's operation. If he judged that his chemicals might help, he then conducted laboratory tests in the mill to help determine what changes to make. But, the testing did not resolve the complexity, as Ned explained that "this test by itself might be extremely complex and require a lot of interpretation because they're not always exact science." The interpretation led to physically testing potential changes by using the new chemicals in the papermaking system and gathering data about the process for a week. This data served as the foundation for Ned's recommendations to the mill:

> I am responsible for deciphering—based on everything I know about the mill, all our tests that we did in the lab, based on the objections or problems the mill might have or the mill's limitations—take the data that we recorded and assimilate all that to say, "Did it work or not?" And it's not always easy to say that it did work. A lot of it is textbook kind of work—there's a certain way of running laboratory tests. But there's also a knowledge base background for knowing "How do these classes of chemicals fit into this kind of paper making and how are they going to affect what happens at the end of the machine?" You read a

couple of lines in a book saying this class of polymers should do this, but it never happens that way and there's always some good reasons why it doesn't. If you've seen the reasons enough times in different applications or different situations, you're going to be alerted or aware of the potential problems before they occur or look for those opportunities when they're there.

Laboratory tests and then actually inserting the chemicals into the paper machine further situated learning in Ned's experience. He used previous experience to analyze and interpret the tests and outcomes. His judgment came from reliance on his experience. Although it isn't apparent in these comments, Ned also mutually constructed these interpretations with others as is noted later in this chapter. Ned's experience eventually led him to what he called a framework for problem solving and decision making. Developing this framework was part of the self-authorship required of employees to effectively deal with the complexity of their work.

Developing Frameworks for Dealing with Complexity.   Once participants understood the complexities of their work, they needed frameworks for handling them. Ned spoke directly to this issue upon being promoted to manager, which started his learning process anew:

> I knew how to do the sales job. The specifics were different in each mill and I couldn't generalize, but at least I had a framework that worked. Now I'm a manager. Decisions are now made on my gut reaction. I'm relying on two things. My value system is one—my internal comprehension of this is right or wrong—I predict how people would feel. The second thing is watching role models, like my boss. People follow him; he cares about people and about doing the right thing for them. I'm watching; there are obvious reasons why he is successful and people follow him as a leader. He is trying to assist me and educate me.

Ned was in new and unfamiliar territory as a manager. He took his sense of what was right with him but also was looking to his boss for guidance to work through the complexities of managing people. He hoped to achieve a framework similar to the one he had developed in the technical sales side of his work, but he did not yet have it:

> It is unsettling to not feel like you know what is going on. Classic issue is making decisions without enough information. Basically given information I have, what is the right thing? It comes down to two types of decisions. First, technical stuff—chemistry, science behind it—no problem there. The ambiguous part

is the human side of the equation. That is where I use the gut reaction, where something feels right or doesn't. There has to be a better framework for this. The gut feeling has to be translated into some kind of classification; then I can make a more objective decision based on historical data or experience. There has got to be something like that system once you get the experiences. Right now I'm at the stage of what the hell do you do? I'm trained as a scientist; technical guy, that's my natural tendency. I do like to have a framework and a theory. I feel like there have to be reasons for action and reaction. From the technical side, that is obvious. From the people side, you have to sort out words, sentences, and facial reactions—distill individualism down to a framework and conceptual reasoning.

Ned brought some values to this process and was taking advantage of every opportunity to mutually construct knowledge with his boss. Yet he needed more experience actually managing people to develop his framework.

Sandra needed a framework for her work as well—counseling teenagers with chemical abuse issues. She described it like this:

I guess it's kind of leaving your emotional baggage at the door. It's a real difficult line to establish boundaries with how close you get with your clients and exactly how much you open yourself emotionally to them. You've got to have some emotion; you've got to establish some kind of relationship with them or it's not going to work. I had a real difficult time with that in the beginning of my work. But now I find it much easier. You have to have real clear boundaries for yourself because if you try to take it all on yourself, then you're going to burn out. Chemically dependent people will use you up that way because they need so much energy and attention, especially the teenagers. But you've got to offer enough emotion so that they get some of that energy and attention. But it's just learning how to spread that out over the team, how to tag team with each other if you feel like you're getting in too deep or if you feel like you just can't take it anymore.

Sandra had worked with chemically dependent teenagers for some time when she shared these thoughts, so her experience helped her develop a framework—her emotional boundaries and how to assert them—to cope with the ambiguity and stress involved. She reported that she benefited from autonomy, good supervision and support from previous colleagues to form this framework. She and her colleagues' tag-team approach meant they supported each other in expressing and staying within their boundaries. This mutual construction helped affirm self-authorship of one's boundaries.

Lindsey took a class to help him develop a framework for his work as a government economist. He explained his work:

> I compute a current estimate for computers. I have people calling me from all around who are really interested in these numbers. It's kind of neat to know that people are actually depending on you, and what you are doing has an impact on what is going on. Essentially this number is composed of about nine components, six of which I get directly from the Bureau of Labor Statistics. The other three I estimate myself from looking though industry literature and specific trade magazines. Essentially these are judgment calls on my part, and I just read a lot of literature and I try to formulate opinions as to what exactly is the percent decline in prices of printers for these quarters.

Due to the importance of his estimate and upcoming responsibilities, Lindsey enrolled in a graduate level course in econometrics:

> I'm going to be in charge of a very large databank, which is essentially again a price index. And there's a lot you can do to price indexes to make them better. You can seasonally adjust them; you can try to correct for certain numbers that just don't look right. And there's about a hundred different ways to go about doing that; and there's about 150 different ways of testing how you just went about that. Essentially my knowledge is very limited as to different procedures for how to do this. I was hoping to get some ideas from this class.

Lindsey was looking for assistance and ideas for improving his price index and finding his way among the many options for working with it. Like Ned and Sandra, he was trying to develop frameworks to understand and manage the complexity of his work.

Dilemmas in Mastering Complexity. Although virtually all participants' employment settings necessitated complex and socially constructed knowledge, not all contexts offered support for employees to respond to the complexities. Lynn offered an example of learning the subtleties of teaching in a rural area:

> I have a learning disabled kid—he tested that way—but his mom wouldn't sign the paper because she didn't want him labeled. He could learn and maybe get out of it, but he doesn't have the basic concepts to continue and he can't be retained. I can talk to the mom, but she hits her children. I hate to call and

> say he's in trouble, because she'll hit him and that doesn't solve anything. I have called and he is sad the next day and doesn't want to go home after school. I just give him love because he doesn't get it at home.

Lynn's processes for dealing with learning disabilities and behavior problems were unsuccessful in this situation, leaving her with few alternatives. She was also frustrated with the complexity of acquiring support for these types of issues:

> Today we had an incident—I deal with it day to day. I had a child last year that was severely abused; the agencies wouldn't help. I finally said, "what will it take, for him to die?" It is eye opening to me what society is doing to deal with this. They say call us, but then they don't do anything. I can't be his mother. He goes home to a drug-infested environment. There is not much support from anyone to deal with these situations. It is discouraging. You try to do job best you can, but we are talking about a life, a child, our future.

Lynn continued to experiment with new approaches from soliciting help from agencies to teaching children how to approach each other. The complexities of the issues were beyond her capability to change in her role as teacher. The magnitude of the situation and the lack of support to deal with it resulted in this experience having little effect on promoting self-authorship.

Amy developed ways to manage complexity and self-author her work in managing a women's boutique despite the lack of support she received. She reported that the storeowners, who were too busy with other stores, gave her responsibility for buying, accounting, selling, hiring, and decorating the store. She needed to learn to deal with the ambiguity of knowing what would sell, how to market her inventory, and competition with other stores. The first year she reported, "They told me I knew best, but I went too heavily into certain things. I'm feeling my way with not much guidance." Amy's interest in multiple aspects of the job led her to invest time in learning how to make judgments despite the lack of guidance. Doing so helped her develop a stronger sense of herself as a manager:

> At first I was frustrated, but now I just tell them what needs to be done. I know what will sell. I doubled August sales from one year to the next. That gave me the confidence that I succeeded. Not having direction, not having a sense of accomplishing anything—it is nice to have people come in and say how nice the store looks, that we have nice things. The store is doing better financially. I rely a lot on intuition—knowing what to buy is mainly from see-

ing what we had in the past, observed what did and didn't sell. Putting things on sale, watching other stores, see what they are doing. Also when things are selling, if things aren't moving. We have a different crowd in August; they have more money so we buy more expensive stuff then. Observe people, what kind of money is available in different months.

Amy worked her way through the complexities of buying clothes that would sell for her particular customers, selecting price ranges and types of items for various clientele, when to put things on sale, and how to make her store inviting. Her success fueled her confidence, which in turn led her to take more initiative to do what she thought was best. In some ways her store-owners' validation of her initially helped her along, although her frustration and financial mistakes could have been lessened had the owners offered a little more guidance.

Translation to Educational Practice. Contexts that helped employees understand and develop frameworks for effectively handling complexity used the three principles to guide employees toward self-authorship. Employees were validated as knowers by being afforded autonomy to understand and work with complexity. Rather than being told what to do, they were guided by written resources, conversations with coworkers and supervisors, and processes for problem-solving particular to their fields. Supervisors taught employees what questions were important to explore to make decisions. They were given samples to use as guides when they approached new tasks. Providing these resources as employees were conducting their work situated learning in the employees' experiences. Employees had opportunities to mutually construct effective ways to work with their supervisors and coworkers. Thus these settings acknowledged complexity, offered employees autonomy to engage in it, and yet offered guidance to help employees develop frameworks of their own to handle complexity and participate effectively in the social construction of knowledge relevant to their work.

If educational practice were to model these work settings in campus work roles, campus employers would give student employees autonomy to understand and work with complexity rather than frame their roles as implementers of others' decisions. Too often teaching assistants, research assistants, para-professional staff, and student service providers simply carry out orders from some higher authority. This simply reinforces authority-dependence. To promote self-authorship (and more effective work performance), supervisors should validate student employees as capable of handling complexity, give them meaningful work responsibilities, and afford them a reasonable degree of autonomy to perform their work. Supervisors would train employees to ask questions, the way Anne's boss taught her to do, to guide their work. Employees would be given opportunities to learn from and with their peers, as Dawn and Megan did. Samples of work, like Barb had, could give employees guidance in doing new tasks. These approaches situate learning in employees' experience and give student employees the guidance they need to learn to handle complexity. Mutually constructing meaning with them about their work offers opportunities for them to observe frameworks others use and to develop their own ways of thinking about their work.

The complexity of participants' work required that they learn on-the-job, extend their understanding beyond their college preparation, remain flexible, work collaboratively with others, analyze data to generate conclusions, and make wise choices. Given the nature of their work, their employers offered them extensive autonomy to use their talents. This autonomy led employees to see that who they were as people—their sense of self—was central to knowing and functioning in their work.

Self as Central to Knowledge Construction/Work

Employers invited participants' sense of self into their work roles because these organizations needed their employees to contribute to their improvement and success. It is unlikely that the personal growth of their employees was their main goal; rather it is likely that employers recognized that developing their employees would lead to more productive and effective work. Supervisors' invitation for participants to incorporate themselves into their work was communicated through autonomy, trust, and freedom to develop a personal work philosophy. These dynamics not only invited the self into the process of knowledge construction, but promoted intrapersonal development in ways that helped participants self-author their career goals and priorities.

Autonomy and Trust.   Participants appreciated supervisors' trust in them. This trust conveyed that employers valued participants' capability, and thus invited the self to become a central part of making sense of and doing one's work. Megan described this trust in her public relations position:

> It's up to me what approach I take to do it, and different angles for things. It's expected for me to improve, but the way I do it is my choice. This gives me a lot of flexibility and creativity, which I like. There's no right or wrong to it, they are my ideas.

Andrew attributed this kind of freedom in work to the management philosophy at his company:

> I'm trying to think how to word it, but I guess the true responsibility they give you, I mean, the freedom of work. Sometimes you may just have a manager who hands you stuff and then you do it. Or you're given a responsibility and then you can define your job from there. You take more initiative, rather than it being dictated to you. They kind of give you the ball and then tell you to go play with it rather than tell you how to shoot hoops. We joke at work, we call it the "dump and run," because sometimes it seems like they don't have a very formal training procedure. But by the same token I think it's good because it allows you to find your niche and do your thing. They take the approach if somebody comes in new, looks at the thing, they may find a better way to do it. So they don't like to say, "This is the way it should be done always." They're not afraid to let people reinvent the wheel, especially if it means they come out with a better wheel.

Andrew appreciated that he could take initiative to define his work. He translated his company's willingness to let people reinvent the wheel to the management trusting the employees to come up with a better wheel. He did clarify that they were not without direction:

> When push comes to shove they give us the direction we need. But for the most part I completely do not feel like I have management looking over me. I feel that I'm making more of an effort to let my management know what I'm doing so they're kept abreast rather than them coming to me and saying, "Well, what are you doing?" And I think that makes just a big difference in the way you feel. Management never really checks up on you; you're given complete trust. Now if you don't perform, I'm sure things would be said. When I was with [my previous company] I just felt like every single thing I had to do had to be checked and looked over. It's like, "I can add two plus two." It wasn't that they didn't think you could do it; it was just that's the way they were, very structured and controlled.

Andrew, having experienced both controlling and autonomous management philosophies, felt more valuable when he was afforded autonomy and trusted to perform. So did Lindsey, whose government position demonstrated that autonomy was possible even when the work was controlled. He reported that, "Essentially someone's going to check up one everyone at every level of this agency. Yet, nobody leans over my shoulder. They basically are relying on me to finish what I need to finish on time for them." Despite the oversight common at every level of this agency, Lindsey was trusted to do his work effectively. Like Andrew, he knew there was an expectation to perform effectively and appreciated being trusted to do so.

Some participants were offered trust and autonomy with minimal guidance. This still resulted in self-authorship, as Justin reported in his job as a recreational therapist for adolescents:

> When they gave me this position they just said, "Do it. Go find an office somewhere and create a program." I just read books and used experiences I've had. I would try to do stuff and it wouldn't work. Then I would know not do it anymore. And then I started making up games to get the kids to play together. It was uncomfortable at first. I was like, "Well, aren't you going to give me some guidelines?" They were like, "We're pretty confident in you." I struggled for a couple of months because I didn't know what to do really. And then I started having little bits of success. Then it started building up. I got a lot more confident and a lot more able to try new things. It's really built some self-confidence in me. I learned that I can do it. I learned not to give up on stuff. I've learned to try to open myself up to other people and learn from them. I've learned to look at things people do and evaluate that in my own mind, then make a decision as to what kind of positive things I can take from that and add to my repertoire.

Initially Justin wanted more direction, but ventured into trying things on his own because his employer validated him as a knower by expressing confidence in him. Success with his ideas increased his confidence, allowing him to take more risks to try new ideas. Trying ideas and keeping those that worked situated learning in his experience. His growing confidence also allowed him to learn from others, evaluating their activities to see what he could add to his approach.

Confidence stemming from freedom to define one's own work prompted participants to formulate their own work philosophies. Will started out in collections work and learned through experience how to find people who owed his company money, how to persuade them to pay their debts, and how to judge alternatives in approaching people whose circumstances varied. Four years after graduation he accepted an automobile financing job. He described how his philosophy helped him manage the autonomy afforded him in this job:

> I have a lot of autonomy. No two deals are same. I use my judgment for who will and won't pay. Ninety percent of the time I

can make my own decision and the manager backs me. Most of the time she'll back me no matter what she thinks. It is a guessing game—the only way we make money is to do loans. I use my past experience, trying to remember people who paid me well, showed stability, residents in the area for a period of time. Job stability and payment history are the two most important things.

Will trusted his own judgment based on his previous success. The freedom to decide for himself furthered his ability to analyze situations and his comfort with responsibility. Four years later he had acquired an internal sense of self that allowed him to take on even more responsibility. He described his new role:

On behalf of a group of gentlemen who've been together for 20 years, I'm acquiring small manufacturing companies. It is a lot of responsibility. The analysis is similar to my previous work. I analyze whether something will be profitable. If I made a mistake previously, it was maybe $8,000; now it is in the millions! I don't want to make a mistake that big. It is not an exact science. We have certain criteria—we only buy a company that has been profitable for five years, no losses; no unusual or big risks like compliance with EPA (Environment Protection Agency) or OSHA (Occupational Safety & Health Administration). There is not a checklist though. [It's a] weighting of things. Some problems can be overcome by strengths in other areas. Their management team is important—will they stay on and be successful? Where is the company in the marketplace—what makes them special? Do they have a competitive advantage? Do they have a niche? We are not out talking to their customers or competitors due to confidentiality—we have to rely on what is publicly available. That is not an exact science either. Creating cash flow statements is an exact science—but growth rates, numbers you plug in are educated guesses. Look back at projections, and sometimes they are not very close. But, if no risk, no return.

Despite all the ambiguity and complexity of this process, and the magnitude of potential mistakes, Will was not stressed with this role. He used his experience to develop a more sophisticated framework from which to analyze information and take calculated risks. Evan, who leases real estate, took a similar stance to make tough decisions, a stance that had emerged from independence to develop his own philosophy (see chapter 5):

The way I go into it now is I just use what I know and then I get a feel for the situation; and then I pretty much know what I have to ask or find out. I've networked enough and I know enough

> people now where I can call someone up or we can talk a situation out and think about what we have to do. So we have enough expertise that we don't completely fail.

These stories suggest that autonomy and trust led to increased confidence and personal work philosophies. These philosophies led participants to take on more responsibility and manage the risk it entailed.

Autonomy to develop their own work philosophies helped participants move toward self-authorship and achieve consistency between their work and self-definition. Lauren described achieving this consistency after changing jobs:

> I know that's where I belong. Before, it was being at a desk all day long, parking in the same spot, sitting in the same chair, using the same pen, using the same phone, having your boss in the same office as you and breathing over you. And now, it's a choice of Lauren decides when she gets up, when she goes to work, when she comes home. I see my boss maybe every three or four months; we communicate, but it's via computer, telephone. And I guess the biggest word would be flexibility. I think that that was one thing that I did not have in my first career. And I think I'm a pretty self-motivated person. With this flexibility, you work as hard as you want; you play as much as you want. And so to me that fits my style of life much, much more. I feel like I'm more my own boss than I was before. I just feel like I have more responsibility, whereas before, I felt like I was being watched. And the nature of my personality, I think, definitely fits in more with the atmosphere of a sales person.

Lauren appreciated her flexibility to manage her own work, to have more responsibility. Reflecting on her previous job, she realized that it was not consistent with her self-definition. The invitation of the self into making sense of one's work led participants to judge work on the extent to which it matched their sense of themselves. This shift in perspective led to decisions about how to perform their work and decisions about work goals and priorities.

Self-Authoring One's Work.   Being externally defined when they entered the workforce after college, most participants focused on learning how to do their work. Encountering autonomy and being trusted to use their judgment in their work prompted a shift in focus from "How does one do this job?" to "How do *I* do this job?" This is another version of Gwen's insight about shifting from "how you know" to "how *I* know" (chapter 1). Participants actively worked on what they perceived as their employers' expectations—that they bring an internally defined sense of self to their work. This required epistemo-logical growth to construct their own knowledge about various aspects of their work and develop their own philosophies about how to perform it. It also required an internally defined self from which these beliefs were generated and which was open to, but not overwhelmed by, the perspectives of others. Ned clearly articulated the process of learning to be himself in his work:

> I'm acting more like myself. The more I like the job, the more my customers like me and want to do business with me. I'm devel-oping my own style. You might have the title of whatever—there's this preconceived image of what that person should do. After a few years of doing it, you realize you aren't that stereo-type and are more successful if you don't act that way. Self-actualization, self-confidence—maybe that's it. Coming out of school I was worried about what people thought of me, how would I make the best impression. In retrospect, you say be your-self, you can be more motivated and do the best job. People judg-ing you hopefully aren't so self absorbed that if you aren't identi-cal to them its okay; hopefully they judge you on results. You figure out the stereotype is wrong but play that role until you change it.

What Ned seemed to be describing was the shift from "How does one do this job?" to "How do *I* do this job?" His story indicates that finding the self and being willing to let it guide his work was the key issue. In response to how this came about, he said:

> Tough question. I wouldn't have thought of it until you asked me. The biggest factor is being around successful people. I have an excellent opportunity to be in many different businesses and observe what works and doesn't. I'm exposed to many different political scenarios, personalities, and historical issues. It's a great grab bag of experiences or examples of people I can observe and choose among. I'm leaving myself open to change—not trying to settle on one style. As I mature, experience different things, I'm open to adjusting. It is changing, not static.

Ned reflected that to a degree, gathering ideas from other people and develop-ing his own style stemmed from the lack of feedback. He compared the regular feedback from grades in school to the annual performance appraisal in the work world, concluding:

> When you get away from the feedback-oriented system to the open structure, you have to fall back on yourself. You decide

> what you'll do until someone tells you otherwise—maybe this is what leads to being yourself. Maybe constant feedback makes people not be themselves and openness leads to being yourself.

Ned's insight suggests that too much feedback can shape people into something other than their own internal definition. Thus effective feedback would promote autonomy and clarification of one's work philosophy. Ned received this kind of feedback from interviews:

> The first time you start to observe yourself is when you are going through interviews. People ask you fundamental questions about what you do. After a couple times you start to put a framework together. Here is why I made these decisions; fundamental philosophies that I've based my life on. That was the point when I did that introspection about "Who am I?" and "What am I all about?" From there, I kept on building on that.

Being asked to explain his thinking and his belief system in interviews offered Ned feedback that prompted him to reflect on a rationale for his decisions, his work philosophies, and their interconnection with his identity. These experiences, along with figuring out how to enjoy his job, helped him make the shift from external to internal self-definition. Rather than feedback that narrowed his options, Ned encountered feedback that helped him clarify and expand his philosophies.

Sometimes being oneself in one's work meant finding boundaries between one's own needs and the needs of others. This was particularly true in the human service arena. Alice reevaluated how she treated clients in her counseling work based on finding this boundary:

> I try to sugar coat things. I have always done that when it comes to confrontation. I'm a real peacemaker. The clients need the honest truth. I realized that I was sugar coating it for me and not for the benefit of the client. [My supervisor] helped me practice being direct; we do some role-playing. This hands-on stuff is making me aware of my own issues that could limit my abilities in counseling also.

Role-playing with her supervisor (situating learning in her experience and mutually constructing meaning) helped Alice recognize how the peacemaker part of herself mediated her work with clients. Her experience suggests that bringing the self to one's work sometimes means that the self needs to grow into the work. Sandra, whose story about working with chemically dependent teens appeared earlier in this chapter, spoke to the same issue of bringing herself to her work in order to make an emotional connection with her clients while simultaneously defining the boundaries to maintain her energy to assist them effectively. Lynn reported a similar struggle in balancing her needs with those of her students.

The emergence of an internal sense of self also prompted participants to stand up for what they believed in work settings. Megan described this dimension of incorporating self into work:

> Someone asked me if I wanted to be right or be liked; I wanted both! Parts of me want to be liked by people so I don't want to be bossy and inflexible. But part of me at work doesn't want to be liked, but rather respected. I'm not a pushover. I learned which battles are worth fighting. I'm changing that way. I'm pretty confident about things I feel should be a way; the right way. We may not do it that way, but I won't back off without voicing my opinion. If I think there is a better way, I'll push for it and try to get as much evidence to present my case as I can. Sometimes it works, other times it doesn't. If we don't do it, I feel better that I have told them to try to save them money or create the best image possible for company. I feel like I am right, but maybe I'm not.

Megan's shift from wanting to be liked to wanting to be respected reflects the shift from external to internal self-definition, a shift that was aided by autonomy and trust she had experienced in previous jobs. Her internal sense of self is evident in her efforts to voice her opinion and push for better alternatives. At the same time, she knows that others may disagree and that her responsibility is to raise the issue rather than take responsibility for the decisions others make. She acknowledged that this was a change from her previous thinking:

> I stand up for what I believe in. One person is irritated with me because he wanted a seminar brought in for another company; we can't do it ethically. I stopped them and got others involved. Up until a year ago, I probably would have said, "well, if he said it is okay, it is okay and they won't find out." Morally and ethically I don't think it is right, but I wouldn't have gone to such lengths as I do now. The longer I've been there, I've just developed more self-confidence. I've learned that I can voice my opinion.

Megan's story illustrates the vast difference in bringing an externally defined self versus an internally defined self to one's work. Employers who want employees to identify and address problems need employees who have an internally defined sense of self that makes stepping forward possible. Before leaving the crossroads, participants were unable to stand up for what they believed if it meant not being liked by others.

Mark offered an example of bringing an internally defined self to his full-time position at a large law firm. It was similar to the example he gave as a law clerk in chapter 2:

> I was asked to write a position statement for a client to the EEOC [Equal Employment Opportunity Commission]; I had no experience with this. I had never seen one. I asked to see one that the attorney who gave me this assignment thought was good. I role modeled from it, changed it according to what I thought was best. Writing is a creative act; you have to invest yourself in it. If you are not seeing yourself in your work, you are losing something. You were hired to put yourself into your work. There are thousands of facts I could put in. The key is prioritizing them. That comes from critical thinking skills I've been working on for as long as I can remember. A lot has to do with educational training. Certain facts are obvious; if the employee is complaining about discrimination due to race, then you put in racial background. Also I have to decide where to put these facts in the statement.

Mark's educational training, his previous experience as a law clerk, and the self-authorship he had developed at this point made it comfortable for him to put himself into his work. He used other attorneys' work as models but adjusted these models to incorporate his own perspective. Like Megan, he felt responsible for putting himself into his work. Putting themselves into their work, or being themselves in their work, made participants valuable employees who raised important questions, who listened carefully to and learned from their colleagues, and who could make and justify effective decisions. It also made their work more enjoyable because work was consistent with their growing internal sense of self.

Dilemmas with Self as Central to Work.   A few participants' supervisors did not invite them to bring themselves into their work, but rather expected them to do as they were told. Experiences in which the growth and inclusion of the self were not supported or actively thwarted yielded a lack of confidence. Because most participants initially defined themselves externally, the affirmation of external others was crucial to getting through the crossroads.

Although a few participants encountered work settings that did not promote self-authorship, Genesse is one of the few who encountered a number of such environments in succession. As a result, her story reveals the negative effect sustained work in this context has on growth. Genesse described herself as "just really timid, afraid of what people would think if I said something" in college. Her initial experience of living on her own started to increase her confidence. Her first job as a marketing representative also increased her confidence. Like others who had autonomy, she forced herself to call on clients and through initial successes was beginning to feel more sure of herself. However, unlike the stories above, lack of support or good supervision over the next few years made this journey very difficult to the point that Genesse identified standing up for herself as the major issue of her twenties (see chapter 1). Ethical dilemmas with her boss in her marketing job created stress that shook her initial confidence:

> Ethically I don't think [the senior marketing representative] is right on line. I'm going to have to work on just toughening up and overlooking certain things that I don't think are right because there's nothing I can do about him because he's higher than me and I can't really blow the whistle on him. . . . They let another representative go—that really got to me because I was fearful for my job too. So I was really stressed about that, so I have had to step back a little bit and let things go. I just can't let him get to me the way that he did because I've got to stay with this job for a while, at least until I get something else because I've got to pay the bills.

Genesse was at the crossroads at this time because her initial successes had begun to strengthen her internal voice. However, it was still overshadowed by external forces more powerful than her. Genesse felt she had no alternative but to overlook ethical violations, even though she thought they were wrong. To escape this unhappy situation, Genesse accepted a job in retail. She found the assertive sales approach her supervisors emphasized uncomfortable because it focused more on sales goals than on what customers really wanted to buy. Although she was promoted to store manager, the long hours and stress involved in meeting sales goals affected her health. After being sick and dropping to 95 pounds, Genesse accepted a job doing placement for a temporary service. Although she found it less pressure to match employees and companies than to do direct selling in retail, the job still had its shortcomings. Genesse prefaced the following story by saying, "You probably think I'm strange, I always have poor managers." Her statement of qualification hinted that she still was not certain whether the problem was her or her managers, a sign that she was still at the crossroads. The story clarifies where the problem was:

> There are different things about this job that frustrate me. Discrimination things. One company wanted a receptionist. The

> first two I sent were black. The first person had just gradated from college, had a clear speaking voice, was very professional. The employer said she liked her, but she wouldn't fit in because she was black. She asked for two more candidates who were white. I couldn't believe it. My boss laughed it off. The sales manager said do what the client wants. I sent them. I didn't know what else to do; I couldn't risk my job. I know it is wrong but my hands are tied.

Genesse had gained some strength to express herself when she thought something was unethical, but when her managers dismissed her concerns, she felt helpless because she could not risk her job. The lack of support from her managers was becoming commonplace in her work experience. To make matters worse, Genesse had difficulty interacting with a colleague who routinely yelled at her. Genesse stayed as long as possible in her attempt to establish a career but eventually felt the need to leave this position. This experience shattered Genesse's confidence. She had to actively process these work experiences to rebuild her confidence, a process in which she was positively aided by her friends and her husband. Her next job as a human resource specialist finally was one where support was available:

> For the first time since college, it seems to be a good situation. I work with normal, mentally stable people. I'm finding confidence from this job. We get emails from the executive secretary— thoughts for day, positive things. It is an optimistic way of looking at things. [It helps me] adjust the way I am thinking. I have always been more passive and timid in the past. I tried to work on it. If something is making me unhappy, I try to act on it, ask the right people, or try to work on going ahead and doing what I think needs to be done. If I think it is right, I go ahead and do it—I'm working toward being more autonomous. I'm not a loose cannon, I still feel like I need approval for things I do; praise, or "yes, that is a good idea."

A little support in the form of positive messages and the apparent absence of ethical digressions made Genesse's work environment a positive factor in her getting back on the journey toward self-authorship. Doing what she thinks needs to be done and working on being more autonomous reveal that she is beginning to author her own life. Her story illustrates that work settings in which employees are told what to do and their concern for clients is dismissed make no contribution to employees growth toward self-authorship. These contexts led Genesse to be unhappy in her jobs and to seek alternatives. They also negatively affected her health. Because her growth was thwarted, she did not become a long-term asset to any of her employers. The lack of validating her as a knower and mutually constructing meaning with her cost both her and her employers.

Translation to Educational Practice. The invitation to incorporate and develop participants' sense of self in the context of their professional work responsibilities enhanced their growth toward self-authorship. Employers' hopes for getting "a better wheel," to use Andrew's analogy, translated to giving participants autonomy to use their skills and thinking. The trust inherent in this autonomy validated participants as knowers and situated learning in their experience. The guidance offered when necessary reflected the principle of mutually constructing knowledge and adjusted use of the principles to match participants' developmental journeys. The combination of these principles helped participants develop their own work styles and blend their personalities with their work in effective ways. Encouragement to stand up for what they believed further reinforced self-authorship.

The first step in translation of these stories to campus work roles is for supervisors to assume that student employees may be able to "invent a better wheel." Too often educators assume that student employees do not have sufficient knowledge or skills to improve upon the task at hand, whether it is teaching, a research project, building good relationships among students, or an office procedure. Adopting the assumption that students are capable of contributing to the work is the precursor to offering them the kind of autonomy that promotes self-authorship. From this autonomy comes trust and validation as knowers. Linked with appropriate guidance in the form of mutual construction makes it possible to afford employees autonomy and still ensure quality service to the students served by the work role.

The second step is acknowledging that self is central to one's work and that developing a sense of self is a key component of campus work roles. Talking directly with student employees about how they might develop their own work style in relation to meeting their specific job responsibilities would introduce this idea to them and validate them as knowers. Inviting student employees to develop their own work styles, to explore their beliefs, and to form frameworks from which to approach their work occurs through mutual construction of knowledge on-the-job. Feedback in the form Ned described coaches student employees to refine their thinking and become cognizant of how their beliefs contribute to their work style. Thus supervision, from initial discussion of job expectations to an autonomous management philosophy to performance feedback, can be organized to promote self-authorship. Approaching supervision this way requires believing that student employees have something to contribute and that their growth toward self-authorship is equally important to the job function they perform.

Mutual Construction

Viewing knowledge as socially constructed and expecting employees to contribute effectively by bringing their sense of self to that process led to the mutual construction of meaning in determining how work would be accomplished. The mutual construction of meaning around how to conduct oneself in one's work provided support for establishing an internal sense of self. That, in turn, helped participants move away from inauthentic interactions with coworkers and clients and toward ones characterized by mutuality. Growth in both arenas helped participants further establish their perspectives in the epistemological realm. The process of mutual construction also kept challenges congruent with participants' progress on the journey. Thus mutual construction of meaning integrated the principles to promote self-authorship. Mutual construction took place with supervisors, colleagues, and clients.

Supervisors as Mentors.   When participants viewed supervisors as mentors, it was often because supervisors engaged the growing edge of participants' development on the journey to self-authorship. Gwen's story (chapter 2) about how her manager helped her form her own conclusions and Evan's mentors teaching him how to make real estate deals (chapter 3) are both about supervisors who accepted employees' external self-definitions but simultaneously invited them to move toward internal self-definition in their work and carefully guided their progress.

One of Lauren's early supervisors understood that her external self-definition prompted her to "beat around the bush" in their conversations. Lauren reported that he routinely responded to her with "So what are you asking?" Lauren's boss pushed her to clarify what she meant by asking her questions when he thought she was hedging. At one point Lauren wanted to transfer but was afraid to ask her boss. When she did approach him, she reminded him that he had encouraged her to be direct. He rewarded her directness with the transfer she desired. He affirmed the importance of expressing her own ideas and needs, a dimension of developing an internal sense of self. Another supervisor affirmed this when Lauren took a new job and received the salary and benefits she directly requested. She reflected on these experiences:

> I think that that was one of the greatest lessons I learned, that even though the answer may be no, it is much better to ask. I

don't think I was always as direct as I've learned to be for fear of what people would think or how that would affect you later. And I think that that's something that I can pull over into my personal life, into my work life, into going to the store and asking to return something. That's definitely a skill that I have acquired. And it still makes me nervous, but you've got to do it.

This comment reveals that Lauren's original beating around the bush came from fear of how people would react, a typical concern from an external location on the journey. As her bosses validated her as a knower and mutually constructed meaning with her, she learned to express herself and strengthen her sense of self in ways that carried over into other arenas of her life. Her supervisors' guidance matched her progress on the journey toward self-authorship and thus supported her growth.

Gavin's boss also matched mutual construction to Gavin's progress toward self-authorship. Gavin described how his boss helped him learn to think for himself:

It's really nice to know that I can just say, "Mr. Smith, I'm having trouble with—I don't understand this." He doesn't always give me the answer. A lot of times he'll throw back questions like, "Well, what do you think about it?" He always tries to get you to answer it yourself. And if he feels differently, he'll tell you. I'm still kind of nervous just because I feel like what I'm asking him is going to be stupid or silly. But he never makes you feel bad. His method of getting people to learn is he always thinks that if you're a bright enough person you really do know the answer or it's easy enough for you to find out. If we disagree, then he says, "Well, if that's the way you see it, do it your way and if it works out let me know." . . . It gives me the impression that if my mindset is that I'm going to do it my way, I can do it that way. If it doesn't work, I'll tell him. And a lot of times he'll say, "Well, you'll feel a lot better with yourself because you tried it." So it's a very, very relaxed atmosphere with very, very professional people. They just know how to—it's like they're being a mentor. It's neat.

Gavin's boss used numerous forms of mutual construction. He helped Gavin reflect on his own ideas and expertise to think through his work. When Gavin needed help, his boss provided it without making Gavin feel incompetent. When Gavin wanted to try something a different way, his boss supported trying it even if he disagreed. Even when Gavin did make mistakes, his boss still encouraged him to try out his own thinking in order "to feel better about himself." His boss appeared to be an expert at using the three principles. Perhaps this support for Gavin's self-authorship contributed to his progress in making his career change to teaching.

One of Sandra's supervisors also helped her think for herself:

> [My supervisor] was terrific. He built my confidence; he trusted me, never second-guessed me. He forced me to explain my reasons. That trained me to do this for myself. I had to think about it, so I got better at it. I knew he would ask. He trained me to do it on my own; thus I made better decisions. He had confidence in me, so I did too. It was a precious gift.

Mutual construction with her supervisor helped Sandra articulate her reasons for particular counseling approaches. His trust validated her as a knower. Through their conversations she learned to think through what she was doing because she knew he would ask. This mutual construction led to increased confidence and an ability to construct knowledge on her own. Like Lauren and Gavin, Sandra recognized the value of this supervision—this precious gift—that helped her move toward self-authorship. Similarly, participants valued mutual construction with colleagues and its contribution to their work and personal growth.

Collaboration with Colleagues.   Mutual construction with colleagues occurred in many work settings, generally aimed at providing a better product or service. Barry offered a typical example of collaboration at his advertising agency:

> We have brainstorming sessions to think of different plans. We get people together and tell them what the goals are, who the company wants to reach, where they want to reach them, local or national, and what kind of sources do you have, what kind of money, celebrity personalities you have access to. Then you start having different ideas.

The value of collaboration in Barry's work was to enrich ideas to meet his companies' advertising goals. Human service professionals, many of them teachers, also found collaboration among colleagues to be a mainstay of making everyday decisions to provide better service to clients. Candace taught at a Paideia school where a team of teachers merged English, foreign language, literature, science and mathematics into an integrated curriculum. She reported loving the job because "the people on my team are very helpful and I've already gotten—the ideas and their knowledge—they're just incredible. I'm learning a lot." Pamela worked in a school where groups of teachers were assigned the same students so they could collaborate. She described her team's approach:

> I can go to my team and say, "I'm having problems with this student. Are you seeing similar things?" Or you can talk about what you're going to be doing the next week. Say I'm doing some math things in science. I can talk to the math teacher and see if they could review this concept with the students so they are not totally lost when they come to science class. It really helps a lot. At first I thought it was just me having the problems.

Pamela blamed herself at first for problems with students, until she took time to explore the problems with other teachers. She reported that when one teacher found something that worked with a student, she shared it with the team. Pamela found this mutual construction helpful in handling discipline and helping students understand content.

Sandra's stories about the team approach in her counseling work show how direct feedback exchanged among colleagues promotes self-authorship in work:

> I've found some very helpful people [in my team] who have a lot of experience in the field and are very willing to talk with you about things and say, "Next time you might want to try that." There are a lot of things that come up in an inpatient setting that kind of surprise you, even after years of experience. We make a big effort to work together as a team. You always have at least one other person to bounce ideas off of—you're not out there by yourself.

Despite having experience, Sandra knew surprises were around every corner and she relied on the support of others to assess her performance. Sandra grew accustomed to bouncing her ideas off others, mutually deciding what to do, and getting feedback from colleagues about her performance. Thus she was pleased that it was a formal part of another job:

> There are a lot of good people on staff. We have peer review meetings for two hours every week. We discuss cases. The team perspective, ideas about what to try, is really terrific. I rely more on them than on my supervisor. If I have a lot of experience, I make my own decisions; that is part of gaining confidence as a therapist. I don't ask about chemical dependency issues because I have a good base of knowledge and can make good decisions. If it is new ground I'll ask a colleague who has more experience

> for their opinion. Usually I say, "Here is what I was thinking about doing, what do you think?" to see if it sounds like a good clinical decision.

Sandra was aware that she had changed the way she solicited others' perspectives. Initially she sought out their opinion about whether she had handled something right; later she formulated her own approach and checked with others to see if it sounded clinically appropriate to them. She attributed this shift to her increased confidence and knowledge base acquired from experience.

These efforts at providing better advertising campaigns or services to clients hinged on the belief that collaboration could produce better work outcomes. This put participants in positions to express their own thinking and acquire feedback from their colleagues. As a result, learning to construct meaning with others helped participants' move toward defining themselves internally and join others from an internally defined sense of self. The shift Sandra described is an example of defining her self and work internally and joining others from this new self-authored perspective.

Once participants were well into authoring their own lives, they intentionally sought out colleagues with new perspectives to expand their thinking. Dawn described gathering ideas from watching other actors in her theater group:

> To watch people taking leaps and bounds with their choices, it was something very valuable for me to learn. If they can do it, certainly I can do it. And it's very rewarding to work with a talented group of individuals. I felt like I could be a little sponge and absorb things from them. You imitate them in a way. You see something that works and you try it. If it works for you, you continue to try it and then it becomes your thing.

Watching others take risks validated Dawn's ability to take risks. Her colleagues modeled choices with which she could experiment. Having the confidence to try these choices helped her figure out what worked for her, helping her decide whether to add it to "her thing."

Adrian spoke to the notion of expanding herself in her work at an advertising agency, the type of job she had held since graduation in two different companies. At the time she shared this story in our eleventh interview, she had developed her own philosophies and was trying to be more open to expanding them through others' ideas. This conversation emerged from her comment that she knew she was competent, to which I responded by asking her if she viewed herself as an expert. She replied:

No way! I work, especially for my boss and around people, whose minds intrigue me, whose opinions and philosophies and ideas only build on my own thoughts and ideas everyday. That would stop if you were an expert. I like exploring ideas with people. That's good for me, because I fall into a mode of "why don't people see it this way—isn't this obvious?" Working through difference of opinion; that process is good. The atmosphere and personality of the company is very open and there is no taboo subject, no one you can't talk to. [We have] really creative people with good ideas. It is the type of environment in which that is fostered. It is good for me.

Adrian already had an internal self-definition that shaped her values and how she saw the world and her work. She recognized that she was placing this value system on other people and at the same time wanted to continue to expand her philosophies by exploring those of others. Her security with herself allowed her to reflect on her expectations of others and to open herself to learning from them. Her comments reveal the capacity for mutuality in relationships with others, a capacity that stems from her internal sense of self.

Collaboration with Clients. Participants often learned to develop and hone their ideas through collaboration with clients. Often, clients had information employees needed to do their work. Gathering this information and analyzing it helped participants move toward self-authorship. Al described this scenario in his initial job in computer consulting:

We started to redesign a new system. You're basically trying to get as much information out of the people who are the end users. You hold a lot of interviews and just try to suck as much information out of them as you can so that you can design the system. What needs to be done here? How can we automate it? What are the different things we need to get done in this system? You have to grasp what they're saying and then organize it. Then you write up the documentation and put together a design of the system. . . . You first start with it on a business level. What are the business functions we need to meet here? And then break it down into technical parts. We need these types of programs to do this. And then you actually write the specifications for those program that are going to solve this business function.

Al had the technical knowledge to identify programs and write their specifications. Before he could use that knowledge he had to mutually construct the business functions needed with his clients. He needed to grasp their information before he could organize it to design the system.

Ned also needed information from clients in order to make good decisions about chemicals for their paper machines. In addition he needed to convince various players at the mill to accept those decisions. Ned used various people who had expertise on different parts of the system to help him solve problems. Once he devised a plan, he explained it to people who would be involved in making or implementing the decision. He described why it was important to get others on board, even if they were not the key decision-makers:

> There are a hundred different people analyzing it from their perspective. So you've got the guy running the machine, who has no education but he's been there for 35 years and he knows this machine and he's thinking, "Don't some college boy come tell me how to run this thing." And then you've got the mill manager, who's been to 49 other mills and probably is not aware of the specific details of how his mill runs. And then you've got the process engineer, who is intimately familiar with his piece of the pie, but not the big picture. So I have to assimilate all that data and kind of filter it. You've got to have the right filter on when you're talking to the specific person.

Ned realized that each person's experience led to a different perspective. He was careful to use the right filter with specific people, connecting his expertise to theirs. His comment about the veteran who ran the machine hints at a dilemma Ned encountered in mutual construction—being younger and less experienced than his clients. He talked about overcoming his hesitation to talk to others:

> It is imposing to talk with experts or important people, powerful people, especially when you're young. One of the things that I've had to overcome for myself is to feel that age should not make anyone more or less equal than the other. I'm not going to get nervous when I talk to a mill manager or when somebody important wants to talk to me. Whereas before I was, "Well, why do they want to talk to me? Maybe I won't say the things that they want to hear or maybe I'll sound stupid."

Asked how he overcame this hesitation, Ned explained:

> It was my job. I've got to talk with these people. The first year or two of my job I was asking my boss a lot of questions before I went into a situation. After a time I just kind of naturally fit into the role I was supposed to be playing because I learned what I

was supposed to say and not say. So I had a confidence factor there; I had some base knowledge that allowed me to know up front that I could get through the situation. So I relaxed and I started asking real questions and getting real answers. As I felt comfortable, it helped me reduce or eliminate mental blocks to meeting and interacting with people and to do things in my job, in my personal life, everywhere. A much more open feeling.

Ned's more open feeling emerged from becoming himself in interactions with his clients. Experiencing success in mutual construction of meaning with older, more powerful people helped bolster his evolving sense of himself. It had this effect because he was given the opportunity to function autonomously in his work and because he was encouraged to be honest when he was unsure. He shared:

You improvise along the way and if you get into a problem you just back up and honestly say, "I didn't know this," or, "I need to find this out." And you find that being honest and trying hard counts a heck of a lot. And it doesn't matter whether you knew it or didn't. They'll teach you, and you'll learn, and they'll accept it.

Because clients appreciated his honesty when he did not know something, he felt comfortable expressing himself. He found support in others teaching him which led to his confidence that he could learn and that others would respect his growing expertise.

Mutual construction with clients was not limited to business contexts. Rosa said working with her students' parents was her biggest learning experience when she started teaching. She explained:

I always had to be really careful with how I approached things with them and using the right words. Even with test results. Parents can interpret them so differently than they're meant to be. So I always had to make sure I stressed how you were supposed to be taking this. A lot of parents took it to heart, like, "Okay, my child should be in sixth grade because she tested out of sixth-grade level in reading." . . . I had a child I had to retain. That was one of the toughest challenges I had with a parent. The mom wanted what was best for the child, but the father said, "If you retain him, I'll pull the kids out of the school." The mother wanted her kids getting a Catholic education. So she was asking me, "How can I tell my husband about this?" I got help from the principal, the school psychologist, and another first-grade teacher.

To accomplish what she thought was best for her students, Rosa had to work effectively with their parents. Communicating effectively with their parents meant learning how to guide their interpretations and help them with dilemmas. Her colleagues engaged in mutual construction with her to help her with tough challenges.

Dilemmas with Mutual Construction.   Not all supervisors invited their employees to participate in mutual construction. When participants had not yet solidified their self-authorship, such environments interfered with their progress. Remember Kelly's experience (chapter 4) when her colleagues voted to strike. At that point Kelly did not have the internal sense of self needed to vote her conscience and was discouraged that her colleagues did not value her opinion. Genesse's story earlier in this chapter also shows the devastating effect of lack of mutual construction during the early phases of the journey.

For participants in the midst of authoring their own lives, lack of mutual construction with supervisors and colleagues was a temporary setback. This was the case for Anne, who changed jobs as part of further defining herself and her professional goals:

> The company I was with wasn't necessarily right for me. I found a job that sounded great, I liked the boss and other people I interviewed with; it sounded challenging. It wasn't the job so much I didn't like; I didn't fit in with the culture. The culture was conservative; they wanted people to be mediocre. People were unhelpful, they thought I wanted to know too much. I wasn't stimulated, so I went back to school.

Anne reflected clearly on her learning from this negative work environment:

> I've learned a lot in the past two years—about myself. I lost a lot of confidence at the last job. People treated me badly, and I started doubting myself. I will never let that happen again—I have talent, I can be successful. I started thinking I wasn't that good, couldn't handle the responsibility. Another person quit after ten months and he felt the same way. We realized it wasn't us; it was them. Going back to school was the first big step; being around people interested in bettering themselves instead of negative attitudes. Doing well at school made me feel good. Meeting other people and the experience at the new job—people telling me I am doing a good job, thanking me. That is the big thing; being successful again. Now I realize the other situation was a one-time incident. If I ever change jobs again, I'll look at

the culture of the company really hard. In my previous job, I felt average and mediocre and it was expected.

Anne succumbed temporarily to the expectations of those around her to be mediocre. This called her confidence and ability into question until she had opportunities for mutual construction with others to identify the problem as the culture of the company. Although her confidence in herself was shaken in the negative environment, Anne managed to recover from it with a stronger sense of herself in part because she had opportunities to mutually construct an interpretation of this experience with others.

Participants who were experienced at self-authorship were least fazed by lack of mutual construction. Candace moved to another school due to budget cuts and found herself at odds with both her principal and her colleagues. She explained how she handled it:

> A student walked out of my classroom. I said that's a three-day in-school suspension. To avoid conflict with the parent, the principal wanted me to just drop it. And I said, "No." He said he wouldn't do it. I said, "You don't have a choice." The way they did our contract this year, all the discipline is grievable through the contract. So I reminded him of that and went to another vice-principal who is an advocate for new teachers. The kid got three days in-school suspension and I got a letter of apology. Since then he's been pretty formal with me, which is just fine.

Lack of support did not impede Candace from implementing what she thought was appropriate discipline, nor did the principal's refusal intimidate her. She found a similar lack of support among the math faculty at the school, reporting that they did not want to share materials or ideas. Candace was not necessarily happy with these dynamics but they did not interfere with her authorship of her own work because it was already established. Lauren reported a similar experience having acquired a new boss who wanted things done his way. Having had previous supervisors who encouraged her to author her own work, she found this boss wanting. Her reaction was, "I wish I had another boss, but you have to make do with what you can. I can't let him ruin my day-to-day activity." Lauren did not question herself when she and her boss disagreed; instead she viewed it as a problem belonging to the boss. This situation did not contribute to her continued growth but at the same time it did not interfere with her already established self-authorship.

Participants who were forming their internal foundations responded somewhat differently to lack of mutual construction. Sandra described this experience with a new supervisor:

I don't know if I don't have confidence in him. I'm trying to give him the benefit of the doubt. I take what he says, but do what I want anyway. That is not the way it should be. If he gives me a direct thing to do, I'll do it. There have been things that I have put off, or done my own way, because I feel like it is clinically more correct. My old supervisor gave me lots of options; my new supervisor shuts down a lot of options with his suggestions. I have been trying to tell him that it seems that it cuts off other options. We butted heads a few times. What would I do without connections with others? I use that a lot. I call people and ask for opinions.

Sandra's growth from her previous job prompted her to want more options in supervision and more mutual decisionmaking with her boss. She perceived his suggestions as closing down her options or as less clinically correct than her perspective. She was trying to work with improving this relationship, but still acted on her own beliefs. Her openness to mutual construction, even when she could apparently get away with just doing what she wanted, demonstrates growth toward interdependence with others. Despite her independent streak, she believed that working out differences with her supervisor was important.

These stories suggest that dilemmas in mutual construction hindered externally-defined participants from moving into and beyond the crossroads, and created problems for those in the midst of authoring their own lives. Only those who were solidly into self-authorship or working on the internal foundation were minimally effected.

Translation to Educational Practice.   Mutual construction validated employees as knowers and situated learning in their experience. Supervisors who helped employees explore, experiment, and learn how to think were regarded as mentors. Participants who encountered these mentors learned how to self-author their ideas and express them to others. Work settings in which collaboration among colleagues was encouraged further aided participants in self-authoring their work through gaining ideas from others, seeing others model various approaches, and getting direct feedback on their performance. They learned to express their ideas and accept feedback in these mutual constructions when colleagues were working collaboratively toward common goals and supportive of individual employee's growth. Skills and confidence gained in mutual construction with supervisors and colleagues helped participants who needed to mutually construct meaning with clients to perform their work. Learning to be themselves in these interactions, be honest about what they knew, and listen to others' perspectives helped them succeed in working effectively with clients.

Achieving these ends through campus work settings means using mutual construction as both a core assumption and a principle for practice. Supervisors should focus on helping employees develop their thinking through the kind of questioning Gavin and Sandra reported, and help employees express themselves the way Lauren's supervisor did. Creating opportunities for student workers to collaborate with other student workers and full-time staff would offer the opportunity to see models, gather ideas about particular work, provide opportunities for exchange of feedback that helps self-authorship, and provide a supportive team approach to accomplishing work goals. Paraprofessional and student leadership roles also have numerous opportunities for mutual construction with clients, in these cases, other students served by these roles. As is the case with translating the other two core assumptions, to use mutual construction means believing that student employees have something to contribute.

Implications for Campus Work Settings

The employment settings described here were primarily focused on enhancing productivity of institutions, agencies, and companies. Employers' beliefs about the role of employees in enhancing productivity, however, meant that a secondary focus was developing employees to be autonomous. Employers invested in their employees in the hopes of long-term gain regarding their ability to learn continuously, adjust quickly, function autonomously, collaborate effectively with others, and make wise decisions. They recognized that in a complex world, employees have to learn to think, analyze and make decisions on their own rather than be told what to do. Oblinger and Verville (1998), in a volume that specifies what business needs from higher education, argue that the contemporary world necessitates flexible organizations. They note that in flexible organizations, employees need teamwork, communication, and interpersonal skills. They also argue that employers want employees who can quickly adapt to their work roles, yet quickly become transformative agents, defined as people who "have ideas, 'think outside the box', cause friction, and look ahead" (p. 77), to help the organization effect change. Gardner called employees with these skills "the *new learning employees*—[who] balance expertise in their content knowledge with strong interpersonal communication, teamwork, and self-accountability skills" (1997, p. 72). Although it is not clear from the participants' stories whether their organizations were actively trying to develop them as transformative agents, their stories do convey many of the major characteristics Gardner, Oblinger and Verville, and others identified as key to evolving organizations, such as communication, teamwork, interpersonal skills, problem-solving, decision-making, creativity, leadership, and continuous learning to name a few.

Despite employers investing in employee development for the employers' benefit, their doing so offered the opportunity for growth to the longitudinal study participants. The stories in this chapter convey that participants learned the skills and competencies for their particular work as well as competencies necessary in the contemporary world of work. Much of the growth participants' described, which I've interpreted through a developmental lens as self-authorship, also captures Peter Senge's (1990) concept of personal mastery. Senge defines personal mastery as a process of lifelong learning in which we continually clarify our visions and our ability to see reality clearly. Senge wrote:

> The juxtaposition of vision (what we want) and a clear picture of current reality (where we are relative to what we want) generates what we call "creative tension": a force to bring them together, caused by the natural tendency of tension to seek resolution. The essence of personal mastery is learning how to generate and sustain creative tension in our lives. (p. 142).

Senge states that our vision "comes from within"; thus it requires an internal sense of self. Acting on this vision through one's work means that it is one's own work, an idea similar to the shift described by participants to "how *I* do this job." Clarifying current reality involves a shift from viewing current reality as an ally rather than an enemy, thus leading to a commitment to truth and openness to change—outcomes many of the stories in this chapter contain. I interpret this shift as similar to the shift from external to internal self-definition. Other characteristics Senge includes in personal mastery, such as inquisitiveness, connection to others, a sense of influence but not control over external events, and continual learning are also consistent with self-authorship and the growth participants described in their work settings. Changes Senge describes as coming from personal mastery also match changes that stem from self-authorship—integration of reason and intuition and greater connection to the world.

It almost seems as though participants' employers read Senge's comments on conditions that are conducive to developing personal mastery: "developing a more systemic worldview, learning how to reflect on tacit assumptions, expressing one's vision and listening to other's visions, and joint inquiry into different people's views of current reality" (1990, p. 173). These conditions were inherent and often explicit in contexts that viewed knowledge as complex and socially constructed, viewed the self as central to knowledge construction, and focused on mutual construction of meaning. The three principles I have advanced to implement these assumptions—validating the learner as a knower, situating learning in the learner's experience, and mutually constructing meaning—would create the conditions for personal mastery.

How do these conditions translate to campus work settings? Some campus work roles focus primarily on getting a job done (e.g., working on the grounds crew); others focus on the dual purpose of getting work done and promoting students' growth as a contribution to the educational mission (e.g., teaching or research assistants). Some even focus primarily on student growth (e.g., student leadership roles). Given the importance of preparing graduates to work in complex, flexible, rapidly changing contexts, it is important to consider conceptualizing the entire campus work environment, to the extent possible, as an *educational* rather than a production function. Conceptualizing the entire campus work environment as educational does require transforming assumptions about the role of students' campus work. Although work outcomes would remain important, student learning would be equally important. Making work settings educational will necessitate more time from supervisors to guide student staff the way longitudinal participants were guided by their supervisors. Supervisors would become educators and thus must be given time in their workload for this responsibility. Although it is possible that student employees could learn to function autonomously and make wise choices, thus providing better service, if students stayed in campus work environments long enough to develop personal mastery and self-authorship, this goal may not be realized in campus work settings. Yet the long-term educational benefits of promoting self-authorship outweigh the short-term costs of using campus work settings for this purpose. Because approximately 60 percent of students work during college (Levine and Cureton, 1998), and many others engage in paraprofessional or leadership roles on campus, the campus work environment has rich potential to enhance the educational mission.

Paraprofessional positions are prevalent in both academic and student affairs arenas, at both the undergraduate and graduate levels. In both arenas, these positions contribute simultaneously to the functioning of the institution and the student's education. These contexts could be organized to promote personal mastery and self-authorship by framing them around a complex, socially constructed view of knowledge, emphasizing self as central to knowledge construction, and engaging student employees in the mutual construction of knowledge relative to their positions. The same is true of campus service roles. Although I have synthesized key suggestions in earlier segments to translate stories about each assumption to educational practice, I integrate those next in the specific campus work roles that exist widely on college campuses.

Paraprofessional Positions in Academic Affairs

The most prevalent paraprofessional positions in academic affairs are research and teaching assistants. One of my colleagues incorporates the three assumptions needed for promoting self-authorship into his work with his research assistants. His research team consists of faculty members, postdoctoral fellows, and graduate and undergraduate research assistants. The team approaches its work from the perspective that scientific facts are tentative and subject to revision. Team discussions revolve around interpreting data, recognizing that each person brings their own perspective to this process, and identifying next steps in the research program. Research assistants, both graduate and undergraduate, are welcomed as members of the team and their perspectives are valued. This context conveys knowledge as socially constructed and complex, models the mutual construction of knowledge among knowledgeable peers, and validates the students as knowers. It conveys that who people are affects their interpretations and decisions. Learning is situated in learners' experience because they participate in running the experiments and the processing discussions. They are afforded autonomy and trusted to carry out their laboratory duties as members of the team based on the team's agreements, rather than simply carrying out orders. Framing the graduate and undergraduate research assistant role this way promotes students' learning and self-authorship while simultaneously enhancing the effectiveness with which they conduct their work.

Graduate and undergraduate teaching assistant positions could be framed similarly. Graduate teaching assistants often teach classes independently with the guidance of a faculty supervisor. A colleague who coordinates a group of graduate teaching assistants (TAs) teaching multiple sections of the same course illustrates using the three assumptions to promote self-authorship among the TAs. A training seminar introduces the TAs to the content and goals of the course, pedagogical theory and practice, and evaluation techniques. Multiple perspectives are included, as is the notion that each instructor must develop her own pedagogy. Prior to teaching, each TA constructs her own syllabus, in consultation with the faculty supervisor, to meet the purpose of the course. Regular teaching seminars during the semester give the TAs an opportunity to process their work as a group, raise concerns, generate solutions and new approaches, and reflect on how their particular style works. Some choose to team-teach, creating another opportunity for mutual construction. TAs are given autonomy and trusted to conduct their teaching and evaluation of students appropriately. The seminar group and faculty supervisor contributes to helping individual TAs address areas they would like to improve or issues they encounter. This context frames knowledge about pedagogy and course content as complex and socially constructed. The self is central to how the TA chooses to implement his or her responsibilities. Mutual construction takes place among the TA group and with the supervisor. Learning is situated in TAs experience as they teach and process their work simultaneously. Autonomy and respect in mutual construction validate their capability to bring their sense of self to their teaching.

Undergraduate teaching assistants are less likely to teach independently and more likely to assist students in understanding the course material and assist the instructor with evaluating students' work. This position can still be framed to promote self-authorship by including the TA as a member of the teaching team. Functioning as a team, the instructor and TA could mutually construct class activities, assignments, and assessment processes. Valuing the TA's perspective of how students are reacting to the material would affirm the TA's voice and perspective. Mutual discussion of ways to help students learn would emphasize the role of self in knowledge construction, as would discussion of what style works for this particular TA to help students learn. Exploring ways of conveying the course knowledge—in class, in study sessions, or in one-on-one sessions—would emphasize the complexity and social construction of knowledge. Mutual construction of evaluation techniques would embody the three assumptions as well. Framing the undergraduate TA position this way makes the TA a valuable partner in the teaching process rather than a person who makes handouts and grades objective tests. Progress toward self-authorship that would emerge from this role would benefit the TA and provide meaningful assistance to the instructor. A related position, one-on-one tutoring, is another context in which to promote self-authorship using this framework.

Paraprofessional roles in computing and technology are increasingly prevalent in higher education. These roles are sometimes filled by students in technical fields for whom the work serves as professional preparation; they are sometimes filled by students with general interest in technology whose major areas of study are totally unrelated to technology. The unique dynamic of these roles is that students often have knowledge and expertise more advanced than that of the full-time faculty and staff. This unique dynamic lends itself to using the framework for promoting self-authorship. Technological knowledge is extremely complex, socially constructed among knowledgeable peers (of varying ages and education), and rapidly changing. Encouraging paraprofessionals to bring their expertise to improving and implementing technology on campus and inviting them into the mutual construction process can promote their self-authorship and maximize use of their expertise. Rather than view these paraprofessionals as staff to assist students and hold late-night laboratory hours, they could be viewed as valuable contributors to educating faculty and staff about technology and to improving technological systems for all university constituents. Job descriptions for these students could be negotiated depending on their expertise and learning goals, supervision would model supervision described in this chapter, and paraprofessionals would be included as important members of the technology team.

Internships or co-operative experiences, although usually framed as part of the curriculum rather than employment, constitute another work setting within academic affairs where self-authorship can be promoted. The longitudinal participants' experiences in employment settings could be mirrored in internship and co-op settings. Faculty supervisors of these settings could use the three assumptions and three principles to communicate to internship sites the type of experience they desire for students. They could also use the assumptions and principles in their supervision of students working in these sites. For example, the graduate program in which I teach requires two internships as part of the curriculum. The faculty and students solicit internship sites that provide meaningful experiences that promote self-authorship. The job description for each internship is created mutually by the student, faculty supervisor and site supervisor to meet the students' educational needs and the sites' functional needs. Evaluation processes are mutually developed by the same players to be consistent with the job description. This approach conveys that knowledge and expertise in the work area is socially constructed, that self is central to conducting one's responsibilities, and that expertise and authority are mutually constructed. Encouraging internship supervisors to teach interns to think for themselves, offer them autonomy with appropriate guidance, and opportunities for mutual construction with others further implements this framework. This process is relevant across internship contexts: business, technical fields, service fields, and student teaching in education. Service learning, another initiative becoming associated with some courses that has potential to promote self-authorship, is addressed in chapter 9.

Paraprofessional Positions in Student Affairs

Paraprofessionals are central to many student affairs functions, including admission, orientation, student activities and organizations, and residence life on residential campuses. Some of these roles are volunteer (e.g., admissions tour guides and student leaders) whereas others are paid (e.g., orientation leaders and resident assistants). Despite the diversity of responsibilities across these roles, all these positions can be framed to promote self-authorship, thus contributing to the educational mission. The student affairs profession's renewal of its original commitment to education via *The Student Learning Imperative* (American College Personnel Association, 1994) advocates framing all student affairs functions as arenas for student learning. Thus paraprofessional positions should promote learning of the paraprofessionals and the students who benefit from their work.

As was the case in the settings in which the longitudinal participants worked, framing paraprofessional positions to promote self-authorship occurs in the context of institutional priorities and needs. Admission and orientation functions are concerned with achieving enrollment and retention goals and thus desire to convey a positive image of the institution. Yet admission and orientation staff know that college choice and adjustment to college life are complex matters, socially constructed by students with their parents, peers, and educators. The incoming students' unique interests, abilities, and goals are also central to both processes. Rather than script the paraprofessional tour guides' or orientation staff's message, which is tempting in an effort to control what prospective students hear, it is more productive to incorporate the assumptions and principles that promote self-authorship. Acknowledging that each student chooses and acclimates to college life in unique ways helps guide paraprofessionals to analyze how they experienced these processes. Teaching paraprofessionals to think about these issues, giving them autonomy to perform with guidance as needed, and opportunities for them to mutually construct as a group how they will perform their duties offers opportunities for self-authorship. Mutually constructing how to convey their perspective and the institution's perspective in a way that allows prospective students to construct their own views helps paraprofessionals function as resources rather than advice givers.

The resident assistant (RA) position is another prime area for promoting self-authorship, both of RAs and students they educate. Student affairs professionals conceptualize residential living as an educational process. Purposes of residence halls thus include creating environments that enhance students' academic success, promote students' personal development, teach self-responsibility, and provide learning experiences beyond the curriculum (Greenleaf, 1974). RA roles thus include role modeling effective academic performance, fostering community development, promoting individual student development, educational programming, confronting behavior problems, and leadership (Winston & Fitch, 1993). RA roles generally involve some administrative tasks that are not necessarily educational (e.g., maintenance paperwork, or provision of supplies).

The majority of RA responsibilities are characterized by complex, socially constructed knowledge. Certainly guiding students toward the interpersonal skills and sensitivity to live productively in community is a complex process, socially constructed among diverse members of the community. This process is mediated by the unique development of the individual members of the community and their ability to effectively mutually construct group norms with their peers. Educational programming is equally complex given central campus issues like alcohol abuse, eating disorders, and relationship violence. The decisions college students face regarding peer and societal pressure are also the content of educational programming. Because the content of RAs work clearly embodies the three assumptions central to promoting self-authorship, the three principles to promote self-authorship should be used to frame their roles.

RA pre-service and in-service training would invite their experiences as students and RAs into the learning process and validate their insights into college life. Autonomy and trust to carry out their responsibilities with appropriate guidance would help them determine how they as individuals would conduct their work effectively. Staff discussions and supervisory meetings would focus on helping RAs develop their own perspectives on their work, determine what they believed, and stand up for it in staff decision-making. Authority and expertise would be shared among staff peers and supervisors in making decisions about educational initiatives and community problem solving. Feedback on their performance would focus on their ability to meet their educational goals for residents as well as their growth toward self-authorship in their work. I have often observed that RA training and supervision focuses more on telling RAs what to do rather than engaging them in mutual construction. If for-profit companies, human service agencies, and educational institutions can share expertise and authority with novice employees, as is evident in the preceding stories, residence life offices can do the same.

Similar opportunities exist for promoting self-authorship in paraprofessional roles related to the commuter population. Commuter center paraprofessionals' work is complex because they focus on helping students of various ages who have daily lives and responsibilities beyond the campus. The complications typical of commuter students' lives—family responsibilities, jobs, traveling, parking—add to the complexity of their college experience. Helping commuter students juggle these complexities with their academic and social learning is a complex process that must be tailored to individual students' needs. Thus the commuter center paraprofessional must be able to validate students as knowers, situate learning in their experience, and engage students in mutual construction of meaning. To do so, the paraprofessional must have guidance to move toward self-authorship.

Finally, leadership roles in student organizations, student government, and Greek life offer opportunities for self-authorship. Rather than belabor the three assumptions and three principles for practicing them any further, suffice it to say that leaders in these roles should be afforded the same combination of autonomy, trust and guidance evident in the longitudinal participants' stories. Shared authority with campus educators and administrators and participation in mutual construction of plans that affect college life would promote leaders' self-authorship and enhance the quality of campus life. Perhaps inviting leaders to be genuine partners would help campus educators progress in solving complex issues—such as hazing in Greek organizations—that they have been unable to solve for decades. As Andrew noted earlier, maybe students could invent a better wheel.

Graduate students often have paraprofessional roles in student affairs. These roles are generally half-time assistantships that help support students through graduate school. They typically are found in residence life, commuter centers, student activities, Greek life, admissions, orientation, learning assistance, student leadership programs, recreational sports, and alumni relations. The same framework and particulars described for promoting self-authorship for undergraduates could be used to promote self-authorship for graduate students.

Service Roles on Campus

Students are often employed in diverse service roles on campus in offices, computer labs, childcare facilities, libraries, recreational facilities, food service operations, and sometimes on housekeeping, maintenance, and grounds crews. These roles are usually focused on the work to be done rather than promoting student employees' self-authorship. This is due, in part, to the roles of their supervisors being defined as getting a job done rather than educating students. In light of the demand for self-authorship in today's society, it seems reasonable to suggest that all areas of employment, student and otherwise, should focus on promoting self-authorship. Managers of these service operations already know they are complex processes that are implemented more effectively when employees have a vested interest in providing good service. Such an interest comes from inclusion in decision-making, trust and respect, and mutual problem solving. Including students in this way would promote their self-authorship and enhance their commitment to their work. This same process, of course, would be beneficial to conceptualizing the managers' positions as well.

Work as Learning

Campus work roles offer rich opportunities for students to learn responsibility, particular skills, collaboration, and problem solving. Framed as suggested above, they also promote the epistemological, intrapersonal and interpersonal complexity needed for self-authorship and personal mastery. Framing work as learning does require that employers establish learning goals for these experiences, just as educators establish learning goals for courses or internships. Training and supervision then proceeds from those learning goals and provides employees with the means to achieve them. Using the three principles keeps employers constantly connected to employees' capabilities to judge how much guidance is needed. Mutual construction helps employers adjust their guidance as employees' capabilities in performance and self-authorship improve.

Opportunities to develop self-authorship in the multiple campus work settings described here are equally important as opportunities offered through the curriculum. As many of the longitudinal participants noted, they often understood something they had learned in class better when they experienced it directly. Thus framing work settings to promote self-authorship is not a luxury, it is essential to students' education. Holton pointed out that "the *process* of succeeding in school is very different from the process of succeeding at work" (1997, pp. 100–01). Offering students experience during college with the process they will need to succeed in work after college is crucial to their success. Promoting self-authorship in the curriculum and in work settings can be strengthened by promoting it in the co-curriculum as well, the topic taken up in the next chapter.

9

CREATING CONTEXTS FOR
SELF-AUTHORSHIP IN THE
COCURRICULUM

In college, if you had a bad class, you got a bad grade. That was just something that happened because you lived with all your friends and there were always things to put that aside. But when you deal with real-life situations, like you've got rent to pay or you bought a house, ups and downs are much, much more emotionally felt because it has a direct impact on how you live. In college you can't really see that. It's a lot more emotional learning once you get out [of college] because before you always knew you could always just give up and go home. Now you can't give up and you can't go home. So you've got to kind of tough it out and make sure that you are doing something you like.

Gavin

Gavin's observation about dealing with real-life situations after college contains a crucial insight about self-authorship and college educators' role in being good company for its development. Gavin's report of setting difficult experiences aside during college, a notion I heard from numerous participants, suggests that these experiences did not connect with Gavin's sense of who he was or who he was becoming. These learning experiences did not promote self-authorship because the self was not emphasized as central to learning. Learning was just a process to endure, with no significant meaning for real life, and no real consequences for failure. The difference with what Gavin calls "real-life situations" is that they do bring self centrally into learning. The fact that "you can't give up and go home" means that *you* have to be centrally involved in making things work. This connection to self, through real impact on everyday life and consequences, creates what Gavin called learning's "emotional impact" after college. Educators, students and the popular press routinely distinguish college life from "real life." If college is going to prepare graduates for real life, college needs to become real life. That is to say, educators must create learning experiences that have substantive meaning for everyday life, require real responsibility on students' part, and that connect to students' internal self-evolution. The cocurriculum is one ideal context through which to accomplish this goal.

The two previous chapters detailed participants' real-life experiences in advanced education and employment that provided good company for the journey toward self-authorship. Their experiences in their communities and their personal lives also offer rich examples of good company or the need for it. Many participants found themselves living and working in diverse communities where others' backgrounds, culture, or customs were different than their experience. Learning to live in diverse contexts highlighted that knowledge was complex and socially constructed, that who people are is central to how they know, and that mutual construction of meaning is necessary to account for diverse perspectives. The exploration of the complexity of diversity was directly situated in participants' own experience, making it real and meaningful. Contrasting their own experience and values to new ones they encountered prompted exploration of their beliefs and sense of self. Mutual construction of meaning with diverse others necessitated an internal sense of self that was not overshadowed by external voices. Stories about these experiences convey how the framework of the three core assumptions and the three principles to connect them to students' development can be translated to campus living arrangements, cultural immersion experiences, and service-learning.

Some participants accepted leadership roles in their communities or pursued volunteer work. The complexity and social construction of knowledge was prevalent in these contexts, as was the need for them to define the beliefs and identity they brought to these roles. Both leadership and volunteer roles required sharing expertise and authority with other people. Again, these experiences were directly situated in participants' experience, making them "real." Dealing with the real consequences of these roles was manageable due to good company from others who validated them as knowers and aided them in mutually constructing meaning about their responsibilities in these roles. These stories reveal how the framework I've advanced for good company can be used in student leadership roles (e.g., student government, student organizations) and service-learning.

All of the longitudinal participants encountered experiences after college that necessitated self-authorship. Nowhere was the difficulty of giving up or going home more evident than in career and relationship decisions. Encountering the core assumption that self is central to knowledge construction in all aspects of life initiated developing an internal sense of self. As this self materialized, career decisions that had been made prior to its arrival, usually on the basis of external influence, often needed to be reconsidered. In some cases this meant significant career changes to bring careers into line with the internal self. In other cases it mean reprioritizing career goals in the grander scheme of life in general. In some cases it meant figuring out how to merge career and family goals. These dilemmas were automatically situated in participants' experience. The degree to which they found good company to validate them as knowers and mutually construct meaning varied. These stories convey how the framework for good company could be implemented in college career services, academic advising, and efforts to mediate the effect of peer culture on career decision-making.

Building and maintaining relationships was also a common experience and challenge for the longitudinal participants. Choosing life partners and building effective intimate relationships reflected all three core assumptions. Uncertainty about how to make these decisions in the face of their complexity was widespread. Dilemmas around maintaining relationships founded on external self-definition also emerged as internal self-definition evolved. Learning how to mutually construct meaning of everyday life and major life decisions was also a challenge. Changing relationships with parents also required self-authorship. Making the transition from parent-child to adult-adult relationships meant intrapersonal and interpersonal changes. In some cases parents' divorce initiated changes in relationship patterns. In other cases, disagreements over marriage or children created stress and warranted revised roles in these relationships. Finally, relationships with coworkers required learning how to participate effectively in mutual construction of meaning. Again, the principle of situating learning in learners' experience was automatic, but validation as knowers and mutual construction varied with the context. Relationship stories illustrate numerous ways the college cocurriculum can offer good company during college including relationship and community building processes in living environments and educational programming regarding identity development, interpersonal communication, creating authentic mutual relationships, mutual decision-making, appreciating diversity, and conflict-management.

I organized chapters 7 and 8 around the three core assumptions to promote in-depth exploration of those assumptions and because those chapters dealt with experience in similar arenas, either advanced education or work. This chapter includes participants' experiences in multiple arenas: community living, community roles, career decision-making, and relationship decision making. I have organized it around those arenas, using it as an opportunity to integrate the three core assumptions and the three principles for educational practice. Participants' stories in each arena are then translated into educational practice to promote self-authorship in particular aspects of the college cocurriculum. The last segment of the chapter synthesizes these recommendations into a call for an integrated cocurriculum, the goal of which would be to promote students' self-authorship by being good company on the journey.

Real-life Experiences that Promoted Self-Authorship

Membership in Diverse Communities

Participants moved all over the country and in a few cases to other countries upon graduation in pursuit of career goals or relationship interests. It was usually the case that they found their new living environments more diverse than the ones they left behind at college. They reported gaining perspective from analyzing experiences in which others' lives were different than theirs. These perspectives contributed to their self-authorship.

Gaining Perspective: On Others, Self, and the World.   Lauren described how making friends with people who were less socioeconomically privileged than her contributed to her growth:

> I also matured in my relationships because people my age were not plentiful, so I did make some new friends that were older. And, also, different types of friends. In high school and college, everybody I hung around with was like me. You should give everybody an opportunity to be your friend regardless of where they work or where they went to school or if they didn't go to school or if their economic background was different than yours. And I can honestly say that I didn't give the other people a chance [before]. And I don't know why. But coming here opened some doors. You just really realize that everybody's different and everybody's unique in their own way. That doesn't mean that they're less because they don't have a college degree, for example. . . . And I'll tell you, too, I think I'm more appreciative right now because from what I see there are so many other sides and walks of life. Everybody's situation isn't like the situation that I have. So maybe a little bit more open, I guess.

Lauren's friendships with people whose economic backgrounds or ages differed from hers expanded her awareness of and appreciation for individual differences. She valued her relationships with new friends and appreciated her own life circumstances more than she had earlier. Membership in this new friendship community expanded her thinking, her sense of herself, and her ability to relate to diverse others.

Adrian's move to New York City due to her husband's work expanded both her perspective and her life goals. She realized how it had changed her when a college friend visited:

> All the different cultures—to me just walking on the street is a learning experience here. It's just amazing. Recently one of my girlfriends from college came to visit. We were fairly similar in college, but we're both getting away from how we were in college. But we're also getting further away from each other. We're just in completely different views on the world. It was obvious that just experiencing the city has changed me and my husband. We don't realize it because it's just happening to us, but when she came to visit it was like, "Oh, yes, I used to be like that," which isn't all bad I guess. Just the things we've been able to do, the museums, seeing Broadway shows, even just walking through neighborhoods that maybe aren't that nice, just knowing that that exists and people live in the street. There are just so many other people, a racially mixed couple is not the end of the world. It's very common. People much older than we are having children, just different lifestyles. It's made me more aware as opposed to my girlfriend. She kind of lives in her own little world, and everything's how she thought it would be and going smoothly and rolling right along. For me it just magnified the fact that I wanted something more.

Exposure to different degrees of privilege, lifestyles, and culture changed Adrian's view of the world and broadened her sense of what she wanted in her own life.

Lydia's membership in a diverse community went a step further; it helped her reinvent herself. She moved to another country due to her husband's military assignment and taught school there. She talked about how the experience changed her:

> It has made me more independent of what I know—more willing to try new experiences and not be so hesitant about it. I was so shy when I started college; not anymore! Because if there is one thing that living in an area that is not yours teaches you, it is that you have to get out there and speak up for what you

believe in and what is right. To not let others roll you over to
their ideas and roll you over to their ways.

Living in another country challenged Lydia to express herself and her beliefs.
Although she expressed not letting others "roll her over," her openness to new
experience led to reinventing who she was:

It was a fabulous experience. I did things I never would have
thought I would do. It makes you feel small; there are so many
other people out there! If you have experienced this much, how
much more is out there? I have a thirst for more. If you stay in
the same place, you get in a rut. It is so exciting! You don't know
what you are capable of; you reinvent yourself as you gain new
experiences. We had earthquakes; we got used to it. We had
[electrical] power-sharing there. There were six months when
between two and four hours a day you had no power. It is fun
to teach when the power goes out; 85 degrees—it gets overwhelming. It got to be a joke. Everybody accepted it. Here, the
power goes out and people are beside themselves. I learned to
be more flexible. When you experience other things and see
other people deal with things, it puts your life into perspective.
The more people you know and more experiences you hear
about, you get stronger. I am a strong person now; we move
and redo everything. I'm fortunate, I've stumbled onto things.
I'm like a cat; land on my feet. Life is too short to be bothered
by little things like moving and being uprooted from job and
friends. There are other jobs and friends.

Seeing how others lived and gaining new experiences helped Lydia transform
herself from a shy to a strong person. Her flexibility, stemming from gaining
perspective on life, helped Lydia make the constant moving typical of military
life an opportunity rather than a stressful experience. Her comment about
other jobs and friends also suggests that she had developed an internal sense
of self, an internal "home," to take with her to new communities.

Scott's opportunity to learn from others' lives came through his work. He
worked for the government his first few years after college. At one point his
work in immigration netted new experiences:

I've matured quite a bit since I joined this agency. I went out
with border patrols several times to rural areas in Texas. There
are border towns—and in between, nothing. You sense the
remoteness, see shantytowns, you can't help but learn. It pro-
duces a little humility. The suburbs of Juarez, Mexico aren't like
Washington DC—they're burning tires in winter to keep warm.
The environmentalists whine about it as a pollution problem.

[I'm thinking,] "Look across the river, idiots!" It is sobering. At the same time you can be thankful for what you do have. I used to whine. I've made it my mission not to do it anymore.

Scott's exposure to other life circumstances put his own life in perspective. He had been in a search for some satisfying career since college graduation, and the new sense of perspective affected that process as well. In the course of acting on this issue, he found himself in yet another context through which to gain perspective. He left his government job and became a bartender while sorting out his career goals. He described how his interaction with his customers expanded his perspective on himself and the meaning of success in adult life:

I tend bar for a lot of people—plumbers, truckers, delivery people, some are professional, factory managers. I have two worlds; people come in less educated than I am, but they are making a lot of money. They feel they are successful without as much education, and therefore they define success differently than college graduates. This helped me realize that I have had a decent life. I need to look no further than some of my customers to see that I am doing okay, that I shouldn't feel pressure because success isn't dependent on job or monetary wealth. The irony is that my current work environment has helped. Some people are retirees; they are in four of my five days; true alcoholics. We watch the stock channel and talk investment every day. These are older men who have nothing to prove anymore. They are comfortable in their lives. That helps.

Scott's exposure to lifestyles different than his own to helped him reframe his conceptualization of success in adult life. Although he had not yet constructed his vision of a satisfying career, he was broadening his perspective of options. His appreciation of his past and current life circumstances and his confidence that he could construct his own life made his career uncertainty manageable.

Membership in diverse communities demanded self-authorship. Cultural and socioeconomic diversity reflected the core assumption that knowledge is complex and socially constructed. Different views of the world and customs reflected the central nature of self in knowledge construction. Living effectively in diverse contexts also necessitated sharing authority and expertise among people. Learning was situated in participants' experience, bringing them face-to-face with others' whose lives differed from theirs. Mutual construction of meaning with diverse others heightened their awareness of their own privilege and expanded their views of relationships, their own life goals, change, and success in life.

Translation to Residence Life and Cultural Immersion Programs.

Residential living offers one of the best opportunities for students to take up membership in diverse communities. Daily living in residence halls entails negotiating space, facilities, noise, visitors, and diverse musical tastes with other students. These negotiations are real, have tangible effects on students' quality of life, and situate learning how to work with others directly in their experience. Residence life educators can capitalize on this intense opportunity to help students gain the kind of perspective Lauren, Adrian, Lydia, Scott, and their peers gained through membership in diverse communities. The challenge of making residential living educational, of course, is that the expectation of mutuality in relationships is generally a developmental stretch for most students. Thus using the framework to promote self-authorship is a way to connect these expectations to students' development, providing them a learning opportunity while simultaneously alleviating problems generally associated with students' ineffective negotiations with each other.

There are multiple means through which residential life educators can implement the framework for promoting self-authorship. One is creating norms for group living among members of particular communities. The University of Nevada—Las Vegas (UNLV) Community Standards Model (Piper, 1997) is an exemplar of this process and intentionally uses the framework for promoting self-authorship. Perhaps the most important dynamic of the UNLV model is its focus on the development and learning of residents in the context of creating healthy community. The standards are "shared agreements that define mutual expectations for how the community will function on an interpersonal level (that is how the members will relate to and treat each other)" (Piper, 1996, p. 14). Participating in the standards process also calls forth students' intrapersonal development as they learn their own values and how to express them, as well as their epistemological development as they work to decide what to believe. The specific rationale for the Community Standards Process is:

1. They provide a means by which resident's expectations of authority to meet their individual needs is shifted to recognize that the resident and the community must work together to create an environment that best meets everyone's needs.

2. They provide the opportunity for residents to express expectations of how they want to be affected by others.

3. They provide a forum for discussion of their different expectations and come to agreement on ways that they can live with the differences or compromise on the differences.

4. They provide a shift of responsibility from the RA to the residents of the community.

5. They empower residents to deal with problems before they mushroom (Piper, Strong, & Buckley, 2000, page unnumbered).

These statements reflect the complexity of creating a living environment that meets multiple needs, brings self to the center in deciding and expressing individual needs, and stresses sharing authority in coming to agreement about ways to handle difference. The experience is real because the students are given responsibility for creating and maintaining the standards within their community.

Facilitating the Community Standards Process effectively revolves around the three principles for promoting self-authorship. First, learning is situated in students' experience because they are creating norms for their own living environment and revising them as their everyday experience warrants. Residents are validated as knowers by the autonomy and trust to choose norms wisely and work with each other to compromise. Mutual construction of meaning is continual as residents generate norms, come to agreements, revise agreements, and engage in community discussions of violations of the norms. Resident advisors provide good company during this process. They introduce residents to the standards model at the outset of the term (although summer mailings also introduce the model to students and parents). They help residents become acquainted and provide a model of how to begin the norm creation process. They moderate discussion, raise questions and issues for residents to consider, and help clarify and synthesize residents' ideas. However, it is the residents who determine the norms and confront each other when they are violated. RAs coach students on how to engage in dialogue with each other around violations but do not take over the dialogue for them. This process gives students real responsibility for managing their living environment and experiencing the consequences of their decisions. Articulating the learning goals of the model often alleviates parents' concerns about their sons or daughters handling interpersonal problems themselves.

There is strong evidence that the Community Standards Model promotes self-authorship. Students participating in the model reported "they had learned to appreciate their uniqueness, had become more self-aware, more responsible, more confident, more capable of standing up for what they believed, more willing to state their opinion, more understanding of others, more able to stand up for what they wanted, and more willing to object to activities and actions they felt were wrong" (Piper, 1997, p. 24). These comments, taken from an extensive assessment of community standards, suggest progress out of the crossroads and into becoming the authors of their own lives. The comments also reflect the same benefits longitudinal participants reported from membership in diverse communities—an increased understanding of one's privilege, a broader view of diversity, and an increased ability to interact effectively with others. A version of this model could also be used in guiding roommate relationships or relationships among members of student organizations or staff groups. I use a version of this process to engage students in my graduate classes in setting standards for our classroom learning. [A complete description of the Community Standards Model can be obtained from Terry Piper, UNLV, Las Vegas, NV.]

A second means to promote self-authorship is through diversity programming within residential life. Processes like the Community Standards Model automatically bring students into contact with difference and negotiating it, but additional programming could focus specifically on understanding multiple layers of diversity. To situate learning in students' experience, programming should initially focus on "manageable" topics. Exploring differences among students from rural, urban, suburban, and city backgrounds in which students could share their experiences with each other would model the kind of experience Adrian described. Students would be validated by respect for their particular values, customs, and views from their experience, yet mutual construction of meaning would engage them in understanding others' values, customs, and views. Similarly, programming on socioeconomic differences would help students understand how values and customs emerge from their own circumstances, the meaning of privilege, and broaden their perspectives about who they might choose for their friends (as Lauren's story illustrated). Being good company in these programs would mean validating students' current experience and perspectives, encouraging their active reflection on who they are as a result of their experiences, and encouraging efforts to understand and engage with diverse others. Progress on self-authorship in these contexts is a key factor in effective diversity programming on more difficult topics such as race and sexual orientation.

Cultural immersion programs in which students gain opportunities to experience another culture are another context for membership, albeit temporary, in diverse communities. Cultural immersion programs emulate the intensity of residential living in their intensity and situating learning in experience. They offer the same kind of experiences Lauren, Adrian, Lydia, and Scott described in their exposure to cultures different from their own. Cultural immersion programs could be framed as service learning, student group activities, paraprofessional staff training, or educational programming. They could be spring break or weekend trips to interact with another culture, sustained involvement with members of another culture (such as tutoring children in inner-city schools), or participation in international exchange programs. To promote self-authorship, these experiences would acknowledge the complexity of multiculturalism, help students explore their uniqueness, and engage students in understanding and negotiating difference. Clear learning goals, support for reflection and risk-taking, and giving students real responsibility would provide good company. Living-learning communities in residential life, particularly those focused on diversity, are another form of cultural immersion experiences.

In addition to these efforts, educators must reevaluate campus norms and practices that limit membership in diverse communities. The selection processes for many student organizations, for example, promote students bringing in members like themselves. Although that is a natural tendency (as Lauren described), working with students to create selection processes that allow diverse membership would promote their self-authorship. An assessment of institutional traditions that limit diverse participation is also important here (Magolda, 2000). Participation in diverse communities not only promotes self-authorship, but also promotes intercultural competence, another aspect of development that combines the epistemological, intrapersonal, and interpersonal dimensions (Storti, 1999). Ortiz (2000) reported that participation in study abroad programs fostered students' intercultural competence. Thus participation in diverse communities also contributes to graduates' ability to function effectively in a diverse society.

Community Leadership and Volunteer Roles

Many participants accepted formal leadership roles within their communities and several involved themselves in volunteer work. These experiences helped strengthen their sense of who they were, build mutual relationships with others, and decide what they believed about various social issues.

Developing One's Own Voice and Beliefs.   Community leadership and volunteer roles often required interactions that participants initially found uncomfortable. Megan offered an example from her work with the Junior League:

> It is a whole different type of learning experience. I worked on a fund-raiser, getting food and drinks for a cocktail party. They wanted everything donated. I hate asking for things. I learned! If people were going to eat, I would have to get things donated. I felt like people would be annoyed. I would stare at the phone

thinking, "I have to make this call;" I felt like a salesperson. I made myself do it and it turned out great. I found out people were willing to give. I wouldn't mind doing it again. The worst thing is people said no, and I said okay. People were nice about it. I would like to be more involved in projects dealing directly with people in the community or with children. A lot of them are during the day and after school, so depending on my work schedule next year I'd like to do those. Perhaps be involved in Fernside (a group that helps children whose parents have died), because having lost my father, I can relate.

Megan had to get food for her function, so she had to make those calls. The validation she encountered, either through affirmative responses or through being turned down nicely, helped her gain confidence to participate further in more intense roles with people in the community.

Kelly was similarly challenged when she took a position as moderator of the deacons at her church. She shared what happened:

It went really well. I think I was youngest moderator they ever had. It was a good experience in life for me to handle a group of adults. I got another hefty dose of learning to deal with people, their difficulties, and their requests. I was the "go to" woman—services, food drives—it was overwhelming at times. I delegated and it worked great! It was a lot of work preparing for meetings, making sure that everyone was doing what they were supposed to. I was on several committees, and couldn't extend myself any further. [Delegating] didn't always work; it was easier to say, "I'll just do it." But I forced myself to say, "This is the problem," passing around the assignment sheet until it was full. It was good for me to be forced into that role.

Being forced into needing others' help gave Kelly experience in delegating work to others and monitoring its completion. This helped her grow in her ability to work collaboratively with others. Her church involvement also yielded an invitation to the National Prayer Breakfast, another growth producing experience as she explained:

I'm still high off the trip! Here is little Kelly from small town USA, sitting in a room with these huge people! We're all the same under God's eyes. There were 3000 people there—including heads of state. It focuses on Jesus as a person, not as Christ; that is how they get people from all different religions to come. There were people from the U.S., Indonesia, Australia—just in our little table of ten people we had the whole world! Amazing. They tell you before you go, to get out of your comfort zone, talk to people you wouldn't talk to. I tried to do that. I went to an urban prayer and worship—never experienced that kind of worship before! It was outside of my comfort zone to be there, but neat. At the luncheon, Arafat and Rabin talked about peace—I learned about relationships between Jews and Palestinians—an educational experience. When you learn about the background, it makes their words take on different meaning. . . . It also made me look at media in a much different way. I saw how the Washington Post portrayed the Breakfast this year. I talked to people about how the media portrays things—asked people about events in Jerusalem and people told how it was portrayed. Watching the news this week, the culminating of impeachment, is it really what it is or just media bonding it all into one story?

Kelly's validation as equal to important leaders in God's eyes helped her venture out of her comfort zone. Her experiences in different forms of worship and learning about events around the world broadened her perspective and made her more critical of what she read. The complexity she experienced at this event helped her think in more complex ways.

Some participants were involved in intense, long-term volunteer roles. These contexts highlight that self-authorship develops in the context of constructing mutual relationships. Al sought out involvement with young people because he felt that was missing in his work. He found satisfaction in joining a big brother program:

Every time we do something I feel like I can be kind of a role model or give him that male perspective of things that he doesn't get. His Mom does a great job; I really respect her. We have a great time. His mother's told me now a few times how much a difference it has made in this kid. So that really makes me feel good about that. Every weekend we usually do something, everything from playing sports to him helping me work on the car to seeing a movie, doing some art-craft kind of things, whatever I can think of. If he seems interested, then we'll do it. It's a lot of fun.

Al enjoyed spending time with his little brother and the boy's mother validated Al as having a positive influence. Al continued this relationship and added other volunteer activities. Two years later, despite working full time and taking premed classes, he shared:

I've had my little brother for two years now. He is nine. We still do stuff almost every week. That's a nice thing. I'm a councilperson on my church singles group. Today I taught the Sunday school class. I'll do Habitat for Humanity once a month. Yesterday we helped build a recreation center for a group of Cambodian refugees. I'm also a Project Safe Place volunteer. It's a runaway shelter. You're trained on what to do and how to deal with them and whether to bring them to the shelter or to your home or whatever else. This volunteer stuff is all stuff I like to do.

The validation Al felt from these activities played a strong part in his career change to medicine. During his first year of medical school he joined another big brother program in his new community, still kept in touch with his original little brother (now two hours away), taught Sunday School, helped with a student health clinic and a rural health clinic, and was President of the Christian Medical Society. His volunteer work kept his life meaningful and contributed to his sense of who he was and his purpose in life.

Anita was involved in a big sister program at a children's home that helped her figure out her own beliefs, clarify her career goals, and learn about herself through interacting with others:

The little girl I have is nine. She has very difficult problems. She was taken away from her mother, who has AIDS. The chances of her going home are nil, but she doesn't know it. We went out for her birthday and she picked out some clothes. When I took them over, she didn't want to see me, she just wanted the gift. Her therapist said I should tell her how I felt, so I did. It went over poorly, she got angry, and now she doesn't want to see me. I also work for the national runaway switchboard. On the switchboard, you have to let them figure things out for themselves; try to turn the conversation around to steer them in a direction without giving them an answer. I'm getting used to not knowing at the switchboard. Nothing you can say is wrong, as long as you are trying to help. The same call could be handled differently by different people. Like with my little sis, I feel like I shouldn't have brought it up, but others said I had to do it. I'm learning to let things go. I'm better at realizing and admitting when I've made mistakes. I'm more humble. Sometimes I hear other calls and I wouldn't have done something that way. I'm trying to figure out for myself if I have the right to an opinion. Like if someone hits them, I have a hard time saying it is wrong. It can lead to an arrest, and make a bigger mess. I have a hard time being as directive as I should. I have to figure out for myself what my own beliefs are. I do have the right to an opinion. I know molestation is wrong, but what will life be like if I make the call?

Anita recognized the complexity of dealing with these situations and was trying to find her own way of doing so. Various situations forced her to weigh what she believed against another person's needs and to find the balance between expressing herself and being truly helpful to other people. This learning, situated directly in her experience, was helping her develop her belief system.

Heather's involvement with a little sister helped her develop her belief system, but more importantly it helped her understand some issues in her own life. It was by far the most intense story of volunteer work that I heard. Initially, it helped Heather expand her perspective as she explained:

> My little sister and her family have had an impact on my life and how I see things. Witnessing a single parent—her mom isn't at poverty level, but needed plenty of government assistance to get there. I was more sheltered, thought people who were on welfare didn't work hard enough. Watching this woman gave me a lot of appreciation—people in those negative statistics are trying to make a better life for themselves. She just found a townhouse. I gave her some contacts, and she is now a home-owner. It's good to watch her hard work pay off. My little sis is 12 this year; I've known her since she was eight. A lot of changes in her life in that time. It is a joy to watch. I work through things with her. She has taught me a lot about how to communicate on a different level; how to be patient. Watching things she has to deal with brought an awareness to my life, a respect. I've watched her family grow up. I appreciate what I have, respect them for what they have to do to get ahead. It is hard some days to maintain a certain level of compassion and caring without driving yourself to the point of depression. I get a lot out of the relationship with her; I see her once every ten days. There are days when I have a million other things to do and it would be easy to put her off. Ultimately I'm glad I don't do that. It is a responsibility I have decided to take seriously.

Heather gained respect for people whose experience differed from hers, became increasingly aware of her privilege in life, and learned to be patient and communicate in a relationship. Although there was a lot of joy involved in this endeavor, it was also difficult, as Heather reported the following year:

> I had the worst crisis with my little sis this past week. I've known her for six years; you hope you have gotten somewhere. Intuitively I know I have done some good. It deflated me emotionally this week. Her home life is as unstable as when I first met her. Sometimes her day to day life is still fragile; I can't control that. Everybody has good intentions, they say, "this isn't your

responsibility," but after six years, it isn't that easy. You can't pull away from someone that is part of your life. Others say you have to draw the line. She is pretty much like a sister to me. If I drain emotionally for her a couple weeks, I'll get it back. She is 14. She can't stereotype teachers because of me, has to explore things she'd rather not explore; she helps me understand that age group.

The complexity of a teen growing up in a difficult environment was becoming more clear to Heather each year. She still benefited from the relationship and remained committed to it because her little sis was now family. Heather made good on her promise to take this responsibility seriously, as was evident in this story a couple of years later:

My little sister was on the run several times, ended up at my house, we would negotiate her return to her house. Each time got more serious, then suicide notes started. It ended up, the last time she ran, she was on the run for four weeks. She showed up at my door, moved in with us from April–July. We entered the process of trying to have the county take over custody of her—took her mom to court. We went through that with her—she had a rough time, and was sick a lot. Because I have no legal right to be her guardian, they put her in the county home. Later we found out she was pregnant. She hid it, but by court order she was forced to get a pregnancy test. I took her, and we found out. It was a volatile situation. She gave birth in January. Then she was released back to her mom by the courts; by then I fell into a slump myself. I came to a lot of realizations about myself, how I live my life.

This intense experience, occurring simultaneously with some other family situations, called Heather's view of herself into question. She tried to articulate it:

I'm trying to think about telling you what I have learned. One of the basic things I have learned is my family is a very compulsive family; very high achievers, motivated, in doing so we didn't nurture the emotional side. I lived life a lot that way to the point where I did things out of guilt or driven by something other than what I really wanted. I got through summer with my little sis because I felt it was my duty. I didn't always do it well; I didn't understand that I was enabling. Fortunately, my husband was great through that summer. I also had a good support group of friends who were close enough to know what was going on. This was validating of me. I was trying to control things in my little sister's life; her happiness.

The complexity of this situation brought home the fact that Heather could not control her little sister's circumstances or her happiness. Facing that fact prompted an exploration of her role that expanded into exploration of herself in her own family relationships. Over the next year Heather worked through many personal issues related to these discoveries and further developed her internal sense of self as a result.

Participants' involvement in community leadership and volunteer roles brought them face to face with the complexity and social construction of knowledge. The diversity they encountered in these roles helped them recognize privileges they had experienced and the responsibilities they might adopt to assist those with less advantage. Trying to cope with this complexity meant further developing their internal sense of themselves and their beliefs. Mutual construction with other people who held multiple perspectives also helped participants express themselves and work toward mutual relationships with others.

Translation to Student Leadership Roles and Service-Learning.

The value of these community and volunteer roles was their grounding in the three assumptions and that the three principles were in place to help participants stretch to the self-authorship required in these roles. This same framework can frame community and volunteer roles on campus. The key factor in implementing the framework in these contexts is trusting students to participate as partners with educators, making their experience in these roles real.

Student leadership roles in student government, judicial boards, student organizations, and Greek life are all opportunities to promote self-authorship, not to mention enhance the functioning of these groups. The first step is letting student leaders deal with complexity. Campus realities such as alcohol abuse, date rape, racial tension, gay bashing, and hazing convey the complex and socially constructed nature of campus life. With the exception of judicial boards, and then in limited ways, student leaders are not genuinely involved in the resolution of these issues. Giving them responsibility to explore these issues, understand the complexities, and work together to generate solutions would involve them in struggling with complexity in their communities. Self as central to knowledge construction would be reflected in the expectation that they as student leaders take meaningful responsibility in the overall effort to address campus issues. Self would also be emphasized as central as student leaders struggled with their own values and beliefs about these issues in order to join others in mutual construction of meaning about them. That mutual construction, the sharing of authority and expertise to generate solutions, would express trust in their ability to make meaningful contributions. It would also convey that they have to change the culture via their own individual values and behavior, as well as their participation in the peer culture. This approach is consistent with Rogers' (1996) recommendations for effective leadership in the 21st century, which include collaborating and engaging in creative conflict, creating environments based on trust and empowerment, and encouraging diverse voices and creating a shared vision, to name a few.

As Ira Shor eloquently pointed out, this approach is "not a know-nothing process" (1992, p. 247) in which student leaders are left to decide whatever they wish. Instead it is a genuine partnership in which they are trusted and validated as capable people to play their part in campus issues, offered learning situated in their own experience, and engaged in mutual construction with educators. Readers who are wondering if students have the capability to contribute to these seemingly impossible problems might consider that educators addressing these without sharing authority with students have made dismal progress despite concerted and good intentioned efforts nation-wide. Scholars of student culture (and culture in general for that matter) stress that cultural change requires change within members of the culture. Promoting self-authorship is a key factor in reducing the peer pressure that contributes to many of these problems, and in helping students develop the internal self that heightens respect for self and others.

Service learning is a popular initiative on college campuses. It is a clear opportunity to organize real experiences that help students gain perspective on themselves, life, and relating with others, much like Al, Anita, and Heather reported. Promoting self-authorship through service learning is more than planning a trip to a soup kitchen or a weekend with Habitat for Humanity. These experiences automatically reflect complexity. However, students must be engaged in making sense of this complexity in order to move toward self-authorship. Service learning framed as a mutual learning endeavor (Kendall, 1990) conveys to students that while they serve others they will also learn about themselves. Rhoad's (2000) argues that such service-learning challenges a participant's sense of self and promotes a caring self, one that is genuinely interested in the welfare of others. He identified three components of structuring service-learning to achieve this goal: mutuality, personalization, and reflection. Rhoads believes that mutual construction of the experience with those served, personal interaction, and thinking through the connections to their academic and personal lives makes service learning meaningful. His three components are consistent with the framework for promoting self-authorship.

Exploration of their reactions to service, to diverse others, and to multiple life circumstances should focus on what they learned about themselves and how these experiences affected beliefs they hold. Opportunities for students who share a service-learning experience to engage in mutual construction of meaning about it is one way for them to explore what they learned. Validation of students as knowers and respect for their exploration helps engage them in genuine exploration to expand their perspectives. Mutual construction, with people served, other students, and educators, can strengthen their internal identities, increase confidence in expressing their voices, and help achieve mutuality in relationships.

Real-life Experiences that Necessitated Self-Authorship

Participants routinely encountered experiences that necessitated self-authorship regardless of whether the framework to promote it existed. The stories that follow illustrate the typical dilemmas participants faced in career and relationship dimensions of their lives and their struggle to resolve these dilemmas depending on their progress on the journey toward self-authorship. Although it is not the role of higher education to prepare young adults for every possible challenge they will face, better company in college to promote self-authorship would benefit both graduates and the communities in which they work and live. Career services, academic advising, and educational programming could make strong contributions to good company during college that would enhance graduates' ability to be productive citizens. This segment of the chapter highlights the challenge of the career and relationship dimensions and translates those challenges into support systems in career services, academic advising, and educational programming.

Career Decision-Making

Although participants left college with their externally acquired formulas for career success, they quickly discovered a major missing piece to the career success puzzle—themselves. Delving into their careers, which most had chosen on the basis of some external influence without regard to their own values, surfaced the assumption that self is central to knowledge construction and one's work. In fact all three core assumptions were present, demanding self-authorship on all three dimensions of development. For some participants working toward self-authorship meant minor career adjustments; for others more substantial adjustments were needed.

Career Changes. Career dissatisfaction sparked exploration of why work was not as rewarding as participants expected it to be. This exploration usually revealed that participants' particular work was discrepant with who they were becoming. Al had this experience (see chapter 4) in computer consulting, prompting his change to medical school. Heather's lack of interest in business led her to return to school to become a teacher. Anita left medical supply sales to pursue social work for similar reasons. Gavin's story illustrates the experiences of those participants whose growing internal selves prompted complete changes of career goals and paths. He learned that getting a degree did not mean getting an enjoyable job:

> We were told if you go to college and get a degree, there will be a job waiting that you enjoy. So many people have had to deal with this not happening. I got into insurance, I did it for the need to work, to get experience. You go into it without knowing what you are after. The first few years are hell, but you feel you have to stick with it. It takes that long to realize that if you aren't happy you need to do something else. It took me three years to realize I wouldn't like it.

Gavin decided to return to school to become a teacher. Explaining how this came about, and why he had not done it earlier, he shared:

> It was something in the back of my mind I wanted to do eventually. I loved school; I had experiences with coaching that sparked my interest. My family reminded me of what I had said, offered reinforcement. There still is this doubt in the back of my mind. Insurance was just a job. This could happen here too. You have reservations when you seemingly fail at something. I never had this attitude toward anything before. . . . I didn't do education in college due to bad information from people that it wouldn't be a career that is financially secure. That's not the truth now that I have looked into it. The way I was brought up, I went to college with the notion that success is based on financial. Through school that held true. This lasted through the first few years out of college. I wanted to be as successful as my family, one notch better. A couple years out of school, I met people who were financially successful and this was the only thing good in their life. I found others who had a good life and were financially okay. They were real life examples rather than reading it in books. Meeting people makes you think differently.

Gavin accepted societal messages he heard about being successful and these guided his choices in college and beyond. He believed people who told him teaching was not a financially secure profession and believed that financial security was the key to having a good life. Only when real people he met interrupted his perception about the relationship of financial security and a good life was Gavin able to return to an idea he had put away—being a teacher. This exploration was, of course, prompted by his dissatisfaction with selling insurance, a dissatisfaction that stemmed from it being incongruent with his sense of himself. The emergence of this sense of self is what prompted Gavin to make the career change decision, which required returning to school, even though he was still unsure of it:

> I wondered, after going to school for four years, then working four years, then working and going to school for two more years, if I was wasting my time—if after all of this, when I finally get my teaching job, was I going to look at this and say, "I really don't like this that much either?" But I really, really, really do like it. Coaching I enjoy, teaching the class I enjoy, I also tutor kids that get expelled from school—I enjoy that too. Two years into it, I think I made a very, very good decision. Even at Miami I thought I would really love to be a teacher. My roommate and I talked about going into the business world for 20 years, making our million, retiring, then going to school to become teachers! Well, I better do that now, because if that is what is going to make me happy, that is what I had better do. And I am really happy. I really enjoy trying to help the kids who aren't the best students. Some teachers talk about students they can't stand— and I kind of like them. My overall theme is trying to help kids.

Gavin's story about he and his friend's plan reveals that he knew he wanted to be a teacher, but external influence prevented him from acting on that. It was not until he traversed the crossroads that he could act on his own interests. A factor in his traversing the crossroads was seeing other models of adult success that were consistent with his growing internal voice. This validation helped him move forward, as did the support he received from his family.

Career Priorities.   For some participants the journey toward self-authorship meant reprioritizing within the career they had begun. Mark's story in chapter 2 about realizing that some of his law school goals were inconsistent with his values illustrates this dynamic. Once the internally defined self became central to work, participants had to consider it in relation to how they framed priorities within their careers and in the context of their overall lives.

The biggest issues were usually reframing definitions of career success and balancing careers with family goals. Anne altered her definition of career success due to a negative work experience, leading her to tell me in our twelfth interview that there was more to life than one's career:

> It's strange, I could see myself being happy doing my current job for the next five years. It doesn't seem like I need the next

promotion. I'm relaxed. I'm satisfied with what I am doing. After
having a bad job, I'm recognizing that there is more to life than
work. In earlier years, I felt I needed to move up, get the promotion—comparing myself to others who started when I did. I
want to do well, it is important for me to be challenged and
stimulated, but being a vice president by a certain age doesn't
seem as important. The lousy job created chest pains, stress;
there is more to life than being in the office 80 hours a week.
Enough is enough. . . . I'm more content. Maybe this is due to
the way I think about things—I was always concerned about
others and comparing myself and how fast they are rising; now
I'm more concerned with improving myself and enjoying
myself. I am happy with where I am right now; I have met some
of my expectations. I'm seeing and doing new things—at a conference last week I met people from all different countries. I feel
like I could do this forever. I'm happy to be more satisfied with
what I have and not so greedy.

Anne's change of perspective is a move away from how she compares to
other professionals and how her career progresses compares to some external
standard. When her work interfered with her health and personal happiness
she began to reevaluate its place in her overall identity. Increasing satisfaction
with herself and an internal self-definition allowed her to self-author her professional boundaries and enjoy her work.

Lauren made this same shift away from comparing herself to others. Her
experience involved reprioritizing what was important to her within her career
area to incorporate her work life and her personal life. She shared, "I always
wanted to be the career person crawling to the top; the price isn't worth it.
This came from me inside. I felt so confident that job is not number one anymore—I knew it was right." Explaining further how the shift from crawling to
the top to the job no longer being number one occurred, Lauren spoke to letting go of competing with others:

It was all consuming—all I thought about was what I should or
could make. Or how I was getting cheated. My husband was
good at putting things into perspective. The career move I made
was huge! I had an opportunity to sell surgical equipment; the
money was double or triple, but it was high pressure, stress,
long hours. I was only focused on the money, thinking I will do
anything for the money. A friend who is a headhunter asked,
"Where do you see yourself in five years?" I said, "Hopefully
working, with children." He advised going to a big company for
benefits and flexibility—more of everything than just totally
work. It was hard for me to hear that because I wasn't pregnant,
that future time wasn't in front of me. Now that I am at that

> future time, I'm glad I did it. I could have done the other job for
> a year or two, but not with a family. It was hard to admit that it
> was going to change—you compare yourself to your friends
> that are doing better than you. You don't look at people who
> have less than you!

The part of Lauren's self that wanted a family created a conflict with the part of her that wanted to do as well or better than her friends. It was clear in hearing her assessment of where the competitive attitude came from that it was rooted in external self-definition:

> As a youngster I was competitive in sports and school; part of it
> is just individual. My brothers aren't like that. Some of it is my
> father's influence. His career was important to him and identi-
> fied who he was. When I was in individual sports, I always
> wanted to be best and win. And the atmosphere at college—I
> identified with friends that thought job was important. Also the
> kind of work I do—selling is competitive, comparing yourself to
> others. Usually with selling, the harder you work the more
> money you make, so there is financial motivation too.

Lauren's experience with winning sports as a youngster, her interest in her father's approval (for which she took her first job which she knew she would not like), the influence of her friends, and the societal message that success is largely financial drove her competitiveness in the career world. This served her well until another side of herself began to emerge that valued family and life beyond work. When the two conflicted (and with the apparent support of her husband), she reprioritized her career goals to be in synch with her internal sense of self. This learning was situated in her experience, she was validated in reprioritizing by her husband, and she mutually constructed meaning about this change with important others around her.

The struggle to determine how to balance family and career pervaded the late twenties as participants prepared to start their families. Ned explored this issue in our tenth interview:

> I would like to have children, but I'm not convinced that [my
> wife] is ready yet. There is no question that we will; it is a ques-
> tion of when. We are both 27, have a couple years here. The way
> the discussion goes right now is, "How do we do this with
> schedules? Does one quit?" It's a big decision regarding how
> kids are raised, how the development cycle goes, arguments
> about socialization. Those are the kinds of decisions, if you make
> the wrong one, ten years later you resent it, there are problems
> with kids or spouse. It's up there with marriage decisions! I don't

know the answer. We've kicked it around a bit; actually I do kind of know the answer. [My wife] wants to work; she enjoys her job and feels she is contributing. Both of our mothers were in traditional nuclear family. We are seeing both of our mothers going through the empty nest syndrome. Their personalities are different than people who are working; different set of values, prioritization of issues. We don't want that to happen. I don't want her or me to have nothing [beyond family]. Our mothers have had a tough time getting back into the job market. [My wife] is also a 21st century woman; she doesn't feel that it is her job to stay at home. She says, "why don't you stay home?" How to balance two careers and have a family at the same time is the biggest question. Financially we are set for retirement by the time we are 30—life is pretty grand. Career is going great. How do you raise a family with career, time and job pressures that are all around you? That is the main reason we haven't started a family yet; we haven't figured it out.

Ned and his wife knew they wanted children and had the financial resources to choose among alternatives for childcare. Their awareness of the complexity of raising children is evident in Ned's alluding to socialization and its potential impact on how children grow up. He and his wife also observed both the benefits of stay-at-home moms in their own experience and the costs to their own mothers later in life. Their financial success, although opening doors to multiple options, did not simplify the complexity of this important decision. Ned and his wife needed to decide what they believed about child rearing and how their own identities would connect to careers and children.

Not surprisingly, the balancing of career and family considerations affected women more intensely than it did men. Recall Alice's story in chapter 1 about her anger that she would have to give up all she had worked for to have a baby and her husband could continue on his career path. Also recall Alice's change of perspective in Chapter 6 after her first child was born. Alice's story is one of continual decision-making as she learned more about her internal sense of self. When Alice realized that she really wanted to stay home with her children, she worked through that perspective to organize her life around her internal voice.

Anita was in the midst of the process Alice had worked through. Anita returned to school to change careers and near completion of her degree she had a son. Her story reveals the dynamics of the struggle to self-author the career-family combination:

I have always thought I couldn't stay home and raise a family. Mom did that, she dedicated herself to her family and lost her identity. She never was able to reenter the workforce due to lack of confidence. This caused strain in their relationship; dad is working in a job he doesn't like, and she sits at home. I have always said I need to have my own thing; now that I have a child, the idea of him in daycare is beyond my imagination. I'm in class one morning a week; it is hard for me just that one day. What if somebody else doesn't love him the way I do, and he gets as aggravating as he can be, how will they handle that? We went out to this business thing; I called three times before 8 o'clock. I don't know where anxiety comes from, it is just there. I have to come to grips with that. My husband joked did I imagine I would be a housewife at 29. I'm worried about becoming nothing else but a fulltime mom. My husband is supportive. He is glad I am home, but would be fine with me going to work. He doesn't expect me to make money; I have the luxury of that decision. Even with all of those options, it is hard to choose. We'd like to have three or four kids; my husband is 37, he would like to do it sooner than later. We'll play it by ear, one at a time. For the foreseeable future, my job is taking care of kids. School is great because I only have two classes, and I feel like I am doing something. Ultimately, when kids are school age, I will have most of my education done and have 20 more years to work anyway. I'm building on something now so that I can have my own life again then. It is hard to think that far out. Four months into it, I love it, but it is confining. I need to find a network. Rare to find people in my situation—not too many who are trying to do both.

Given Anita's observation of her parents, she was certain she would not stay home to raise her family. Yet when her son arrived, her emotions were such that daycare was unimaginable. Even though she planned to use daycare to complete her degree, she was considering fulltime motherhood for the coming years. The uncertainty of the decision was apparent in these comments:

I feel guilt from our families, both mom and mother-in-law expect me to be home because I don't have to be someplace else. I don't have to do it because they say so, but I didn't know what I was going to do, or know how I was going to feel. One of the hard things since we moved to [a new city] is that I haven't found girlfriends I feel close to. One of my friends says it is selfish [for me to consider working] because I don't need to work. Others who are working feel like, "don't let that [kids] happen to me." I just had a friend here visiting; she had good time but was ready to leave! It is difficult. At times I get angry about being at home all the time and doing laundry. Then I think, I am the only one making myself do this. There is no one to be angry at. I

have to figure out what I want and whatever I choose won't be perfect.

Anita was bombarded with opinions from her family and friends about what was right. Yet she was clear that *she* had to figure out what she wanted. She was trying to understand her inner feelings, which often conflicted, and knew that no decision would be perfect.

Career issues, particularly their relationship to life in general and raising a family, demonstrate that real life is characterized by the three core assumptions, and thus demands self-authorship. Knowledge regarding career and family was clearly complex and socially constructed within multiple perspectives and options. The self was central in terms of reflecting on one's own experiences, understanding one's own emotional feelings and identity as related to career or parenthood, and dealing with one's own conflicting feelings and beliefs to make these choices. Mutual construction was complicated by parents' and in-laws' values and expectations, friends' experiences, and mutual cooperation between partners regarding each one's career and parenting needs. The participants' stories demonstrate that making real life decisions necessitates a lot more than a few external formulas for success.

Translation to Career Services, Academic Advising, and Peer Culture.

The magnitude of career decisions, particularly the emotional and financial cost of changing careers or of family-career decisions, warrants more emphasis on good company via career services and academic advising during college. Typically career services and academic advising processes help students explore complexity and convey to students that their values are an important factor in career decisions. However, this occurs in the context of external self-definition, pressure to choose a major, and societal pressure regarding career success. Students' initial external self-definitions make them prone to accepting authorities' advice as the truth. Even if they are in the crossroads, external pressures often outweigh their own initial ideas. Parents and peers often pressure students to choose majors before they are ready to do so, as do curriculum requirements and institutional policies. Societal definitions of success as monetary wealth and prestige mediate students' choices of major until they have traversed the crossroads. To complicate matters insufficient time is allotted for counseling and advising appointments on most campuses.

Framing academic advising and career services to promote self-authorship begins with immersing students in the complexity of various career options. Situating learning in their experience can be achieved through internships, shadowing professionals in their fields of interest, information interviews with practitioners, interviewing practicing professionals about the values that permeate particular careers, and interactions with alumni. Interactions with older students in particular majors would help undecided students gain perspective on these majors and how others chose them. Throughout these experiences, students must be challenged to explore their reactions to this information, assess their skills relevant to these roles, and reflect on how their values compare to these career options. This introduces the self as central to one's career choice. Most current approaches to career exploration introduce the self as central through workbooks (see, for example, Hettich, 1998), activities that focus on values clarification or career interests, or inventories that synthesize personal interests. Faculty who teach first-year career development courses and career services personnel who assist students in career exploration often report, however, that students look to these activities and inventories as means to find the external truth about career choices. This stems from students' external self-definitions and their reliance on external authorities to determine the right career path. Direct, concrete experience is needed to adequately convey the notion that self is central to career choice. Thus these approaches will be more effective if coupled with the direct interactions with professionals and alumni who first-year students perceive as authorities.

The self as central can also be emphasized by giving students real responsibility in the counseling/advising relationship. Given guidance and resources to explore and reflect, students should be held accountable for preparing for advising sessions so that they can engage in mutual construction with educators. Failure to prepare should entail consequences, such as rescheduling after they have prepared (as is typical in the real world after college). Academic advisors and career counselors should challenge students in these dialogues about why they are in a particular major or career path and how their values relate to those choices. Major and career choices should be reviewed with juniors and seniors whose internal voices might be materializing in potential conflict with their plans. While parents and students do not want to face changes in major late in college, perhaps it is still less costly than doing it four years after graduation. Typical career planning efforts such as resume writing and mock interviews should also move away from external formulas and technical information to encourage students to bring themselves centrally into their resume or interviews. Helping students define values and how to communicate them in these settings is equally, if not more, important than font size. Focusing on helping students choose an appropriate job rather than on just getting a job would also promote self-authorship and wise decision-making.

Obviously these suggestions require time and effort on the part of educators and students. Institutional policies such as timing on declaring majors or staffing of advising and career services would need to be reviewed to make the framework for self-authorship possible. Given its importance in the longitudinal participants' stories, and its potential to promote self-authorship, making career exploration and decision-making part of the curriculum may be warranted. Teaching career counselors and academic advisors about the journey to self-authorship and the framework to promote it is necessary for them to be good company. The same is true for faculty who could use the framework in their classes, giving students another opportunity to determine the consistency of their courses and major with their internal voices. Conceptualizing career services as a comprehensive system beginning with exploration and ending with transition to post-college work environments is necessary. Extensive efforts in recent years in programming for first-year students focused on increasing student-to-student interaction, faculty-to-student interaction, student involvement, linking the curriculum and cocurriculum, and increasing academic expectations and academic engagement (Barefoot, 2000). These interactions and students' engagement in academic and campus life can be structured in ways that help students begin the journey toward self-authorship in the career arena as well as in other dimensions of their lives. Programming for seniors about work environment expectations, processes through which to reflect on and learn from one's experiences, and guidance on how to make decisions about dissatisfaction, promotions, and career changes would provide support for this transition. Chickering and Schlossberg (1997) take the position that "the critical purpose of higher education is to help students become effective agents for their own lifelong learning and personal development" (p. 37). They identify the senior year as "the best opportunity to encourage that sense of agency and to supply experiences, concepts, and perspectives that help them move on" (p. 37). Alumni could be central in these programs to offer students role models and connections beyond the campus. Similar programming or individual advising regarding the career/family issue could also be facilitated by alumni. Students could be aided in exploring their values about family and work, learning mechanisms for exploring these issues, and how to analyze an employment culture for family benefits if they are certain children are in their future.

Peer culture, particularly on traditional-age campuses like the one my longitudinal participants attended, often mediates progress toward self-authorship. When many students are in the external portion of the journey, they listen to authorities, to general societal messages, and to each other in hopes of gaining approval. Peer culture can pressure students to choose careers without serious exploration just to have something to say when a peer asks, "What is your major?" Peer culture also pressures students to choose prestigious careers or careers with high earning potential. Gavin's story demonstrated how societal and peer pressure mediated his ability to follow his own internal voice to become a teacher. Transforming peer culture is a complex challenge. Reviewing institutional policies and practices that send these messages is one step. For example, do publications or panels that highlight student or alumni achievements offer a narrow view of adult success? Do career services cater to business students? Do cocurricular selection processes or awards favor particular models of success? Every attempt to reduce competitiveness in the cocurriculum, as well as in classroom learning, is a step toward broadening students' ability to listen to their internal voices. The inclusion of recent alumni into the work of student organizations, particularly those focused on majors, could provide alternative perspectives to those prevalent in the student culture. Opportunities for meaningful interaction beyond the student culture, such as internships or the campus work settings in chapter 8, can reduce the blinders sometimes created by one's own corner of the student culture.

Finally, working with parents to support their student's self-authorship can be useful. Parent's hopes for their offspring often mediated their ability to validate their students' internal voices. Sharing stories of alumni with parents and students, either in publications or through direct interaction, and programming to broaden parents' understanding of career options would help parents be better company for their students' journeys to self-authorship. Typically campus offices that interact with parents do so around individual problems or fund-raising. Inviting parents to join in educating their children may be another avenue of promoting self-authorship.

Building and Maintaining Relationships

Choosing and Maintaining Relationships with Partners.
As Gwen articulated in chapter 1, the "how you know" question is huge in choosing relationships with spouses and partners. Gwen's story in chapter 2 shows that she was fortunate to get through the crossroads before making a marriage commitment. Lowell (chapter 4) and Sheila (chapter 5) described the trauma involved when the internal sense of self is incompatible with marriage commitments. Participants knew on an abstract level that a commitment to significant relationships was a complex issue, yet from the external phase of the journey, even this aspect of life took on the external formula dynamic as Jim explained:

> Before I met [my girlfriend], I had this vision that I would meet this perfect girl, we would get married and live in bliss the rest of our lives. Fights would not be a problem, and the relationship would just naturally happen. There wouldn't be any work involved. Now I'm realizing—I'm learning that relationships are just a lot of work. From the beginning we've had some minor things we've got to get worked out. But when we're together we have an incredible time. Not always, but definitely way more good times than bad. But it's been interesting to see that relationship develop. What's going to happen next is kind of where we are right now.

Jim's vision of relationships as bliss existed despite his own parents having divorced. He was beginning to recognize that relationships involved work, yet still clung to his vision of the right relationship. As it turned out, "what happened next" was a disillusion of his current relationship on the assumption that it was not the right one. He explained:

> She is an awesome lady—not right for me. We talked about it a lot—we are both committed to marrying and keeping it. I was thinking, "It may or may not work." That isn't the way it should work. Not fair. We're both from divorced families, so pretty strong about that concept. One of things that led to our splitting up was a friend of mine from college said at his bachelor party it may not work. I talk [to friends] about finding the right one, looking for that relationship that is magical, what if I don't find it? A natural, be together type thing, where things fall into place. Marriage is the craziest concept—two people who are different and live their lives together. Insane! But we all want to do it. Has to be some magic, natural, liking some things—"no matter what you do I'm in love with you" type thing. It wasn't that way with [my girlfriend] and I.

Jim's uncertainty about whether this relationship would work as a marriage, in conjunction with his commitment to marry and keep it, led him to let it go. Although he recognized the complexity of two different people living together, he was still after the magical relationship in which love would prevail over all else. Jim was still strongly influenced by friends' opinions, as is evident in his being shaken by his friends' comment about the workability of Jim's relationship. Two years later Jim was also on the verge of marrying a woman whom he felt that he loved, but he reported that "She annoyed me. I would sit at dinner with her, she was talking, I didn't care. I knew this was not it. We were so compatible in many ways though." It seemed he was still holding out for the "right" relationship.

Even when participants found what they thought was the "right" relationship, it did not resolve the uncertainty and complexity of working through relationships with significant others. There were days when participants wondered if they had chosen wisely, and it was hard to adjust their initial romantic ideas about relationships to reality. The comment below captures this sentiment:[1]

> I always had this fairy tale idea about marriage. I never heard any real people say that—it was only in movies. But that is what it came down to. You should see the movie "Three Weddings and a Funeral!" There is a point in that where one guy says, "I just want to meet somebody I really like, and thinks I'm not repulsive." It's almost like that. I won't say I settled on that whole concept, we do have a physical and emotional attraction that I haven't found with anyone else, but it isn't a fairy tale. I wondered that day [wedding day], "Do I want to do this?" I have doubts about whether it was the right decision, then I see [my spouse] at the end of the day and say, "Yeah, this is a good thing for me."

Most participants found that significant relationships were complex, required self as central to participating in the relationship, and required mutuality and interdependence. After two years of marriage, Adrian summed it up as "No Hallmark card":

> I think the whole thing is a learning experience. Learning how to live with someone who's not a roommate or a mother or a brother and just understanding again that someone else might not share exactly the same feelings about exactly the same things. Just because you get married, you don't have one brain and become one person. . . . No Hallmark card here! . . . But I think all of marriage for me has been learning, I mean, about myself probably more than anything. Plus just trying to decide—I mean, it's hard enough for me to decide what I want to do, let alone what we want to do together, where we want to be. It just brings one more thing into the mix and one more thing to consider, which is good I guess. I wouldn't trade it.

---

[1] I use this quote anonymously to avoid harm to the participant who shared it. Although I do not use the real names of participants, I do use their "assigned" names consistently to keep their stories in context. Because I share my written accounts with participants, who in turn often share them with their partners or families, attributing these comments to the participant could result in discomfort for the parties involved. Respect for participants and their families outweighs my interest in consistency in this instance as well as in others where sharing information could potentially result in harm to participants at some future time.

Learning about the other person also meant learning about herself. Adrian's comment about people not having one brain just because they are married sounds obvious, but many participants did not realize just how much work it would be to get two brains working in the same direction. Adrian offers a crucial insight in her awareness of the difficulty of deciding what she wants, then adding the complication of mutual decision-making.

Differences between participants and their partners were a primary source of the work that had to be done to maintain relationships. Al offered an example:

> My wife has a fairly dependent personality. She needs support and is used to more time from significant others. I can't do it. It has been hard for her. When I do have time, that is my first priority. I don't need that near as much; that sort of bothers her. To her it means I don't care. She is getting used to that and I'm adjusting to getting away from being a completely independent self. We've had some struggles. It is hard to be married to a medical student or doctor. [The relationship] is work. In my case, given my wife's personality, it has been a lot of work. When she gets frustrated, there is nothing I can do—as a medical student, I have no say. Once I'm through residency, I'll have a little more choice in practice and we can live a reasonable life. The relationship thing has to be factored in there.

Al had given up his volunteer work to devote his energy and what little time he had as a medical student to his relationship. He and his wife were working to understand each other's personalities and their meaning. Al talked two years later about the road from independence to interdependence:

> Marriage has been a learning process—learning to go from an independent person, to having to check things before I do things—I'm still adapting, but getting better. I'm a very independent person. I don't need to have somebody around; my wife is the opposite. Things that don't phase me, phase her a lot—we have to learn what is a big deal. Marriage is a lot harder than being a doctor at times. It's still worth it, and I'm adapting to the learning process. For somebody like me, when I was dating, they were 5th on the priority list. When you get married, that has to change! The third year of medical school was harder because I was gone a lot, working a lot of hours. My wife was used to being together all the time.

Although part of Al's struggle was the demand of medical school, he reflected that part of it was shifting from independence to mutuality. Learning what was a big deal to each person was hard enough; learning to work with those issues was even more difficult.

Differences about how to deal with relationship issues also arose in many relationships, often due to past experiences. The next story reveals these complexities:[2]

> I'm hesitant to talk about these things. Growing up, my parents never fought—they are divorced. My mom swept problems under the rug. My mom and I are very close. She didn't put energy into marriage—she is on her third one now. I look at that, not as an excuse, but part of my past. [My spouse] goes right at it. I was unhappy about something, but said it was fine. [My spouse] can pick it up. It's scary. [My spouse] was right, I didn't want to talk about it. Getting it out is positive, but the other problem is, I have emotions I want to work through myself—[my spouse] wants to put it on the table. I like to get feedback from people but [my spouse] deals with problems internally, or shares with a best friend. I want to talk to people who've experienced the same thing. [My spouse] doesn't want other people knowing our business—wants us to talk only to each other. [My spouse] would have a fit if [s/he] knew I talked to you about these things.

These differences in whether to talk about issues or who to talk to about them caused friction as partners tried to coordinate their own styles and past experiences to making relationships work. As was the case in these stories, many participants worked at maintaining their own voices while simultaneously adjusting to meet the needs of partners.

Transforming Relationships with Parents. The twenties were a time of transforming roles with parents from child-parent to adult-adult relationships. Lauren described that process in chapter 5 as she made the decision to move to another state to pursue a significant relationship. You will recall that despite her parents' support, Lauren still identified "leaving her parents" as the hardest decision she had made. Some participants, like Adrian, transformed relationships with parents while living in the same town. Adrian and her spouse had lived elsewhere for two years, and upon returning to the locale of their parents were interested in stronger family connections. Adrian described how they approached it:

[2.]This story is also used anonymously, and the participant's gender disguised, to avoid potential harm to the participant.

We do a lot of family things but we're not getting caught up in them; we are starting our own pattern. We're breaking some old traditions and staring new ones; like having a holiday dinner at our house. We had Christmas day here; we've always been the ones to drive and cart things around. There wasn't too much dissension. . . . We are also fixing up an old house. The house is a good medium for my relationship with my father; he is handy. On Saturday morning, dad comes over; [my husband] is at work. That is time for us to spend together. We are closer and I can learn from him; he feels needed and appreciated. It's a different level of relationship. My husband's family is here too—all within ten minutes. I was skeptical at first but it works out well. Everyone calls first instead of dropping in. . . . Our families are proud of us. We don't need to live up to any one else's expectations. When parents were paying for school I felt that. Now they trust my judgment. We have adult relationships with the family. After moving back here, we spend real time, not visiting time. We can get a sense of our parents' relationship daily; they know that about us. It is more down to earth, more real.

Adrian and her husband established adult relationships with both their families by maintaining their independence (establishing their own patterns and not living up to others' expectations) and by spending quality time together. Their families, like Lauren's parents, were supportive of this shift to adult relationships.

Some participants made independent decisions of which their parents did not approve, making the transformation of the relationship more difficult. Usually parental disapproval stemmed from wanting the best for their children; yet it made the son or daughter's decision more difficult. Phillip shared his experience with his parents in chapter 4, revealing that their wishes for him constrained his perspective for a while. He did decide to move to pursue his career and they supported him in the process. When participants' perceived parental disapproval, even if it was not explicit, it weighed heavily on them. Kris offered one such situation:

I'm really struggling with the relationship with my Mom. That relates to the pregnancy. She's just not real excited about it, which really is very difficult for me. She hasn't talked about coming down when I have the baby. And I'm not sure how to handle that. I don't feel like I can approach her on it because as soon as I do she'll take offense and get real defensive. And I know that from experience with her. I thought about writing a letter, but as soon as I do that it's all there in writing and she misinterprets it and it all comes back. I've toyed with talking to my Dad about it, but that puts him in the middle in a really bad situation because there's jealousy there anyway that I'm Daddy's girl. So that makes that even tough to handle. So right now I'm just trying not to let it affect me, but it does. . . . I spent a couple of days in tears, trying to decide how to handle that situation. And basically, in this case, the decision I made was not to handle it, not to confront it or approach it, which isn't the best option. But right now it's the only option for me.

Kris was disappointed about her mother's lack of excitement but did not see any good options for working through it with her mother. It was part of a bigger issue, as became clear when she continued:

I've discussed it with my sister. She said that she doesn't understand it either. The first time I felt the baby move I told [mom] and she was like, "Oh, that's nice." Just no excitement, no enthusiasm, no "What did it feel like?" I guess I was really hoping that this would help draw us closer together. A lot of it stems from she doesn't approve of my marriage. I feel like [my husband] doesn't fit the image that she had of the man she wanted me to marry. She just doesn't want to accept him. I see that and then I see my sister, who's dating a guy that she met at college who is an accounting person for one of the big ten companies or the big six or whatever that is. I see the way that [Mom] reacts to him. The sun rises and sets in him, where [my husband], the sun could rise and Mom wouldn't even know.

Kris knew her parents were not excited about her marriage to an older man, but thought these issues had receded in the years between the marriage and her pregnancy. Her ability to have an adult relationship in which she could share her excitement about her first child was hindered by unfinished business between them about the choice Kris had made.

Some of the most difficult transformations occurred with new in-laws. Wedding plans and religion seemed to be the major sources of contention as newlyweds tried to act on their own interests. Cara's story in chapter 6 conveyed her mother-in-law as an external force she "swayed to" initially, but then after moving out of the crossroads stood her ground with. Genesse reported a similar experience:

I found just different moral and ethical values with [my husband's] parents. His church is old school. You'll go to hell if you do X—I am angry sometimes when we come out [of the service]. He feels guilty because his family goes to this church. I

> love his family, but I don't want to be expected to be there. We
> have gone to a Methodist one that I love. We went there yester-
> day and he enjoyed it too. That was a turning point. We both
> need to enjoy it. If we break away [from his parents] now, they
> won't expect us to do everything they want. They never say
> anything, but you know how they are thinking. You feel guilty.
> Disapproving, you know they are disappointed. The minister
> said we might want to do something on our own. His parents
> are very nice, fine people. They brought him up very well. But
> we are establishing our own household—clinging to each other.

The minister validated Genesse and her husband in pursuing their own interests. Genesse conveyed that she perceived her husband's parents as disapprov-
ing of their not attending his original church, although it isn't clear in her story
whether they ever expressed this concern. The sense of what parents and in-
laws expect had a strong influence, even when it was not stated.

Anne and her husband had more explicit disagreements with their parents
and dealt with them openly. Anne explained:

> I was kind of shocked at how the adults behaved regarding the
> wedding. We wanted to have the wedding at Miami, and the
> families said they wouldn't come. They wanted to have it in
> their church. We try to be understanding, hoping they will real-
> ize we are happy. We spent Thanksgiving weekend with his fam-
> ily. We clashed—his mom felt I was too strong willed; I asked
> her to talk about it. I'm not going to cry about it; it is her prob-
> lem. This isn't worth it, I'm a good person, we are happy. Last
> year I would have been crying, talking about it all the time. I
> think I put so much energy into work, my CPA, my husband—I
> don't have time to deal with these things. I am trying to be
> understanding—our parents are adjusting. We are their first
> kids to get married.

Despite their disappointment, Anne and her spouse tried to understand their
parents' views and their need to adjust. However, as Anne became the author
of her own life, she challenged her mother-in-law to work through their differences, determining that the problem belonged to her mother-in-law.

For a few participants, transforming relationships with parents meant role
reversals due to difficulties the parents experienced. Evan spoke to this in
chapter 6 when he described his role in the extended family as more central
after his parents' divorce. He also reversed roles in a way with his father by
taking care of his father's needs while he was incarcerated. Heather experienced transformations with her parents as a result of their divorce as well:

I'm emotionally challenged like never before. My parents are going through a divorce right now; it has been dragging out for a year. My father did not want this, so it is a heartache for him. Mother has really changed as far as who she is and how she interacts. I have three younger sisters. I am the typical oldest, take on everything! Dealing with the divorce, we grew up in a family where we were emotional; let it out. We were emotionally close, even though our parents didn't have a close relationship. We feel things strongly. It's been an emotional year with all of this; some days I go on whatever reserves I have. It's a strain on my relationship with my husband, a hard thing to have so much. I'm talking to either parent everyday for a two-week span; one of those things that people advise me to pull back on, but my personality doesn't fit that.

Heather's routine conversations with each parent revealed her involvement in the situation. She also took responsibility for helping her younger sisters cope with the family situation. Yet she kept some perspective on it:

There have been days when I shut down. But I never felt like I couldn't keep going. Every person's scenario is the reality they live in. Last spring I worked with kids at age 14 who had more issues than I've dealt with. I shouldn't deprive myself of my emotions because of that, my reality, relevant to my own experience. I get strength from the courage of kids I have dealt with. My husband has been helpful, an understanding and supportive spouse. My parent's divorce could ultimately be the best thing for them. I don't want to admit that, but when we get through it, it could be best. I had to get through the grieving process. I have known for a long time that their relationship wasn't strong. I resigned myself to them staying together. They were not a good couple, didn't nurture each other, or communicate. It is hard to see the family broken apart. I grieved the loss of family; then went back to what I intuitively knew was best.

Heather's experience in her inner city teaching put her own problems in perspective. She also had support from her husband. She also knew, once her grieving had occurred, that divorce was probably best for her parents. After the divorce, Heather reported that she and her father became closer and she was able to have candid conversations with him about their lives. His trauma brought them to an adult-adult relationship.

Developing Effective Relationships with Colleagues. Regardless of their line of work, most participants routinely needed to interact effectively with their colleagues. Mutual construction of knowledge and work decisions among colleagues was often aimed at providing better service to clients, but it required the ability to construct mutual relationships with others participants usually did not know well. This was true even in work settings where one would expect to operate independently, such as in teaching. Team teaching contexts were not uncommon. Candace, a math teacher in a paideia school, described how her group of educators mutually constructed meaning:

> We meet about three times a week as a whole team. And then I meet at least once a day with at least one other teacher on our team to plan either the science labs or my math labs or to find out what they're doing in whatever the other disciplines are. Lots of times I'll be finding out Spanish words for things that I'm doing. . . . And then even outside my team, with my seminars, I have two seminars, and I'm on three of the other teams, as far as seminar is concerned. So I have to read and discuss seminar with each of their readings; and they're all different.

This mutual construction across disciplines was necessary to provide an integrated set of lessons for students. Candace found this intellectually stimulating and felt responsible for working with her colleagues to come up with good lessons. This was a stark contrast to her previous experience in another school where teachers were competitive and did not communicate with each other (see chapter 8).

Teachers of special education also engaged in mutual construction in co-teaching with regular teachers to assist their learning disabled students as Kris described:

> We try to plan our lessons together. Now she has a pretty good idea of what she wants to teach because she's just been through this workshop on applying math to daily life, which is what the special education student really needs. So I pretty much let her do the teaching, and I kind of work one-on-one if somebody has a question. Or if there's a discipline problem, a lot of times I'll deal with that. In decision-making, there are a lot of things now that I still consult other people and I really take into consideration their opinions before I make the final decision. But legally the final decision is mine because I am the special education teacher.

Kris's students benefited from her effort to work effectively with other teachers. The stories in chapter 8 revealed that regardless of the context—human services, business, finance—clients benefited from employees working effectively with coworkers.

The need for mutuality in relationships permeated participants' adult lives regardless of circumstance. Those getting married or looking for life partners needed interpersonal and intrapersonal self-authorship to connect effectively. As they pursued their own adult lives, they needed an internal sense of self and ability to connect in mutual ways with their parents. This mean working through parents' expectations—real or perceived—which represented one of the hardest sources of external influence to let go. Contemporary work settings made success, even in jobs that seemed autonomous, contingent on effective sharing of expertise and authority with colleagues to make good decisions and meet goals. Thus despite varying levels of support, the participants were all confronted with the complexity of building and maintaining relationships in their lives and the need to establish their own internal selves to bring to those relationships.

Translation to Residence Life, Educational Programming, and Counseling.

Some educators argue that preparing graduates for relationships in young adulthood is beyond the scope and purpose of college. I disagree. In the light of campus issues—relationship violence, hazing, peer pressure's mediation of alcohol abuse, lack of civility, and tolerance of diversity—attention to relationship building is crucial to improve the campus community and make it a safe, civil, educational environment. The value of helping students build relationships with diverse others is also supported by research suggesting that having different types of friends is associated with more complex moral reasoning (Derryberry & Thoma, 2000). The increasing interdependence, globalization, and multiculturalism of contemporary society necessitate better preparation of college students for productive citizenry. Social problems, such as domestic violence or violence in resolving disputes (i.e., fatal fights over children's sports games), also suggest that better company for self-authorship is an important part of producing a healthy society.

Getting along with one's college roommates is often a challenge for many students. Residence life staff spend innumerable hours working with roommate conflicts. Roommate contracts, a process in which roommates make agreements about how they will treat each other, are often used to help students manage these relationships. Using the framework for promoting self-authorship to shape this contract process would teach students to explore their own values and beliefs, how to express those to roommates, and how to negotiate compromises to handle differences between roommates. I envision this as a mini-version of the Community Standards Model. RAs could introduce residents to this concept as a group, sharing steps in the process and typical issues roommates usually need to negotiate. Residents' own experiences in building and maintaining relationships would be welcomed to help everyone learn how to build effective relationships. Roommates would then work on their agreements privately, consulting the RA or other residents for help as needed. As is the case with the Community Standards Model, students would maintain responsibility for dealing with conflicts as they arise. The staff would assist them in engaging in effective dialogue with each other but would not take the problem away from the students or solve it for them. This approach would situate learning in students' experience, validate their ability to work on relationships, and teach them how to mutually construct meaning. Negotiating with roommates in this context would provide exposure to expand beliefs, encourage self-exploration and expression, and teach interdependence in relationships. This same process could be used in building and maintaining relationships among student staff members and among members and leaders of student organizations.

Educational programming about relationships, provided by various student affairs offices, offers another context to promote self-authorship. These programming efforts should help students understand relationships as complex and socially constructed, emphasize the central role of self in effective relationships, and describe the nature of mutual construction of meaning in healthy relationships. Programs on building relationships with friends could help students identify what they want from a friendship, how to communicate this to others, and how to negotiate different needs in friendships. Students' own experience in friendships would be validated in these programs and they would be engaged in mutually constructing meaning about what makes a good friendship. Pairs of friends could be invited to programs to strengthen their relationships, as could groups of students who live together or work together in a student organization. These efforts would have a dual focus on students developing their own identities and developing mutual relationships with others from the vantage point of those identities. Programs on considering what groups to join could also help students develop their internal voices by exploring what they are looking for from group membership. Student affairs educators' expertise in student, group, and community development offers a sound foundation from which to organize these efforts.

Programs on choosing, building and maintaining relationships with significant others would also begin with helping students identify what they want in these relationships, emphasizing the importance of identifying the self they bring to these relationships. Addressing the myth that these relationships are magical is important to help students understand the complexity of these relationships and the work that is necessary to maintain them. Including recent graduates who could speak to their experiences and share stories like the ones in this chapter could engage students in an exploration of these relationships. Teaching students frameworks for handling differences and mutually constructing meaning is also important given the stories here. Interpersonal communication, conflict-management, and mutual decision-making would be important components of all relationship programming.

Programming should also address relationships with parents. Students begin to transform their relationship with their parents during college. As students gain autonomy and new perspectives, they often expect less direction and more freedom from their parents. Parents have to adjust to changes in their student's expectations of them as well as changes their student's beliefs due to exposure to multiple perspectives. Some of this programming would interconnect with the issues I noted earlier in academic advising and career services; some would directly address how to alter roles with one's parents as college proceeds. Parents could be involved in this programming through joint parent-student programs on parents' weekend or in orientation. Student affairs offices could include information in publications or newsletters for parents about these changes and how their students' growth toward self-authorship might affect family relationships. Tips for how to engage in productive discussion about these issues could be useful to parents and students alike.

Divorce is becoming increasingly common in this country, and parents sometimes divorce after their children have left home. Thus a common concern for many college students is their parents' divorce while they are in college, or soon after they graduate. Programming that helps students clarify their understanding of divorce, work through their feelings about it happening to their family, understand what it means to their sense of self, and helps them with ways to maintain relationships with each of their parents would alleviate some of the trauma these events produce. Programming on maintaining relationships for children of divorce would also be helpful given the longitudinal participants' hesitation about marriage when their parents had divorced.

Partnerships between student affairs educators and academic programs whose disciplinary content is relevant to relationships would enhance these programming efforts. Communications faculty could contribute expertise toward teaching students interpersonal communication skills. Psychology faculty could contribute expertise on identity and relationship development. Family Studies and Social Work faculty could contribute expertise on family dynamics, violence in relationships, and divorce. Faculty in Women's Studies or Ethnic Studies could contribute expertise in gender and ethnic identity development and working with diversity in relationships. Faculty working in organizational development or leadership could contribute expertise in developing personal mastery and skills needed in work relationships (e.g., conflict-management, mutual decisionmaking). Partnering with faculty in these disciplines would incorporate the knowledge of their disciplines into programming while student affairs educators would connect that knowledge to students' development.

Counseling Center staff are often involved in conducting outreach and group programming or as consultants in programs other student affairs educators organize. Inclusion of Counseling Center professionals is essential given the crisis proportions of some events in students' lives. Although much of the journey to self-authorship can be aided through the avenues I've described here, in some cases in-depth individual counseling is necessary to move through the journey. Many of the longitudinal participants took advantage of professional therapy in their twenties to explore their dissatisfaction with life and develop their internal voices. Devoting more resources to counseling services may be another means of helping students make meaningful progress on self-authorship during college.

An Integrated Cocurriculum as Good Company for Self-Authorship

The translations to practice throughout this chapter focus on particular arenas, yet they all share a common framework. They all address all three dimensions of self-authorship in these particular contexts. The longitudinal participants' stories reveal that success in young adulthood requires more than a complex mind. It requires a complex mind (epistemological self-authorship) and a complex self (intrapersonal and interpersonal self-authorship); in fact, the two are inseparable. Thus preparing students for life after college requires engaging their minds and their internal selves to work toward the complexity they will need for success. Given the magnitude of the journey from external to internal self-definition, students need as many experiences as possible that promote self-authorship. The more coherent those experiences are, the more likely they will contribute to self-authorship. The framework of the three core assumptions and the three principles for educational practice is a means to achieve this coherency and stay connected to student development. The framework is a way to make college life real as opposed to an abstract, unconnected exercise. This is a framework for good company.

An integrated cocurriculum to promote self-authorship will emphasize development on all three dimensions. Although intrapersonal and interpersonal development is clearly in the foreground of student affairs education, the journey to self-authorship requires complex epistemological development as well. Helping students explore, expand, clarify and decide what they believe about themselves and the world is integrated into helping them decide who they are and want to be and how to engage effectively with others. Integrating the far-flung parts of the cocurriculum around the goal of self-authorship brings coherence to the cocurriculum. Partnerships among student affairs educators' to coordinate their efforts would help implement the framework to promote self-authorship effectively. Programming on relationships, for example, connects to the use of the Community Standards Model in residence life or to career services' programs on balancing career and family. Service learning in battered spouse shelters could bring perspective to relationship violence on campus. Conceptualizing the learning goals of these efforts together could result in a more coherent and powerful cocurricular learning environment.

To implement this integrated cocurriculum using the framework to promote self-authorship does require a significant transformation in the minds of student affairs educators. This core of this transformation relates to student affairs educators' assumptions about students. Just as I advocated (chapter 7) that faculty need to accept students as adults capable of knowing in the academic arena, student affairs educators need to accept students as capable of knowing in the cocurriculum. Student affairs as a profession has always advocated student responsibility but the reality on many campuses is more control-oriented than student responsibility-oriented. Student life is messy because it is real, whether institutional administrators are aware of it or not. Rather than treating things like alcohol abuse, relationship violence, and eating disorders as situations that can be controlled, student affairs educators (and the institutions in which they work) must accept the messiness of helping students bring their self-evolution into these areas of their campus life. One of the principles for good practice in student affairs is engaging students in active learning (Blimling, Whitt, & Associates, 1999). "Active learning invites students to bring their life experiences into the learning process, reflect on their own and others' perspectives as they expand their viewpoints, and apply new understandings to their own lives" (ACPA and NASPA, 1997, p. 3). This definition emphasizes both welcoming student experience and helping students expand their perspectives. As I have argued elsewhere, "our task is to make what and how students think center stage, respect that experience, and create learning environments that are meaningful to that experience yet facilitative of remaking it" (Baxter Magolda, 1999c, p. 31). Using the framework for promoting self-authorship means less control and more partnership with students in remaking their experience.

The framework I advocate is not, as Ira Shor said, "a know-nothing process" (Shor, 1992, p. 247). Shor, talking about empowering education, noted that partnership with students did not mean abandoning existing knowledge and expertise. Rather it means including students' own lived experiences and questions in exploration of knowledge and mutual construction among members of the knowledge community. Riane Eisler's notion of a partnership society is useful here. Describing two basic models of society, she wrote:

> The first, which I call the *dominator* model, is what is popularly termed either patriarchy or matriarchy—the *ranking* of one half of humanity over the other. The second, in which social relations are primarily based on the principle of *linking* rather than ranking, may best be described as the *partnership* model. In this model, . . ., diversity is not equated with either inferiority or superiority. (1987, p. xvii)

Eisler clarified that transformation from a dominator model to a partnership model meant those in the dominate group giving up their right to dominate in order to join others in partnership. Educators have traditionally dominated students. Promoting self-authorship requires a move to a partnership model in higher education.

The challenge of implementing an integrated cocurriculum for self-authorship is to define the cocurriculum as central to promoting self-authorship and to institutional missions. Defining the learning goals of both the overall cocurriculum and its specific parts is the foundation of building and justifying the cocurriculum to achieve them. Just as faculty groups specify learning goals of courses and majors, student affairs must articulate what learning is to be achieved in residence life, student activities, student organizations, and etceteras. The profession's most recent philosophical statement, the *Student Learning Imperative* (American College Personnel Association, 1994) supports this approach. Explaining how this learning contributes to desired qualities of graduates, as well as desired capacities in the academic arena, connects the cocurriculum to the larger mission of the institution.

Connections with other arenas are crucial to create a coherent experience for students. Opportunities for student affairs and academic affairs partnerships abound in the campus work settings shared across the two divisions, in student affairs educators helping faculty deal with student development, and in faculty helping student affairs connect intrapersonal and interpersonal growth to students' academic lives. One arena in which this is occurring is learning communities. A learning community is characterized by faculty and students creating shared goals, working collaboratively toward them, sharing responsibility to teach and learn from each other, and de-emphasizing competition (Goodsell Love, 1999). Influenced by the shift from knowledge acquisition to knowledge construction (Goodsell Love, 1999), learning communities are conceptually consistent with the framework for promoting self-authorship. Collaboration among peers and with faculty in learning communities offers opportunities for developing social networks among peers as well as exposure to multiple perspectives and ways to restructure what one knows (Cross, 1998; Goodsell Love, 1999). Partnerships among faculty, students, student affairs professionals and academic administrators are common in the learning community movement and models of various learning communities are already in place (for details see Levine, 1999). Virginia Polytechnic Institute, for example, has an extensive array of learning communities that span learning contexts from architecture to mathematics (see http://www.lrncomm.vt. edu/ for information). Schroeder (1999) offered examples of such partnerships at various institutions addressing the success of first-year students, making student government a learning organization, fostering civic engagement through service-learning, strengthening community to enhance learning, establishing and articulating institutional expectations, and using values exploration to reinvigorate undergraduate education.

Student affairs organizations collaborated to conceptualize educational partnerships in a joint document, *Powerful Partnerships* (American Association of Higher Education, American College Personnel Association, and National Association for Student Personnel Administrators, 1998). Forging educational partnerships that advance student learning is also one of the principles for good practice in student affairs, about which Schroeder advocated that we "be willing to leave the comfort, predictability, and security of organizational boundaries and take some reasonable risks" (Schroeder, 1999, p. 155) to develop and sustain educational partnerships. Student affairs educators have the advantage of understanding student development and automatic direct intense experience with students. Making college life real, and making room for the self to be a central part of it, is a major challenge. Student affairs educators have the knowledge base and skills to take leadership to helping higher education move in this direction.

EPILOGUE: MUTUAL PARTNERSHIPS TO PROMOTE SELF-AUTHORSHIP

The journey toward self-authorship is complex and arduous. The narratives in this book convey the magnitude of the shift from external control to internal self-authorship. Becoming the author of one's life—in essence bringing the source of meaning making inside the self—is a life changing transformation. For the longitudinal participants, it meant having an internal home from which to make sense of the complexity of their everyday lives, a solid sense of self from which to join others in mutual relationships, and a sense of peace in an ambiguous and complex world. Their self-authorship enabled them to meet the demands of their personal, work and public lives.

Paths through the crossroads became visible when participants realized that the self is central to making meaning of the world, oneself, and connections with others. Many were assisted in navigating these paths by others who invited them to join in mutual partnerships to further develop the self and define mature relations with others. These other people were good company because they made space for participants' selves to be central to meaning making, yet offered mutual partnerships to support the meaning-making process. Like Robert, the tour guide for the downhill bicycle trek with which I began this narrative, they offered basic instruction and hand signals as appropriate, yet they insisted that participants control their own bicycles.

Too many college contexts promote external control by virtue of not letting students control their own bicycles. The college experience often looks more like a tandem bicycle ride. The front rider on a tandem bicycle is called the captain; the back rider is called the stoker. In many college experiences, the educator takes the captain's role, assigning the stoker position to the learner. The captain steers the bicycle and shifts the gears. The stoker's role is to contribute to the forward motion by pedaling. The stoker is not called upon to make self central to the journey because the journey is externally controlled by the captain. Although it is possible for the two riders to be in partnership, the captain maintains control of the journey. The longitudinal participants' stories suggest that their advanced educational contexts, their work settings, and their personal lives required taking the captain's role or riding their own bicycles. Their experience as stokers did not necessarily prepare them for the self-authorship required to direct and manage the journey.

Colleges must offer a new kind of partnership to prepare graduates more effectively for the self-authorship demanded by contemporary society. The tandem bicycle partnership could offer good company if educators took the stoker role. From this vantage point, the educator could offer guidance and advice as appropriate, help fuel the ride, yet still allow the learner to take the lead in directing and managing the journey. Learning the captain's role would invite the self into the direction and leadership of the journey. Learning to manage the journey could lead to not needing the stoker and the ability to ride one's own bicycle when necessary. Experience in the mutual partnership could also enhance learners' ability to construct mutual relationships in the areas of their lives that involve tandem journeys. These mutual partnerships mean giving learners more control and responsibility for their journeys and their lives. They mean reducing external control and enhancing internal self-authorship. To be most effective, these educator-learner partnerships should permeate the entire college experience from the curriculum to the cocurriculum, from campus work settings to governance. I hope the journeys depicted here, both in their achievements and their struggles, prompt readers to encourage learners to be captains. Transforming higher education in this way makes it possible for learners to navigate the crossroads during college.

REFERENCES

American Association of Higher Education, American College Personnel Association, National Association of Student Personnel Administrators (1998). *Powerful Partnerships*. Washington, DC.

American College Personnel Association. (1994). *The student learning imperative*. Washington, DC.

American College Personnel Association and National Association of Student Personnel Administrators. (1997). *Principles of good practice for student affairs*. Washington, DC: Authors.

Arons, A. B. (1989). *What science should we teach?* (Curriculum development for the year 2000): Biological Science Curriculum Study, Colorado Springs, CO.

Association of American Colleges (1990). *Liberal learning and the arts and sciences major, Volume 1: The challenge of connecting learning*. Washington, DC.

Bagby, M. (1998). *Rational exuberance: The influence of generation x on the new American economy*. New York: Penguin.

Bakan, D. (1966). *The duality of human existence: An essay on psychology and religion*. Chicago: Rand McNally & Company.

Barefoot, B. O. (2000). The first-year experience—Are we making it any better? *About Campus, 4*(6), 12–18.

Barr, R. B., & Tagg, J. (1995). From teaching to learning—A new paradigm for undergraduate education. *Change* (November/December), 13–25.

Baxter Magolda, M. B. (1992). *Knowing and reasoning in college: Gender-related patterns in students' intellectual development*. San Francisco, CA: Jossey-Bass.

Baxter Magolda, M. B. (1994). Post-college experiences and epistemology. *The Review of Higher Education, 18*(1), 25–44.

Baxter Magolda, M. B. (1995). The integration of relational and impersonal knowing in young adults' epistemological development. *Journal of College Student Development, 36*(3), 205–216.

Baxter Magolda, M. B. (1998). Developing self-authorship in young adult life. *Journal of College Student Development, 39*(2), 143–156.

Baxter Magolda, M. B. (1999a). Constructing adult identities. *Journal of College Student Development, 40*(6), 629–644.

Baxter Magolda, M. B. (1999b). *Creating contexts for learning and self-authorship: Constructive-developmental pedagogy.* Nashville, TN: Vanderbilt University Press.

Baxter Magolda, M. B. (1999c). Engaging students in active learning. In G. Blimling & E. Whitt (Eds.), *Good practice in student affairs: Principles to foster student learning* (pp. 21–43). San Francisco, CA: Jossey Bass.

Baxter Magolda, M. B. (1999d). Learning-centered practice is harder than it looks. *About Campus, 4*(4), 2–4.

Baxter Magolda, M. B. (1999e). The evolution of epistemology: Refining contextual knowing at twentysomething. *Journal of College Student Development, 40*(4), 333–344.

Baxter Magolda, M. B. (2000). Interpersonal maturity: Integrating agency and communion. *Journal of College Student Development, 41*(2), 141–156.

Belenky, M., Clinchy, B., Goldberger, N., & Tarule, J. (1986). *Women's ways of knowing: The development of self, voice, and mind.* New York: Basic Books.

Blimling, G. S., & Whitt, E. (Eds.). (1999). *Good practice in student affairs: Principles to foster student learning.* San Francisco, CA: Jossey-Bass.

Brown, L. M., & Gilligan, C. (1992). *Meeting at the crossroads: Women's psychology and girls' development.* Cambridge, MA: Harvard University Press.

Bruffee, K. A. (1993). *Collaborative learning: Higher education, interdependence, and the authority of knowledge.* Baltimore, MD: Johns Hopkins University Press.

Chickering, A. W. (1969). *Education and identity.* San Francisco, CA: Jossey-Bass.

Chickering, A. W., & Reisser, L. (1993). *Education and identity, second edition.* San Francisco: CA: Jossey-Bass.

Chickering, A. W., & Schlossberg, N. K. (1997). Moving on: Seniors as people in transition. In J. N. Gardner & G. Van der Veer (Eds.), *The senior year experience: Facilitating integration, reflection, closure and transition* (pp. 37–50). San Francisco: Jossey-Bass.

Clinchy, B. M. (1996). Connected and separate knowing: Toward a marriage of two minds. In N. R. Goldberger, J. M. Tarule, B. M. Clinchy, & M. F. Belenky (Eds.), *Knowledge, difference, and power: Essays inspired by women's ways of knowing* (pp. 205–247). New York: Basic Books.

Clinchy, B. M. (2000). Toward a more connected vision of higher education. In M. B. Baxter Magolda (Ed.), *Teaching to promote intellectual and personal maturity: Incorporating students' worldviews and identities into the learning process. New Directions for Teaching and Learning* (pp. 27–35). San Francisco: CA: Jossey-Bass.

Cross, K. P. (1998). Why learning communities? Why now? *About Campus, July/August, 3*(3), 4–11.

Denzin, N. K. (1994). The art and politics of interpretation. In N. K. Denzin & Y. S. Lincoln (Eds.), *Handbook of qualitative research* (pp. 500–515). Thousand Oaks, CA: Sage.

Derryberry, W. P., & Thoma, S. J. (2000). The friendship effect: Its role in the development of moral thinking in students. *About Campus, 5*(2), 13–18.

Dewey, J. (1916). *Democracy and education.* New York: The Free Press.

Dykstra, D. I. Jr. (1996). Teaching introductory physics to college students. In C. Twomey Fosnot (Ed.), *Constructivism: Theory, perspectives, and practice* (pp. 182–204). New York: Teachers College Press.

Eisler, R. (1987). *The chalice and the blade: Our history, our future.* San Francisco, CA: HarperCollins.

Erikson, E. (1968). *Identity, youth, and crisis.* New York: Norton.

Evans, N. J. (2000). Creating a positive learning environment for gay, lesbian, and bisexual students. In M. B. Baxter Magolda (Ed.), *Teaching to promote intellectual and personal maturity: Incorporating students' worldviews and identities into the learning process. New Directions for Teaching and Learning* (pp. 81–87). San Francisco, CA: Jossey-Bass.

Fontana, A., & Frey, J. H. (1994). Interviewing: The art of science. In N. K. Denzin & Y. S. Lincoln (Eds.), *Handbook of qualitative research* (pp. 361–376). Thousand Oaks, CA: Sage.

Fries-Britt, S. (2000). Identity development of high-ability Black collegians. In M. B. Baxter Magolda (Ed.), *Teaching to promote intellectual and personal maturity: Incorporating students' worldviews and identities into the learning process. New Directions for Teaching and Learning* (pp. 55–65). San Francisco, CA: Jossey-Bass.

Gardner, P. D. (1997). Are college seniors prepared to work? In J. N. Gardner & G. Van der Veer (Eds.), *The senior year experience: Facilitating integration, reflection, closure, and transition* (pp. 60–78). San Francisco, CA: Jossey-Bass.

Gilligan, C. (1982). *In a different voice.* Cambridge, MA: Harvard University Press.

Glaser, B. (1978). *Theoretical sensitivity.* Mill Valley, CA: Sociological Press.

Goodsell Love, A. (1999). What are learning communities? In J. H. Levine (Ed.), *Learning communities: New structures, new partnerships for learning* (pp. 1–8). Columbia, SC: National Resource Center for the First-Year Experience and Students in Transition, University of South Carolina.

Granrose, C. S., & Kaplan, E. E. (1996). *Work-family role choices for women in their 20s and 30s: From college plans to life experiences.* Westport, CT: Praeger.

Greenleaf, E. A. (1974). The role of student staff members. In D. A. DeCoster & P. Mable (Eds.), *Student development and education in college residence halls* (pp. 181–194). Washington, DC.: American College Personnel Association.

Hake, R. R. (1998). Interactive-engagement versus traditional methods: A six-thousand-student survey of mechanics test data for introductory physics courses. *American Journal of Physics, 66*(1), 64–74.

Hamilton, K., & Wingert, P. (1998). Down the aisle. *Newsweek.* July 20: 54–57.

Hettich, P. (1998). *Learning skills for college and career, second edition.* Pacific Grove, CA: Brooks/Cole.

Holton III, E. F. (1997). Preparing students for life beyond the classroom. In J. N. Gardner & G. Van der Veer (Eds.), *The senior year experience: Facilitating integration, reflection, closure, and transition* (pp. 95–115). San Francisco: CA: Jossey-Bass.

Hooks, B. (1994). *Teaching to transgress: Education as the practice of freedom.* New York: Routledge.

Hopkins, R. L. (1994). *Narrative schooling: Experiential learning and the transformation of American education.* New York: Teachers College Press.

Howard-Hamilton, M. F. (2000). Creating a culturally responsive learning environment for African American students. In M. B. Baxter Magolda (Ed.), *Teaching to promote intellectual and personal maturity: Incorporating student's worldviews and identities into the learning process. New Directions for Teaching and Learning* (pp. 45–53). San Francisco, CA: Jossey-Bass.

Ignelzi, M. (2000). Meaning-making in the learning and teaching process. In M. B. Baxter Magolda (Ed.), *Teaching to promote intellectual and personal maturity: Incorporating students' worldviews and identities into the learning process. New Directions for Teaching and Learning* (pp. 5–14). San Francisco, CA: Jossey-Bass.

Jordan, J. V. (1997). A relational perspective for understanding women's development. In J. V. Jordan (Ed.), *Women's growth in diversity: More writings from the Stone Center* (pp. 9–24). New York: Guilford Press.

Josselson, R. (1987). *Finding herself: Pathways to identity development in women.* San Francisco, CA: Jossey-Bass.

Josselson, R. (1996). *Revising herself: The story of women's identity from college to midlife.* New York: Oxford University Press.

Kegan, R. (1982). *The evolving self: Problem and process in human development.* Cambridge, MA: Harvard University Press.

Kegan, R. (1994). *In over our heads: The mental demands of modern life.* Cambridge, MA: Harvard University Press.

Kendall, J. C. (1990). *Combining service and learning: A resource book for community and public service.* Raleigh, NC: National Society for Internships and Experiential Education.

King, P. M. (1978). William Perry's theory of intellectual and ethical development. In L. Knefelkamp, C. Widick, & C. Parker (Eds.), *Applying new developmental findings* (Vol. 4). San Francisco, CA: Jossey-Bass.

King, P. M., & Kitchener, K. S. (1994). *Developing reflective judgment: Understanding and promoting intellectual growth and critical thinking in adolescents and adults*. San Francisco, CA: Jossey-Bass.

King, P. M., & Kitchener, K. S. (in press). The Reflective Judgment Model: Twenty years of research on epistemic cognition. In B. K. Hofer & P. R. Pintrich (Eds.), *Personal epistemology: The psychology of beliefs about knowledge and knowing*. Mahwah, NJ: Erlbaum.

Kitchener, K. S. (1983). Cognition, metacognition, and epistemic cognition. *Human Development, 26,* 222–232.

Kohlberg, L. (1984). *Essays on moral development. Volume 1. The philosophy of moral development*. New York: Harper & Row.

Ladson-Billings, G. (1994). *The dreamkeepers: Successful teachers of African American children*. (1st ed.). San Francisco, CA: Jossey-Bass.

Ladson-Billings, G. (1995). Toward a theory of culturally relevant pedagogy. *American Educational Research Journal, 32*(3), 465–491.

Levine, A., & Cureton, J. S. (1998). *When hope and fear collide: A portrait of today's college student*. San Francisco, CA: Jossey-Bass.

Levine, J. H. (Ed.). (1999). *Learning communities: New structures, new partnerships for learning*. Columbia, SC: National Resource Center for the First-Year Experience and Students in Transition, University of South Carolina.

Loeb, P. R. (1994). *Generation at the crossroads: Apathy and action on the American campus*. New Brunswick, NJ: Rutgers University Press.

Loevinger, J. (1976). *Ego development: Conceptions and theories*. San Francisco, CA: Jossey-Bass.

Magolda, P.M. (2000). The campus tour ritual: Exploring community discourses in higher education. *Anthropology and Education Quarterly, 31* (1), 24-46.

Maher, F. A., & Tetreault, M. K. T. (1994). *The feminist classroom: An inside look at how professors and students are transforming higher education for a diverse society*. New York: Basic Books.

National Research Council. (1991). *Moving beyond myths; Revitalizing undergraduate mathematics*. Washington, DC: National Research Council.

National Science Foundation (1996). *Shaping the future: New expectations for undergraduate education in science, mathematics, engineering, and technology*. Washington, DC: National Science Foundation.

Nelson, C. E. (1989). Skewered on the unicorn's horn: The illusion of tragic tradeoff between content and critical thinking in the teaching of science. In L. W. Crow (Ed.), *Enhancing critical thinking in the sciences*. Washington, DC: Society for College Science Teachers.

Nelson, C. E. (2000). Effective strategies for teaching evolution and other controversial topics. In National Science Teacher's Association (Ed.), *The creation controversy and the science classroom* (pp. 19–50). Arlington, VA: NTSA Press.

Noddings, N. (1984). *Caring, a feminine approach to ethics & moral education.* Berkeley: University of California Press.

Oblinger, D. G. & Verville, A. L. (1998). *What business wants from higher education.* Phoenix, AZ: Oryx Press.

Ortiz, A. M. (2000). Expressing cultural identity in the learning community: Opportunities and challenges. In M. B. Baxter Magolda (Ed.), *Teaching to promote intellectual and personal maturity: Incorporating students' worldviews and identities into the learning process. New Directions for Teaching and Learning* (pp. 67–79). San Francisco, CA: Jossey-Bass.

Palmer, P. J. (1993). *To know as we are known: A spirituality of education.* San Francisco, CA: HarperCollins.

Palmer, P. J. (1998). *The courage to teach: Exploring the inner landscape of a teacher's life.* (1st ed.). San Francisco, CA: Jossey-Bass.

Parks Daloz, L., Keen, C. H., Keen, J. P., & Daloz Parks, S. (1996). *Common fire: Lives of commitment in a complex world.* Boston: Beacon Press.

Parks, S. (1986). *The critical years: Young adults and the search for meaning, faith, and commitment.* San Francisco, CA: HarperCollins.

Pascarella, E. T., & Terenzini, P. T. (1991). *How college affects students: Findings and insights from twenty years of research.* San Francisco, CA: Jossey-Bass.

Perry, W. G. (1970). *Forms of intellectual and ethical development in the college years: A scheme.* Troy, MO: Holt, Rinehart, & Winston.

Piaget, J. (1950). *The psychology of intelligence* (M. Piercy and D. Berlyne, Trans.). London: Routledge & Kegan Paul.

Piaget, J. (1970). *Structuralism.* New York: Basic Books.

Piaget, J. (1977). *Equilibration of cognitive structures.* New York: Viking.

Piper, T. D. (1996, November). The community standards model: A method to enhance student learning and development. *Association of College and University Housing Officers-International Talking Stick,* 14–15.

Piper, T. D. (1997). Empowering students to create community standards. *About Campus,* 2(3), 22–24.

Piper, T. D., Strong K., & Buckley, J. (2000). *UNLV Community Standards Institute.* (Workshop Manual available from Terry Piper, Associate Vice President of Student Affairs, University of Nevada, Las Vegas)

Rhoads, R. A. (1997). *Community service and higher learning: Explorations of the caring self.* Albany, NY: SUNY Press.

Rhoads, R. A. (2000). Democratic citizenship and service learning: Advancing the caring self. In M. B. Baxter Magolda (Ed.), *Teaching to promote intellectual and personal maturity: Incorporating students' worldviews and identities into the learning process. New Directions for Teaching and Learning* (Vol. 82, pp. 37–44). San Francisco, CA: Jossey-Bass.

Rogers, J. L. (1996). Leadership. In S. R. Komives & D. B. Woodard (Eds.), *Student services: A handbook for the profession* (3rd ed., pp. 299–319). San Francisco, CA: Jossey-Bass.

Schroeder, C. C. (1999). Forging educational partnerships that advance student learning. In G. S. Blimling & E. J. Whitt (Eds.), *Good practice in student affairs: Principles to foster student learning* (pp. 133–156). San Francisco, CA: Jossey-Bass.

Senge, P. M. (1990). *The fifth discipline: The art and practice of the learning organization.* New York: Doubleday.

Shor, I. (1992). *Empowering education: Critical teaching for social change.* Chicago: University of Chicago Press.

Shor, I. (1996). *When students have power: Negotiating authority in a critical pedagogy.* Chicago: University of Chicago Press.

Straub, C. (1987). Women's development of autonomy and Chickering's theory. *Journal of College Student Personnel, 28,* 198–204.

Strauss, A. (1987). *Qualitative analysis for social scientists.* New York: Cambridge University Press.

Strauss, A., & Corbin, J. (1994). Grounded theory methodology: An overview. In N. Denzin & Y. Lincoln (Eds.), *Handbook of qualitative research* (pp. 273–285). Thousand Oaks, CA: Sage.

Storti, C. (1989). *The art of crossing cultures.* Yarmouth, ME: Intercultural Press.

Twomey Fosnot, C. (Ed.). (1996). *Constructivism: Theory, perspectives, and practice.* New York: Teachers College Press.

Willimon, W. H., & Naylor, T. H. (1995). *The abandoned generation: Rethinking higher education.* Grand Rapids, MI: William B. Eerdmans Publishing Company.

Winston, R. B. Jr., & Fitch, R. T. (1993). Paraprofessional staffing. In R. B. Winston, Jr. and S. Anchors (Eds.), *Student housing and residential life* (pp. 315–343). San Francisco, CA: Jossey-Bass.

Zohar, D. (1997). *Rewiring the corporate brain: Using the new science to rethink how we structure and lead organizations.* San Francisco, CA: Berrett-Koehler.

LONGITUDINAL STUDY METHODOLOGY
AND METHODS

I have operated from a constructivist perspective from the start of the longitudinal project because I view the dimensions of development as constructed by individuals making meaning of their experience. Both Perry (1970) and Belenky et al. (1986) emphasized their theories as possible windows through which to understand epistemological development, rather than the objective truth. Thus although I used their theories to inform the college interview (Phase 1), I employed an open-ended interview and an inductive analysis to allow new possibilities to emerge from the context. In sharing the findings of the college phase, I emphasized them as possibilities stemming from a particular context, useful in other contexts depending on the reader's judgment of transferability. I continued this constructivist approach in the postcollege phase (Phase 2) to continue to allow participants' constructions of their experience to emerge. Consequently, the intrapersonal and interpersonal dimensions became major themes in the interviews. Because this book synthesizes data from the postcollege phase, I will concentrate here on postcollege methods, highlighting college-phase methods as necessary. Descriptions of this method have been previously published due to the longitudinal nature of the study.

Participants

The 39 persons upon whom this book is based are participants in a 14-year longitudinal study that began in 1986 when they entered college. The study began with 101 traditional age students (51 women and 50 men) who attended Miami University of Ohio, a state institution with a liberal arts focus. Admission is competitive and the entering class of which the participants were a part had a mean ACT score of 25.8 and 70 percent ranked in the top 20 percent of their high school class. Their majors included all six divisions within the institution, and cocurricular involvement in college was high. Of the 70 participants continuing in Phase 2 of the study, 59 graduated within 4 years and the remaining 11 in 5 years. Twenty-one of the Phase 2 participants pursued additional academic preparation after college graduation, including law school, seminary, medical school, and various graduate degrees. Their occupations included business, education, social service, ministry, and government work. During the years after college, 7 participants withdrew; others were lost due to address changes or inability to schedule interviews after repeated attempts. Seventy participated in the fifth year. The most substantial drop occurred between the fifth and sixth year with only 51 participating in Year 6. Participation remained fairly stable in Years 7 (48), 8 (42), 9 (41), and 10 through 14 (39). Gender remained balanced over these years, resulting in 22 women and 17 men in Year 14.

Of the 39 participants who continued through Year 14, 30 were married, 2 were divorced, and 15 had children. Seventeen had been or were pursuing advanced education: 12 had received master's degrees in education, psychology, social work, business administration, and economics. One had completed seminary, 2 received law degrees, and 1 was in medical school. One was taking undergraduate teacher education courses; another completed a doctorate. The most prevalent occupations of these 39 participants were business (16) and education (9). Areas within business included sales in varied industries, financial work, public services, real estate, and marketing. Educators were secondary school teachers. The remaining participants were in social work, law, homemaking, and Christian ministry.

One dynamic of this context is the small number of students from underrepresented groups on the campus. Only 3 of the original 101 participants were members of underrepresented groups, 2 of whom continued into Phase 2. Although none of these 3 withdrew from the study, all were unreachable by Year 10 due to changing addresses. This book offers a vision of development based on these 39 participants. This vision is offered as a possibility and it is not assumed to fit any young adults outside of this context. Transferability to other students and contexts is left to the judgment of the reader, based on the thick description of participants' stories (Denzin, 1994).

Interviews and Rapport: Developing a Partnership

The qualitative nature of the college interviews was continued during Phase 2 to allow participants' stories to be the primary focus. Phase 2 interviews were unstructured (Fontana & Frey, 1994). Because few researchers have explored development after college via a longitudinal approach, it was particularly important for the interview to allow participants to set the agenda and to allow their perspectives to emerge freely. The annual interview began with a summary of the focus of Phase 2 of the project, which was to continue to explore how participants learn and come to know. The participant was then asked to think about important learning experiences that took place since the previous interview. The participant volunteered those experiences, described them, and described their impact on her or his thinking. I asked questions to pursue why these experiences were important, factors that influenced the experiences, and how the learner was affected. Each year, I used participants' reactions to the conversation to revise and improve the interview process. The interview became more informal as the study progressed and addressed what life had been like for participants since we talked last. These conversations included discussion of the dimensions of life they felt were most relevant, the demands of adult life they were experiencing, how they made meaning of these dimensions and demands, their sense of themselves, and how they decided what to believe. Inherent in these dimensions was their sense of themselves in relation to others and their involvement in significant relationships. Interviews were conducted by telephone and ranged from 60 to 90 minutes. A sabbatical during Year 12 allowed me to visit 10 participants for face-to-face interviews in their homes.

Rapport established from our long association contributed to the richness of the interviews. Throughout the project, I provided direct information to participants about my research interests and procedures. I shared annual summaries of my interpretations of the collective interviews and invited participants' reactions. Upon completion of the college phase of the study I sent copies of *Knowing and Reasoning in College* to all remaining participants. Over the next few years I continued to send annual summaries, including excerpts from published works. These efforts on my part to both keep them apprised of my interpretations and to solicit their interpretations altered our relationship from the traditional researcher-participant to partners in understanding young adult life.

This partnership contributes to the intimate nature of the interviews, apparent in narratives throughout this book. Participants routinely commented that they had few opportunities to talk about themselves with someone who listened. Their friends and families tended to give them advice, share their own similar experience, or try to alleviate participants' concerns. My focus on hearing their stories, constantly asking for the meaning behind their thinking or how they arrived at their current perspective, provided opportunities for self-reflection. As Ned shared in chapter 5, the interview was an opportunity for introspection:

> I don't often get the opportunity for someone to ask these tough questions to figure out my framework. It is very parallel to discussions with my close friend—at the beginning I had no idea what I'd say; then I recognize things I need to think more about.

Over the years participants became accustomed to this opportunity to explore during our conversations. They also came to anticipate the questions in my mind as they shared their stories. The information, conversational nature of the interview meant that they were given autonomy to define and pursue significant topics. I had no pre-determined questions; instead I asked questions to gain an in-depth understanding of the stories they told. My questions included: "What does that mean for you?" "What do you mean when you say that?" "How did that perspective come about?" or "What are the experiences that led you to that notion?" I also asked how various perspectives related to each other or to earlier perspectives from previous interviews.

I conveyed my respect for participants' privacy in numerous ways, another important dynamic of our partnership and participants' willingness to share intimate reflections on their lives. I invited them to choose the focus of the interview and to offer dimensions of their experience for discussion. Participants were aware of my interest in the epistemological, intrapersonal, and interpersonal dimensions of development from my writing and our previous interviews. In cases where our interview focused on one dimension over another, I often noted this observation and asked if there were other dimensions that warranted our exploration. Participants knew, however, that I would not push them to discuss areas they were uncomfortable sharing. Their willingness to share insights across dimensions, including personal and relationship issues, was likely heightened by my emphasis on confidentiality. I have never revealed their identities over the 14-year study and have routinely consulted with participants when I wanted to publish their stories extensively. Although I have had participants' permission to share some very personal experiences because participants believe this would benefit others, I have sometimes chosen to withhold those stories from published work out of concern for their privacy. In this book I have shared some of this material anonymously rather than connecting it to the psuedonames used throughout the

14-year project. Our overall rapport has conveyed to participants that I have a genuine interest in their well being and respect their privacy.[1]

Interpretation: Mutually Constructing Narratives

My constructivist approach to this project and the partnership developed over the course of the study both mediate data interpretation. My constructivist approach led to using grounded theory methodology (Glaser, 1978; Strauss, 1987; Strauss & Corbin, 1994) to analyze interview responses. Data collection and interpretation are "guided by successively evolving interpretations made during the course of the study" (Strauss, p. 10). Each year transcriptions of the taped interviews were reviewed and divided into units. The units were then sorted into categories to allow themes and patterns to emerge from the data. Rereading data for each participant across years resulted in successively evolving interpretations and further development of patterns. Credibility of the themes and patterns is enhanced through prolonged engagement to build trust and understanding, and member checking to assure accuracy of interpretations. Two research partners joined me to reread and analyze the postcollege data. Each of us prepared summaries of themes individually followed by meetings in which we discussed and synthesized our perceptions. This use of multiple analysts helped mediate our subjectivities and increase the adequacy of our interpretations.

Despite these methods, the question of whose story is told in this book is important. The issue of representation, or the degree to which a qualitative inquirer presents participants' stories versus her own, has been explored by numerous scholars. In light of my constructivist bent and the three core assumptions central to Part II of the book, I approach this question using those three core assumptions. Viewing knowledge as complex and socially constructed (the first core assumption) yields the notion that no one true journey toward self-authorship exists; rather multiple journeys abound. These journeys stem from the complex lives of individual participants, their meaning-making of their experience, and their social construction of meaning with those around them. From

---

[1]This kind of rapport is essential to an in-depth study of human development. Peers who suggest that this rapport has altered the participants' development, a matter seen as a potential problem from a positivistic perspective, have sometimes challenged me. I concur that participation in this project probably has altered participants' development due to the self-reflection involved, the opportunity to read about others' development, and exposure to the overall developmental process. I remind readers, given this issue, that I make no claims that these participants' stories or my interpretations of them are generalizable to others but rather particular constructions that may be transferable.

this vantage point, the phases of the journey toward self-authorship—in fact the concept of self-authorship itself—are offered as possibilities for understanding how young adults view knowing, themselves, and their relationships.

Social construction of knowledge is inherent in another core assumption; authority and expertise are shared in the mutual construction of knowledge among peers. My participants and I mutually constructed the narrative of this book. They offered their narratives and their meaning making in the context of my questions and quest for understanding their lives. I interpreted their meaning making by merging their stories with my understanding of human development. I routinely consulted them, sharing my interpretations for their reaction and feedback. My part in this mutual construction was mediated by another core assumption; self is central to knowledge construction. The meaning I made of their narratives was mediated by who I am—my personal experience of my own development, my experience as a student and scholar of human development theory, and my experience as a faculty member who interacts intensely with students of this age group.

While not professing to write the "true" story of these participants' lives, I am committed to offering a reasonable interpretation of their narratives. This has involved balancing what Clandinin and Connelly call "falling in love" with participants and maintaining some distance from them (2000, p. 81). Full involvement with participants, or in this case going into their stories, gaining access to intimate details of their lives, and caring about their well-being, yields rapport and understanding. Yet Clandinin and Connelly emphasized that researchers "must also step back and see their own stories in the inquiry, the stories of the participants, as well as the larger landscape on which they all live" (2000, p. 81). This tension is congruent with the tension between self as central to knowing and knowledge as mutually constructed. One must bring the self to the knowing process, yet simultaneously make space for others' narratives and from the two, construct a perspective.

The story told here—the four phases of the journey toward self-authorship—is my construction. It is mutually constructed with others, primarily my longitudinal participants. My construction has benefited from the perspectives of others including the two research colleagues who helped read transcripts and others who provided feedback on the construction. I offer it here for continued mutual construction with readers to contribute to educators' understanding of young adult life and the nature of good company for that journey.